Deep Blues

Deep Blues

Human Soundscapes for the Archetypal Journey

Mark D. Winborn

Deep Blues
Human Soundscapes for the Archetypal Journey

Published simultaneously in Canada, the United Kingdom, and the United States of America by Fisher King Press. For information on obtaining permission for use of material from this work, submit a written request to: permissions@fisherkingpress.com

Fisher King Press
PO Box 222321
Carmel, CA 93922
www.fisherkingpress.com
info@fisherkingpress.com
+1-831-238-7799

Many thanks to all who have directly or indirectly provided permission to reprint their work, including Stanley Crouch (for the postlude), Tom Smith (photos), and Kevin "Chopper" Peshkepia (cover art). Every effort has been made to trace all copyright holders; however, if any have been overlooked, the author will be pleased to make the necessary arrangements at the first opportunity.

Contents

Acknowledgements

The blues has provided great satisfaction, comfort, and joy in my life. However, the opportunity to write about the blues would not have been possible without the support of a number of individuals, especially my parents, my wife Lisa, and my sons Benjamin and Aaron.

I would also like to thank: Stan Perlman who provided early encouragement about this project; Adam Gussow, professional bluesman turned professor of English and Southern Studies at the University of Mississippi, for generously sharing resources; and Mel Marshak (1926 – 2010), whom I gratefully count as my mentor and the greatest influence in my development as a psychoanalyst.

There is deep appreciation for the bluesmen and blueswomen of Memphis, Tennessee, who keep the blues alive, and especially for those musicians who invited me to play with them at Blues Hall on Beale Street: Blue Blake, Mark Ross, and Eric Hughes.

Finally, I would like to express a special thanks to the artists associated with the imagery of Deep Blues. Tom Smith of Winthrop Harbor, Illinois graciously provided permission to use his exquisite black and white photographs, taken between 1976 and 2006 (all photographs © Tom Smith 2006), which capture the gritty essence of the Maxwell Street Market area of Chicago. All of the photographs in Deep Blues are the work of Tom Smith. More of his photographic artwork can be seen at www.maxwellblues.com. The cover art for Deep Blues is the creation of Kevin "Chopper" Peshkepia. Chopper's evocative artwork can be viewed at www.peshkepia.com.

Prelude

"Is There Harm in Singing the Blues?"
—Sermon by the Reverend Emmett Dickinson:
Paramount Records, 1930

(Spoken)
I'm speaking to you from this subject
It's no harm to sing the blues
There's so-called preachers all over this land
Are talking about the man or woman who sings the blues
You don't know the meaning of the blues
The blues is only an outward voice to that inward feeling
And way back yonder
When Adam and Eve was put out of the Garden of Eden
To till the earth
He began to sing a song
I don't know what he sang
But I imagine he sang

(Sung)
I didn't know my burden was so hard
Oh I didn't know my burden was so hard
Oh I done made up my mind
Oh how I had some preachin' kind
I didn't know my burden was so hard

(Chanted)
Way back yonder
Uh when Israel crossed the Red Sea
On dry land
And landed on the other side
I'm told that they sang a new song

I don't know what they sang
But I call that the Israelite blues
I imagine they sang
"I just made my escape
And got over yonder"
And way back down -
When Paul and Silas
Was in the Philippian jail
Paul said, "Silas
Uh do you feel like singing"
Silas says "I never felt as much like singing before
In all my life"
I call that the jailhouse blues
They tell me that Silas sing
Or prayed
The old jail reeled and rocked like a drunken man
The chains fell from their hands
The shackles fell from their feet
The old jail doors sprang open
Uh but they done kept on singing those
Jailhouse blues
Way early in the morning
The jailer came
And saw the jail was standing ajar
And he just drew back his sword
To take his own life
Uh but Paul said "Just stay your hand
For we are all here"
I imagine they continued to sing
The jailhouse blues
Way down yonder
Uh when our foreparents was in slavery
They sang George Washington offer his song
The sang Abraham Lincoln on his song
I call that the slave time blues

1

Introduction

"In the beginning was noise. And noise begat rhythm. And rhythm begat everything else."
—Mickey Hart

I started listening to blues music when I was about 13 or 14 years old. I didn't know why I was attracted to the blues but I knew it resonated with something in me as soon as I heard it. The gritty, visceral, deep feel of the blues expressed something for me that I couldn't express for myself. The blues has allowed me to experience these emotions long enough to "get it" on the inside. Bill Willeford calls this influence of the blues the "education of the heart" and sometimes I think of it as deepening or expanding my emotional vocabulary.[1] The blues is a way of maintaining an ongoing dialogue with myself because it allows access to some fundamental aspects of myself which might otherwise remain hidden. The history and tradition of the blues is also appealing; allowing the experience of continuity in felt relationship to, and participation with, the blues tradition.

However, writing about the blues is a difficult task because I am trying to express in words what can only ultimately be experienced aurally. On some level I am uncomfortable with, or resist, the idea of reducing or conceptualizing the blues because the blues is not a thing, an object to be examined; it is an experience. Words cannot fully convey what the blues is about because the blues is about hearing and resonating with the pain, suffering, joy, or sadness in the blues singer's voice. In the final sense, words cannot fully express an understanding of the blues or capture the experience of the blues. This situation is similar to C.G. Jung's statement about images: "Image and meaning are identical; and as the first takes shape, so the latter becomes clear. Actually, the pattern

---

1 "Abandonment, Wish, and Hope in the Blues." In N. Schwartz-Salant and M. Stein (Ed.) *Chiron: Abandonment,* pp.173ff.

needs no interpretation: it portrays its own meaning."[2] Words and concepts cannot avoid being a reduction of the blues. Author Charles Keil characterized writing about the blues in this way: "There are really no blues critics - the very title seems either self-contradictory or altogether empty of meaning."[3] Paul Garon echoes these sentiments by asserting that we are unable to describe in secondary process terms the nature of our primary process response to the blues.[4] However, while acknowledging these limitations, I will highlight certain aspects of the music which are salient and relevant to my own experience of the blues.

Jungian analyst Paul Kugler hypothesizes that there exist "acoustic images" as well as visual images. If his hypothesis is correct, one could say that the blues operates within a particular set of archetypally based acoustic images.[5] Archetypes are inherent universal potentials to experience aspects of life in a particular manner. Therefore, the archetypally based acoustic images that make up the blues need no interpretation, only an experience of them to potentially constellate a response in the listener. The blues is like a Talmudic statement about dreams: "The dream needs no interpretation, it is its own interpretation." The blues, like the dream, only need a vessel to resonate in. The blues speaks for itself.

Throughout this book I'll be drawing on ideas from the field of Analytical Psychology, the school of psychoanalytic theory and practice created by C.G. Jung, to facilitate the exploration of the blues. Very little has been written about the blues from the perspective of Analytical Psychology: only two works written from a Jungian perspective have been published to date. An essay by Bill Willeford gives a general introduction to the blues and then explores the intimate relationship between the blues and feeling or emotion, both as experience and process.[6] He illustrates this relationship through the examination of archetypally based emotional themes such as abandonment, wish, and hope. Willeford utilizes the attachment and separation processes of the mother-infant relationship to interpret some of the emotional activity portrayed in blues performances.

---

2   C.G. Jung, "On the Nature of the Psyche," *The Structure and Dynamics of the Psyche*, CW8, par. 402. NOTE: CW refers throughout to *The Collected Works of C.G. Jung.*
3   *Urban Blues*, p. 163.
4   *Blues and the Poetic Spirit.*
5   *The Alchemy of Discourse.*
6   *Abandonment, Wish, and Hope in the Blues.*

Another article, by Stephen Diggs, approaches the subject from a significantly different perspective.[7] Diggs frames his observations within the conceptual framework of Archetypal Psychology[8] and he explores the phenomenon of the blues primarily from a collective or cultural perspective. He envisions an "alchemy of race" existing in contemporary America in which the dominant conscious attitude is the "white mind" which is still largely entrenched in the European tradition. Diggs argues that the blues, emerging out of the experience of black African-Americans, is "doing therapy on the soul of Western consciousness" by bringing it into relationship with depression, passion, and Dionysian energies. Unfortunately, Diggs does not explore how Western consciousness has influenced African consciousness; missing an opportunity to examine the possible reciprocal nature of this influence.

There are a few books within Analytical Psychology that deal with more general aspects of music. Books of particular interest are *Music and the Mind*, by Anthony Storr, *Sounding the Soul*, by Mary Lynn Kittelson, and more recently *Music and Psyche* by Paul Ashton and Stephen Bloch (Eds.). Storr's work, the most general of the three, examines the origins and functions of music, the patterns of music, the effect of music on the brain and soma, and the inner experience of the composer and listener. Storr focuses most of his attention on classical music, hence deeply rooted in the Western tradition which, while illuminating, limits the applicability of some of his observations to the topic at hand in our discussion.

Kittelson's work focuses on the broad experience of sound, hearing, listening, and silence, especially as it takes place within the frame of the analytic encounter. She uses the image of "the acoustic vessel" to draw attention to the unique form of *temenos*[9] created by listening at deeper levels to the acoustic patterns transpiring within a therapy hour. Kittelson also explores the role of sound in music, poetry, and other healing arts. Her understanding of the general aspects of sound sheds light on various aspects of musical experience.

Music and Psyche by Ashton and Bloch is an exploration of the interface between music and psyche as mediated through analytic understanding. It is a collection of essays covering a range of topics related

---

7 "Alchemy of the Blues." *Spring*, vol. 61, pp. 16ff.
8 Archetypal Psychology, developed originally by James Hillman, is a subset of Analytical Psychology.
9 *Temenos* – "A Greek word meaning a sacred, protected space; psychologically, descriptive of both a personal container and the sense of privacy that surrounds an analytical relationship." – (Sharp, *Jung Lexicon*)

to the interaction of music and psyche, from individual psychological transformation to recent findings from neuroscience and the healing powers of music's spiritual dimensions. *Music and Psyche* explores the nature of music's impact and resonance in the psyche, and with psyche's self-expression through music.

While I am sure that there are other works that I have overlooked, the limited number of books and articles discussed illustrates how little work has been done from a Jungian perspective on the interpretation of music, especially the blues. Naturally, there are a number of authors from other disciplines that have written on the psychological, historical, sociological, and anthropological aspects of music as well as works specific to the blues.

Blues and the Poetic Spirit, by Paul Garon is one of my favorite books. Garon examines the blues from the perspective that the blues is poetry and then likens the bluesman to poets such as Robert Frost, T.S. Eliot, and Allan Ginsberg. He also utilizes surrealist philosophy and psychoanalytic theory to explore the various themes present in the blues, such as Eros, aggression, humor, work, or male supremacy. Garon is one of the few authors who make an attempt to understand the blues from a psychological perspective, even though some of his arguments sound dated and rather fixed in the cultural revolution of the 1960's.

The first book on the blues by an African-American author was *Blues People*, by LeRoi Jones. Working sociologically, Jones traces the development of the blues from its origins in slavery through to its influence on the contemporary jazz idiom. Jones pays particular attention to the values within African-American culture which gave birth to the blues and the shift in those values which caused an eventual decline of the blues within the African-American culture. He also traces the influence of the blues on white America.

Charles Keil, in *Urban Blues*, makes an important contribution to blues scholarship by identifying the close parallels between the role of the bluesman in the African-American community and the role of the African-American preacher. He provides insight into the importance of psychological "commitment" on the part of the audience and how that relates to the capacity of the music to affect an emotional shift in the audience. Building on this insight, Keil proposes that the role of the bluesman is more of a "belief role" rather than a "creative role" and more "priestly" than "artistic."

Blues and Evil, by John Michael Spencer, is a rather intriguing book written from a more Afro-centric perspective. Spencer's position is that other blues scholars have all accepted the stereotype of the blues being seen as inherently secular music, both in terms of form and function. He disagrees with this perspective and presents arguments for the existence, within the blues, of underlying mythologies, theologies, and theodicies (i.e., explanations for the existence of evil in the world created by God). Spencer is the only author I came across, outside of Analytical Psychology, who utilizes some of Jung's theories, especially Jung's perspectives on evil, in laying out his positions.

Nothing but the Blues, edited by Lawrence Cohn, is primarily a historical and biographical account of the blues. It is an enjoyable and scholarly introduction to the personalities and styles associated with the blues. The book traces the developments in the blues from its most primitive origins, through country blues, classic blues, vaudeville, gospel, urban blues, white country blues, East Coast Piedmont blues, and jump blues, as well as the blues revivals of the 1960's and later. Most of the chapters are written by ethnomusicologists and are primarily descriptive rather than interpretive. One of the added pleasures of the book is an excellent discography covering a wide variety of blues styles.

Jeff Titon explores the blues from the perspective of a musicologist in his book, *Early Downhome Blues*. His work provides an extensive examination of the musical structure, form, and content of early country blues. He also explores the cultural context in which country blues developed. Titon provides an extensive catalogue of song lyrics to support his analysis of the music.

Finally, I will mention *Blues Fell This Morning*, by Paul Oliver. The subtitle of the book, "Meaning in the Blues," is somewhat misleading because Oliver never explores this topic from a depth perspective. Instead, Oliver's work, originally published in 1960, focuses primarily on identifying and categorizing the various content themes found in blues recordings. Each chapter brings together a large number of blues songs with a common theme such as travel, love, or work. After reading the book one is left with a greater awareness of the vast area covered by the blues, but without a greater appreciation of the depth and vitality of the music. Oliver has difficulty moving from the position of an outsider in his observations on the blues and African-American culture, lending a somewhat stereotypic tone to his comments.

An underlying theme which will emerge in the chapters that follow is similar to a premise presented by Maud Bodkin, namely that it is possible to identify themes in poetry (or the blues) which, "have a particular form or pattern which persists amid variation from age to age, and which corresponds to a pattern or configuration of emotional tendencies in the minds of those who are stirred by the theme."[10] Bodkin uses the term "archetypal pattern" to refer to that, "within us which . . . leaps in response to the effective presentation in poetry of an ancient theme." Her premise is especially relevant since poetry itself was originally presented in the form of a song. Our discussion will initially explore the archetypal foundations of blues music and the development and history of blues music as a specific musical form. As our musical journey unfolds, I will use the concept of "unitary reality" proposed by Erich Neumann to organize various themes observed in the blues.[11] We'll examine the idea that the blues reflects a state of "unitary reality," a state which articulates an essential characteristic of the blues experience and accounts for the depth and richness of blues music. Neumann defines unitary reality as, "A reciprocal co-ordination between world and psyche . . . a co-ordination which is based on the archetypal structure which embraces both, or of which both are partial aspects . . ."

---

10 *Archetypal Patterns in Poetry*, p. 4.
11 *The Place of Creation.*

and which "leads to an emotionally toned unitary experience."[12] As such, the blues is a manifestation and containment of the archetypal field that constitutes unitary reality. It is the development of these ideas around unitary reality and the blues that contribute to the unique perspective of this book. These ideas are further developed through an examination of the role of the bluesman and the blues performance. Ultimately, the blues has an innate healing potential: it is a form of therapy which incorporates elements of humor, alchemical imagination, personification, and the narrative impulse.

12　*The Place of Creation*, p. 27.

2

The Genesis of the Blues

"Music gives a soul to the universe, wings to the mind,
flight to the imagination, and life to everything."
—Plato

Origins

The blues has been around a long time. The blues existed before there was ever something called the blues. Perhaps the blues began when mankind first developed sufficient consciousness to be aware of subjective feelings. It was certainly present in the time of the ancient Greeks; after all, they developed the dramatic form commonly referred to as Greek tragedy. According to Joseph Campbell, "The sufferings revealed through the episodes of a [Greek] tragedy are not accidental or occasional, but 'grave and constant,' archetypal of human life."[13] Campbell's description of the Greek tragedy could well be used to describe the typical content of the blues.

Perhaps Orpheus was the first bluesman. In ancient Greece, Orpheus was the greatest musician among the mortals. He was married to Eurydice but immediately after the wedding she was killed by a viper. Orpheus' grief and love was so great that he vowed to go to the underworld and try to bring Eurydice back. His grief, expressed through his songs, was so great that even the dreaded goddesses, the Furies, were wet with tears. He sang the following song to Hades, lord of the underworld, and his queen, Persephone:

O Gods who rule the dark and silent world,
To you all born of a woman needs must come.
All lovely things at least go down to you.
You are the debtor who is always paid.
A little while we tarry on earth.
Then we are yours forever and forever.

---

13 *The Inner Reaches of Outer Space*, p. 135.

But I seek one who came to you too soon.
The bud was plucked before the flower bloomed.
I tried to bear my loss. I could not bear it.
Love was too strong a god. O King, you know
If that old tale men tell is true, how once
The flowers saw the rape of Persephone.
Then weave again for sweet Eurydice
Life's pattern that was taken from the loom
Too quickly. See, I ask a little thing,
Only that you will lend, not give, her to me.
She shall be yours when her years' span is full.

Others who heard the song of Orpheus were profoundly moved by it. The song of Orpheus "drew iron tears down Hades' cheek, and made Hell grant what love did seek."

Of course, being a blues song, the situation didn't turn out happily ever after for Orpheus and Eurydice. Hades agreed to release Eurydice to Orpheus under one condition: that he wouldn't look back on her as they made the journey to the upperworld, much like the bargain Yahweh made with Lot and his wife.[14] Unfortunately, Orpheus looked back to reassure himself of her presence just before they reached the upperworld. Immediately she slipped away into the darkness and the only word he heard her speak was "farewell." Forsaken, he wandered the countryside alone, until he came upon a band of Maenads who tore him limb from limb and flung his severed head into the Hebrus River.[15] The link between Orpheus and the blues is so strong that Peter Guralnick, in his book *Searching for Robert Johnson,* describes Robert Johnson as a modern-day Orpheus.[16]

However, the link between ancient Greece and the blues does not end with Orpheus. The blues is also present in the journeys of Odysseus and in his fights with his wife's suitors upon his return to Ithaca. The blues also exist in Demeter's grief for her lost daughter Persephone and the blues is present in those driven mad by music of Dionysus or Pan. So it would seem that we have always had the blues.

---

14 *Holy Bible*, Genesis Chap. 19.
15 This mythic summary of Orpheus was adapted from Hamilton, *Mythology,* pp. 104ff.
16 Robert Johnson is widely considered to be the greatest bluesman to ever be recorded. He reportedly made a pact with the Devil to obtain his prodigious skills on the guitar. Johnson was just 27 years old when he died in 1938 at the hands of a jealous husband.

The blues sound is generally raw and primitive. It has some basic but fluid forms. It is culled up out of the *prima materia*[17] and has never lost touch with the base elements of life. The origins of the blues reflect its humble beginnings with early blues performers relying only on guitar, harmonica, and vocals to communicate their message. The overarching themes are emotional and spiritual, not rational. The word "blues" originally had nothing to do with sadness, but seems to have meant a state of mind more akin to boredom. By the early 1800's, however, the term "blue devils" came to signify contrary spirits that hung around and caused sadness.[18]

The early influences of the blues originate in West Africa, transported to America by African slaves. African-American blues historian John Reese eloquently states the deep connection between the music and the history of the people:

> Blues was such a strong part of our history and how we got here. There is an urgency to this music. When black people were brought here, they didn't have time to pack their bags. It was chaos, but out of that chaos came all this beautiful music. We had to find some way to get a handle on this. The field hollers, the chants, if not for that music, nobody would have survived. That's the closest one will have to the presence of God, when blues and jazz are performed. A lot of people don't want to stare that power in the eyes. But that power goes from the source to the performer to the audience. To express ourselves in a strange land in strange conditions, we had to take whatever ability we had and make the best of it. Or there wouldn't be any blues or jazz.[19]

In West Africa there is a term, *griot*, which is used to refer to a tribal singer but also refers to a tribe's archive of musical stories which preserve the tribe's history and culture. The blues carries on this tradition of musical lore with timeless songs that are continuously remade because of the emotional depth and wisdom that they possess. The *griot* singer commonly accompanied himself on an instrument referred to as a *halam* or, in other African dialects, the *banjo*. It is made of an elongated dried gourd with five strings. Musicians were still using banjos

---

17 *prima materia* – "An alchemical term meaning 'original matter,' used psychologically to denote both the instinctual foundation of life and the raw material one works with in analysis - dreams, emotions, conflicts, etc." - (Sharp, *Jung Lexicon*)
18 Brian Robertson, *Little Blues Book.*
19 Quoted in J. Gentry "The Subway Lounge." *Living Blues*, Issue 132, p. 55.

made of gourd as late as the 1840's. This instrument was brought to the Americas and as it evolved it became the most common instrument of the plantation South as well as providing the first instrumental accompaniment for the blues singer.[20]

The first generation of African slaves sang African songs and chants. By the second generation those songs were replaced by work songs with the conditions of their American environment as the focus. White slave owners repressed traditional African drumming and worship of African deities for fear that those influences could incite revolts. Westerners also considered African music primitive because it emphasized rhythm rather than harmony and melody.[21] Perhaps this reaction occurred because rhythmically based music appeals more directly to the body and encourages movement. Thus the blues might be considered the shadow[22] or anti-thesis of Western musical forms.

West African music typically has a layering of rhythm, a complex weave of beats, and an avoidance of a single stressed rhythm; it is polyrhythmic as opposed to the typical mono-rhythm of Western music. In the blues this is maintained with a, "floating accent, associated with the vocal line despite the regularity of the accompanying rhythm, often anticipating the chord change rather than accenting on the chord change."[23,24] This polyrhythm may also take the form of the vocal rhythm falling into a two-beat (double) rhythm while the accompaniment is being played in a triplet rhythm, or it may take the form of an alternation between double and triple rhythms throughout the song.

West African music also has an antiphonal emphasis, a call and response - theme and comment pattern, which is a characteristic that has also carried over into African-American blues and gospel. The call and response pattern and the repetition of certain phrases, as found in African music, can also be heard instrumentally in the repetition of certain patterns of notes that form a riff in jazz and blues.[25]

A particularly good example of these African influences can be heard in the sacred blues of Blind Willie Johnson who is considered the fore-

---

20   Charters, "Workin' on the Building." In L. Cohn (Ed.). *Nothing but the Blues.*
21   Jones, *Blues People.*
22   Shadow – "Hidden or unconscious aspects of oneself, both good and bad, which the ego has either repressed or never recognized." - (Sharp, *Jung Lexicon*)
23   Charters, "Workin' on the Building."
24   This characteristic can be heard in the Muddy Waters song - *Still A Fool.*
25   Jones, *Blues People.*

most example of the mixing of the blues style of music with a sacred theme.[26] His performances were emotional onslaughts that were powered by howls, growls, cries, and vibrato that were intended to constellate the religious fervor of the listener, to excite the believer and convert the non-believer. Johnson typically sang in a gravelly, false bass voice. These features suggest a lineage with certain African sacred rituals. In these African rituals, the masked singer adopts a shift in voice tone that accompanies the change in appearance associated with the donning of the mask. Deep chest growls, false bass tones, and strangulated shrieks were all part of the masked singer's repertoire of vocal effects.[27]

Despite the similarities between West African music and the blues, there also exist some significant differences. In West African music the concept of the solo performer, i.e., playing and singing by oneself, is relatively nonexistent. Also, the themes of West African music are largely about the tribe itself: their gods, work, nature, and the conditions of man's life.[28] Hence, West African music is largely about the collective and collective themes. In the blues, the emphasis is predominantly placed on individual experience even though the themes may be universal. Diggs asserts that the emergence of the solo performer of the blues and his focus on individual experiences was a result of the introjection of the "I," or ego of the West by the rural, unskilled African-American.[29] Hence, the blues reflected a movement from collective community to individual consciousness. The importance of individual experience and expression in the blues is further emphasized by Diggs:

> Blues was a music that arose from the needs of a group, although it was assumed that each man had his own blues and that he would sing them . . . As such, the music was private and personal . . . it was assumed that *anybody* could sing the blues. If someone had lived in this world into manhood, it was taken for granted that he had been given the content of his verses . . . Given the deeply personal quality of blues-singing, there could be no particular method for learning the blues.[30]

---

26   An example of this is Blind Willie Johnson's performance of *Motherless Children*.
27   M. Humphrey "Holy blues: The Gospel Tradition." In L. Cohn (Ed.). *Nothing but the Blues*.
28   Jones, *Blues People*.
29   Diggs, *Alchemy and the Blues*.
30   Diggs, *Alchemy and the Blues*, p. 82.

Blues went back for its impetus and emotional meaning to the individual, to his completely, personal life and death. Because of this, blues could remain for a long time a very fresh and singular form of expression. Though certain techniques and verses came to be standardized among blues singers, the singing itself remained as arbitrary and personal as the shout. Each man sang a different blues . . . The music remained that personal because it began with the performers themselves, and not with formalized notions of how it was to be performed.[31]

The Birth of the Blues

It is impossible to identify when the unique pattern of musical form, now labeled the blues, first emerged. However, most evidence suggests that it originated in the Delta cotton country of northwest Mississippi. The blues, as a particular musical form, may have emerged, during the late 1800's, out of a broader class of music called "reels" which was a catch-all term for social music, especially dance music.[32] However, it's clear that the blues also developed out of the work songs of slaves, sharecroppers, and chain gang prisoners. These work songs and field hollers were also known as "arwhoolies." Arwhoolies are short rhymed verses of one or two phrases which were used to communicate between patches of sharecropping farms and allowed prison gangs to work together in a coordinated manner. This is consistent with bluesman Son House's 1965 account of how the blues began: "People keep asking me where the blues started and all I can say is that when I was a boy we always was singing in the fields. Not real singing, you know, just hollerin', but we made up our songs about things that was happening to us at that time, and I think that's where the blues started."[33]

These arwhoolies were associated with the, "African-influenced five-note pentatonic scale, as opposed to the European eight-note diatonic scale."[34] The pentatonic scale is most often used when the blues are sung unaccompanied but when performed with accompaniment, utilizing Western instrumentation, the utilization of the diatonic scale is required. Blue notes (usually the flattened third, fifth, and seventh scale degrees) are created using tones of the European diatonic scale, either by raising or lowering the pitch of the note which allows the

31 Diggs, *Alchemy and the Blues*, p. 67.
32 Humphrey, *Holy Blues*.
33 Quoted in Charters, *Workin' on the Building*, p. 13.
34 Robertson, *Little Blues Book*, p. 4.

sound of the pentatonic scale to be recreated and a minor key tonality to be evoked.[35] Blues songs with twelve bars of 4/4 meter was the most commonly utilized form as early country blues emerged as a distinct musical genre. The song lyrics usually fell directly into three-line, AAB, stanzas where the second line repeats, sometimes with slight variation, the words in the first, and the third line completes the thought, with a rhyme at the end.[36]

Harmonically, in primitive country blues there may be a one or two-chord "drone" found throughout the entire song which results in rather hypnotic inductive effect. However, most blues are based on the tritone interval (tonic, subdominant, dominant chords) which is considered to be the most dissonant of all intervals, carrying tremendous tension.[37] Thomas Moore addresses the tritone interval in more depth:

> Musical therapy, therefore, does not imply any harmoniz-ing of life as avoidance of dissonance. Stability, evenness, calm, order, control, happiness and peace - these are not the goals of musical therapy. Dissonance has a place and even an energizing function. In music, sound dissonance creates climax and provides expressiveness, it gives bite and spice to an otherwise unsavory mixture of tones. For centuries one of the most dissonant intervals was the tri-tone or diminished fifth, sometimes called *diabolus in mu-sica*, the devil in music.[38]

Moore's comments have implications for the healing properties of the blues which will be explored in greater detail later.

There is also a clear link between the blues and spirituals, with many performers of the blues crossing over to perform spirituals as part of their repertoire. Jones says, "The blues is formed out of the same social and musical fabric that the spiritual issued from, but with blues the social emphasis becomes more personal, the 'Jordan' of the song much more intensely a human accomplishment."[39]

Because of the link with slavery, sharecropping, and prison life, the blues is closely associated with the experience of oppression. In fact, according to Spencer, without oppression and racism there would be

---

35 Cohn, *Nothing but the Blues.*
36 Jeff Titon, *Early Downhome Blues*, p. XVIII.
37 Diggs, *Alchemy and the Blues.*
38 *Musical Therapy*, p. 133.
39 Jones, *Blues People*, p. 63.

no form of music identified as the blues.[40] Paul Garon expressed similar sentiments:

> Only the very specific sociological, cultural, economic, psychological, and political forces faced by working class African Americans - forces permeated with racism - produced the blues. Nothing else did! . . . Only the complex web of racist oppression suffered by blacks at the hands of whites produced the blues, regardless of the many types of suffering with which the blues deals in the manifest content of songs.[41]

In the process of analytic therapy, we frequently observe how the repressive and suppressive influences of the psyche operate similarly to the oppressive forces within a collective and can create the conditions necessary for the development of the blues and its manifestation in the form of grief, depression, worry, and loneliness. The psychic cost of the blues, both individual and collective, exists side by side with the psychic renewal imparted by the blues, as pointed out by blues singer Noble Sissle: "The music did not just happen. There is a history to the birth form of our music. There is an element of life in it - religion, romance, tragedy, faith, hope, and primitive abandon - brought together and paid for at a tremendous price."[42] Sissle's comments can be seen as an implicit acknowledgement that the emergence out of collectivity into individuality is an inherently suffering experience in itself. It seems that Sissle is describing a process of individuation,[43] initiated through the institution of slavery. In fact, Sissle also seems to be redeeming the unrecognized shadow aspect of slavery; an institution which destroyed so much, also served as a catalyst for a movement from a collective consciousness into an individual consciousness. This paradox is one of the wellsprings of the blues.[44]

The blues might be seen as a means of transcending the immediate experience of oppression through expression. For example, love is the

---

40 Spencer, *Blues and Evil*.
41 Quoted in Titon, *Early Downhome Blues*, p. 275.
42 Quoted in Spencer, *Blues and Evil*, p. XXVI.
43 Individuation – "A process of psychological differentiation, having for its goal the development of the individual personality." - (Sharp, *Jung Lexicon*)
44 Of course, one must be careful to consider that the possibility that the interpretation of slavery as an individuation process is merely the imposition of a Western conceptual framework onto African culture, i.e., valuing individual consciousness over the collective. As Kawai (1988) points out, concepts such as ego, Self, and individuation take on a different connotation when examined in the context of the Japanese culture.

vehicle of potential transcendence in Robert Nighthawk's *Sweet Black Angel*:[45]

I've got a sweet black angel, I likes the way she spread her wing
When she spread her wings over me, I gets joy and ev'rything

If my black angel should quit me, I believe that I would die
If you don't love me black angel, please tell me the reason why

The oppression that served as the gestation for the blues remained even as the blues evolved. Until recently few blues singers were given copyrights to their songs and they typically only received travel expenses to the recording sessions and a one-time payment for recording the songs that day. It was extremely rare for an early blues singer to receive royalty payments for the records which were sold.

As Keil points out, the blues has always been a migratory music.[46] At first it was carried by men moving from town to town in search of work and then later it became associated with traveling medicine shows, circuses, and later touring troupes or musical revues. In this way, it parallels some of the migratory patterns north of the Mason-Dixon Line by emancipated slaves and later of African-Americans leaving the agricultural economy and Jim Crow laws of the South. In fact, over one million blacks moved northward from Southern states between 1915 and 1930.[47] During this massive migration the blues evolved. The role of the solo bluesman diminished and blues bands became prominent as the blues moved into louder urban settings, eventually leading to the electronic amplification of the instruments and a greater emphasis on dance oriented rhythms. However, Richard Wright does not feel that the blues lost its importance or vitality as the blues moved off of the plantation and into the cities: "On the plantation our songs carried a strain of otherworldly yearning which people called 'spiritual'; but now our blues . . . are our 'spirituals' of the city pavements, our longing for freedom and opportunity, an expression of our bewilderment and despair in a world whose meaning eludes us."[48]

---

45 Often throughout this book only selected stanzas or lines of songs will be presented, rather than the complete lyrics.
46 Keil, *Urban Blues*.
47 Spencer, *Blues and Evil*.
48 Quoted in Spencer, *Blues and Evil*, p. 122.

Defining the Blues

But what is the blues? The blues is a form of music with a particular sound and feel but the blues also describes an emotional state usually characterized by sadness, grief, or depression. The blues is a more evocative way of describing an internal state; an internal state that seems much richer when communicated through the blues than through psychological language which can seem rather sterile in comparison. Listen to the depiction of a fragmenting inner world described in Stevie Ray Vaughan's lyrics to *Tightrope, "Caught up in a whirlwind, can't catch my breath, knee deep in hot water, broke out in cold sweat, can't catch a turtle in this rat race, feels like I'm losin time at a breakneck pace."* The blues also describes specific experiences such as the loss of a lover, a friendship betrayed, or a bad drunk. Finally, the blues may refer to an entire lifestyle or philosophy of life. When used in this manner it is sometimes talked about as "living the blues." Paul Oliver summarizes these threads as follows: "Though the blues may frequently be associated with a state of depression, of lethargy, or despair, it was not solely a physical, nor a mental state. It was not solely the endurance of suffering or a declaration of hopelessness; nor was it solely a means of ridding oneself of a mood. It was all of these, and more: it was an essential part of the black experience of living."[49]

When a blues musician refers to himself as a "bluesman" he is not only referring to the type of music he plays but also the type of life he has led and the attitude he has about life. It is in this last sense that the blues begins to comment upon or amplify the *anima mundi*, or world soul. An awareness of the *anima mundi* can be detected in many blues songs, e.g., T-Bone Walker's - *Mean Old World*, "*This is a mean old world to live in by yourself*," or Elmore James' - *The Sky is Crying*:

> *The sky is crying, look at the tears roll down the street*
> *I'm waiting in tears for my baby, and I wonder where can she be?*
> *I saw my baby one morning, and she was walking down the street*
> *Make me feel so good until my poor heart would skip a beat*
>
> *I got a bad feeling, my baby, my baby don't love me no more*
> *Now the sky been crying, the tears rolling down my door*

The blues philosophy implicit in the blues includes the idea that the blues is something to be accepted; not something to be gotten rid of or fixed:

Going Down Slow - Mance Lipscomb

> *Don't send no doctor, he can't do me no good.*
> *It's all my fault, mama, I didn't do the things I should.*

Willeford describes the blues philosophy in this way, "In the imaginative world-view of the blues, joy is born of pain; pain is not to be denied. Joy is not simply the denial of pain but represents an order of value of its own right. Irony [in the blues] assures that pain is not denied, is taken into account, as the value of joy is affirmed . . . One must remain open to the reality of human misery."[50] This stance of acceptance is reflected in Junior Kimbrough's lyrics "*most things haven't worked out*" and "*I done got old.*" In listening to Kimbrough's music one has the sense that Kimbrough is making an observation, not a complaint. Within this philosophy of acceptance the blues is seen as something ubiquitous and pervasive, penetrating into all areas of life:

---

49 *Blues Fell This Morning*, p. 283ff.
50 *Abandonment, Wish, and Hope in the Blues*, p. 181ff.

I've Got Too Many Blues
—Mabel Richardson and Sam Price's Blusicians

I've got too many blues, I'm worried all the time
Don't know if I'm goin' or comin', I just about lost my mind

I've got blues for breakfast, blues for lunch
Blues for supper, by the bunch
I've got too many blues and I'm full of misery
Just as sure as you're livin' someone has put bad luck on me

I get the blues when I'm high, the blues when I'm low
Ol' man blues just won't let me go
Why he keeps on followin' me, I sure cannot see
Come on in mister blues and have a drink on me

I've got blues by the dozen, blues by the score
I've got so many blues I can't stand no more
I've got too many blues for any poor girl to bear
Can't you see I've got more than my share

Blues Everywhere - Yas Yas Girl

Well it's blues in my house, from the roof to the ground
And it's blues everywhere since my good man left town.

Blues in my mail-box, 'cause I cain't get no mail
Says blues in my bread-box, 'cause my bread got stale.

Blues in my meal-barrel and there's blues upon my shelf
And there's blues in my bed, 'cause I'm sleepin' by myself.

Everyday I Have The Blues - Memphis Slim

Everyday, everyday I have the blues
When you see me worryin' baby, yeah it's you I hate to lose

Whoa nobody loves me, nobody seems to care
Well worries and trouble darling, babe you know I've had my share

The blues is experienced, accepted, and survived; not conquered or overcome. One hopes to eventually feel better but the intent is to acknowledge and cope with the deeply visceral experience of the blues:

Groaning the Blues - Willie Dixon

I'm so tired of moanin, tryin to groan away my blues
I keep weepin and cryin every time I think of you
I rather die of starvation, perish out in the desert sun
Than to think of some other man holding you in his arms
My heart gets so heavy, Lord I shakes down in my bones
I can't love another but I'm forced to weep and moan

Trouble in Mind - Muddy Waters

Trouble in mind, and I'm blue
Oh you know I won't be blue always
You know the sun is gonna shine in my back door some day

Always underlying the effort to survive the blues is the assumption and acceptance that the blues will return again later to be dealt with again; the ongoing cycle of the fall and redemption, death and resurrection, the mythologem of the Great Round. This is reflected in the title of a song by Muddy Waters, *No Escape from the Blues*, and also in the following songs:

Hard Times Ain't Gone Nowhere - Lonnie Johnson

People raving about hard times,
I don't know why they should.
If some people was like me,
They didn't have no money when times was good

Southern Blues - Ma Rainey

Your house catches on fire and ain't no water 'round
Throw your trunk out the window, let it burn on down.

Willeford elaborates further on this aspect of the blues philosophy: "When one has the blues, one hopes that one will find the path to not having them, and that when one does not have them, one fears that one may already be on the path to having them. Having the blues and not having the blues exist, metaphorically speaking, at a distance from one another. And knowledge of both conditions is assumed and drawn upon in a blues performance."[51] This same attitude is reflected in Jung's comments in *Answer to Job*:

> It is far better to admit the affect and submit to its violence than to try to escape it . . . the violence is meant to penetrate to a man's vitals, and he to succumb to its action. He must be affected by it, otherwise its full effect will not reach him. But he should know, or learn to know, what has affected him, for in this way he transforms the blindness of the violence on the one hand and of the affect on the other into knowledge.[52]

Upon first hearing the blues one might notice a parallel with the First Noble Truth of Buddhism – i.e., that suffering exists and is unavoidable in birth, old age, sickness and death. The acknowledgement of suffering and the need to accept the presence of suffering in life is also present in the blues as Jeff Titon points out: "Though some blues songs express satisfaction and others are resolved happily, most concentrate on trouble. To feel blue is not merely to feel sad; it is to feel a complex of emotions, as the narrator begs, brags, threatens, cries for help, stoically accepts his situation, or exits with an ironic parting shot."[53] However, there are other facets to the blues, for often the blues is a celebration of life, living, sensuality, and joy. An example of this would be *Good Times*, recorded at various times by Koko Taylor, B.B. King, Bobby Bland, and others:

Hey everybody, let's have some fun.
You only live once
And when you're dead, you're gone.
So let the good times roll.

The books and articles reviewed in the introduction of this book contain dozens of useful definitions of the blues, but I like to think of the blues as joyful participation in the sorrows of the world. Charles

---

51 *Abandonment, Wish, and Hope in the Blues*, p. 177.
52 *Psychology and Religion*, CW11, par. 562.
53 *Early Downhome Blues*, p. 182.

Keil says the blues is about soul, which he describes as an "unspeakable essence."[54] According to Willie Dixon, one of the greatest blues composers, the blues is, "the facts of life, the heritage of the black race, and a thousand generations of poverty and starvation."[55] John Lee Hooker's words underscore the universality of the blues: "And so when you gets the feelin' it's not only what happened to you - it's what happened to your fore-parents and other people. And that's what makes the blues."[56] Paul Garon says, "That the blues is poetry is beyond doubt."[57] The blues are defined as, "a sad thing and a rejoicing thing," by blueswoman Van Zula Hunt.[58] Little Jr. Parker says, "The blues is based on somebody's life; it hits 'em in the heart and the love comes out. You think of your last love, or the girl you're with, or the troubles you've had."[59] Some say the blues simply tries to decipher the relationship between men and women. This is certainly the perspective of Son House who said, "I don't know who it was that started this thing, this blues business. You know it ain't but one way you - the blues exists, and that comes between male and female bein' in love. Uh-huh. And when one has been deceived by the other. And then he gets the blues, that is, if they love each other. Yeah. Then they get the blues."[60] A longer definition is provided by Robertson:

> The blues shares with poetry the basic quality of offering a skillfully condensed and intensified "snapshot" of an experience. The essence of the music is simple and direct, as are the lyrics, and for that reason it seems to me the great blues singers are America's Zen masters. They are men and women deeply in touch with the here and now who tap into the very essence of human experience, longing, and loss through the simplicity and direct truths of their songs. The feelings in the blues are not limited to sadness, for a person can find undisputed joy in the music and can benefit from an attitude that speaks and sings of a kind of cosmic comedy. In the blues, the line between tragedy and comedy is frequently blurred. Willie Dixon explained it all by saying, 'You can have the blues one day because your

---

54 *Urban Blues.*
55 Quoted in J. O'Neal."I Once was Lost but Now I'm Found: The Blues Revival of the 1960's." In L. Cohn (Ed.), *Nothing but the Blues*, p. 378.
56 Spencer, *Blues and Evil*, p. 74.
57 *Blues and the Poetic Spirit*, p. 1.
58 Quoted in Spencer, *Blues and Evil*, p. 39.
59 Quoted in Keil, *Urban Blues*, p. 166.
60 Quoted in Titon, *Early Downhome Blues*, p. 179.

woman went away. Then you can have the blues the next day because she came back.[61]

All of these are wonderful examples of defining characteristics of the blues but it is the blues songs that provide the best definition. Please note the individual differences reflected in the same song, recorded in the same era, by two prominent female blues artists of the time:

The Blues Ain't Nothing But - Georgia White

Oh the blues ain't nothin' but a woman wanna see her man
Cause she wants some lovin', you women will understand

Oh the blues ain't nothin' but a low down heart disease
Just lovin' your man, he's so hard to please

Oh the blues ain't nothin' but a woman lovin' a married man
Can't see him when she wants to, got to see him when she can

Oh the blues ain't nothin' but a good woman feelin' bad
Always downhearted, blue, disgusted and sad

Oh the blues ain't nothin' but a feelin' that will get you down
Fallin' out with your man, you feel like leaving town

Blues Ain't Nothin' Else But - Ida Cox

Oh the blues ain't nothin' but your lover on your mind
The man that keeps you worried, and always cryin'

Oh the blues ain't nothin' but a good woman wanting to see her man
She can't get when she want him, gotta catch him when she can

Oh the blues ain't nothin' but a slow achin' heart disease
Just like consumption, it kills you by degrees

Oh the blues ain't nothin' but a woman that cries night and day
Cryin' about her lover, another woman took him away

Oh papa papa papa, mama done gone mad
Oh the blues ain't nothin' but a good woman feelin' bad

---

61   *Little Blues Book*, p. xv.

Both of these women are singing the same song which vividly describes the feeling of the blues and some of the conditions which contribute to the development of the blues. Yet, each of the singers places her own idiosyncratic stamp on the song; personalizing that which is universal.

3

The Blues and Unitary Reality

> "Music is feeling, movement, law, and spirit, in the
> form of something not purely psychic but pointing
> beyond itself to something real . . . the unitary reality."
> —Erich Neumann

Little Whitt Wells, a Georgia bluesman, says, "You know, the blues is a trance music. If it can't take you there, it ain't worth the effort, and if folks can't get there, well I guess it's not meant for them . . . The blues is where it's at with me. I am the blues, it's my life."[62] His comments have some psychological implications which I hope to make explicit in the following passages. Wells' discussion of the blues as being "trance music" and his statement that the blues "take you there" imply that the blues evokes a shift from one state of consciousness to another. The blues "takes you" from ordinary consciousness into a blues conscious-ness, in which the yearnings and sufferings of the soul are brought clos-er to one's subjectivity. Also implied in his comments is the idea that individual responsivity is part of the equation in this shift. Without the appropriate attitude or responsivity one is unable to make the shift into a blues consciousness.[63] Finally, Wells also speaks about the movement past the distinctions between subject and object, self and experience, individual and collective. These implicit meanings in Wells' comments reflect a state of "unitary reality" which I contend is an essential charac-teristic of the blues experience and accounts for the depth and richness of blues music.

---

62 Quoted in Herman , Big Mo and Little Whitt Sing the Moody Swamp Blues."
    Blues Revue, Issue 32, p. 32.
63 Wells' comments are reminiscent of the interaction between Christ and the disciples in Matthew, Chap. 13 where he is telling the parable of the mustard seed and then says, "Who hath ears to hear, let him hear." The disciples then said, "Why speakest thou unto them in parables?" To which Christ respond-ed, "Because it is given unto you to know the mysteries of the kingdom of heaven, but to them it is not given." Like Wells, Christ is addressing the issue of receptivity to a particular experience.

Erich Neumann's work on unitary reality was originally published in the 1952 *Eranos Yearbook* and he could be considered, along with C.G. Jung, one of the first intersubjective theorists.[64] His theory of unitary reality anticipates similar work in the area of intersubjectivity by authors such as Robert Stolorow, George Atwood, and Thomas Ogden. At the same time Neumann's work is broader, more encompassing, than the authors he antedates. Neumann proposes that there are two types of consciousness: "conscious knowledge," associated with the ego-complex, which splits experience into polarized categories, and "perceiving" or "extraneous" consciousness, which is knowledge that is beyond the ability of the ego-complex to process.[65] He indicates that an excess focus on conscious knowledge has resulted in a diminished awareness of the world's unity and continuity, as well as its aliveness and significance, which Neumann contends is primarily experienced through feelings and intuition. Neumann points out that the term *abaisement du niveau mental*[66] is used somewhat pejoratively as though no consciousness is present in these states where extraneous knowledge dominates. He desires to resurrect the idea of *participation mystique*[67] from being a label used to characterize a primitive form of thinking in which the distinction between subject and object is blurred, to one in which a specific type of knowledge, which he refers to as "field knowledge," is exchanged between one being and another existing within the same "reality field."

Neumann's work in this area builds on Jung's theories about *participation mystique*, the psychoid realm, synchronicity, the archetypal structure of experience, the *anima mundi*, the *unus mundus* and the *unio mentalis*. Neumann reminds us that the archetype is both a fact in the outside world and a potential image in the reality of the psyche, hence it bridges the gulf between inner and outer. Neumann indicates that when a personality is immersed in an archetypal field it means, "There is a reciprocal co-ordination between world and psyche . . . a co-ordina-

---

64 Most simply, intersubjectivity is the sharing of subjective states by two or more individuals. The concept of intersubjectivity is a "field or systems theory in that it seeks to comprehend psychological phenomena not as products of isolated intrapsychic mechanisms, but as forming at the interface of reciprocally interacting subjectivities." (Atwood & Stolorow, *Faces in a Cloud*, p. 178)

65 *The Place of Creation*, p. 5.

66 *Abaisement du niveau mental* - "A lowering of the level of consciousness." – (Sharp, *Jung Lexicon*)

67 *Participation mystique* – "A term derived from anthropology and the study of primitive psychology, denoting a mystical connection, or identity, between subject and object." - (Sharp, *Jung Lexicon*)

tion which is based on the archetypal structure which embraces both, or of which both are partial aspects and which "leads to an emotionally toned unitary experience."[68] According to Neumann, synchronistic and magical phenomena operate within unitary reality fields. He states that unitary fields also encompass interactions between human beings, between human beings and animals, between human beings and things, and between animals and their environment. The infant's initial lack of distinction between mother and infant is seen by Neumann as the first experience of unitary reality.

Neumann indicates that a primary feeling experience of unitary reality is the sense that something is being unified, something previously split is coming together again and redeemed, or that something previously in exile or banishment is reclaimed.[69] He also indicates that experiences of relatedness, mutual sympathy, Eros, or interconnectedness are also indicative of unitary reality. This certainly applies to the blues, which brings one into felt connection with repressed feelings and desires. These experiences of oneself are being reclaimed and at the same time are experienced as taking place within the larger context of a felt community of other people engaged with the blues, hence the awareness of unitary reality is constellated via a relationship with the blues.

One of the primary reasons that Neumann's concept of unitary reality is pertinent to our exploration of the blues is that Neumann identifies expressions of the creative process as belonging to the meaningful order discernible through this "extraneous knowledge dimension." Neumann's observations coincide with Joseph Campbell's observations on the parallels between the mystic and the artist:

> For the reality in which the artist and the mystic are exposed is, in fact, the same. It is of their own inmost truth brought to consciousness: by the mystic, direct confrontation, and by the artist, through reflection in the masterworks of his art. The fact that the nature of the artist (as a microcosm) and the nature of the universe (as the macrocosm) are two aspects of the same reality.[70]

---

68 *The Place of Creation*, p. 27.
69 An interesting sidelight is that fact that "In Greek mythology Harmonia [hence our words harmony, harmonica, harmonics] was honored as Goddess of the bringing-together of opposing forces . . . The syllable *ar* or *har* means the uniting of opposites to a whole." (Streich, "Music, Alchemy and Psychology in Atlanta Fugiens of Michael Maier." In M. Maier *Atlanta Fugiens*, p. 29)
70 *Inner Reaches of Outer Space*, p. 121.

An experience of unitary reality is not exclusive to blues music and in fact Igor Stravinsky indicates that, "A new piece of music is a new reality."[71] Likewise, Patricia Skar says, "Listening to and playing music help us rediscover an inner place of 'unitary reality,' where we are rooted in the cosmos and also in our individual selves."[72] Both Skar, explicitly, and Stravinsky, implicitly, are making statements about the close relationship between unitary reality and musical experience. Indeed, any music can facilitate an experience or emergence of unitary reality. However, the blues has some specific characteristics which make it an especially vital example of unitary reality.

We can hear the allusions to unitary reality states in the lyrics of the blues. Consider the following lyrics from Robert Johnson's *Hellhound on My Trail*:

> *I got to keep movin', I've got to keep movin'*
> *Blues fallin' down like hail, blues fallin' down like hail*

---

71 Quoted in Storr, *Music and the Mind*, p. 75.
72 "Music and Analysis." In M. Mattoon (Ed.). *Zurich 95: Open Questions in Analytical Psychology.*, p. 402.

And the days keeps on worryin' me, there's a hellhound on my trail.
Hellhound on my trail, hellhound on my trail

This hellhound is the element of the psyche that pursues but is subjectively experienced as threatening or monstrous.[73] Clearly, in these verses the blues is something that Johnson is intimately connected with and living out. The distinction between inner state and outer situation is unimportant. The blues is something that surrounds him, chases him, alters his internal state, urges him to compulsive action, and connects him with inner images which vividly depict his unitary world. These same characteristics can be found throughout the blues idiom:

Blow Wind Blow - Muddy Waters

Don't the sun look lonesome
Setting down behind the trees?
Don't your house look lonesome
When your baby's packed to leave?

The Sky is Crying - Elmore James

The sky is crying, look at the tears roll down the street
I'm waiting in tears for my baby, and I wonder where can she be?

I saw my baby one morning, and she was walking down the street
I saw my baby one morning, yes she was walking down the street
Make me feel so good until my poor heart would skip a beat

I got a bad feeling, my baby, my baby don't love me no more
I got a bad feeling, my baby don't love me no more
Now the sky been crying, the tears rolling down my door

All My Love In Vain - Robert Johnson

I followed her to the station with a suitcase in my hand
And I followed her to the station with a suitcase in my hand
Well it's hard to tell it's hard to tell, when all your love's in vain
All my love's in vain

---

73 A similar psychic situation is presented in Francis Bacon's poem, *The Hound of Heaven.*

When the train rolled up to the station, I looked her in the eye
When the train rolled up to the station, and I looked her in the eye
Well I was lonesome I felt so lonesome, and I could not help but cry
All my love's in vain

When the train it left the station, was two lights on behind
Well the blue light was my blues and the red light was my mind
All my love's in vain.

Graveyard Dream Blues - Ida Cox

Blues on my mind, blues all around my head
Blues on my mind, and blues all around my head
I dreamed last night that the man that I love was dead

I went to the graveyard, fell down on my knees
And I asked the gravedigger to give me back my real good man please

The gravedigger look me in the eye
Said "I'm sorry lady but your man has said his last goodbye"

I wrung my hands and I wanted to scream
But when I woke up I found it was only a dream

The blues is a manifestation and containment of the archetypal field that constitutes unitary reality. Neumann points out that inner and outer are merely categories of a conscious knowledge system, not reality. In the field of unitary reality, the distinction between inner and outer is diminished, psychical and physical are no longer opposites, and the boundaries of form defining a person and the Other become blurred. Here he is talking about the "transgressive character" of the archetype, i.e., the capacity of the archetype to move beyond dichotomous reality, as defined by Jung,[74] and hence he is associating the unitary reality with the structure of the archetypal field. Through a transcendence of opposites, the blues moves us deeply into the realm of unitary reality. A good example of this is the lyrics to T-Bone Walker's *Stormy Monday*. He sings, "*The eagle flies on Friday and Saturday I go out to play*," invoking the listener's anticipation of payday and the associated pleasures, perhaps excesses, which will take place on Saturday night. But as the

---

74 See "Synchronicity: An Acausal Connecting Principle, "*The Structure and Dynamics of the Psyche*, CW8, par. 964.

song continues Walker sings, *"Sunday I go to church and I kneel down 'n' pray, and this is what I say, baby, Lord have mercy, Lord, have mercy on me. You know I cried, Lord, have mercy, Lord, have mercy on me."* In making this movement within the song, Walker juxtaposes the sacred and the profane. Mircea Eliade describes the sacred and the profane as "two modes of being in the world, two existential situations assumed by man in the course of his history" but also describes an "abyss" which divides the two modalities.[75] Within the unitary world of blues consciousness there is a coexistence of the sacred and the profane in which a conflict between the opposites is not constellated. According to Storr:

> Nietzsche realized - no one more vividly - that the only life we know is constituted by opposites. Pleasure is inconceivable without pain; light without darkness; love without hate; good without evil. The pleroma may contain no opposites, but in life, heaven and hell march hand in hand; it is only the never-never land of the afterlife that they become separate entities. This is why the greatest art always includes tragedy; why it must embrace tragedy as well as triumph; why the denial of suffering is the negation of life itself.[76]

We can see from this passage that the blues belongs among the great arts because of its extraordinary capacity to embrace, embody, and transcend the experience of the opposites, especially as they become manifest in the experience of tragedy and suffering.

The blues removes us from the polar reality of non-unitary experience because it doesn't tend to separate experience into polar categories in which one pole cancels out the Other. Oliver felt the bluesman was above all a realist who was not repulsed by the uglier side of the world in which he resided but instead accepted the presence of both evil and good.[77] The blues reconciles opposites by its focus on the relationship between men and women as its predominant theme while maintaining the paradoxical tension of the affinity and antinomy between men and women. Spencer claims that this perspective reflects a worldview rooted in an Afrocentric, holistic perspective on the world and personhood.[78] Similarly, James Cone says the blues, by focusing on sexuality as a dominant theme, rejects the distinctions between body and soul, and em-

---

75   Eliade, *The Sacred and the Profane*, p. 14.
76   *Music and the Mind*, p. 158.
77   *Blues Fell This Morning*.
78   *Blues and Evil*.

phasizes the idea that there can be no wholeness without sexuality.[79] Often love and hate (or aggression) exist side by side in the blues just as they do in the unconscious. Only when our ego defenses are constellated is there an attempt to separate love and hate in order to reduce the anxiety associated with this ambivalence. Within the unitary reality of the blues, good and evil, love and hate, staying or leaving coexist side by side without an experience of internal contradiction.

The transcendence of opposites can be found throughout the blues. For example, in one song B.B. King may sing about his "woman" who gives him gasoline to drink when he asks for water and in the next song he may sing about his "baby" who generously gives him a $20 bill when he asks her for a nickel. Likewise, in *Kind Hearted Woman Blues*, Robert Johnson sings of a woman who will *"do anything in this world for me"* but who also *"studies evil all the time."* Another example is reflected in a verse found in many blues songs: *"I love you, baby, ain't gonna tell you no lie, but the day you quit me, that's the day you die."* A final example of the transcendence of opposites is contained in the following song:

If I Make It Over - Bumble Bee Slim

Well, I'm blue and evil, so many things to learn
So many days to worry, so many ways to turn

I had so much trouble, swear my nerves are weakenin' down
I would swing on a freight train, but I'm afraid to leave the ground

Whistle keeps on blowin' an' I got my debts to pay
I've got a mind to leave my baby, Lord I've got a mind to stay

This coexistence of opposites is part and parcel of the blues world and contributes to the fullness of the experience of life. What appears to non-blues consciousness as ambivalence or paradox is not oppositional within the consciousness of the blues. In analytic therapy, it is often a patient's difficulty in tolerating ambiguity or ambivalence which leads to symptoms of anxiety, avoidance, withdrawal, or the activation of splitting defenses.

---

79 Cited in Spencer, *Blues and Evil*, p. 36.

Alterations in Time Consciousness

Changes in the experience of time are another manifestation of unitary reality in the blues. German philosopher Georg Hegel maintained that music was the first art to give us the sense of unification occurring in time rather than in space.[80] We can see an aspect of unitary reality in Igor Stravinsky's distinction between ontological time (time as it actually is, as it is measured) and psychological time (the subjective inner experience of an individual which varies according to his inner state, whether he is bored, excited, in pain, aroused).[81] Stravinsky believed that music, which is primarily expressive of the composer's "emotive impulses," substitutes psychological time for ontological time. The listener, if he becomes engaged in the music's drama, often finds that his perception of the passage of time becomes altered. Thus the listener and the performer have entered into a shared unitary reality in which even the passage of time becomes altered. Because the blues is so emotionally charged, it has a unique capacity to evoke this aspect of unitary reality. Time distortion for both patient and analyst frequently occurs in the emotionally charged setting of analytic therapy. When there is significant emotional energy constellated in a session it often seems as though the session flies by or there can be a movement into a sense of timelessness whereby the end of the session is encountered as a surprise to both participants.

Neumann indicates that the threefold time (past, present, future) of consciousness is an artifact of the ego-complex, and that within unitary reality, time is autonomously occurring but not passing.[82] This is similar to the way in which Jung speculates on the relativity of time within the unconscious.[83] Thus Hegel's and Stravinsky's observations support the idea that music in general, and the blues specifically, are avenues by which one can become aware of and participate in an experience of unitary reality. An alteration in time consciousness, and other sensory perceptions, can often be experienced in the improvisational interaction between musicians in a blues performance. Two such experiences are described by blues harmonica player, Adam Gussow, of the Harlem street blues duo, *Satan and Adam*:

---

80 Storr, *Music and the Mind*, p. 173.
81 Storr, *Music and the Mind*, p. 185.
82 *The Place of Creation*, p. 44.
83 "The Soul and Death." *The Structure and Dynamics of the Psyche*, CW8, par. 815.

The music seems to play itself, an endless streaming glide, hard good work poured into a bottomless sweet spot . . . the 125th Street groove was special. One cold windy March afternoon we were slamming hard on "Ode to Billy Joe," whirling each other in circles like a couple of dizzy square dancers . . . The bustle and roar of Harlem suddenly trembled and fell away. Harlem was there and wasn't, I was here and wasn't, Mister Satan was everywhere and nowhere. We had entered the Zone. The Zone was beyond words, deeper than language. It was a flaming nuanced frenzy, fully articulated in all dimensions, sustained at the barest fraction below all-out effort. We stayed in the Zone for an endless moment . . . Mister Satan's eyes were closed; he rocked on his hi-chair, unfurling three-octave electrical storms. Time shivered. Suddenly - Bam! - he gave a ferocious yank, stopped playing, fell back in his chair. I stopped on a slippery dime . . . 'I forgot I was playing!' he [Mister Satan] gasped, eyes crinkling, tickled. 'I got so far into the groove my hands started moving by themselves!' [84]

Mister Satan was singing the song about pretty girls, working his harsh rasp . . . I bit down hard, worked each reed, followed his vocal curves and swerves with my inner ear - doubling, echoing, urging - and felt myself sinking into a warm low free place, as though whatever I'd been standing on had suddenly softened and given way. I had infinitely more time between phrases than I'd realized. Each seemed to flow effortlessly out of the next. There was room to move down here, to stretch out your elbows and take a deep breath. Aaaah. Feel that? What would you call it? And then, with a small pang of disappointment, I floated back up through the music and found myself on the street.[85]

This alternation of time consciousness can also be detected in the following lyrics to *Future Blues* by Willie Brown:

Can't tell my future, can't tell my past.
And It seem like every minute sure gonna be my last.
And the minutes seem like hours, hours seem like days
It seems like my woman ought to stop her low-down ways.

---

84 *Mr. Satan's Apprentice: A Blues Memoir*, p. 107ff.
85 *Mr. Satan's Apprentice: A Blues Memoir* p. 166.

4

Archetypal Manifestations in the Blues

"The archetype is . . . a dynamism which makes itself
felt in the numinosity and fascinating power of the
archetypal image."
—C.G. Jung

Archetypal Themes and Complexes

The themes associated with the blues are the building blocks of human experience: love, sex, work, travel, gambling, abandonment, loss of autonomy, addiction, adultery, relationship, trust, jealousy, joy, betrayal, and death. One could say the darker aspects of the Greek myths are present in the blues: the ecstasy, abandon, and drunkenness of Dionysus, the anger and revenge of Zeus; the love and sexuality of Aphrodite; the jealousy of Hera; the suffering and darkness of Hades' underworld; and the physical affliction of Hephaestus and Chiron. The blues certainly does not reflect the characteristics of the light carriers, Apollo and Athena. Diggs indicates that there is a tremendous breadth to blues lyrics but that the two core themes are depression and libido: "Depression and passion in the blues finds a strong association with Dionysos' blueness as 'somber madness' and instinctual sexuality . . . and so the blues . . . is most at home in our modern temples to Dionysos: juke joints, night clubs, bars, whorehouses, and 'blue light' districts."[86] Through these lyrics, the blues underlines the importance of the emotional life of the individual and yet points to the universality of these experiences.

Overall, there is a parallel between experiencing the blues and being in an autonomous complex. One author, uses the term "autonomous" to characterize an aspect of the blues and he indicates that he is using it to describe something out of the mainstream and therefore less affected by mainstream influences.[87] Hence, the blues functions like the com-

---

86 *Alchemy of the Blues*, pp. 35ff.
87 Jones, *Blues People*.

plex, outside of the mainstream of the collective conscious influences. Mance Lipscomb describes an encounter with an autonomous complex in the lyrics from *Goin to Louisiana*:

> *Soon one morning, the blues knocked on my door.*
> *Come here to stay with you, won't be leaving no more.*

Blues music attempts to amplify basic human experiences through both lyrics and tone. The standard blues scale incorporates flat and sharp notes in order to create a sound that is more discordant and expressive of inner experience than the standard scales. Notes are also "bent" to make it sound as though the instrument is screaming or crying. At times the experience is expressed through the shouts, moans, wails, and cries of pain from the performer. An example of this is the introduction to Howlin' Wolf's *Moanin' for My Baby*, which literally opens with a long, plaintive moan expressing the pain associated with his separation from his woman. Similar vocalizations are heard on Little Walter's *Rollin and Tumblin*. Neumann indicates that the experience of archetypes, just as with the feeling-toned complexes of the personal unconscious, can be disturbing to our conscious minds and there is likely to be a concomitant effort from our conscious mind to distance ourselves from these entities experienced as emanating from the deeper layers of the psyche.[88] In parallel fashion, the blues can be disturbing. The wails and moans of the singer, the discordant rhythms, and the dissonant chord structures can evoke deeper responses than anticipated by the conscious mind and are often experienced as disruptive to the ego-complex. For the psychoanalyst or therapist, it can be disturbing when a patient's verbalizations give way to a deep guttural wail – communicating a pain for which words simply aren't adequate.

Mother and Infant Blues

The presence of the mother-infant dyad is strongly felt in the blues. Kenneth Wright discusses the importance of non-symbolic, nonverbal means of expression and communication in the mother-infant dyad: "Infant and mother are in nearly constant communication, but this communication does not use words. It takes the form of the cry, the smile, and the tantrum; the touch, the holding, and the tone of voice."[89] Given Wright's statement, it becomes easier to understand the significance of a common blues phrase, "*cryin' the blues.*" Interestingly, Storr cites research which suggests that all music originates from the ritualized verbal exchanges which go on between mothers and babies during the first year of life.[90]

Garon's ideas about the appeal of the blues are consistent with the material presented by Wright:

> We can speculate that at least some decisive contributions to the force of appeal in the blues can be found in the listener's infancy; perhaps the soothing voice of the parents, or more likely, the infant's own crying. The crying as symptomatic of a painful state produces pleasure in the listener insofar as it can be identified with "from afar" - thus the aesthetic disguise operates in such a way that painful emotions can be recalled and mastered when listening to the blues, the aesthetic illusion maintaining the distance necessary for mastery.[91]

While I am in agreement with Garon's statement regarding the role infancy plays in the ongoing appeal of the blues, I disagree with his assessment that listening to another's pain is pleasurable via the working

---

88   *The Place of Creation.*
89   *Vision and Separation*, p. 253.
90   *Music and the Mind.*
91   *Blues and the Poetic Spirit*, p. 13.

of an aesthetic disguise. I propose that the pleasure is obtained by having a sense of understanding by another as well as the sense of being
connected to a more universal human experience, much in the same
way Jung proposes that myths and fairy tales contribute to the understanding of individual experience by providing a broader, more universal context for that experience.

Given the importance of the mother-infant dyad in the development of communication and music, it is not surprising that the mother
archetype is prominent in many blues songs:

Mother Blues - Jimmy Gordon

I've treated my dear old mother, I've been treatin' her so unkind
Without a mighty change I believe I'm gonna lose my mind.

So many men are in trouble and their mothers have been their slave
So much grievin' and worryin' I've carried her to her grave.

Motherless Children - Blind Willie Johnson

Motherless children have a mighty hard time
When mother is dead.

Goin Down Slow - Mance Lipscomb

Write my mother,
Tell her the shape I'm in.
Tell her to pray for me,
Forgiveness for my sins.

Won't Somebody Pacify My Mind - Sonny Jones

I'm gonna leave here walking, make home my second stop.
I'm gonna find my mother, she's the only friend I got.

This association with the mother archetype and maternal language in
the blues is consistent with Neumann's perspective that: "Creative man

lives in a state of being not quite split off from the mother-archetype and its world, and this naturally expresses itself in the accentuation of the child-archetype in his psyche."[92] As I mentioned earlier, Neumann views the mother-infant dyad as the first experience of unitary reality. Wright also recognizes in psychoanalysis and the mother-infant dyad, the same qualities that can be detected in the blues:

> Words . . . are a singularly poor vehicle for conveying to others our deepest selves - those 'thoughts that do often lie too deep for tears'. . . This objective form operates by creating a resonating echo within another subject. My 'barbaric yawp' creates a sympathetic and resonating response in you by arousing in you the latent patterns I have idiosyncratically expressed. There has been a resonating recognition of iconic patterns of experience, made possible through the mediation of an external form that embodied in some analogical way the primary pattern.[93]

In this passage Wright is referring to nonverbal communication as it interacts with archetypal patterns of experience. It is just such an experience of the "deepest self" that is reflected in Leroy Carr's *Midnight Hour Blues*:

> *In the wee midnight hours, long 'fore the break of day,*
> *When the blues creep on you and carry your mind away.*
> *While I lay in my bed, and cannot go to sleep,*
> *While my heart's in trouble, and my mind is sinking deep.*

Wright goes on to discuss the importance of developing a maternal mode of language, which serves the inner needs of the subject, rather than the usually encountered paternal mode of language, which functions for the civilizing and societal needs of the object. The maternal mode "retrieves the self from its unspoken limbo."[94] It is within this maternal domain of language, the mother tongue, which I believe the blues function.

Through its emphasis on the emotional life of the individual the blues harkens back to our earliest experiences, the mother-infant dyad, and the development of the subjective sense of self. John Bowlby discusses the importance of emotions as the most basic datum of communication:

---

92 *The Place of Creation*, p. 103.
93 *Vision and Separation*, p. 254ff.
94 Wright, *Vision and Separation*, p. 263.

> There are, in fact, no more important communications be-
> tween one human being and another than those expressed
> emotionally, and no information more vital for construct-
> ing and reconstructing working models of self and other
> than information about how each feels towards the other.
> During the earliest years of our lives, indeed, emotional
> expression and its reception are the only means of com-
> munication we have, so that the foundations of our work-
> ing models of self and attachment figures are perforce laid
> using information from that source alone.[95]

Heinz Kohut also hypothesizes that music accesses preverbal, primitive modes of psychological experience.[96] Garon, drawing on the work
of Kohut, speculates that the blues deals primarily with primary process, i.e., unconscious mental activity, rather than secondary process,
i.e., ego-directed rational mental activity.[97] References to these earliest,
most primitive experiences are found throughout the lyric content of
the blues. In the following blues songs paranoia, aggression, omnipotent destructiveness, and omnipotent power, characteristic of Melanie
Klein's description of the paranoid-schizoid position,[98] can be heard:

The Blues What Am - Jazz Gillum

Don't want my rooster crowing after the sun goes down
Don't bring peanuts in my house, it will make a coffin turn around.

I don't want nobody to lay their bare hands on my head
I don't eat everybody's cooking, I'm suspicious of my cornbread.

Don't touch me with your broom, don't let my lamp get low.
Don't let the dogs start howling 'cause somebody got to go.

Take your hat off my bed and hang it on a nail
If I sit down on your trunk, I am bound to go to jail.

---

95 *A Secure Base*, p. 156.
96 "Observations on the Psychological Functions of Music." *J. of the American Psychoanalytic Association*, vol. 5, pp. 389ff.
97 *Blues and the Poetic Spirit*.
98 The paranoid-schizoid position is a psychological state proposed by Melanie Klein which depicts the psychological functioning of early childhood
but which is also present to varying degrees in adults. It is characterized by
internal part object relationships. Part objects are a function of the splitting
defense which takes place in phantasy. In this developmental position, experience is primarily perceived as all good or all bad. See "Notes on Some
Schizoid Mechanisms," In J. Mitchell (Ed.) *The Selected Melanie Klein*.

I don't want my brother to put his bare feet in my shoes
Somebody stole my rabbit's foot, and I've got the suspicious blues.

Tin Pan Alley - Stevie Ray Vaughan

It was the roughest place I've ever been,
All the people down there living for the whisky wine and gin,
I heard a woman scream, I peeped through the door,
Some guy was working on her, Lord, with a two by four

Sawmill Man Blues - Pleasant Joe

I didn't build this world, but I sure can tear it down.

Mad Mama Blues - Violet Mills

Want to set this world on fire, that is my mad desire,
I'm the devil in disguise, got murder in my eyes.

Now if I could see blood runnin' through the streets
Could see everybody lying dead right at my feet

Give me gunpowder, give me dynamite
Yes, I'm gonna wreck the city, gonna blow it up tonight.

In a similar fashion, the hyperbole, which Heinz Kohut associates with the grandiose infantile self,[99] can be heard in the following songs:

Just To Be With You - The Paul Butterfield Blues Band

On a ship that's made of paper,
I'll sail the seven seas.
I'll even fight sharks with a toothpick,
Darlin, whoa baby, just to bring you home with me.

---

99 Kohut describes the grandiose infantile self as the self that emerges out of the normal infantile experience of oneself as the centre of all experience and omnipotent. See Ernest Wolf, *Treating the Self.*

I'm Ready - Muddy Waters

I got an ax handled pistol on a graveyard frame
That shoots tombstone bullets wearin' balls and chains.
I'm drinkin' TNT. I'm smokin' dynamite.
I hope some screwball start a fight,
'Cause I'm ready, ready as anybody can be.
I'm ready for you, I hope you're ready for me.

Black Panther - Johnny Shines

My baby gets unruly, thinks she can stop a train,
Hold up her hand, stop the lightin' and the rain.

Christopher Bollas elaborates on the connection between mood states (i.e., complexes) and the infant-child self in a manner that helps us understand why the blues, through its capacity to communicate emotionally laden material, is such a moving musical form:

> If a person enters a mood, he approximates in this form of psychic activity another means of establishing and elaborating elements of the infant-child self . . . some moods establish fragments of former self states . . . moods are complex self states that may establish a mnemic environment in which the individual re-experiences and recreates former infant-child experiences and states of being.[100]

In a complementary passage Jung discusses the archetypal basis of the affects (i.e., moods):

> At the same time they [archetypes] have a "specific charge" and develop numinous effects which express themselves as affects . . . Thus we regularly find that unexpected or otherwise inhibited unconscious contents break through and find expression in the affect. Such contents are very often of an inferior or primitive nature and thus betray their archetypal origin.[101]

---

100   *The Shadow of the Object,* p. 100ff.
101   "Synchronicity: An Acausal Connecting Principle." *The Structure and Dynamics of the Psyche,* CW8, par. 841.

The power of the constellated archetypal affects being described by Jung can be detected in the following description by bluesman Luther "Guitar Junior" Johnson of his early exposure to the blues: "Walking past a juke house, I'd hear the music of B.B. King, Jimmy Reed, T-Bone Walker, Son House, and Howlin' Wolf. The music gave me goose pimples. People hollering and screaming. I was too young to take it, the feeling was so powerful. I couldn't eat, drink, or sleep when I heard the music."[102]

In listening to the blues one can also often experience a void created by unfulfilled desires or needs. Wright, coming from a psychoanalytic perspective, describes the void that can be the subjective experience of one's inferior function:[103]

> There is a speechless want . . . that gives itself a body and knows itself by looking for an equivalent in the system of available significations . . . First we sense there is something there, then we grope around it and toward it; finally, perhaps, if we are fortunate, we grasp it . . . So it is that we use this gift of the Other to speak those things that 'stir in our middles,' . . . which would otherwise remain mute and unformed. We give birth to ourselves through language.[104]

This "speechless want" is reflected in the lyrics of *I Be's Troubled* by Muddy Waters, "*Baby, I just can't be satisfied and I just can't keep on cryin.*" Willeford also addresses this area of the speechless want when he states, "One function of the blues performance is to articulate the not-yet-articulated, even though what is thus expressed is in some sense already known."[105]

---

102 Quoted in M. Cooper, "Luther "Guitar Junior" Johnson: You Got to Have a Feeling for People." *Living Blues*, Issue 142, p. 45.

103 In Jung's model of typology, the inferior function is the psychological function which is closest to the unconscious and lags in development and differentiation (see *Psychological Types, CW6*, pars. 763ff).

104 *Vision and Separation*, p. 138.

105 *Abandonment, Wish and Hope in the Blues*, p. 177.

5

Blues Play: Performers and Performance

"Whoever speaks in primordial images speaks with a
thousand voices; he enthrals and overpowers.
—C.G. Jung

Some writers on aesthetics have theorized that there is a shared "entrainment" between listener and composer at the unconscious level.[106] This process of entrainment is particularly present in the blues. Keil, in elaborating on the similar roles played by both the black preacher and the blues singer, says:

> The word 'ritual' seems more appropriate than 'performance' when the audience is committed rather than appreciative. And from this, it follows, perhaps, that blues singing is more of a belief role than a creative role - more priestly than artistic . . . Bluesmen and preachers both provide models and orientations; both give public expression to deeply felt private emotions; both promote catharsis - the bluesman through dance, the preacher through trance; both increase feelings of solidarity, boost morale, strengthen the consensus.[107]

Keil's description accurately portrays the shared emotional state and "entrainment" that seems particularly prominent in the relationship between the blues performer and the audience. Keil's observations, with his emphasis on ritual, also underscore the implicit spirituality in the blues performance. According to Robert Moore, ritual has the capacity to transform profane space into sacred space.[108]

Neumann indicates that for the true evocation of an archetype to occur, "a concurrence between the tendency to form a psychic image of a certain kind and a factor in the world outside is indispensable in

---

106 G. Rolla, *Your Inner Music: Creative Analysis and Music Memory.*
107 *Urban Blues*, p. 164.
108 "Ritual, Sacred Space, and Healing." In N. Schwartz-Salant and M. Stein (Eds.), *Chiron: Liminality and Transitional Phenomena.*

every case."[109] Neumann is pointing out the essentially inter-dependent nature of the field of unitary reality and as such he provides explanation for the broad appeal that the blues have come to have world-wide. The blues performance is an activating event that is congruent with a pre-existent psychic image based in deep affective experiences, especially suffering, which results in the evocation of the archetype. The significance of Neumann's perspective will become more evident as I discuss the inter-dependence of the blues performer and the listener or audience.

Intersubjectivity in the Blues

Attending a blues performance is a shared experience of the unitary field of blues consciousness. The blues performer and blues audience are both making an internal reference about what it is like to have the blues and realizing that the other one knows. While all blues singers implicitly invite the audience to identify with the singer and the song, some blues songs, like the ones represented below, make that invitation more explicit:

Five Long Years - Eddie Boyd

Have you ever been mistreated, and you know what I'm talkin' about
Now you know I work five long years for one woman,
She had the nerve to put me out

I finally learned a lesson, you know a long long time ago
The next woman that I marry, she got to work
And bring me some dough

Yes I been mistreated, you know what I'm talkin' about
Now you know I work five long years for one woman,
She had the nerve to put me out
She had the nerve, She had the nerve, She had the nerve to put me out

---

Roll and Tumble Blues - Hambone Willie Newbern

And I rolled and I tumbled and I cried the whole night long
And I rose this mornin' mama and I didn't know right from wrong

---

109   *The Place of Creation*, p. 82.

Did you ever wake up and find your dough roller gone
And you wring your hands and you cry the whole day long

Nine Below Zero - Sonny Boy Williamson II (aka Rice Miller)

Yeah, ain't that a pity, people ain't that a cryin' shame
Ain't that a pity, I declare it's a cryin' shame
She wait till it got nine below zero, and put me down for another man

I give her all my money, all of my lovin' and everything
All of my money, all of my lovin' and everything
It done got nine below zero and she done put me down for another man

Nine below zero, the little girl she done put me down
Nine below zero, the little girl she done put me down
She know I don't have nowhere to stay, and I don't have not one dime

Daniel Stern's work with infant development proposes that the development of a subjective sense of self is significantly contributed to by the process of affective attunement or a sharing of affective states and "knowing" what another person is feeling, i.e., the movement toward a state of unitary reality. He describes this process between parent and infant as follows:

> For there to be an intersubjective exchange about affect, then, strict imitation won't do. In fact, several processes must take place. First, the parent must be able to read the infant's feeling state from the infant's overt behavior. Second, the parent must perform some behavior that is not a strict imitation but nonetheless corresponds in some way to the infant's overt behavior. Third, the infant must be able to read this corresponding parental response as having to do with the infant's own original feeling experience and not just imitating the infant's behavior. It is only in the presence of these three conditions that feeling states within one person can be knowable to another and that they can both sense, without using language, that the transaction has occurred.[110]

This mutuality of experience is echoed in Atwood and Stolorow's description of intersubjective theory:

> Intersubjectivity theory is a field theory or systems theory in that it seeks to comprehend psychological phenomena

---
110 *The Interpersonal World of the Infant*, p. 139.

not as products of isolated intrapsychic mechanisms, but
as forming at the interface of reciprocally interacting subjectivities. Psychological phenomena . . . cannot be understood apart from the intersubjective contexts in which
they take form.[111]

It seems clear that Carl Jung anticipated many of these intersubjective trends in psychoanalysis, an example of which is his work, *The
Psychology of the Transference*:

The transference . . . alters the psychological stature of the
doctor, though this is at first imperceptible to him. He too
becomes affected, and has as much difficulty in distin-
guishing between the patient and what has taken possession of him as has the patient himself. This leads both of
them to a direct confrontation with the daemonic forces
lurking in the darkness. The resultant paradoxical blend of
positive and negative, of trust and fear, of hope and doubt,
of attraction and repulsion is characteristic of the initial
relationship.[112]

These descriptions also provide insight into the power of the shared
blues experience. In such an experience the blues performer locates a
particular feeling state within himself and then attempts to communicate that feeling state through his lyrics, voice intonation, physical
and facial gestures, and instrumental accompaniment. The members
of the audience resonate with the performers' internal state by locat-
ing a similar affective experience, either from their current affective
state, or from affective memory. The audience then communicates their
resonance to the performer through applause, vocal encouragement, or
dance. Hence, a blues performance, like parent-infant interactions and
intersubjective experiences, also involves a form of mutual mirroring,
and at times a degree of *participation mystique* in which there is a diffu-
sion of boundaries or fusion between subject and object, performer and
audience.[113] As Diggs points out, "In the blues, the union of communal
and individual consciousness allows the individual to be affirmed without the oppositionalism of subject and object. The individual speaks
of himself, but with a language that services a commune of things and
ideas of which he is one."[114] A similar thought is presented by Blacken-

---

111   *Faces in a Cloud*, p. 178.
112   *The Practice of Psychotherapy*, CW16, par. 375.
113   Michael Balint (*The Basic Fault*, p. 66) refers to this situation as a "harmo-
nious interpenetrating mixup."
114   *Alchemy and the Blues*, p. 38.

ing who says, "Through musical interaction, two people create forms that are greater than the sum of their parts, and make for themselves experiences of empathy that would be unlikely to occur in ordinary social intercourse."[115] Blackening's comments highlight the positive aspect of *participation mystique*, which Neumann is seeking to redeem, as well as pointing out the operation of the transcendent function within musical interaction.

The two previously mentioned authors, Diggs and Blackening, are pointing out the transcendence of subject and object separation in the performer-listener dyad. In his observations on art, M.C. Cammerloher points out that there also exists a potential transcendence of the subject-object dichotomy existing between art and artist: "Thus nature [through art] ceases to exist as a mere object. It becomes subject and object in one. It is nature that in the consciously perceiving and creating man, the artist, who is himself nature, becomes aware of itself, experiences itself, in so far as it is perceptive. Thus the dichotomy of subject and object, of seeing and being seen, is resolved: the two have become one."[116] The comments of Little Whitt Wells, presented at the beginning of the fourth chapter, indicate that this transcendence of the dichotomy between art and artist is also central to the blues.

We can detect an experience of unitary reality and "field knowledge" in the following description by musicologist Larry Cohn of a performance by bluesman Son House:[117]

> I saw Son House's first performance when he was rediscovered, in New York City, and I thought I'd have a heart attack. I had never seen or imagined that anyone could sing with such intensity and not drop dead on the spot. Because every song was like a complete catharsis. I mean it was so emotional, you know, he'd just throw his head back, and I used to wonder, my God, this is 1965 - what was he like in 1930? I mean it was just absolutely incredible.[118]

It seems apparent that Cohn was experiencing a transcendence of art and artist as he witnessed Son House become the blues and the blues became Son House. In like fashion, we can hear the unitary aspect of the blues reality in the following description of the effect of the blues

115 Quoted in Storr, *Music and the Mind*, p. 21.
116 "The Position of Art in the Psychology of Our Time." In J. Campbell (Ed.) *Spiritual Disciplines: Papers from the Eranos Yearbooks*, p. 427.
117 Son House, who was rediscovered during the blues revival of the 1960's, was a contemporary of legendary bluesman Robert Johnson.
118 Quoted in O'Neal, *I Once Was Lost But Now I'm Found*, p. 360.

on an audience from Keil: "It unites all the people within listening range through a steady irresistible pulse. As long as the band is playing, people are necessarily involved with each other via a common rhythm and are kept in a state not only of active participation but of keen anticipation as well."[119] Observations by Bruce Richman echo Keil's description of the typical blues performance: "Music is the 'language' of emotional and physiological arousal. A culturally agreed-upon pattern of rhythm and melody . . . that is sung together, provides a shared form of emotion that, at least during the course of the song, carries along the participants so that they experience their bodies responding emotionally in very similar ways."[120]

The Role of the Bluesman

An understanding of the role of the bluesman is important to the exploration of the relationship between the blues and unitary reality. Humphrey indicates that: "For the bright and artistic black men of the Depression-era Delta, the roles of preacher or performer of social music were the primary alternatives to agrarian indentured servitude, and the personality traits that contributed to success in either role were similar in this environment . . . Little wonder, too that elements of 'churchy' delivery began to bleed into blues performance, or that blues phrasing would creep into the church."[121] Meanwhile Keil says, "A blues singer's personality and life style represent a heightened model or type of Negro masculine behavior in general. The bluesman is in a sense every man: the country bluesman is an archetype of the migrant laborer; the city bluesman, a stereotype of the stud, the hustler."[122] And finally, William Barlow indicates that, "blues personas achieved mythical stature in the black community, constituting a black pantheon separate from - and in many ways antithetical to - the white heroes and heroines of middle-class America."[123]

According to Garon, "The blues singer functions as a poet through his or her refusal to accept the degradation of daily life. The essence of the blues is not to be found in the daily life with which it deals, but in the way such life is critically focused on and imaginatively transformed."[124]

119 *Urban Blues*, p. 117.
120 Cited in Storr, *Music and the Mind*, p. 7.
121 *Holy Blues*, p. 132.
122 *Urban Blues*, p. 152.
123 Quoted in Spencer, *Blues and Evil*, p. 9.
124 *Blues and the Poetic Spirit*, p. 70.

Oliver also equates the role of the bluesman with that of the poet, but with that of the philosopher as well, seeing in the bluesman's craft the capacity to turn his eyes through "brutal self-examination" on "the inner soul within and recorded his impressions and reactions to the world without. The result was a capacity to recount his desires, acknowledge his faults, and state his thoughts with almost frightening honesty."[125] Bodkin, in her eloquent description of the role of the poet in a culture, also provides a way of understanding the role of the bluesman in his culture:

> When a great poet uses the stories that have taken shape in the fantasy of the community, it is not his individual sensibility alone that he objectifies. Responding with unusual sensitiveness to the words and images which already express the emotional experience of the community, the poet arranges these so as to utilize to the full their evocative power. Thus he attains for himself vision and possession of the experience engendered between his own soul and the life around him, and communicates that experience, at once individual and collective, to others, so far as they can respond adequately to the words and images he uses.[126]

I once witnessed a performance by an older black bluesman from Mississippi named T-Model Ford - The Taildragger. Ford opened his performance by saying, "I don't know how to read. I don't know how to write. I don't know how to spell. But I know how to play this here guitar so let's go!" For Ford, the blues is synonymous with life. Keil indicates that there is an inseparability of the man who plays the blues from the role of the bluesman, i.e., that the bluesman's work is his life and vice versa.[127] What Keil is describing may be interpreted several ways. He may be describing a complete identification of the individual's ego with his performance persona, or perhaps that the blues and the blues life is experienced as the best possible expression of that individual's psychic life, whereby a natural individuation process occurs. The later interpretation, if correct, supports Neumann's hypothesis about the transcendence of subject-object distinctions. Neumann says: "We know that creative man is closer to the unconscious and to the world of archetypes; we also know that he is closer to what we have described as the unitary reality. What distinguishes him is . . . a greater proximity to the world of man's primordial origins . . . it is precisely his openness to

---

125 *Blues Fell This Morning*, p. 27.
126 *Archetypal Patterns in Poetry*, p. 8.
127 *Urban Blues.*

the original wholeness."[128] It seems Neumann has captured the essence of the bluesman's role with this statement.

The idea that there is little distinction between an individual and his or her performance persona seems supported by the statements of the bluesmen themselves. When asked, "What does your audience expect from you?" Little Junior Parker responded, "They expect what you are."[129] Willie Dixon, perhaps as a reflection of this incorporative process, titled his autobiography *I Am The Blues* and Jazz Gillum titled one of his recordings *The Blues What Am*.

Blues Mythology

The blues and the role of the bluesman have some specific mythological themes (mythologems) which provide the archetypal underpinnings to the songs and the blues personas. Kittelson describes the link between song and myth and the importance of myth to our lives: "Over the centuries, the deepest, the most musical-sounding and re-sounding of stories have become our myths. They have carried our cultural sense of symbolic meaning, via sound, through the acoustics of story-telling . . .

---

128 *The Place of Creation,* p. 101.
129 Quoted in Keil, *Urban Blues,* p. 166.

They help us comprehend, if only vaguely, the patterns we are bound to follow, as individuals and as cultures."[130] These mythologems can be heard in Diggs' description of the blues:

> The blues revolution is Dionysos inciting the instinctual maenads to pull Pentheus from the treetop back down to earth and then tear his detached vision to bits in a dreadful nigredo. It is Huck and Jim traveling down the Mississippi together to escape the abuses of the white patriarchy and find some sense of truth. These images are congruent with the strong association between blacks, women, and youth within the revolution. In the Western imagination, both women and blacks are assigned the qualities of instinct, body, and primitiveness and both carry the repressed and projected qualities.[131]

Spencer also uses mythological elements to describe patterns in the blues: "In African-American folk-heroic literature, such personages as the trickster, the conjurer, and the badman [recurrent figures in the blues] were partial answers to the 'problem of evil.' Having long helped African-Americans of the old South to adapt to the recurring evil of racial oppression, these heroes were fashioned and refashioned out of conscious and unconscious needs that resulted from the oppressive conditions . . . these figures were essentially tragic heroes."[132] Based on the tendency toward boasting and hyperbole[133] in the blues it seems apparent that many blues singers sought to established themselves in the hero role.

Garon states that the blues myths are not universal, but instead represent the African-American response to a historical moment.[134] I believe that Garon's view is limited in this respect and that the blues myths reflect universal patterns of human experience, which accounts for the endurance of this style of music over a hundred year period. The same songs that were recorded ninety years ago are often re-recorded by contemporary performers and are just as relevant today as they were in 1920. A specific historical moment did create a window for this manifestation of the collective psyche to erupt into the collective consciousness, as a means of coping with that moment and the product of that eruption is now referred to as the blues. As Marie-Louise von

---

130 *Sounding the Soul*, pp. 49ff.
131 *Alchemy and the Blues*, p. 41.
132 *Blues and Evil*, p. 6.
133 For examples see the lyrics of *I'm Ready* and *Just To Be With You* provided earlier (see index for page numbers).
134 *Blues and the Poetic Spirit*.

Franz points out, myths are always bound to the culture in which they originate and serve as a compensation for movement occurring within the collective consciousness of the time.[135] Like myths, the archetypal patterns recounted in the blues are also universal and give continued solace to everyone's daily oppressions, addictions, lost loves, sexual frustrations, and misunderstandings between the sexes.

Perhaps the most prominent archetypal figure in the blues is the image of the badman. From the beginning the blues has operated on the periphery of the collective, a response to the oppressive conditions of slavery and the repressive influences of Christianity. Therefore, the blues has been frequently characterized as "the devil's music" and the blues performer seen as morally suspect. Even the musical instruments of blues performers, specifically the guitar, banjo, and fiddle, were at one time thought to be "devil's instruments." According to Spencer, "the black blues singer was traditionally viewed by the constituency of the 'overculture' (the culture of white dominance) as a 'bad nigger'. . . From within the 'underculture,' however, blues singers characteristically were not perceived as 'bad niggers.' The good minstrels were 'badmen' whose personalities were rooted in the traditions of the African trickster and conjurer."[136] Elsewhere, Spencer indicates that "the blues singer's 'badman' qualities - trickiness, capriciousness, lawlessness, and rampant sexuality - have been, from the Victorian or Eurocentric perspective, interpreted as demonic rather than holistic."[137] A natural continuation of Spencer's hypothesis, regarding the holistic impulse in the blues, would be that these men and women are expressing aspects of the repressed side of our human personalities, our shadows, both personal and collective. Indeed, rather than seeing the blues performer as a badman, Spencer interprets the blues performers as, "prodigal sons and daughters whose belief system took them to the periphery of the strict doctrinal enclave of Protestant Christianity - a location of human openness and mythological potentiality."[138]

However, the perception of the bluesman as badman wasn't just from the perspective of mainstream influences of the collective, it was also a perspective that the performers themselves also identified with and promoted:

---

135 *Interpretation of Fairytales.*
136 *Blues and Evil*, p. 7.
137 *Blues and Evil*, p. 12.
138 *Blues and Evil*, p. 13.

Black and Evil Blues - Alice Moore

And I'm blue, black and evil, and I wish I had made myself
I would fix this man of mine, so he couldn't have nobody else.

When I get so blue, black and evil, I get blood all in my eyes
When I catch my man with his woman, he starts to tellin' lies.

I'm so blue, black and evil, until I can hardly see
Caught my man with a girl last night,
That was supposed to be a friend of me.

Two By Four Blues - Merline Johnson

I been talking to you man, and I ain't gonna talk no more.
Well, one of these mornings, I'll cut your head with my two-by-four.

I don't want to hurt that man, just goin' to kill him dead.
I'll knock him to his knees, go back to the man I once have had.

When I leave home, your other woman is knocking on my door.
I'm going to stop so much talking and raise heck with my two-by-four.

The badman role or persona can be seen in the blues persona of Peetie Wheatstraw. Wheatstraw was a powerful performer who was the self-proclaimed "High Sheriff of Hell" and the "Devil's Son-in-Law."[139] Wheatstraw's life, or at least his blues persona, embodied the mythology of the badman motif which Spencer describes.

Gangster Blues - Peetie Wheatstraw

I am gonna take you for an easy ride, drop you off on the riverside.
I've got the gangster's blues, I got the gangster's blues,
I've got the gangsters, boys I am feelin' mean.

I'm gonna bind your mouth so you can't talk,
Tie your feet so you can't walk.

You can start your screaming but must give in,
I'm gonna tear you to pieces and put you back again.

---

139   Robertson, *Little Blues Book*.

Drinking Man Blues - Peetie Wheatstraw

The dealer ask me, "Peetie, how come you so rough?"
Well, now, I ain't bad but I just been drinking that stuff.

That stuff will kill you, but it just won't quit
It will get you to the place that you don't care who you hit.

I been drinking that stuff, and it went to my head
It made me hit the baby in the cradle and kill my papa dead.

The identification with the badman motif is also seen in the life of Little Walter Jacobs, an extraordinary Chicago harmonica player who died from wounds inflicted during a fight following a performance, and in the life of Robert Johnson who died by being poisoned by a jealous husband. There is also Johnny Ace who died playing Russian roulette during the intermission of a performance; Scrapper Blackwell who was shot to death in an alley; and John Lee "Sonny Boy" Williamson who died after being stabbed seventeen times in the head with an ice pick. Naturally, there are also numerous deaths associated with various addictions, including: Paul Butterfield, Juke Boy Bonner, Leroy Carr, and Jimmy Reed. The following song, *Canned Heat Blues*, by Tommy Johnson, celebrates his lifestyle of drinking Sterno, shoe polish, hair tonic, and rubbing alcohol - an alchemy of self-destruction:

Crying canned heat, canned heat, mama, crying sure Lord killing me.
Crying canned heat, mama, sure Lord killing me.
Takes alcorub to take these canned heat blues.

Crying mama, mama, mama, you know canned heat killing me.
Crying mama, mama, mama, crying canned heat is killing me.
Canned heat don't kill me, crying babe I'll never die.

I woke up this morning crying, canned heat 'round my bed.
Run here somebody, take these canned heat blues.
Run here somebody, and take these canned heat blues.

Initiation at the Crossroads

Ritual initiation at a crossroads is an important archetypal motif that exists in the blues mythology. Usually this is an initiation at the hands of the blues god, typically the devil. One New Orleans conjurer described the initiatory process this way:

> If you want to make a contact with the devil, first trim your finger nails as close as you possibly can. Take a black cat bone and a guitar and go to a lonely fork in the roads at midnight. Sit down there and play your best piece, thinking of and wishing for the devil all the while. By and by you will hear music, dim at first but growing louder and louder as the musician approaches nearer. Do not look around; just keep on playing your guitar. The unseen musician will finally sit down by you and play in unison with you. After a time you will feel something tugging at your instrument. Do not try to hold it. Let the devil take it and keep thumping along with your fingers as if you still had a guitar in your hands. Then the devil will hand you his instrument to play and will accompany you on yours. After doing this for a time he will seize your fingers and trim the nails until they bleed, finally taking his guitar back and returning your own. Keep on playing; don't look around. His music will become fainter and fainter as he moves away. When all is quiet you may go home.[140]

Robert Johnson is generally considered to be the greatest bluesman who ever recorded and his initiation at the crossroads is the most widely recounted. According to the myth associated with Johnson, it was a midnight encounter at the crossroads with the devil, much like the one described above, that enabled him to be transformed from a mediocre entertainer to a virtuoso. His payoff to the devil - his own death - is foreshadowed by his song *Crossroad Blues*, *"I'm standin' at the crossroad, babe, I believe I'm sinkin' down."* His pact with the devil also seems to be the reference point for *Hellhound on My Trail* and *Me and the Devil Blues* - *"Me and the Devil was walkin side by side."* Popular acceptance of the myth was reinforced by reports of Robert Johnson's acquaintances, who indicated that he was a very poor guitar player initially, that he had disappeared for a period of time, and that he had then reemerged with stunning ability on the guitar. In the old South, it was generally believed among African-Americans that any sudden acquisition of

---

140 Quoted in Spencer, *Blues and Evil*, pp. 28ff.

luck or talent was the consequence of conjuration.[141] Therefore, Robert Johnson's sudden acquisition of virtuosity on the guitar would be seen as the act of a conjurer.

We know from mythology that crossroads are associated with the trickster, Hermes, and that the stone pillars deposited at crossroads were called *herms*. According to Julio Finn, the African god *Legba* is also associated with entrances and crossroads.[142] More generally, intersections were also associated demons, evil spirits, ghosts, and fairies, as well as being burial places for suicides and murderers and a dumping ground for parricides, e.g., the murder of Laius by Oedipus at "a place where three highways meet." Crossroads are also believed to be rendezvous points for witches and a place to offer sacrifices to the gods. From these examples, it is clear that crossroads are points of numinosity for the psyche as are nodal transitions of all kinds, for example, the point of meeting between the ocean and the shore. These nodal points reflect a radical change in medium, substance, or direction. They represent being in a borderland, on the edge between conscious and unconscious. The belief about going to the crossroads to obtain musical powers from the devil was a variation of black folk belief in which going to the crossroads to meet the devil was done for the purpose of attaining good luck throughout life.[143] A black cat bone was a prerequisite for making the trip to the crossroads. The black cat was thought to be a witch in disguise and the bone was obtained by boiling the flesh off the cat and then tasting the bones until a bitter one was found.

Even apart from the archetypal image of the crossroads, the trickster motif is closely associated with the blues. Spencer indicates that the trickster image in the blues is:

> . . . centered on the African trickster-god, a personage that is both superhuman and subhuman, female and male, sacred and profane, benevolent and malevolent, and who walks with a limp because one foot moves in the realm of the mundane and the other in the realm of the divine. This trickster figure is not only symbolic of what blues is when personified, but prototypal of a paradigm of personality and morality in African-American cultural history. Given the synchronous duplicity or holistic tenacity of African-American culture, the blues singer is one of many African-American personages that fits within the personal-

---

141 Spencer, *Blues and Evil.*
142 *The Bluesman.*
143 Spencer, *Blues and Evil.*

ity scheme of the trickster and that shows the blues to be a symbol of black cultural and ontological reality.[144]

Blues guitarist Paul Geremia seems to support the trickster element present in the blues: "Blues is a funny thing. It's the kind of music that reinvents itself with everybody it comes in contact with. Everybody has his own idea of what is the blues and what is or isn't real for him."[145] Geremia's perspective is similar to the perspective presented by David Rothenberg: "Because music is the art that leaves as soon as it arrives, it always comes to us suddenly, and it departs the same way . . . You don't need to understand in order to know it or to love it."[146]

The blues is the trickster Mercurius, shape-shifter, always changing, always standing for different things, always evolving, and yet always retaining something of the original essence. When the bluesmen began to migrate from the country to the cities, new lyrical motifs emerged. Gradually solo performers gave way in popularity to blues bands. When their instrumentation became electrified the sound evolved, eventually giving birth to rock and roll. As swing elements from jazz were incorporated a new style called jump blues was created. The evolution of the blues from one form of the blues to another is frequently lamented by blues aficionados who often fail to see that the blues is like Hermes, always the same and always different. The blues is not defined only by its form; there is something intangible, a mysterious reality that exists beyond the form.

The Bluesman and the Shaman

The role and activities of the bluesman have some close parallels to the role and activities of the shaman. As we will see, many shamanic elements have relevance to the experience of the blues performance and the blues myth as well. Noted mythologist Mircea Eliade identifies a number of specific characteristics of the shamanic role: the shamanic calling, the initiatory sickness, the obtainment of shamanic powers, the shamanic initiation, the shamanic cosmology, and the shamanic cure which was often facilitated by the use of trance.[147] Because shamanism is an aggregate of religion, magic, art, ritual, and performance, it is clear

144 *Blues and Evil*, p. XXVI.
145 Interviewed in Tom Townsely, "Paul Geremia: Looking for the Sound." *Blues Revue*, Issue 42, p. 11.
146 "The Necessary Note." *Parabola*, vol. XXIII, p. 4.
147 *Shamanism: Archaic Techniques of Ecstasy.*

that shamanism falls within the domain of unitary reality, just as the blues does.

Of initial interest are the characteristics of the shaman and his audience. In a shared, participatory interaction, such as shamanistic healing rites, a unitary reality is constructed. According to Claude Levi-Strauss:

> This fabulation of a reality unknown in itself - a fabulation consisting of procedures and representations - is founded on a threefold experience: first, that of the shaman himself, who if his calling is a true one, undergoes specific states of a psychosomatic nature; second, that of the sick person, who may or may not experience an improvement of his condition; and finally that of the public who also participate in the cure, experiencing satisfaction which produce collective support . . . These three elements of what we might call the "shamanistic complex" cannot be separated. But they are clustered around two poles, one formed by the intimate experience of the shaman and the other by group consensus.[148]

In similar terms, Julio Finn suggests that the bluesman assumes the role of a religious "elder" and the audience assumes the role of a ritual "initiate."[149] The purpose of the "musical convocation" is to invoke the "spirit of the blues" and thereby unite the ritual participants. Finn's view of the bluesman as religious elder seems supported by bluesman Willie Dixon's comments: "The blues are supposed to put thoughts in the minds of people . . . The blues was made for wisdom . . . this wisdom of the blues can be used all through life and that's why most blues songs are written as a statement of wisdom."[150]

There is a close link between the personal experience of the shaman, the shaman's emotional involvement in process, and the efficacy of the shamanic ritual. This is similar to Jung's belief that the analyst could only take the patient as far as he himself had come, and that the analyst must be open to influence from the patient if he is to influence the patient.[151] An essential feature of the bluesman's role, which parallels that of the shamanic role, is his active interaction or participation in the psychological state, mood, or environment he is communicating in his song. Bluesman J.B. Lenoir says, "Nobody can sing the blues if he has

---

148 *Structural Anthropology*, pp. 179ff.
149 *The Bluesman*, p. 207.
150 Quoted in Robertson, *Little Blues Book*, p. xi.
151 "Problems of Modern Psychotherapy," *The Practice of Psychotherapy*, CW16.

never been blued; nothing can come out of you unless it's in you."[152] Similarly, Oliver says, "The blues singer did not comment on a world as seen through a window but as a member circulating within it."[153] Levi-Strauss elaborates on these themes in the following passage:

> In treating his patient the shaman also offers his audience a performance . . . We shall say that it [the performance] always involves the shaman's enactment of the "call," or the initial crisis which brought him the revelation of his condition . . . The shaman does not limit himself to reproducing or miming certain events. He actually relives them in all their vividness, originality, and violence. And since he returns to his normal states at the end of the séance, we may say, borrowing a key term from psychoanalysis, that he abreacts . . . In a sense, the shaman is a professional abreactor . . . the type of abreaction specific to each shaman . . . might symbolically induce an abreaction of his own disturbance in each patient.[154]

Like the shaman, the bluesman cannot merely repeat his own songs or the songs of others. For Keil, "It is the intensity and conviction with which the story is spelled out, the fragments of experience pieced together, rather than the story itself which makes one bluesman better than another."[155] The blues performer must feel the songs he is singing for it to be the blues. Only by being affected by the songs he is singing can the bluesman create a response in the listener. This may be a form of mutual resonation, a form of projective identification,[156] or both processes may be occurring simultaneously. Part of the listener's experience is determined by what the listener is projecting onto the blues performer, and part of their experience is determined by what the listener introjects from the performer. To some degree the performer's experience of himself is influenced by the listener's experience of him. This is somewhat like Heinz Kohut's concept of the selfobject relationship in which there is a self-sustaining function that the Other provides through their presence or activity to evoke and maintain the self of the subject.[157]

---

152 Quoted in Garon, *Blues and the Poetic Spirit*, p. 227.

153 *Blues Fell This Morning*, p. 277.

154 *Structural Anthropology*, pp. 180ff.

155 *Urban Blues*, p. 161.

156 Projective identification is a defense mechanism operating through unconscious fantasy in which the subject psychological inserts a part of themselves into an object in order to harm, possess, or control it (Laplanche & Pontalis, *The Language of Psychoanalysis*, p. 356).

157 Wolf, *Treating the Self*.

RITES &
DESIRES

BY
Amanda Cherry

COVER ART BY
LEE MOYER

TABLE OF
CONTENTS

*To every kid
who ever wrote
a fanfic*

ACKNOWLEDGEMENTS

There are so many people to thank for the existence of this book; I guess I should start at the beginning. I have to start by thanking my late mom, Polly, for always having a book in her hand, and for leaving out all that typing paper (that's what we called printer paper back then) and a green Pilot Precise pen while wrapping Christmas presents when I was six—otherwise my very first book might never have been written. And my dad, Tommy, for having that little kindergarten masterpiece printed and bound.

To Mrs. Bonifay, who loved my love for books in first grade, and to Mrs. Fillingim, who taught me to diagram a sentence. To Matthew, my first writing partner: we're almost due to pull that old story out and give it another go. To my high school friends who passed around my notebooks full of fiction, and who clamored for the next chapter when it was ready. To Tara, who has always loved a good book and who grew up to share that love with the next generation.

To Sharon, the wind beneath my wings, who supported me in everything I ever did. You were gone far too soon. I miss you every day.

To Chuck, Kace, Kevin, Cherie, Fran, Barbara, and co. for adopting me into the author tribe and keeping me believing in myself. To my Tosche Station family, the Drowning in Moonlight team, and my whole Star Wars circle; your love, acceptance, and support have been invaluable.

A giant shout out to Dawn Vogel and Jeremy Zimmerman, for not thinking I was silly when I said I wanted to join them in Cobalt City, and for walking me through every step of this crazy process. You two are excellent writers and amazing friends, and I wouldn't have wanted to go through this madness with anyone else. To Nathan Crowder, for creating the Universe and for being so welcoming to a newbie who said she wanted in. To the whole Cobalt City club, for just being awesome, with extra love to Erik Scott de Bie, who had no problems with my treatment of Stardust in this book (I was terrified you'd be mad!).

And finally: to my amazing husband, Andrew, and my silly son, Mac. Thanks for the patience and the understanding. Thanks for the space and the time for the writing, editing, plotting, planning, and all the other things that make a book happen. Thanks for being my sounding board and my cheerleaders. I love you forever.

PROLOGUE

The initial impression most people got of Ruby Killingsworth was that of a wicked queen from a fairytale film reimagined as a mid-century pinup. She wore tailored dresses, fascinators, seamed stockings, and had a collection of coats so extraordinary it was rumored in some circles she'd had them looted from the tombs of long-dead royals. Fair skinned with long ginger hair, Ruby was a buxom woman—petite but curvy. Her bearing and mannerisms were those of someone much taller, giving her an imposing air her genuine size could not account for. People feared Ruby Killingsworth, even when given no immediate impetus to; that was Ruby's favorite thing about humanity.

Gods, on the other hand—

Gods could be troublesome, the one she'd come seeking today particularly so. He certainly had no fear of her. He feared no human she was aware of, even those with powers as incredible as Ruby's. She had been equipped from childhood with a measure of innate magic that made her uniquely formidable among mortals. She could have had any segment of humanity at her feet at any moment she chose. But those from beyond the mortal realm were, lamentably, immune to her particular abilities. Whatever the nature of her power, the origins of which she'd never managed to determine, it had no effect on those with supernatural qualities of their own. More than one of Cobalt City's resident superheroes had inadvertently outed themselves to her by virtue of their resistance to her thrall. And she'd yet to meet a god of any tradition who wasn't similarly immune. Any dealings with immortals had to be done without the aid of her own magic.

Not that her power was working for her at all at the moment. It was indeed that very difficulty that had brought her through the Coil in search of assistance today. The place wasn't easily reached by a mortal, but Ruby had been here before. She knew the way. And even without her own innate power to aid her, ritual magic behaved as it should throughout the Coil—as long as the ritual was performed correctly. Never in her life had Ruby Killingsworth failed to perform a ritual correctly.

The longhouse stood in tall grass at the end of a well-worn path coming up from a rocky coastline. Ruby clutched her sable wrap tighter around her shoulders to ward off the chill of the wind. Gusts off the water continuously whipped the feather in her hair sharply against the side of her face, causing her no small discomfort as she started toward the longhouse. The weather here was never pleasant, and she cursed under her breath as she trod carefully up the path, trying with some success to keep the patent heels of her stilettos from sinking into the soft ground and gravel.

As she reached the front of the longhouse, the door swung open slowly, revealing its occupant: the Immortal whose assistance she'd come to implore.

A tall man with ginger hair to rival Ruby's own stood in the doorway, wearing a full suit of crimson velvet and a smirk that said he'd known she was coming.

"Loki, darling," she greeted him, "that is quite the dashing cape you're wearing." Years of experience had taught her that opening with flattery was never a bad tact when dealing with this particular Immortal, and she did find his silk-lined cape quite lovely. Loki had always been a dandy—and he was more than a little bit nice to look at.

"I'd show you the emblem on the back," he replied wryly, "but I don't fancy spending the next week mending knife wounds."

"Oh, you're not still mad about Bayreuth?" she challenged, frowning at him incredulously. She inclined her head in a gesture that told him she awaited an invitation to enter.

"Indeed," he drawled, stepping aside and pulling the door with him, gesturing as he did for her to come in.

"You can't be serious," she asserted as she swept past where he stood. Ruby surveyed the room for a moment before committing to a location. Where the moss-covered exterior of the longhouse would have fit into any Iron Age Viking settlement, the interior was the height of Georgian opulence. Brocade clad walls met thick velvet carpets in a room filled to brimming with intricately carved furniture and marble busts of the god who called this place home. It was a glamour, she was sure—cast either to impress or to intimidate; he needn't have bothered, but Ruby appreciated the effort. Though it wasn't at all her taste, she could appreciate the aesthetic. And knowing he cared to make an impression gave her a slightly more powerful position from which to strike the bargain she'd come seeking. It was also far more comfortable in here than she figured it was ordinarily. He'd made it cozy in here, warm and pleasant; the smoke from the fireplace mingled with the diffuse scents of amber and bergamot in a familiar amalgam that seemed intrinsic to Loki. She unclasped her wrap from around her neck and spun it over the back of a red leather chair before easing herself to reclining on a silk settee.

"It was Wagner," Loki replied, still standing in the doorway.

"It was business," Ruby rebutted, straight-faced as she began working her gloves off her fingers. "And anyway, that's ancient history."

"I find it amusing the things you mortals can refer to as ancient," he drawled, crossing the room to sit across from her on a sleek horsehair sofa.

"Touché," she said, her eyes narrowing as the beginnings of a grin tugged at the corners of her mouth.

"To this day, I cannot understand how you got one over on me."

Ruby let her smile come to fruition. This was good. They were having a friendly chat. It was all very civilized and social: exactly what she had been hoping for when she'd thought to come to him for help.

"You weren't prepared," she answered with a shrug. "You didn't see me coming. And you and I both know it couldn't happen again."

"Do we, now?" he asked, quirking an eyebrow at his guest as though sizing her up in a whole new way.

"Loki, darling," she sang, "I am very good at what I do, but I also got very, very lucky. If you'd had so much as an inkling ahead of time… Well, suffice to say I'm well aware I never should have succeeded in the first place. And if you hadn't found the humor in the whole thing and let me get away with it, then I surely wouldn't have succeeded in the long run."

The god eyed her knowingly. "I must say I am surprised you have such insight into the matter."

Ruby grinned. "I'm a narcissistic, power-hungry bitch," she admitted, "but I'm no fool, Loki. I know better than to think I could have bested a god in any real way. I got the better of you in the moment, and then you let me win."

"And I let you live," he reminded her.

"Because I amuse you."

"Indeed. And as much as I am enjoying this little walk down memory lane, I am quite certain you have not come all the way out here simply to make a social call. So forgive me for my abruptness in asking, but what do you want, Ruby?"

"I seem to be having trouble with my powers," she admitted, cutting directly to the chase. She and Loki had a contentious enough history and were enjoying an uneasy enough peace at the moment for her to dare try for obfuscation. "I don't know if they've gotten weaker or if they're gone altogether. And I don't know what the hell is causing it, but there's something gone terribly, horribly wrong."

"And you think I'm behind it?" he asked.

Ruby wasn't sure, but he seemed displeased at the notion of her blaming him for her difficulty. "No," she answered plainly. "As bothersome a fly in my ointment as you've been at times, I do not think this is any of your doing. I know when and how it started; a ritual that got interrupted last December. I thought it might be temporary, but here we are months later, and I'm still completely mundane. Although it's the kind of thing I wouldn't put past you, I am sure my current predicament is in no way your fault."

"Then why are you here?"

"I want your help."

"Oh, that's rich. What in the name of all that's ever been holy makes you think I'd agree to do that?"

"Because you want to," she answered coolly.

"Remember: your powers don't work on me," he chided.

"I just told you," she snapped, "they don't work on anyone."

"What if I like you better this way?" he asked, obviously amused at having the clear upper hand.

"Aww, darling, you like me?" Her tone was half teasing, half flirting, and had just enough edge to it that she was sure Loki understood the game was about to get serious. "I'd never have guessed by all the ways you've tried to have me killed."

"If I'd have really tried, you'd be dead."

"Perhaps."

"I mean it, Ruby," he said. "Why did you come to me for help? Why should I be the one to help you with this?"

"Because you can," she answered. "And because you will. We're too much alike, Loki. That's why we can't seem to get along for more than an hour at a time. We ache for the same things in life. Controlled chaos: all of the little peasants in chaos, with ourselves in control. You appreciate having me to ride herd over the whims and passions of the proletariat whether you like to admit it to yourself or not."

"You run a record company, Ruby," he reminded her, his voice oozing with derision.

"Media empire," she corrected.

"You're not that important," he declared lazily.

"But you're still going to help me."

The god ran his fingers through his tousled hair and flopped down sideways to lounge gratuitously on the horsehair sofa.

"What's in it for me?" he asked.

"Anything you want," she answered. It was a plausible half-truth. She knew that, as a god, Loki had access to knowledge and power beyond anything she was capable of providing, but his usual haunts when visiting the mortal realm could surely use the kind of upgrade being owed a favor by a billionaire could affect. She was sure he was in want of enough corporeal pleasures that he could find something worth his time and energy, which she'd be able to realize without undue difficulty. Loki raised his eyebrows and leaned toward her.

"Anything?" His voice dripped with innuendo they both knew was insincere.

Ruby couldn't help but to laugh out loud. "Now, now Loki darling, don't go getting all lascivious on me. You and I both know that what you're insinuating is not what you're really going to ask for."

"You think me above demanding such in exchange for my services?"

"Stars, no! Not at all! But I do know where your buttons are," she reminded him, letting her gaze settle on his known sensitive spots as she looked him up and down menacingly. "As soon as I have your pants off, you're putty in my hands. We get into bed together, and you're at my mercy. That's not something you're going to walk in to willingly ever again—no matter how much you stand to enjoy it."

"Touché," he echoed her earlier sentiment. "Well," he considered for a moment. "The truth is, I could use some new digs. You know I enjoy the occasional visit to your section of the Coil."

"You do still have an avatar." Ruby had her suspicions in that vein, but that was a card she was playing close to her vest at the moment.

"Yes," Loki allowed casually, "but he's become rather indisposed of late."

"Jail, institution, or mortuary?" Ruby asked then. Teasing and toying with Loki was always fun, and seeing as she had a pretty good idea what had become of Loki's avatar, she knew this particular line of jokes wouldn't raise his ire enough to get her kicked out without what she'd come for.

Loki frowned in a way that told Ruby he was on to her. Was she really going to make him say it?

"Let's just say, that he's out of town for the next... four to eight years." Never one to give a straight answer, Loki had still told her enough.

Ruby's face lit up. "So it is true," she contended, and then mouthed the word, "President," with her eyes wide and her posture expectant.

Loki shrugged. It was the least regal gesture Ruby had ever seen him make. "I can neither confirm nor deny the veracity of your assertion."

Ruby covered her mouth as she laughed out loud. "Now, now," she chided lightly, speaking through the remnants of her barely controlled laughter, "watch your language. You're beginning to sound like a politician yourself. It doesn't suit you."

Loki threw his head back and groaned.

Ruby was glad to know her suspicion had been on point. President Prather was, and had been for some time as best she could tell, an avatar of Loki. But Loki's perceived attitude toward the man's elevation to the title of Leader of the Free World made Ruby wonder if maybe it hadn't been the god's idea for him to seek that office. Her mind was spinning with ways to manipulate that relationship for her own benefit. Being on good terms with the fellow who literally owned the President of the United States could not possibly be bad for business. But that was a conversation for another day. Her priority was getting her powers back. She had four to eight years to exploit Prather.

"You want a deal?" Loki said then, turning the conversation back to the topic at hand.

It seemed as though he was uncomfortable with this discussion of Prather and the Presidency. She'd keep that little tidbit in her back pocket until she needed it. "I want a deal," she affirmed, the affable smile gone instantly as they resumed talking business.

"Then I want a place in town. I want a shrine. Fetishes. A place I can center my power and manifest in your fair city without having to trifle with one bothersome avatar or another. And I think I'd like to try someplace a little more, shall we say… upmarket?"

Ruby quirked her lip. As much as Loki liked to pretend she was beneath his notice, clearly he'd been keeping up on her activities. He was obviously referring to the newly refurbished Ruby Tower at Starcom Center. Ruby had purchased the building as part of a downtown revitalization project in concert with Jaccob Stevens and a few other billionaires. All of them had at one time tried to pretend they were being altruistic with their investments, but really they were just making excuses to gentrify the struggling neighborhood—filling it full of ivory towers created in their own images from which they could sit and pass judgment on those below. Loki enjoyed sitting in judgment as much as the next god; of course he would want in on that.

"How does the forty-sixth floor sound?" she asked bluntly. This was her business face. She may have come here full of charm and sass, but deep down, Ruby Killingsworth was as shrewd a businesswoman as ever there had been. Supernatural powers of persuasion notwithstanding, she had the kind of business acumen that left others in awe. And she had come here with something to offer him, or else she wouldn't have dared to darken his doorstep. She'd suspected he'd ask for this very thing as strongly as she'd suspected the newly inaugurated demagogue in D.C. was indeed Loki's main connection to the mortal realm. This was the crux of her pitch, and although she was sure he wasn't thrilled to be getting in to bed with her again—even figuratively—he might stand to gain a little from this exchange. So he was willing to hear her out.

"And where are you?"

"Forty-eight through fifty."

"Who's on forty-seven?"

"No one. Offices. Gear, equipment, barely anything so far."

Satisfied with her answer that it wouldn't be another tenant, Loki went on. "Balcony?"

"Two. And a great view of Starcom Tower."

The god's expression changed then. His eyes grew wider as his eyebrows knitted in the center of his forehead and his mouth fell open a little. "You're sleeping with Stardust," he said, as sure of his words as he was of the sunrise.

"Now, now, darling. Don't get ahead of yourself."

"Ah. You're not sleeping with Stardust yet."

Ruby grinned and inclined her head. "Not yet," she confirmed.

"You do know he's married?"

"Is this the part where you ask me if I care?"

"You'll be hard pressed to get next to him without your powers."

Ruby grinned wickedly, showing a version of her true face she rarely shared with others. "Well, that's where you come in, isn't it?" she replied, reminding him with those words why she had come here in the first place.

Loki reached out and took her hand, bringing her knuckles to his lips for a kiss that lasted just a moment longer than was absolutely proper.

"Indeed," he replied, "that it is."

CHAPTER
ONE

Ruby fidgeted behind her desk on the newly furnished forty-seventh floor of the Ruby Tower. She hated fidgeting—she found it to be a sign of a weak constitution. She hated that she was even capable of such a plebian display. But there was no other term she could think of for her current state of unsteadiness. For the last hour or more, she'd been bogged down in the minutiae of owning a skyscraper—shuffling through Starpads to find which one of them held her tenancy agreements and cursing the very idea of a paperless office.

Shifting the company's files to digital had been the idea of Arsho Barsamian, the building's usually brilliant (although occasionally troublesome) manager. It had seemed a good enough idea when Arsho had presented it, but Ruby was now firmly of the opinion that moving all her different-looking and otherwise easily identified papers onto identical devices was an idea that scored as less than brilliant. It was frustrating. And she was annoyed.

Of course, it was almost surely not solely the fault of the so-called digital upgrade that Ruby was in such a foul humor. If her fidgeting was a sign of a weak constitution, then at least she could point to the cause of the weakness. The fact that she hadn't had a full-scale breakdown was more than ought to be expected of anyone under the circumstances.

It had been months since she'd gone to see Loki about her powers, and so far, nothing had come of it. She'd gone to work setting up his icons in the space she'd promised him immediately upon her return to the mortal realm. The entire forty-sixth floor was festooned in his livery. She'd even gone so far as to arrange the purchase of some significant historical items from overseas, at no small personal expense. But her immortal neighbor had yet to set foot in the place, as far as she could tell. It would be just like the trickster god to have her set aside an $11 million penthouse condominium for him that he never intended to use. Still, she had held up her end of the bargain, and it seemed as though he hadn't made even a single move toward upholding his.

Ruby had spent the last several weeks getting settled into her own new penthouse and overseeing the setup of the studio and offices in the Tower. Goblin Records was happily functioning in its new home amidst the shiny and evolving skyline of downtown. She'd even received flowers from Jaccob Stevens welcoming her to the neighborhood. That little touch had been the one bright spot in this interminable period of frustrated waiting. Seeing as she meant to seduce Cobalt City's preeminent billionaire and superhero immediately upon the return of her powers, it was nice to know she already had his attention.

But mostly she'd been keeping her head down, burying herself in paperwork, and doing her best to appear busier than she actually was. The busier she looked, the easier it was to avoid people. And the easier it was to avoid people, the happier Ruby Killingsworth would be—at least until Loki came through with some assistance. Every interaction with another person without her powers to aid her left a bad taste in Ruby's mouth, so she'd been doing all she could to keep from speaking to anyone. It had been months since her powers had first failed her, and living without them hadn't gotten even one iota easier. It was frightening, unknown territory, and she didn't like it one bit. She'd done everything in her power to get her magic working on her own—from the staggeringly obscure to the blatantly obvious—all with varying degrees of success. But none of the rites, rituals, or geas she'd tried had netted her any real, sustained, innate magic.

Everything in her power had been decidedly not enough. Now it was time to try everything in Loki's power. If he'd ever get back to her. Ruby was frustrated with the god's months-long silence, but mostly she was frustrated with the lack of magic and this all-new digital office landscape conspiring to not let her get anything done. And the more frustrated she got, the less she cared to deal with anyone.

Fortunately, one of the perks of the paperless office was instantaneous electronic communication that didn't involve actually having to speak with another person. From her phone, Ruby shot off an email to Arsho. She asked them rather less than nicely to please come collect these Starpads and put labels on them, or sync them to some secure cloud thing somewhere so she could get all her documents from anywhere on a single device, or hire someone to do that for them if they had neither the time nor the inclination. She watched the swirling icon on her screen that told her the mail had sent. Satisfied her directive was on its way to its intended recipient, she grabbed her bag and headed for the elevator.

One of the things Ruby loved most about her new office and residence being custom built one atop the other was the elevator system. There were public elevators and semi-public elevators going through the retail shop on the lower floors and to the office and residential space on the middle floors. And there were semi-private elevators, accessed through a separate lobby, for those who had business with Goblin Records on the forty-seventh floor. And then there were Ruby's private elevators. Accessed through biometrics, there was an express elevator that brought Ruby straight from one of her private entrances to either her inner office or her sitting room. Across a private marble lobby from Ruby's personal elevators, her doorman could also allow access to an additional express that would take visitors straight to either her outer office or what served as the front door to her penthouse.

As she stepped into the brass and mirrored surroundings of the lift that would take her from her office to her home without the need to interact with anyone, she once again affirmed her decision to move into the tower full time. Her house in Regency Heights was luxurious enough, and she had no intention to sell the place any time soon, but commuting by elevator absolutely beat rush-hour traffic any day of the week.

She'd barely been home long enough to open the balcony doors and kick off her shoes before there was a knock at the door from the elevator lobby. Ruby cursed under her breath as she slipped her suede stilettos back on; the doorman was supposed to call before letting anyone up. She hated breaking in new employees. Why the hell couldn't people just do things the way she wanted them to? Ruby shook her head as she crossed to the door. Because she didn't have her powers, that's why. This would not have been a problem if she'd been able to use magic when instructing the doormen.

Ruby pulled open the door, ready to let out a swear word, sure it must be Arsho or one of their assistants that the doorman let up without bothering to call. The doorman might be new, but any employee who got past him wouldn't be; they should know better than to come up unannounced. Whoever it was had more than earned the dressing down they were about to get.

"What the—?" she caught herself, stopping her half-articulated tirade when she saw who was standing in her vestibule. The nearest thing she had to compare this moment to was a surprise invasion of trick-or-treaters. But Halloween was months way, and these people at her door were not children. And they weren't exactly costumed, although their manner of appearance was in many ways cartoonish.

There were seven of them—teens and young adults mostly, although a few might have been over thirty. Her best guess was they were a band that had been sent to meet with her in the office and had somehow been sent up the wrong elevator. She was trying to form the words to ask when the thin, ashen boy in the middle held out a note. A young girl with red-to-orange-to-white chin-length ombre hair tried to snatch the note away from the sallow youth, but he pulled it out of her reach and presented it again to Ruby. Having no idea what else to do in the moment, Ruby took the paper and began to unfold it.

"You'll want to wash your hands," the girl with ombre hair said as Ruby looked back and forth between the group and the note. She noticed quickly that it wasn't written on paper, but parchment, and it had been folded neatly and creased with a second, smaller page secreted inside it. The smaller page contained a drawing with a few sentences scrawled around it, and the larger a letter in handwriting with so much flourish to it she had no trouble in guessing from whose pen it had come.

"You'll want the item in the drawing" the note read. "Should be able to get you some answers—maybe even get your powers back. Last known location was a vault in the custody of the CCPD. I sent the Blights along to help you. Use them however you choose. Regards, -L".

"Loki sent you?" Ruby asked the group of them. There was a chorus of nods. Ruby shrugged and moved out of the way of the door to let the bunch inside. Leaving them all in her elevator lobby wasn't going to get anything accomplished. "Blights?" she asked the group as they entered. "Forgive me, but I'm not familiar."

"Tulpas," an androgynous, emo-looking youth answered from the back. "Thoughts-made-flesh."

Ruby eyed the speaker ruefully.

"Am I going to have to worry about pronouns with you?" she asked sharply. The tower's manager, Arsho, was never guaranteed to present as the same gender two days in a row—and keeping up with the right pronouns had at times proven frustrating. When Arsho had finally settled on using "they" full-time, it had been a welcome relief, even if Ruby still occasionally fouled it up. She wanted to know what she was in for with this bunch. The youth shook his head.

"No," he answered, "I'm going to be unhappy with whatever you say. I'm Discontent. This is Fire," he continued, pointing to the girl with the ombre hair. Discontent then pointed out his other cohorts in turn. "You've got Plague," he said with a gesture toward the wan-looking boy who'd handed her the note. She really would want to wash her hands. "There's Pestilence, Doubt, and the twins: Ruin and Decay."

"And you're the—" Ruby was trying to wrap her mind around what she was hearing.

"Physical manifestations of the totality of thought regarding these blights on humanity," Doubt piped up. Of all of them, Doubt seemed to be the one Ruby would relate to the most. She was an average height, average-looking woman who could be seventeen or thirty, with sandy brown hair and wire frame glasses.

"So," Ruby began, trying to digest what Doubt had just told her, "people think on, or worry about, for example: Ruin, and—"

"And I am sustained," Ruin piped up to answer. He was a short man, stocky, and as ageless as the rest of them, who looked as though perhaps he had seen the bottom of one too many vials of anabolic steroids in his day. His brother, Decay, resembled him only in bone structure and hair color. Decay was obese, breathing loudly, and didn't seem to have two teeth left beside each other in his mouth.

"But do you have powers?" she asked the group.

"We are the result," Fire told her, "but we can also be the cause."

"So you can—" Ruby began.

"Set things on fire?" the girl answered pleasantly. "Yeah."

"That's why I didn't let her hold the note," Plague's raspy voice chimed in.

"Not everything I touch catches fire," the girl snapped.

Plague just rolled his eyes and crossed his arms over his chest.

"That—" Ruby began. Then she paused. She surveyed the group

of them, considering for a moment what might be required of her in order to look after seven blights on humanity. "That's a good thing."

The sound of laughter interrupted her then, and Ruby turned her head toward it. The sound had come from outside her apartment, and it was giving her the seed of an idea.

Her nearest neighbors, and the only ones with whom she shared this level of the sky, were Jaccob Stevens and his family. Their penthouse on top of Starcom Tower was actually one story above hers, but she had a clear view of their living space from her sitting room and its adjoining balcony. And every now and then, when the glass was open and the wind was just right, she could hear the things that went on out on their terrace.

The family was enjoying themselves, Jaccob was cooking something on his grill, and the divine smell wafting in through her open windows reminded Ruby she hadn't eaten today. Ruby signaled to the androgynous youth to come closer. An idea had hatched. She could, at the same time, both advance her agenda and test the mettle of these minions Loki had sent her. "Discontent?" she addressed him.

"Yeah?" he answered, sounding just as unhappy as his name might have implied.

"Do you see that woman up there—the blonde one?" Ruby pointed across the way, at the statuesque form of Elizabeth Stevens where she lounged against the balcony railing.

Discontent nodded.

"I want her out," Ruby instructed.

"Out?" Discontent asked, seeming not to have understood the request.

"Out," Ruby affirmed. "Elsewhere. Gone. Unmarried. *Discontented*. And get her to keep the kids away if you can."

Discontent smiled slyly and nodded his head. "Got it, boss. It might take a couple of days, but I can do that."

"Excellent," Ruby affirmed, patting Discontent on the arm as he turned to go. Ruby turned her attention back to her neighbor and his wife.

Elizabeth Stevens was someone Ruby just couldn't help but hate. Tall and blonde, naturally thin, toned and tanned, she was the kind of woman who'd always made shorter, plumper women feel somehow inferior. She'd helped her husband build a multi-billion-dollar tech empire and had only recently retired from running Starcom Industries to pursue a full-time life of philanthropy.

But none of that really mattered to Ruby. What mattered to Ruby was the fact that the esteemed Mrs. Stevens was the one thing standing between her and bedding the most powerful man in Cobalt City. And that just wouldn't do. Even if Jaccob and Elizabeth's happy marriage turned out to be a sham, Ruby had no illusions that she could steal a man from a woman who looked like that, presuming the playing field was level.

But Ruby Killingsworth had no intention of playing fair. She figured she'd be waiting to conquer the man in the super suit until after her powers had been fully restored, but it appeared as though the opportunity to get the wife out of the way had just presented itself. There was no way she wasn't going to jump at it.

Having the services of the living embodiment of discontent was an opportunity she just couldn't pass up.

Now to figure out what the hell to do with the other six.

CHAPTER
TWO

Standing only 5'3" and with a curvy figure closer to the ideal of a bygone era, Ruby Killingsworth was well aware that she wasn't conventionally beautiful. But over the years, she'd learned to use what assets she did have to her advantage. And she knew that she'd never looked more fetching than she did as she made her way to lie on her balcony in the late afternoon sunshine.

The swimsuit she wore was a two piece: white with giant red polka dots; it had a high waist and a halter top and accentuated all her best features—pushing up her bosom and nipping her in at the smallest part of her waist. Her hair was pinned up on top of her head and her nails were painted the same shade of red as her lips. She looked like she belonged painted on the nose of an antique aircraft, and she knew it. She may not have been beautiful in the generic sense of the word, but Ruby had her own brand of sexy that served her quite well.

Today, her oversized white sunglasses were serving her best of all as she lay on her comfy chaise and pretended to be gazing out into space. She was, of course, gazing at her neighbor. It had been a week since the Blights had come into her life, and five days since she'd watched gleefully through her bedroom shades as Elizabeth Stevens had walked out on her husband. And since then, neither she nor either of her grown children had come to darken the doorstep of Starcom Tower. If Ruby had needed proof of the power of these Tulpas Loki had sent her, that had been enough. Discontent had done exactly as he said he would. It certainly inspired confidence in their ability to help her retrieve the item in the drawing. Fortunately, the six remaining Blights seemed to have no problem biding their time until she figured out what it was and how to get her hands on it. She'd quartered them in one of the as-yet unused studios on forty-seven with the instructions to "record an album, or something" while she worked on the problem.

She'd hoped to be in touch with Loki again by now, but he'd remained noticeably absent from his prepared space on forty-six. And another trip through the Coil was out of the question; she'd scarcely been able to scrape together the resources to work the ritual when she'd gone before, and lacking her innate magic left her without the ability to garner more. But it had occurred to her, as her mind had buzzed with questions about the sketch and the Blights, that she had a decidedly more mundane way to reach out to her immortal friend.

It had taken her assistant less than half an hour to provide her with a phone number that bypassed the White House switchboard and got her in touch with Lyle Prather. Loki had made it sound like he was rather put out with his avatar's recent elevation to Leader of the Free World, but Ruby certainly felt otherwise. The man's abominable politics aside, Prather could prove to be the best president of Ruby's lifetime—or at the very least, the most profitable one.

Had any other man occupied the White House currently, Ruby was sure she'd have had a beast of a time getting a direct number to call. There was a chance any correspondence between herself and any other sitting president would have been handled entirely by assistants and media managers. But not this president. This president loved the limelight, he thrived on media attention, and he craved the company of celebrities. When word reached him that the head of an entertainment empire the size and scope of Goblin Records was trying to get in touch, she knew Prather would be forthcoming with his digits.

She used her business phone to make the call. She wanted to make certain the President's caller ID reported it was Goblin Records' CEO calling. There was something a little obscene-feeling about making a call to the White House from her terrace while wearing a bikini and stirring a pitcher of margaritas, but it was what it was.

"And what can I do for you today, Ms. Killingsworth?" Prather's smarmy drawl answered after only the second ring.

Ruby was glad this was only a voice call, and not video; she was free to wear her disgust on her face.

"I'm calling in regards to a mutual friend of ours, Mr. President," she answered. She had no desire to tease or to obfuscate. All she cared about was getting in touch with Loki. But still, there was the possibility this call was being monitored or bugged, so she had to be a little vague. "A red-haired friend," she clarified, "who lives far away, and likes velvet capes."

Prather sucked in a breath. "Have—" he began, his voice suddenly a stutter with all its bluster missing. "Have you heard from him? He doesn't talk to me. Does he talk to you?"

Ruby frowned. "Not in a while, Mr. President," she replied, emphasis on the title as a reminder to the man on the other end that someone was almost certainly listening in. "I was hoping you had. But if that's not the case—"

"I'm sure he'll be in touch soon, Ms. Killingsworth," Prather said, seeming to have recovered from the initial shock of having realized Ruby was calling more for Loki than for him.

"Well, then," Ruby said, "you'll tell him I asked after him?"

"I suppose I might be persuaded," he replied.

Ruby rolled her eyes. He was doing that thing where he decided he was going to have the power in the conversation, and Ruby wasn't having it. She may not have her magic to aid her, but she had years of experience with self-important assholes informing her next move.

"Well, I appreciate that," she said, "and I know you're such a busy man that I won't take up any more of your time. Thank you very much, Mr. President. Have a lovely rest of the afternoon." And with that, she moved quickly to punch the button to end the call. If Prather wasn't fully in bed with Loki at the moment, then she had no use for him.

Her questions were for Loki, not his avatar.

She'd spent the last week practically obsessed with the sketch he'd sent along with his note. There was no further information provided: just a hand-drawn likeness of an item with a few notes on its size and color. She hadn't the slightest idea where it had originated nor anything about how it was supposed to work. She hadn't even been able to discern the name of the thing, so there was no real way to confirm it was in the vault of the CCPD. She had, at least, been able to discover that the vault in question actually existed, and had begun the preliminary recon work to figure out where to find it and exactly how she might go about breaking in.

She was thinking hard on the possibility of just breaking down the door of the vault and having a look around when she heard an overwhelming noise coming from the direction of Jaccob Stevens's balcony. He'd been out there tinkering with some device or another for the better part of an hour. Ruby hadn't been able to tell what he was working on, but it had been his presence in her line of sight that had gotten her onto the balcony in a swimsuit to begin with. And now he'd made a racket so loud that she felt no compunction about peering openly over the top of her sunglasses.

Jaccob waved.

Ruby waved back, grinning wickedly at the knowledge that he'd noticed her. She took a deep breath and forced herself to look away. She was enjoying a sip of the tart margarita she'd been slowly nursing when she noticed the noise was getting gradually louder. She turned her head to catch the rather unexpected sight of Jaccob Stevens approaching her balcony from above. She'd known, of course, that as his alter-ego, Stardust, Jaccob possessed devices that gave him the ability to fly. But she hadn't ever seen one up close.

He arrived at the foot of her chaise aboard some bastardized combination of a rocket and a skateboard with what looked like an upcycled bicycle handlebar on a pole for a handhold. The thing was loud, and by Ruby's best guess, unfinished, but here was Jaccob Stevens on her balcony. And unpleasant noises or no, that was progress.

"Well howdy, neighbor," she greeted him, inclining her head and shooting him her friendliest smile.

"Sorry about the noise," he said, stepping off the board and onto the polished concrete of the balcony.

Ruby waved her hands in a gesture of dismissal. "I'm sure you're not used to having neighbors fifty stories up," she said.

"That I am not," he affirmed.

"Never a dull moment," she commented, smiling coyly as her lips just brushed the rim of her miniature margarita glass.

"No," a fidgeting Jaccob said in reply, "I guess not."

"Just promise you won't make a habit of doing this at four in the morning," she said, gesturing to the board at his feet, "and I think we'll be okay."

"I'll do what I can," Jaccob replied, suddenly seeming less off balance. Ruby was getting the distinct sense he was starting to enjoy this exchange. "But if the city needs me—"

Ruby threw her head back in far more demonstrative laughter than was really necessary. He was being cute on purpose, and the least she could do was reward him with an unmistakable reaction.

"Of course," she drawled, "I moved in next to Stardust. Surely I can't expect too much peace and quiet."

"Well, you're right about that," he agreed, gesturing to the board on the deck, "So I guess this is 'welcome to the neighborhood.'"

Ruby chuckled. "Have a seat," she offered, gesturing to the chaise beside hers. It was mostly in the shade of her giant umbrella and much closer to the pitcher of margaritas than Ruby's own chair. "Have a margarita," she added, "and tell me what this is."

Jaccob looked lost for a moment. Maybe "have a seat and pour yourself a drink" was more than he was ready for so soon after Elizabeth had left. But the hesitation was over in a moment. Jaccob did as he had been invited to and seated himself on the edge of the next chair. He poured himself a drink from the glass pitcher as he answered her.

"I call it the StarBoard," he said. "It's something I'm developing for times when I need to get off the ground, but can't get to the Suit."

"Ah," Ruby said, raising her glass to clink against the one he'd just poured himself. "So I guessed correctly—it's superhero stuff. Also helpful in case of a fire alarm, if you don't care to walk down fifty stories of staircase."

Jaccob laughed as he took a sip of his drink. "Other than the possibility of a fire drill, how are you liking high-rise living?"

Ruby nodded. "It's nice. I like having a forty second commute home from the office. And," she added, tilting her head to look at him over the top of her sunglasses again, "the neighbor seems awfully nice... if a little noisy."

Jaccob's face flushed a little. He could tell she was flirting. And he wasn't walking away. This was good. He averted his gaze for a moment and then looked back up at her and changed the subject. "You know," he said awkwardly, "my son was really excited to learn you were going to be next door. He wants to be a musician. He was pretty keen on the idea of my living next door to the biggest record label on the East Coast."

"Is he any good?" Ruby asked.

Jaccob shrugged. "Honestly, I have no idea. My taste in music is hardly modern."

Ruby genuinely laughed out loud at that. "Just between us," she said candidly, "I can't tell the good from the bad anymore, either. If you look at my playback history, you'll see hits of the 80s, a few one-hit wonders from the 90s, Wilhelm Furtwängler conducting Wagner, and the greatest hits of Benny Goodman."

Jaccob seemed both amused and surprised at her revelation.

"But I can tell what's bankable," she added. "You know, we're always looking at new artists. If you want, send over his contact information. I'll get him hooked up with one of our development people."

"And what if he isn't any good?" Jaccob asked.

Ruby shrugged. "Then he washes out of development and that's that," she answered plainly. "But you're still father of the year because you got him the meeting with the big, important record label."

"And you'd do that?" he asked. "For me?"

Ruby shook her head. "Jaccob," she said pointedly, "if it wasn't for you and your neighborhood revitalization efforts, then I wouldn't be sitting on top of this glorious building from which I can direct my empire. The least I can do is listen to your kid play guitar… piano?"

"Guitar," Jaccob affirmed.

Ruby smiled. She knew that, of course. She'd seen Mike Stevens playing his guitar through the windows of the neighboring penthouse more than once, but she couldn't very well tell Jaccob that. "It's really no problem," she assured him.

"Thank you," Jaccob said sincerely, taking another sip of his cocktail. "This is good."

Ruby nodded again. She sat up on the edge of the chaise and reached for the pitcher, refilling his glass and then her own and giving him basically no choice but to look her in the cleavage as she did it. As much as she was aware of her own shortcomings, Ruby also knew how to use her assets. And she had always had an awfully nice rack.

"You thank me now," she allowed, "but you'll be cursing my name when he's a giant success and suddenly too cool to come home for Christmas." Ruby sat back with her glass in both hands and pretended like she hadn't noticed him looking.

"Nah," Jaccob commented after another sip of margarita. "For one thing, we're Jewish. And anyway, that's more likely to be his mother's problem than mine."

Ruby shot him her sweetest and most sympathetic smile. The tabloids had only just started to get ahold of the story of the Stevenses' recent split, and she hadn't wanted to bring it up. She wanted him thinking about just about anything but his wife. Reaching over and patting his hand where it sat on the chaise beside him, she declared, "Well, that's a problem for another day. No use in borrowing trouble. And anyway, I have a much more pressing problem to deal with at the moment."

"Yeah?" Jaccob asked, sounding genuinely interested. "What's that?"

Ruby quirked her lip. Was it really going to be this easy? "How," she began, screwing her face into an expression of feigned seriousness, "am I going to convince you to stay for dinner?"

CHAPTER
THREE

Ruby sat at her desk and tried not to sulk. Lawyers were bothersome. Music rights were bothersome. Ever since the loss of her powers, just about every single interaction she'd been forced to have with another human being had been bothersome. Ruby had never particularly cared for people in general. But at least with the power to influence and manipulate them, she'd seen to it throughout her life that each interpersonal encounter she'd been made to suffer had at least been fruitful to whatever purpose she was seeking. Now, as the head of a Fortune 500 company, and without the benefit of even the little power she'd been born with, Ruby's world had descended into unacceptable chaos.

She still wasn't sure why that alien had chosen to abduct her for their machinations, but she'd been grateful for the powers it had gained her, even though the ordeal had been somewhat less than pleasant. She'd enjoyed the additional power immensely. Ruby had always wished her innate magic had been more powerful, so she'd more than welcomed her supernatural gifts from outer space. It hadn't taken long for her to get the hang of the additional abilities and integrate them into her day-to-day bag of tricks. Which had made the tragedy last Christmas all the more horrible.

Bolstered by her new and improved magical abilities, Ruby had been sure... *sure*... she'd be able to work a ritual that would finally give her the thrall over her supernaturally gifted peers that her magical abilities had thus far failed to give. Everything had been perfect, until her well-meaning building manager had suspected dark magic and set off the fire sprinklers to stop it. Up until that moment, she'd had no idea that Arsho was familiar with ritual magic. And how was she supposed to guess that her Turkish underling was actually Armenian, and that there were specifics of iconography she'd missed in setting up the ritual?

Magic hadn't been the same since.

At first, she'd thought the magic loss would be temporary. It had been the largest and the most powerful ritual she'd ever attempted. Having it interrupted could have just burned her out—it wouldn't have been the first time she'd needed a few days to rest and recharge after working powerful magics. But days had gone by, and then weeks, and there was no sign of her powers returning. Her initial feeling was that she'd only lost the powers that the alien had somehow gifted her, which she could have accepted, since she had lived without those powers for most of her life. But as the weeks went on, she realized she had lost all of her power—even that little but well-honed magic she'd had with her since childhood was nowhere to be accessed.

And that was bad.

It was, indeed, bad enough to send her through the Coil to knock on Loki's door.

She had to have magic to function. She wanted all of her power back, but she needed, she *required*, her original power returned. It had been nothing short of torturous to deal with the world and run her business without the magical ability she was accustomed to. It was tantamount to losing a limb. And she couldn't stand it.

It was high time she did something about it.

The best information she'd managed to glean about the item in Loki's drawing had come from a roundabout set of sources. She'd thought to do a search for items known to be in the occult vault of the Cobalt City Police—the one that supposedly housed the item in question. It turned out that all the artifacts stored there were considered "evidence" from the various investigations that had brought them into police custody and were therefore subject to the Freedom of Information Act. Finding out the contents of that vault was as easy as clicking a link.

Each item was listed individually, catalogued with intake information, case numbers, investigating officers' information, chain of custody, and other pertinent details. There were all sorts of magical wonders stored there. Ruby thought for a moment about how she could make millions by cleaning the place out and re-selling those trinkets to those who might use them to create mayhem. Of course, that was only a fleeting thought. She already *had* millions. What she didn't have were her powers.

Each item in the vault had been photographed, too. Deep in the case file, once a person figured out where to click, there were several images of each piece of evidence, photographed on at their intake as proof of the condition of the things upon entering police custody.

But there was no sign of the stone-in-metal she'd seen in Loki's drawing. Maybe he'd been wrong. It wouldn't be the first time the god had been mistaken about things. Or perhaps his information was just out of date. The item may have once been in the vault, but wasn't any longer. There was a long disclaimer on the front page of the evidence custodian's website about property being returned to its rightful owner upon the disposition of a case. Just because Loki had heard that the item's last known location was in this vault didn't mean it was still there. He may have been a god, but he wasn't omniscient. The thing could have been quietly returned to its proper owner and he would never have heard of it.

Ruby had dwelled hard on that possibility and even found herself actively sulking about it for the better part of the day after she'd had dinner with Jaccob Stevens. But by the time she'd sat in her living room watching him tinker with his Stardust suit the next night, it occurred to her to dig deeper. She'd gone back to the website and carefully read every detail of every item listed as being in CCPD custody, this time keeping tabs on any entry that mentioned magical power in its description. She'd then combed through those pictures again. What if the item were somehow disguised? It could have been buried in or attached to any number of the larger pieces in the evidence vault.

After what must have been several hours of this, and long after Jaccob Stevens had put down his super suit to turn in for the night, she'd hit what she guessed to be the proverbial jackpot.

It was called the Eye of Africa. Not the most original name, but Ruby didn't so much give a damn. She hadn't noticed it in the photos on her first pass because it didn't look at all like itself. In fact, all that was pictured was a hardened metal case—lead, if she *had* to guess— with shock wires wound around it attached to what looked like an antique six-volt battery. That *had to* be it. There was no chance at all any of the other items in the vault contained what she was looking for. All of them had been too extensively photographed, and there was no sign of anything even remotely resembling the item in the drawing.

But this Eye of Africa? It was an item so powerful that the police kept it in its protective case. The case, she learned, had come from a museum. When she'd clicked through and downloaded a PDF of the case notes surrounding the Eye, she was quickly convinced she had the right thing. The jewel, as it was described in some of the older paperwork, was said to have originated in another dimension. Some slave some thousands of years ago had pulled it from a mine in Ethiopia—King Solomon's Mine, according to some sources—and presented it to the Queen of Sheba. Apparently that's where the name came from. No one was sure of all the hands it had passed through over the centuries, but everyone was sure it gave its wielder far more power than any one human ought to have.

It had come into the possession of the Cobalt City Police Department before even the Icons were around. Upon disposition of the case of the mad wizard in whose custody it had been found, it had been decided that the Eye was far too dangerous to be returned into private hands. The talisman had sat in the CCPD vault for some time before finally being donated to the British Museum, where it was locked away and never displayed.

And in January of 1933, the British had unceremoniously sent it back. There was a scan in the file of a handwritten note from one of the museum's curators at the time; although the handwriting was difficult to read in places, Ruby got the gist. The thing was too powerful. They didn't want it. And, by the way, the fanatic who's just been elected Chancellor of Germany has occult leanings, and let's keep this thing as far from his clutches as possible. They'd even sent it back in this handy-dandy, hard-to-steal, heavily warded and dangerously electrified carrying case.

Well, that part at least made sense. No possibly infinitely powerful items for Hitler—check. And it seemed the CCPD hadn't known what to do with it after that. So it had sat in its case, collecting dust in the vault ever since. Neither the Icons, nor the Protectorate (who'd had a vault of their own at the Keep), had dared to move it into superhero custody. That *had* to be the thing she was looking for. Something so powerful that even the British Museum was uncomfortable housing it—much less the city's most notable superheroes—seemed like just the kind of thing Loki would point her to. She'd have asked him in person, but he still had yet to make an appearance in her building. The more time that passed, the more she was becoming convinced he really had just tricked her out of millions of dollars of real estate with no intention to ever use the place.

She decided to bring the Blights to her office just after the last of the damned lawyers had left for the day to finalize plans. She'd even gotten Plague to brush up against the most irksome of the attorneys in hopes of giving him a cold. That would show him for making her meeting run over. Well, probably not, but she'd spend the weekend enjoying the occasional thought of him feeling as miserable as she had while he'd droned on about the nuances of renewing expiring artist contracts.

She'd have no need to understand nuance if she just had her powers back!

And she'd be well on the road to that in just a few hours if all went well. Tonight they were going after the Eye. It was nearing five o'clock now, and if history was any indication, the sun would be down by eight or so. And Ruby knew as well as anyone else that the ostensibly fiscally responsible CCPD wouldn't be staffing non-essential positions like evidence clerks on a Friday night, even at the occult vault. The place was likely to be empty. It almost sounded too easy.

Almost.

And the Blights were turning out to be a lot of help, much more help than she'd expected from any friends of Loki's. Other than Doubt (who spent the whole evening being, well, doubtful), they'd been generous with suggestions as to how they might help with a break-in. The small but critical differences in the way the powers of Ruin and Decay manifested themselves were particularly interesting and, of all the Blights Loki had sent, those two clearly made the most sense to have along for a heist.

They were deep in the throes of walking through the night's strategy when an unfamiliar sound disturbed their conversation. The unusual, repetitive, digitized beeping concerned the lot of them at first; this was a new building and the noise might be attached to any number of alarm systems. Fire was quick to assure the group that the building was, at least, not currently burning. And while a relief, it did nothing to solve the mystery of where the noise was coming from.

It was Doubt, up and pacing and certain that none of the others' theories were any good, who spotted the source of the offending klaxon. "Your phone is ringing," she declared flatly, pointing at the diminutive device where it sat on Ruby's desk.

Ruby, who was seated at the small conference table on the far side of her office, popped out of her chair and frowned distinctly. That was pretty well impossible. The Starphone Ruby had left out on her desk was her personal one. She had several similar devices, each differently accessible to others. There was a phone for building matters that only Arsho knew the number to, a phone for top-level business matters that only her most lucrative artists and their managers had access to, and she even had one connected to the business network that her receptionists were able to put office calls through to. But the one sitting on her desk was her personal phone, and it was new. Literally no one had the number, so why in hell was it ringing?

Ruby stalked over to her desk, wondering if maybe Loki had some power to ring a phone without knowing the number, and at the same time steeling herself for the tirade she was about to lay down on whatever unsuspecting telemarketer had randomly dialed her private number. She considered for a moment just hitting the "ignore" button, but decided she was mad enough to need to confront whoever had caused this disturbance.

"Yes?" snapped Ruby as she punched the button that allowed the call to come through the speaker, her tone making no secret of the fact that she was not happy with whomever was on the other end of the call.

"Ruby?" the voice on the line answered.

Ruby sucked in a deep breath and took a seat in her desk chair, regarding her Starphone with potent curiosity. "Jaccob?" she asked, having taken just a moment to process that his was most certainly the voice she had heard.

"Hi," Jaccob Stevens answered, sounding friendly and familiar, as though he genuinely had no idea that this call was an oddity.

"Hi," she replied as sweetly as she could while still completely baffled. "Please don't take this the wrong way, but how did you get this number?"

Jaccob chuckled nervously. "It's pretty easy to get anybody's number when you own the network," he admitted sheepishly.

It was Ruby's turn to chuckle.

"You don't think that's creepy, do you?" he asked after a moment. "I mean, I sort of wondered if it was creepy, but then I thought maybe you wouldn't mind and—"

"Actually," she interrupted him, "I think it's kind of cute." In all honesty, had it been anyone else, she *would* have found it creepy and off-putting. But when coming from the man who she had every intention of seducing presently, and coupled with such an adorably contrite attitude about the whole thing, she found it rather endearing.

"Oh, good," Jaccob answered with an audible sigh of relief. "I was a little worried."

"Well, don't be," she reassured him. "Now, to what do I owe this benign stalking? You didn't just call me for no reason."

"No," Jaccob admitted, "I didn't." He took a deep breath.

Ruby looked up at the Blights and shrugged.

Doubt rolled her eyes, and Plague seemed totally uninterested, but the others appeared to be almost as curious to hear the next bit as Ruby herself was.

"I was just thinking," he began again, his nerves clear in his voice, "I really enjoyed our dinner the other night—"

"As did I," Ruby encouraged, hoping to assuage a bit of his obvious trepidation. He was about to ask her out. She knew it the same as she knew that corporate lawyers were annoying, and she couldn't help but grin wickedly at her phone as Jaccob continued.

"So I thought," he added, hesitating only for a moment. "Do you think you'd like to get dinner tonight?"

Ruby's heart sank. Tonight she had plans. *Big* plans. Plans she'd been working on for days, plans she was not at all keen to cancel.

Quickly, she weighed the pros and cons in her mind of putting the heist off another week. Having dinner with Jaccob was a lovely development and a step in a direction she absolutely intended to go, but having her powers back was paramount. And after all, dinner with Jaccob would only go better once she was restored to her proper self. With her powers fully returned, she could easily make him forgive her for turning him down now. With a sigh and a scowl, she answered quietly.

"I have a business thing tonight," she droned. "It's pretty import-ant, and I can't get out of it." She hoped that by sounding as disap-pointed as possible, he would get the hint to ask her out for another day.

"I know what that's like," he replied, seeming barely disappointed with her answer.

Ruby smiled. Of course he knew what that was like. He ran an even larger corporation than she did.

"And I also know how much fun those things aren't," he added. "So how about after? I know a place down in Quayside with a fantastic late-night happy hour. What do you say? Around ten?"

Ruby's face brightened into a grin she hadn't worn since her powers had gone missing. "Can we say ten-thirty?" she asked. That would surely give her enough time to acquire the item and get over to Quayside.

"We certainly can," Jaccob answered, his easy tone telling her he was more than a little bit pleased with this development.

"Well then, it's a date."

"Excellent," Jaccob declared. "I'll text you the address. See you tonight."

"See you tonight," Ruby affirmed. "G'bye."

"Bye," Jaccob managed to say, just as Ruby's finger found the button to end the call. Well, that had been an interesting development. She was still grinning from ear to ear when she looked up from her phone to address the Blights.

"So," she said, rising from her seat to take a deep, self-satisfied breath, "we have a hard end time. Do we need to change our plans at all?"

CHAPTER FOUR

The Cobalt City Police Department kept their super-secret occult vault separate from their standard evidence lockers. Ruby remembered reading about it having been broken into a few years back, although at the time she hadn't been bothered to find out details. This whole week she'd been kicking herself for that. Maybe in the future she'd pay some attention to the news and not just the entertainment rags. But in the present, all she'd really needed was the location of that vault. She'd sent Plague and Pestilence to the public library to do some digging. She'd chosen the two of them because they looked the most like the students she saw coming and going when she occasionally drove past. Fire would have fit in as well, with her copious piercings and brightly colored hair, but Ruby was wary of the possibility of burning the place down.

Ruby mostly detested public spaces and willingly declared her distaste for the unwashed masses. She found a kind of sick humor in having sent the two Blights she most equated with the kind of people who hung out in the central library. The two of them had managed, with little difficulty, to ascertain the location of the vault. It was on one of the less-populated streets in one of the more populated parts of town. Approaching would pose little difficulty.

Pestilence would be meeting the rest of them there, having gone ahead to rally the neighborhood sewer rats into chewing up the wiring of the CCPD's security system. Ruby tried not to think too hard about sewer rats, but was glad at least to have Pestilence on her side. She would hate to be fighting *against* the person who could amass a spontaneous army of feral vermin.

The rest of the party all arrived separately at the nearest public car park, Ruby in her town car and the Blights by various means of public transit. In case of street-side surveillance, she'd thought it better that they muster at the last possible moment.

Never one to be less than perfectly attired for any occasion, it occurred to Ruby as she closed the distance between her car and the alley where she was to meet the others that she looked a bit cliché. In her black leather leggings, low-heeled boots, and moto jacket, and with a knit cap pinned securely to hide her copper locks, she cut every bit the figure of the comic-book cat burglar. Of course, there was a reason stereotypes arose in the first place, and Ruby found her ensemble to be both functional and appropriate.

When the group gathered in the alley adjacent to the police building, only Doubt commented on Ruby's outfit. The others immediately busied themselves with breaking in. Pestilence made it clear that not only were the security cameras down for the moment, but the four-legged cause of that condition would be easily identified. A malfunction would seem far less suspicious when it had clearly come from a rodent infestation. That was the good news. The bad news was that if the proper replacement cables were in the building, it wouldn't take long for the system to be back up and running.

That meant they needed to work quickly. They'd decided to make their entrance via a fire door that opened into a narrow alley between the police building and the art school that backed up to it. During the day, this alley would likely be full of hipster art students smoking clove cigarettes, complaining about the high prices at the Alibi Room, and planning their takedown of the establishment. But after dark on a Friday night in summertime, the place was blessedly empty. Doubt spent her time in the alley making sure it stayed that way. She had no problem changing the minds of any innocent passers-by who thought for a moment about using the alley as a short cut.

Ruin had no difficulty popping the lock on the door and at the same time seeing to it that the attached alarm wouldn't sound. Beyond the door stood a narrow landing to a concrete staircase that seemingly switched back endlessly both above and below.

"Basement," Plague whispered, pointing downward. Ruby took point as the group of them clambered onto the landing and headed to the lower levels where the vault was installed. She led them down the stairs, pausing with only momentary panic when the energy-saving motion-activated lights flickered on. They proceeded down the stark hallway outside of the fire stairs and turned the corner at a sign clearly marked "Vault" with arrows pointing in the prescribed direction.

"I can't believe they're really that dim," Ruby commented quietly.

Doubt shook her head. "They just presume anyone down here has the right to be down here," she reminded Ruby. "If someone needs to check something into that vault, the last thing anyone wants is to have them wandering the basement looking for it."

Ruby shrugged. Doubt could be a real stick in the mud sometimes, but she had a point. The signage was definitely there to steer anyone with legitimate business toward the vault. There was a hanging tile outside of the door to the anteroom and a prominent sign on the door itself. The solid metal door was locked, but Ruin had no more trouble getting through it than he had with the exterior, and soon the lot of them were inside.

On the surface, the anteroom for the CCPD occult vault looked like it could be any evidence room in any police station anywhere in the world. Just as they had done in the hallway, the lights switched on automatically to show that the place was, as Ruby had suspected, currently unoccupied. There was a counter straight ahead of them, separated from the rest of the room by a glass partition, with a locking bolt on a sliding section at one end. There were shelves visible on the near side full of empty boxes, bags, and crates, and labels and signs all over touting such sage wisdom as "Authorized Personnel Only" and "Have Documentation Ready". A door on the far right seemed to lead from the reception area back behind the counter. Ruby inclined her head toward it just in time to see that Ruin had already done his thing, and the door was standing wide open.

The group passed behind the counter and crossed immediately to an overlarge blast door hidden behind some flimsy metal shelving. It was double dead-bolted and hung with half a dozen placards informing would-be intruders of exactly which codes and statutes non-authorized entrants were violating. Ruby, of course, didn't give a damn. Ruin was through that door in scarcely more time than it had taken him to get through the previous two, even though it was clear to all observing that this door was made of sterner stuff than the others.

Beyond the blast door, they found their quarry. There was no mistaking the door to the occult vault for anything but what it was. The giant round door with its spindled handle and multiple dials took up the better portion of the wall before them.

"Uhhhh—" Ruin blanched, stumbling over what to say about it.

Ruby guessed he had never been called upon to open a lock of this magnitude before.

Decay placed his hand on his brother's arm and shook his head. "I got this," the portly man said. He jerked his head sideways in a "follow me" motion and turned promptly on his heel. The group of Blights followed him wordlessly through the anteroom and out from behind the counter.

"You've got what?" Ruby asked, clearly confused as she followed them out of the vault room and into the hallway. "Where are we going?"

"Can't use the door," Doubt piped up. "He has a harder time ruining things he can't see, like the tumblers in the locks in that vault."

"You want in quick," Decay piped up as he led the group around the corner, "then we're going through the side."

Ruby frowned. But her look of consternation turned to one of amazement as Decay turned to face the wall.

He ran his hand gently over the putty-colored concrete and as he did, it began to come apart. As though brushing the crumbs off a cookie and watching it crumble in reply, the concrete began disintegrating into sand-fine particles, raining down a fine dust onto the floor. It only took a few passes for him to get a feel for the process, causing the dust to spill from his fingers at an alarming rate. It was scarcely a minute before Decay was up to his knees in the crumbled concrete. The others had moved back, as to not become buried themselves.

Ruby stood just on the edge of the ever-growing dust pile and watched as the indentation grew.

It seemed effortless. With every pass of his hand, a swath of the wall turned to powder and fell. The air was growing thick with the concrete dust, and Ruby had to cover her mouth with her sleeve. Difficulty in breathing notwithstanding, she was exceedingly pleased. Her glee came to an abrupt halt just minutes into the process when Decay's expert ministrations uncovered a mesh of steel rebar buried nearly a foot into the wall of the vault.

"Oh, for fuck's sake," Ruby exhorted. Maybe they would have had better luck with the door after all.

Fire pushed past her cohorts and then past Ruby as she shook her head and rolled up her striped sleeves.

"This is all me," she declared. She sidled up to Decay. "Get me a good void around them."

With a few scoops of his hands and strokes of his fingers, Decay managed to clear out all of the concrete on all sides of the exposed metal, leaving the criss-crossed steel bars hanging in the air of the meter-wide hole.

Fire turned and shot Ruby a smirk.

"Does steel even burn?" Ruby asked Doubt quietly.

"Everything burns," Fire announced, clearly having overheard her boss's comment, "if it gets hot enough." She turned her attention to the steel bars, running her fingers and then her hands over them in a motion some people might have thought bordered on obscene.

But the steel heated. At first it was only the smell of hot metal that heralded the change, but soon enough the bars began to glow red-orange from Fire's repeated caresses. The melting steel heated the room around them, causing uncomfortable perspiration to form at the base of Ruby's neck. Her hairstyle was likely being destroyed along with the rebar, but she wasn't going to let that dampen her spirits now.

One by one, Fire knocked the glowing steel with her fist, causing the now-brittle rods to break apart at their junctions and fall in chunks to the floor. They landed in the chalky concrete dust, which Ruby could only hope wasn't flammable—at least not at the same temperature the rebar was vulnerable to.

Doubt looked dubious about the whole operation, but none of the others seemed to be too concerned.

Ruby wasn't sure how long it took (save that it was just long enough for her to have to blot the perspiration from her upper lip twice and seriously consider unzipping her jacket) but in relatively short order, the meter-wide hole was free of its metal reinforcements, and Decay was back to crumbling away the concrete. Ruby's toes twitched as the indentation became an opening. There was a tiny hole at first, which quickly opened wider and wider as Decay made final passes over the crumbling concrete. Ruby was grinning with replete fulfillment as she gauged the size of the opening.

She was surprised the wall hadn't been thicker. Knowing the nature of the items stored inside the vault, she had pictured something

more substantial. Of course, she figured two solid feet of steel-rein-
forced cast-concrete would be enough to deter most people. Ruby
Killingsworth was not most people. Once she was sure the hole in the
vault's wall was large enough for her to squeeze through, she signaled to
Decay that he'd done enough and made her move toward the opening.

Leading with her left leg, she deftly slinked through the opening
in the concrete and into the vault. She pulled a tiny flashlight from the
pocket of her jacket and passed it around the space. The ceiling was
lower than she'd expected, likely reinforced to discourage would-be
thieves trying to break in from the ground floor. There was a row of
fluorescent lights hanging from the ceiling that made it feel lower still.
Along the near wall was a counter with bundled sage, pots of salt,
and boxes of differing materials lined up on it. Ruby guessed these
were the things the CCPD deemed necessary to have on hand should
anyone need to interact with the items stored in this vault.

On the far side was a cage of black metal, beyond which stood
a series of plain-faced lockers of varying sizes. "Damn." Why did this
have to be so complicated? "Ruin," she called out through the hole in
the wall, "get in here!"

"No can do, boss lady," Ruin answered her, sticking his head and
hands into the opening. He rotated his hands, framing the hole with
them as he shrugged. "There's no way I'd fit."

Ruby snarled, "So make the hole bigger!" She hadn't gotten this
far just to be foiled by a damned chain link fence and a bunch of
school lockers. If the hole needed to be larger so Ruin could get in and
help her, then she would stand there and wait.

"I've got this," Fire sounded before Decay could move into place
to start back in on the concrete. She stepped easily through the narrow opening and brushed past Ruby on her way to the metal cage. She
cracked her knuckles as she approached the padlocked door.

"Are you sure you can do this?" Ruby asked the girl, shining her
flashlight on the combination lock to give Fire a better view.

Fire shook her head and frowned at the older woman. "I'm a torch," she responded. Fire turned back around and took hold of the lock by the shank with her fingertips. In no more than the blink of an eye, the metal heated up to glowing. Scarcely a moment later, the body of the lock fell to the ground, cleaved neatly on both sides by the heat from Fire's fingers. She thumped the left behind half-circle of metal through the loops in the cage door and pulled it open for her boss to pass through.

Ruby crossed intently toward the row of lockers, passing the flashlight over each of the doors as she did. Truly, she had no idea what she was looking for. She was sure there wouldn't be a sign—*super-scary-powerful Eye of Africa inside*—but she'd had it in her head somehow that she would be able to identify the thing when she got close. Now it was literally right in front of her, and she had no idea which door to open.

"We pop them all," she declared after a moment. It just made sense. Open only one door, and it would be obvious what they'd been after. Open all the doors, leave the whole place in chaos, and it may take significantly longer for anyone to figure out what exactly had gone missing—hopefully long enough for Ruby to have the Eye of Africa safely in the heavily warded basement of her house in Regency Heights, and to have discerned and removed any magical trackers it may have had placed on it. There was no record of the Cobalt City Police Department having anyone with magical ability on staff, but Ruby wouldn't bet against that being the case. If she were to come regularly into custody of coveted and powerful magical items, she'd find a way to hex a beacon onto them in case of theft.

"Here," said a quiet voice behind Ruby. She spun on her heel, ready to strike out at whoever was there and realized it was just Doubt who had snuck up behind her.

Doubt was holding out a crow bar with a stern look on her face. "When in doubt," she commented wryly, "smash everything."

Ruby couldn't help but chuckle. Doubt had mostly been a wet blanket on the whole operation, but this was not the first time she'd come through when it mattered. Ruby traded Doubt her flashlight for the crowbar and began working at the first of the twenty-odd locker doors against the wall of the vault.

The lockers, as it turned out, were more for organization than they were for security. Each of the doors popped open with minimal effort on Ruby's part. Their contents were oddly varied, not all of them obvious with occult potential. Ruby reckoned some of the items to be sham, but supposed the CCPD would rather be safe than sorry—and if a patient in the Fermi Institute claimed an item in their possession was magical, then it was better to lock the thing up just in case. There were books and scrolls, candles and incenses, cauldrons and athame, one locker filled to brimming with voodoo dolls, and plenty of trinkets of varied sizes and shapes that were likely talismans of some stripe. It was only when she'd gotten through a particularly sticky lock and found salt pouring out onto her boots that she felt like she'd hit paydirt.

For a moment, she was surprised and aghast at the idea of getting salt in her ankle-high Manolo Blahnik stacked heel boots, but when it hit her that only the most frightening and powerful items would warrant such a precaution, she figured it was a small price to pay. What was a little salt in her shoes compared with getting her powers back? She tucked the crowbar under her arm and used her gloved hands to scoop out the remaining salt from the locker. She'd have salt in her gloves, too, but it didn't matter. It was only a few sweeps of her hands before the locker gave up its contents.

She had found it. She had found the Eye of Africa.

CHAPTER FIVE

The tool that Loki had suggested would bring her powers back was now in her possession. Doubt shone the flashlight on the thing as Ruby turned it over in her hands. The case was smaller than she'd figured from looking at the picture, no larger than a child's metal lunch box. It was heavier than it looked, the little aluminum case almost certainly lined with lead, and Ruby was careful not to touch the thick mass of copper wire spooled around it and connected to a World War II-era lantern battery.

It looked like a ramshackle science project, but it was what they had come here for. Ruby was grinning wildly. She threw her head back in satisfied laughter but was stopped short when a blinking red light in the corner of the room caught her eye. "Damn!" she said, shoving the crowbar she was still holding back into Doubt's grip.

"What is it?" the other woman asked, clearly stunned by her boss's abrupt change in demeanor.

"That!" Ruby snapped, pointing up at the little beacon as she darted through the wire cage and back into the vault proper.

"What's *that*?" Doubt questioned, following Ruby out through the giant hole Decay had provided and rolling her eyes at the sudden haste.

"It's an alarm," Ruby explained, stumbling through the cement dust and turning toward the exit. "A motion sensitive, *silent* alarm," she emphasized. "It's a Starcom Security thing—only for certain clients, like the police department or the building next door to Starcom Tower." She'd been shown just this model when deciding on security for her business and her penthouse.

"Damn." Doubt finally repeated Ruby's initial curse.

"And that's not the worst of it," Ruby insisted as they rounded the corner toward the door to the stairwell.

"What is?" Fire piped up from the rear of the group.

"The damned thing summons Stardust," Ruby answered tersely as she tugged open the door to the stairs and started up, "and it locks down the building in the process."

Fire shook her head and turned around. She ran out of the stairwell and into the basement.

Ruby was not about to halt her retreat, but called out "What the hell are you doing?" after the girl. It was only a moment before she realized what it was. The overhead lights in the stairwell switched on as the deafening sound of an alarm klaxon echoed through the hollow concrete stairwell.

"They won't lock down the building if it's on fire!" Fire asserted as she caught up to the others in the doorway to the alley.

Sure enough, there were other people beginning to file out of the station's other fire doors. There was no one else in the alley where they emerged, but the throngs of uniformed officers spilling out onto the sidewalks at the front and rear of the building were easily spotted. Fire, Pestilence, and Doubt rushed past the others and farther up the concrete stairs as the rest of the group made for the exit.

"Where are you going?" Ruby asked, daring to pause long enough to listen to their answer.

"The roof!" Fire replied, never breaking her stride toward the next flight of stairs.

"Why?" Ruby challenged.

"The hell do you think Stardust is coming from?" Pestilence snapped, still running up the stairs. "Do you want us to cover your escape or not?"

Ruby nodded. She understood. She and the others continued into the alley and moved toward the rear of the building, where officers and others were steadily streaming from the doors. The confusion seemed to be enough to allow them to blend in, but still Ruby hoped Doubt would be paying enough attention from the roof to keep her from being recognized.

They were scarcely ten meters from the end of the alley when Ruby realized she was still holding the very conspicuous lead and aluminum case containing the Eye of Africa. Even if the no one in the current ranks of the CCPD had ever seen the thing before, and even if no one on the street would possibly recognize it, the case still looked suspiciously like a bomb. And anyone walking around the side of a police station wherein the fire alarm had just activated, carrying something that might have been a bomb, was likely to raise suspicion.

She held out the case to Decay. "Can you get through the wires?" she asked him as the group slowed their progress toward the ever-growing crowd of police and civilians on the street.

Ruin took the case from her hands before Decay had the chance, and immediately the wires began to fray. One by one, the copper strands came apart until they fell away entirely, landing on the asphalt and immediately blending into the assorted detritus native to the alley. He fumbled for a moment with the aged clasp, crusty as it was with the corrosion of the metal in the mixture of salt and leaked eighty-year-old battery acid. When the case came open, it was cleaved in two—falling apart at the hinges and the clasp.

Ruby tossed the lid aside and reached into the other half. Not caring whether she damaged the already sloughing purple velvet of the structure that kept the Eye from rattling around inside of its case, she snatched up the muslin-wrapped item tucked inside. "Take these back to the Tower," she instructed the Blights, as she thrust the piece of metal case back at Ruin.

Quickly, Ruby unwrapped the heavy item in her hand from its oiled and smelly muslin casing, just enough to get a glimpse. If her instincts had been wrong, if this *wasn't* the Eye, then it would be better to know now than find out after having done the work to get away with it. One glimpse was all it took for her to be sure. This was it. The fire in the black opal and the peculiar shape of the metal surrounding it were exactly as Loki's drawing had depicted. She had it. She held the Eye of Africa in her hands.

Ruby quickly stashed the jewel in the right-hand pocket of her biker jacket and zipped it up before slipping casually into the crowd on the street behind the police station. There were sirens in the distance, no doubt racing to respond to the fire alarm in the CCPD station.

But the sound of the most concern to Ruby as she tried her best to blend into the milling mélange of officers and passers-by was the droning roar of Stardust's suit approaching. Living just across the street from him had given Ruby a singular ability to recognize the sound of his proprietary rockets. She wondered as she made her way through the throng on the sidewalk toward the parking structure where her car was waiting if anyone else had even noticed the sound yet. Stardust was about a minute out, from what her ears were telling her. She was likely to have made it to the garage by then, but still she was thankful for the hat she wore. A black knit cap would blend in to the crowd a whole lot better than the mane of bright red hair underneath it.

But even with the cap on, she'd feel better once she was off the street and out of view. It was highly unlikely Jaccob would recognize her, what with the mayhem of the arriving fire vehicles and the chaos of the ever-growing throng of people that would undoubtedly continue to increase once Stardust showed up. But the idea that he might was making her nervous.

She moved toward the parking structure as quickly as she could without arousing the suspicion of any of the hundred or more police on the sidewalks. Ruby had never been one to choose the stairs over the elevator in any situation, but under the circumstances, she thought better of standing still in the semi-exposed vestibule of the parking garage. She decided instead to make a mad dash up the concrete steps to where her car was waiting.

Ruby had told her driver before she left not to get out and open her door upon her return. Fortunately, the magic he was under had everything to do with the contract she'd had him sign when he'd first come to work for her, and nothing to with her missing powers. She got into the town car on her own and let herself breathe for a moment, secure in the knowledge she wouldn't be spotted.

She was pleased to discover that, from the safety of her back seat, she was able to watch the next events unfold at the police station. Through the rear windshield of her town car, Ruby watched as Stardust descended heroically toward the roof of the building. He was accompanied by another person springing across rooftops who Ruby eventually recognized as Wild Kat.

The two of them made it onto the roof just as the first of the fire trucks pulled up to the building. There was smoke pouring out from the lower floor windows now, and it was beginning to waft out of the upper floor windows as well, leaving Ruby to wonder just what Fire had done to the building.

She was easily spotted on the roof, her brightly colored hair drawing attention to her even in the presence of two superheroes. She was standing with her face tilted skyward as a burst of flame erupted under Stardust's boots.

Ruby winced as she watched him fly back into the air again briefly and then land in the middle of the ball of fire. It occurred to her then that she hadn't ever made it plain that the Blights were absolutely not to do Stardust any permanent harm. Doubt seemed to have a good enough head on her shoulders to have figured that out, but there was no telling about the other ones. And Ruby was unsure of the rules that governed the Blights under her purview. It's not like Loki had sent them with an instruction manual. Were they aware of her intentions somehow, extensions of her will, or were they only subject to her orders?

It was no small sense of relief Ruby felt when she saw that Stardust's suit seemed to be fireproof. Whether or not she'd thought to tell Fire and Pestilence not to hurt Jaccob, it looked like he'd be able to handle himself against them. Having her date for the evening injured by her own henchmen would make this night suddenly a lot less wonderful.

But then she saw Jaccob beginning to act as though maybe he'd somehow been burned through the metal of his suit. He was writhing almost, moving uncomfortably this way and that, and as the flames died down beneath him, Ruby couldn't tell what was causing it.

It was Wild Kat who drew Ruby's gaze to the root of the problem. The utility of having Pestilence along for this caper also became clear as Ruby watched. Wild Kat, having been poised low on the rooftop, pounced at Stardust's feet. A dark gray ball (that Ruby instantly recognized as a rat) flew from her paw and over the side of the smoking building.

Fire engines were pulling in on all sides at street level, yellow-clad men and women dragging out hoses and connecting to hydrants as they mustered in front of the station to plan their assault on the fire within. But Ruby's gaze couldn't help but be drawn to the now constant stream of rats and mice climbing up the brick walls from every direction to assault the two heroes on the roof.

The rodents were swarming the rooftop, enveloping Wild Kat up to her knees in a solid, writhing mass of gray and brown fur that turned Ruby's stomach. She tried to look away from the grotesque scene of Wild Kat slashing through the vermin with her claws and Stardust trying to fling them off the places where they had climbed up and begun gnawing at the joints in his suit. She looked for Fire, who she found standing on the far side of the roof from where Pestilence and his rodent army were taking on the heroes. She had no idea what Doubt was doing at this point, but she was sure it had to be something, as the woman's gaze was firm and fixed on Stardust as he continued to do battle with the onslaught of rats and mice that streamed nonstop up the walls and onto the two heroes.

It was gnarly and not unlike a train wreck—even though Ruby was sure in her gut that she did not want to look at the weaponized rodents for another moment, she was somehow unable to force herself to look away.

So she was oddly relieved when a wall of flame kicked up between herself and the battle that blocked her view of the superheroes and the Blights they were dueling. She decided that was as good a time as ever to stop watching and get the hell out of there. They had all agreed before the night began that everyone was on his or her own to get back to the Tower, so it wasn't like there was anything she was waiting for. "Go," she said to her driver. The car obediently started forward and Ruby sat back in her seat.

There was nothing more she needed to see on that roof. She trusted that the Blights would be able to handle themselves without too much difficulty; after all, they were on loan from Loki, and she had confidence he wouldn't send her assistants who needed too much minding. They had plenty of power between them, and there was no reason to worry about their ability to get through the battle and get the hell out. And she'd seen enough to know Stardust was going to make it out okay as well. It was time to get away from this crazy place and to her next appointment.

Jaccob might be a little late to meet her, thanks to the mayhem on the station roof, but in the event he might show up on time, Ruby wasn't about to let herself be late.

CHAPTER SIX

Changing her clothes in the car was an act Ruby had practically made into an art form in the months and years she'd spent climbing the entertainment and corporate ladder. The fact that she was a couple of years out of practice didn't stop her from making it part of the plan. She had no problem changing from her black leather vault-robbing costume into a purple to brown ombre chiffon high-necked mini dress and brown knee-high boots. She fluffed her hair out of its loose up-do, combing her fingers through the gentle curls that had been formed by buns and heat. She'd figured it would look intentional, and as best she could tell via her compact mirror, it did. Jaccob would never suspect she was coming out for drinks straight from a heist.

She glossed her lips as the town car pulled up in front of the address Jaccob had texted her earlier in the night. She made one final check of her face in the rearview mirror, then slipped the Eye of Africa into her bag before stepping out onto the sidewalk. She hadn't had much time to pay attention to it on the way over, and she felt a little bit like a kid on Christmas morning—forced to go to church before playing with her wonderful new toy. Fortunately, a date with Jaccob would be a hell of a lot more fun than a church service; she was sure she'd be enjoying herself enough in his company not to be bothered too much by having to wait to get close to the Eye. If only getting out of skin-tight leather pants in the back seat of her town car hadn't been such a chore, she'd have had more time to stare at it. Had it been anyone other than Jaccob Stevens she was scheduled to meet, she'd have likely called to cancel, but her intentions concerning him were almost as powerful as those concerning the Eye, and the opal in her handbag would be coming home with her tonight.

Of course, there was every chance that Jaccob Stevens might be coming home with her tonight as well. But that was a problem for later. For now, she made her way across the crowded sidewalk and into the little restaurant Jaccob had recommended. It was a tiny place, with a storefront barely as wide as its double doors. The entry was curtained with heavy brown velvet on the inside, and there was nary a window in the front. No wonder this was where Jaccob had wanted to meet. If a person didn't want to be seen having a drink with another person, this was surely the place to make that happen. In fact, the only indication there was an establishment at all behind the darkened, curtained glass doors was the poorly lit etched copper sign above them reading simply, "Durian." That was definitely the name of the bar Jaccob had given her.

The place was dark inside in a way that reminded Ruby of gangster movies from the 1950s. It was exactly Ruby's kind of place. The candles on the little round tables provided the only light, save some amber tinted bulbs behind the bar that took up the entire length of the south wall. Few of the liquors on the shelves behind the tall, Asian bartender were of an ilk commonly found on offer at commercial establishments. She recognized several bottles of rare and unusual spirits among the more commonplace, but still high-end varieties. The ambiance was exactly her style, but her best guess was that the top-shelf libations had been what put this place on Jaccob Stevens's radar.

Ruby had scarcely made it two meters into the room when she

was met by a petite African woman who greeted her with a bow of the head. "You are Miss Ruby," the woman said.

Ruby's eyebrows rose; she didn't like to be at such a disadvantage, but she nodded in affirmation anyway.

"Welcome. Mr. Stevens apologizes for his tardiness," she added. "But he has instructed us to take care of you until he arrives."

Ruby nodded again. She couldn't help but smile at that. Jaccob had been called out to save the city, and yet he'd thought to phone the bar and tell them to look after her. That was a delightful revelation.

Her smile grew wider as the woman led her through a curtain adjacent to the bar and into a tiny back room. There was only one table—an intimate round one with a brown velvet semi-circular bench seat behind it and a bundle of orchids laying between a pair of copper and wooden folders on top. The woman gestured for her to have a seat, and Ruby did so. Sliding across the plush velvet bench, she gave the woman a nod by way of dismissal.

Ruby wished she'd worn a watch. She didn't dare reach into her bag to pull out her phone; she was practically itching to handle the Eye of Africa, and she knew that once her hand grazed it, she'd be hard pressed to leave it be. And the last thing she wanted was for Jaccob to walk in and find her in possession of the stolen article he'd just been called in to deal with. That would end this budding relationship before it had the chance to begin. She was reaching for one of the copper-clad menus when she noticed a slip of paper on the table beneath the orchids. She slid it out from under the three stems, careful not to bruise the blooms hanging just off the edge of the table.

She recognized the flowers as Gold of Kinabalu, one of the rarest and most costly per-bloom flowers on the planet. She'd tried to have a few stems included in her office arrangement when she'd moved in a few months back, but had learned they only bloomed two months out of the year, and March wasn't one of them. She didn't have to open the note to know who they were from. The question remained as to whether or not he'd somehow known of her failed flower order, just figured out her fondness for the colors these orchids displayed, or had made a very lucky guess when going for the most expensive blossoms he could have delivered in late May. It didn't matter.

The flowers were lovely, and they were definitely from Jaccob. Ruby was more than a little pleased. She had been greeted personally with an apology and found $18,000 worth of orchids waiting for her on the table. This was perhaps a better start to the evening than had Jaccob been on time. And it only got better when she read the note.

"Apologies," it read. She thought she recognized Jaccob's handwriting on the folded cardboard. Had he really taken the time to write this note himself before running off to answer an alarm at a police station? That would be just like him, wouldn't it? "I don't know how long I'll be," the note continued, "and I'll forgive you if you don't wait. Please have a drink, and I will get there as soon as I can. Hope to see you, Jaccob."

Ruby grinned. She could hang around for a while. After all, it wouldn't be too long before Fire and Pestilence would let up and make their exit. She had no idea what Doubt was up to, but was pretty sure she'd be leaving with the others. They had only gone to the roof in the first place to cover her escape, and she was sure they would know she was away by now. She hadn't yet sussed out by what means they were connected to her exactly, but she was aware they were somehow. Whatever method Loki had employed to bind them to her had done a pretty good job of keeping them where she wanted them, so it only stood to reason that they would know when it was safe to beat a hasty retreat.

Ruby also had no idea how long the fires would keep burning without Fire there to sustain them. If things inside of the station had truly caught fire, then she supposed the Fire Department would handle it in due course. But if it was as she suspected, and the fires would only burn for as long as Fire remained present, then it wouldn't take

long for the heroes to breach the building. And seeing as the alarm
that had been triggered was inside of the occult vault, it would practically take no time at all for them to find the damage and see that
whatever dastardly villain had breached the vault had clearly gotten
away. Jaccob would be joining her soon after that.

Stardust might be Cobalt City's preeminent superhero, but he
was no super sleuth. Once he had determined with reasonable certainty that there was no perpetrator to apprehend, he'd be on his way.
Oh, she was sure he would be *aiding* in the investigation into the missing item, lending all manner of technological assistance in trying to
ascertain what had been stolen, its powers, its history, and its possible
uses. But that wouldn't be tonight. Tonight he would excuse himself
while the CCPD went about securing the crime scene and gathering
evidence.

Ruby wasn't concerned about evidence. She knew the Blights
didn't have fingerprints, and she was confident Pestilence had done
away with the video surveillance as he had claimed. Add to that the
fact that *nobody* in Cobalt City knew she'd ever had any powers—
much less that she had lost them—and she could be secure in her
confidence that no one was going to suspect her.

She was on her second plate of foie gras pastilles and her third
durian cocktail when Jaccob finally made his appearance. The bar, it
turned out, was named after the exotic South-Asian fruit they special-
ized in featuring in their mixed drinks. It tasted something like garlic
spun into caramel and folded into whipped cream, and Ruby wasn't
sure she liked it. But as she finished her first rather strong-yet-odd
martini, the waitress had come by to suggest she try the chef's favorite
food pairing. Having nothing else to do with her immediate future,
Ruby had decided to give the pastilles a try.

One bite in, she remembered she'd failed to eat dinner and realized she was incredibly hungry. She'd wolfed down the first plate of
foie gras just fast enough for it not to last to the end of her second

martini, but just deliberately enough to understand that the chef knew what she was talking about—the two menu items definitely played well together. So she'd ordered more of both the next time the waitress came by.

She still didn't know what time it was, and she was beginning to get the feeling the staff was talking about her behind her back. *She* might know what was going on, *she* might know she wasn't actually being stood up. But the kitchen and floor staff in this bar probably didn't. They probably had no idea that a police station across town had been broken into, a valuable and dangerous item stolen from their vault, and their building set on fire to cover the perpetrator's escape. And she was sure they had no idea that the police station in question had been equipped with an alarm that specifically summoned Stardust to their aid.

Even knowing all of this, Ruby didn't enjoy being the object of pity nor of ridicule from the serving staff. She had resolved to finish the food and drink in front of her and then call for her car and excuse herself for the evening. But she hadn't needed to.

The chips of ice had barely begun to melt in her glass when a smiling Jaccob Stevens clambered through the door. His face was flushed, his hair still damp from sweat, and his clothing not as tidy as Ruby was used to seeing it. But he looked equal measures pleased and relieved to see her waiting for him at the table. "I'm really sorry I'm so late," he said as he slid into the booth to sit beside her.

"Think nothing of it," she replied. It did her no harm to be magnanimous now. He didn't need to know she'd practically had one foot out the door when he arrived. "I take it you were saving the city from certain doom?"

"Something like that," Jaccob answered, giving a wave to the waitress who'd just poked her head into the room. The waitress nodded at Jaccob and then took off again.

"Then it's no problem," Ruby insisted.

"Really?" Jaccob asked, sounding oddly surprised.

Ruby reached over and patted his hand. "Jaccob," she addressed him, scooting a little closer to where he sat as she looked him in the eye. "I knew who I was agreeing to go out with. And it's not as though Stardust is exactly a secret identity. I am well aware that, from time to time, there will be larger concerns that take you away for an hour… or several. And if I'd had a problem with that, then I would never have said yes when you asked me out in the first place." She patted his hand again as she went on. "The last thing you need right now is someone who's new in your life trying to keep you from being the person you've been all along. I'm never going to be angry that you put the needs of the city ahead of any appointment you have with me."

Jaccob turned his hand over and squeezed her fingers.

"And the orchids are lovely," Ruby added, "I appreciate that you cared to send them. But I promise a text or an email will suffice in the future."

"I appreciate you saying that," Jaccob said. He sat up straighter then, and his face was suddenly much more serious. "And, wait, you're already saying you'd go out with me again? Even after I made you sit here for… how long has it been?"

"Long enough for you to save the city," Ruby answered, smiling. "And yes, I'd like to think this won't be the only time we get to go out for a drink together."

Jaccob nodded.

The waitress made another appearance then, bringing with her a tray covered in dishes which she expertly unloaded onto their table. There were a pair of martini shakers, and two small cylindrical vessels made from ice nested in silver bands with curved handles, along with four plates of hors d'oeuvres that included a third serving of foie gras pastilles.

Jaccob poured the two little ice cups full of the whitish liquid from one of the martini shakers as the waitress gave a nod and left the room again. Jaccob slid one of the ice cups toward Ruby and then picked up the other by its handle. Ruby lifted hers as well.

"To good company," Jaccob offered, as the two of them clinked their glasses together.

Ruby inclined her head in agreement as she moved to take a sip of the sweet-smelling liquid. It was good: more tropical and refreshing than the durian martini had been, but still containing the fruit's unmistakable notes of chives and powdered sugar.

"Now," Ruby said as she put down her glass and picked up a tiny croquette from one of the plates on the table, "tell me all about it... if you can." Ruby really wasn't sure what kind of non-disclosure agreements Cobalt City's superheroes had with the local police, but she hoped Jaccob would talk about what he'd been up to tonight. First off, it would keep her from having to make up details of a work meeting she hadn't really gone to. Secondly, it would make her look like the kind of woman who would be content to sit back and listen to a man talk about himself all night long, and men always seemed to like that. But most importantly, it would give Ruby the best possible insight on what the police had figured out about what had gone on in their vault.

Jaccob rolled his eyes and took a pronounced swig from his drink. He reached for the shaker to re-fill the cup as he looked at Ruby and answered. "There was a break in," he began, topping off his drink from the silver shaker, "at the CCPD's occult vault."

"The CCPD has an occult vault?" Ruby asked, playing both dumb and interested at the same time.

"Yeah," Jaccob answered, taking another sip from his cocktail. "They do. It's full of... magic stuff."

Ruby chuckled. "Magic stuff," she repeated, bringing her glass to her lips.

Jaccob shook his head again. "I hate magic," he said.

Ruby's eyes went wide for a moment, but she managed to keep a hold of herself. "Hate's a strong word," she contended.

Jaccob shrugged his shoulders. "It doesn't make any sense," he replied. "I like code. I like numbers. I like machines. There's logic to tech. I like logic. There's no logic to magic. No discernable rules."

Ruby took a pronounced gulp from her drink and fought the impulse to explain the intricacies of differing magical traditions, the rules that governed them, and the critical distinctions from one tradition to another. Now was not the time to deliver a treatise on the orderliness of magic. She needed to hear what he knew about the break in at the vault, not spend the rest of the night debating the relative merits of the supernatural versus the technological.

"Okay," she managed to allow, popping another croquette into her mouth.

"And the CCPD's got a whole vault of this stuff," Jaccob went on. "Magical stuff. Some of it they understand, and some of it they really don't. Sometimes the stuff is just evidence in a case, and they give it back to its rightful owner after the case is disposed. But sometimes the bad guy gets convicted and the police or whoever decide the items in question are too sinister or too powerful to be returned, so they put them in this giant underground concrete vault surrounded by salt and lead and whatever is supposed to repel magic, I guess."

"You guess," Ruby teased.

"Like I said," Jaccob replied, "I don't understand magic."

"Do you think whoever it was tonight used magic to break in?" she asked, trying not to sound too interested.

Jaccob shrugged. "No idea," he allowed. "The police don't know, either. But I am sure they used magic to get away."

"How do you know that?" she asked, again trying her best to seem somewhere between dispassionately interested and idly curious.

"They got away across the roof," he answered her, frowning as he reached across the table for one of the narrow spring rolls on a triangular plate. "There were a bunch of unexplained fires and... I think—" His face screwed itself into a confused frown. "—a swarm of rats and mice, and then—" Jacob shuddered as he continued. "—ants, maybe, and cockroaches."

Ruby frowned then, too. She was glad she hadn't hung around to watch that portion of the proceedings. Rather than dwell on that mental picture, she decided to focus on something else Jaccob had said. "You think?" she asked.

Jaccob frowned as he took a bite of his spring roll. "I think," he admitted. "It's weird. It's like I remember it, but then I don't. I think I saw something or did something, but then I doubt it happened at all."

Ruby nodded her head and reached for her discarded martini. She used the wide brim of the glass to hide the smile she couldn't suppress as she took another sip. Doubt had surely earned her keep if Jaccob couldn't even properly remember his conflict with the Blights less than two hours ago.

"That's odd," Ruby commented coolly when she was able to gain control of her expression again. She polished off the rest of her martini before pushing the glass to the far side of the table and turning her attention back to the ice cup and its contents.

"The whole thing is odd," Jaccob concurred, "but it's magic, so that's just par for the course."

CHAPTER
SEVEN

The rest of the night had gone exceedingly well. Ruby and Jaccob had talked on and off about magic, and all its attendant quirks and foibles, Ruby pretending not to know even a fraction of what she actually did. And she'd managed to get him to share everything he knew about what had gone on at the police station.

Nobody was sure yet what was missing from the vault. Fire had apparently done a real number on the building, and they were still waiting for the place to cool off enough for authorized personnel to get in and take inventory. Ruby was singularly pleased to learn that Pestilence really had wiped out all manner of surveillance in the place, and the police had absolutely no leads. She'd pushed on that one, too, asking, "Who breaks in to a police station—really?"

Jaccob had said everyone's best guess was there might be a new supervillain in town, and they were bracing for more occult crimes to come.

That was all very good news, in Ruby's opinion.

It was a lovely night altogether. For hours, they had sat and talked and eaten and drank. Jaccob was an interesting guy. He shared that he liked comic books, classic rock, and disaster movies. His favorite thing about this bar was the cocktail in the ice glasses, but he also had been known to call ahead and get an order of green bean spring rolls, sweetbread croquettes, or those divine little foie gras pastilles brought out to him in his car to eat in between afternoon appointments around town. He had excellent taste in food and drink and even better taste in flowers. Ruby was already hoping to see some evidence of his taste in jewelry some time in the future.

She was sure by the time the two of them sauntered out a side door arm-in-arm that the place had long since closed to the public. But if Jaccob made a habit of being here after hours, Ruby certainly wasn't going to complain. It wasn't the first time she'd been given such special consideration after all, and she'd never been one to contest the VIP treatment. A light rain had begun to fall as the two of them laughed their way out of the restaurant and into Ruby's waiting town car.

When Jaccob had confessed to having sent the Stardust suit back to his place without him, Ruby had been uncharacteristically amused by the mental picture of its flying there all on its own. But she'd also been able to discern from the remark that he hadn't exactly arrived at Durian by car. Seeing as she'd had her driver standing by all night, there had been no hesitation on her part in inviting him to ride back downtown with her. After all, they were neighbors; it just made sense not to make him call for a car when they were going to practically the same place.

After a distance of only a few blocks, they came to an irksome and unexpected halt. When Ruby sent the driver out to investigate, she found herself particularly glad of the enchanted contract she had the man under. Not only was he magically unable to speak of anything that went on in the car, he was all but completely enslaved to her will whenever she was inside it. Ruby had been pleased to find that these bits of magic she'd worked on her underlings had held fast even in the face of the loss of her personal powers. And as the rain grew heavier, pelting the roof of the town car with its noisy downfall, she was certainly thankful she didn't need to get out to check on things herself.

When the driver returned, it was not with good news. The bridge that would take them back across the river to downtown was closed for unspecified reasons, as were several other bridges in the vicinity. Apparently there was something criminal going on—not an unusual turn of events in Cobalt City by any stretch, but an odd thing for Stardust not to know about.

"Should you—" Ruby asked Jaccob as the driver began turning the car around to at least get them out of this traffic jam. "I mean... should Stardust be—?" She gestured in the general direction of the police lights and chaos just outside her window.

Jaccob, apparently wondering the same thing, was already tapping at a device on his wrist that strongly resembled a wristwatch, but which Ruby was decidedly certain was not. "I guess not," he answered after a moment. He seemed to be scrolling through data on his wrist display, and was, in Ruby's estimation, looking a little forlorn. "At least," he added with a noncommittal shrug, "nobody called me."

Ruby nodded, looking out her window to get as good a look as possible at the goings on across the bridge. There was every chance this was just the kind of ordinary mayhem that peppered the streets of Cobalt City every Friday night, but there was an equal chance the Blights had had something to do with it. They'd made no secret of the fact that, while they were at her beck and call while in her custody, hers weren't the only orders of business they would be seeing to in town. As long as they didn't get caught, Ruby didn't give a scrap of a damn what they did when she wasn't using them. And as the next hint of a plan began to hatch in her brain, she was ready to give them not only credit, but some small measure of reward.

"Just head out to the house," Ruby instructed the driver, who nodded in reply but gave no audible answer as the boss turned her attention back to Jaccob. "I have a place in Regency Heights," she told him, "the opposite direction from where all of this stuff is going on. We can stay there tonight and come back into town in the morning—after all of this madness has been cleaned up and put away."

Jaccob's gaze shot up suddenly. His whole body tensed, and he swallowed hard. He reached over and took Ruby by the hand, averting his gaze from hers before he spoke. "Ruby," he began softly, "I'm sorry if I—"

It was clear to Ruby that Jaccob had no way to say whatever it was he was trying to say. She sat quietly and waited for him to gather his thoughts.

It might have been a whole minute before he took a deep breath and started again. "Look," he started, still unable to meet her eyes, "I like you, and I've had a really good time tonight. And I don't want you to think that—" He trailed off again, but Ruby was beginning to get the gist of what he was trying to say. "It's just," he began again, "well, it's really soon, and—"

"Jaccob." Ruby interrupted him before he was able to get any more words out. She was sure now she'd figured him out. He was adorable, and she was about to score some serious points with him. Ruby brought her free hand to his chin and tilted his face up until she could look him in the eye. "It's a mansion," she said. "I have five guest rooms."

Jaccob's jaw fell slack and a slight flush came to his cheeks. "You have five—" he repeated.

"Guest rooms," she finished the sentence for him. "You can take your pick." She smiled gently and nodded.

Jaccob shut his eyes and leaned back against the seat, shaking his head and clenching his jaw shut. "I'm sorry," he said after a moment. "That was awfully presumptuous of me."

Ruby squeezed his hand and shrugged. "Nah," she countered. "I suggested you come home with me and spend the night. Your assumption was pretty standard. And besides," she added, grinning a little more wickedly now, "it's not that I wouldn't. It's just I know things are complicated for you right now. And I don't want to be the reason things get more complicated. And I'm not trying to make you uncomfortable. We'll get there, or we won't. But that's not a question for tonight. Tonight the only question we need to answer is how we can get enough sleep to function properly in the morning without having to resort to napping in the car while trying to get home."

Jaccob nodded and smiled. "Yeah, good idea."

Ruby had been sure the Eye would be warded. The idea that anyone would create an item with as much power as this one supposedly held and not put some sort of magical shielding on it was absurd. No sorcerer capable of the creation of such a thing could possibly lack the foresight to see that others would try and steal it; over the course of centuries, one or more of those attempts was bound to be successful. Putting in your own flavor of magical security was the best way to assure you had time to steal the thing back before a thief had the chance to use it against you. It was a strategy as old as time, and so Ruby was not at all surprised when her first attempts at magically accessing the Eye had been wholly unsuccessful.

After bidding Jaccob a friendly farewell over breakfast, she'd headed to her sanctum to work on the gem. She'd begged off riding back in to town with him with a fib about a conference call she'd likely miss due to traffic. Never mind that it was a Saturday. Jaccob had made it clear he had no clue how the entertainment business operated, and Ruby was quick enough to use that to her advantage. She told him she'd drive herself into town after the call, and even teased that she would give him a ride in her sports car later on if he asked nicely. When he'd countered with a promise to give her a ride on the Stardust suit someday, she'd practically giggled at the blush that followed. He hadn't meant the innuendo, but he'd caught it as soon as he'd said it. Ruby had just winked and called him a tease. He'd stumbled over his next few words, and Ruby had brushed it off and shooed him out the door.

It was less that she wanted to be rid of him, and more that she was beside herself with anticipation of finally getting to work on the Eye. She'd slept with it under her pillow, knowing sometimes the dream state could be a key to accessing certain kinds of magic. But it was evident the ward around the item was far too powerful for the item's energy to be tapped so easily.

Ruby didn't mind—not really. She had expected as much. She knew about wards, and she knew about breaking them. She was an expert on this kind of magic, on how it was created and might come to be destroyed. It was only a matter of time before she would be able to crack the Eye and gain access to its power.

It had been a fortunate twist of fate that had found her in the mansion this morning instead of at her penthouse. The Tower, as opulent and as convenient as it was for most purposes, lacked any prepared magical space. There was some shielding, of course—what little she had been able to spin in her newly mundane state—but it was scarcely enough to protect her from external casting. It certainly wasn't set up for any major ritual undertakings. The mansion, on the other hand, was singularly equipped for such things. Surrounded by earth, lined with lead, tiled in natural salt, and with wards that had taken her days to construct at the height of her power, the sanctum in the mansion's basement was the only place Ruby would dare to fiddle with magic as powerful as that contained within the Eye of Africa.

This was doubly true considering some of the things Jaccob had shared with her over drinks. Apparently, as he started to feel his liquor, his tongue got a little loose. As it turned out, he seemed to really enjoy talking about superhero stuff. Ruby hadn't been sure if it was some misguided attempt to impress her or whether he was just unaccustomed to having someone willing to listen to his tales. Either way, some of the information he'd inadvertently spilled could prove invaluable in the long run. Most specifically pertinent to her current purposes, Jaccob had mentioned a young woman who could see and hear the spirits of places and structures. These spirits told her things—things about the goings-on of the people in the area and about anything these spirits found to be unusual or suspicious.

The earthen layer around Ruby's sanctum should be enough to stop the spirits from prying. The wards, the salt, and the lead would keep out any other type of snoop, technical or magical. In this room, she felt safe enough to start serious work on the Eye. Its power would be hers. It was only a matter of time.

But time, it seemed, was not going to cooperate. And neither was the Eye of Africa. Magic had been eluding Ruby since the unfortunate incident last Christmas, and the gem wasn't making its return easy. Hours spent in the ritual space with the Eye of Africa, and so far she'd failed to so much as touch its power.

The day had been, to say the least, frustrating. Ruby had been prepared for the Eye to be the most heavily warded, most powerfully protected magical item she had ever encountered. But she hadn't had even the foggiest inclination that a full day's work would get her nowhere. But more than nine hours into her wasted Saturday, that had certainly been her experience.

The whole process had been infinitely frustrating. She'd tried everything she knew to get through to the thing and it just didn't seem to do her any good. Finally admitting defeat and giving in to hunger and thirst, Ruby emerged from her work space to discover it was far later in the day than she had figured. She was exhausted, physically and magically. And she needed to recharge. Leaving the Eye in her own cast circle in her own prepared workspace would not only be the safest way to keep the thing for the time being, it also might do a little to aid in getting through to it, her own magic perhaps able to dilute whatever was protecting it by simple osmosis of energy.

She made quick work of changing from her magical vestments

into an outfit more suitable for driving back into town. Ruby enjoyed her little sports car. Bright red, with a high-performance engine and the word MAVEN emblazoned on its license plate, the convertible was Ruby Killingsworth in mechanical form. And although she usually preferred her town car in the city, four p.m. on a Saturday was hardly rush hour, so the drive back to her penthouse was pleasant enough, lacking Cobalt City's usually high traffic volume.

She had met with a tiny snarl as she turned onto the Quayside Bridge. A couple of minor superheroes were going about some business at the far end, and the traffic in both directions had slowed to get a look. Ruby thought it a little ridiculous that with all the superhero activity in this town, people still stopped to so shamelessly rubberneck. Of course, when she got close enough to the action to see the two heroes for herself, she felt doubly sure her decision to leave the Eye in her workspace had been a sound one. She instantly recognized one of them as Kensei—the young woman Jaccob had described as being able to talk to spirits. Ruby knew a thing or two about spirits, and she was sure any in the area would likely sound an alarm were such a powerful item to cross their sphere. Much better, she figured, to have the Eye tucked safely into a shielded place across town. Even with her hair beneath a scarf and her face behind her overlarge sunglasses, between her vanity license plate and the fact the top was down, Ruby was easily identifiable driving her little sports car. Even if she were able to get away, it was unlikely it would be for good.

She vowed then and there to keep the Eye right where it was until she was sure she could shield it with magic of her own. Even with the relative anonymity of her town car, she would still be exposing herself were she to bring it forth. And there was no safe way to do anything about it outside of that space anyway.

The Eye of Africa was safe. It was secure. And Ruby Killingsworth would find a way to make it her own.

CHAPTER
EIGHT

etting into her building and up to her penthouse was as easy an exercise as Ruby had designed it to be. When she'd first met with the architect in the early stages of planning the Ruby Tower, she'd been very particular about how her private access was to be handled, but until today, she'd yet to fully test the system. This was the first time she'd brought the car into the city since relocating to her penthouse, and she had to say she was impressed. At least something had gone right today. She'd have to send Arsho a text thanking them for getting this stuff right. Her building manager, as infuriating as their meddling had been at times, was perhaps her most capable employee. This fact was proven out again when Ruby was able to pull into her private garage, park her car, and get into and out of the elevator without having to encounter another living soul.

Sure, Ruby loved publicity. She thrived on the occasional "accidental" brush with the paparazzi. She adored seeing her picture emblazoned on the front page of the Times or circulating the internet as the highlight of some viral tidbit or another. But as much as she enjoyed her fame, she valued her privacy more. What the public would never know was that those pictures—even those that looked as though they'd happened spontaneously or without her consent— were all a part of a carefully curated image. She only let herself be photographed when she wanted to be. And today, she had no patience for the public.

It wasn't five minutes after she'd come up the elevator and deposited her keys on her marble-topped entry table that Ruby had changed into a favorite pair of silk chiffon lounging pajamas and a satin robe. She snagged a bowl of dates, a wheel of brie, and some almond crackers from her kitchen before settling down on her sofa. A carafe of burgundy and her computer were still there from Friday afternoon, owing to a standing instruction to her household staff never to disturb items on the coffee table. With the platter of fruit and cheese on the sofa beside her, Ruby poured herself a low tumbler of the unctuous red and absently flipped on the television. As the opening sequence of the Cobalt City Evening News began to fill the room, Ruby pulled her computer onto her lap, determined to plumb the depths of the internet for better information on the Eye of Africa and how she might go about making it do as she willed.

She'd barely begun her online searching, and was already cursing her lack of technical prowess, when she heard a knock on the terrace door behind her. There was only one person who could possibly be there. She had to admit she was surprised not to have heard him coming. Either he'd made marked improvements to the noise level of his StarBoard, or the construction foreman had not been exaggerating when he'd told her about the noise-dampening properties of the glass walls of her penthouse. Either way, Ruby was pleased at Jaccob's arrival. The news anchors were just getting into their top story—the theft of the Eye of Africa—when Ruby turned around and called out, "come on in!"

Jaccob was shaking his head as he pulled the door open and came inside. "I hope I'm not intruding," he said as he carefully closed her terrace door behind himself. "I saw your light was on—"

"No," Ruby insisted, turning down the television volume, "Not at all." She moved the tray of fruit and cheese from the sofa onto the coffee table and patted the now vacant seat beside her. "Come, sit," she invited.

"You shouldn't leave your doors unlocked," he chided as he crossed the room to sit beside her on the couch.

"On the fiftieth floor?" she rebutted. "Really, Jaccob, who's going to surprise me up here?"

"In this town," he answered, "I think you'd be surprised."

Ruby rolled her eyes and gestured to the wine. "Drink?" she offered.

"Sure," He sat back on the sofa and looked somberly at the television. "This is the thing that was stolen last night," he told her, regarding the picture the news was showing of the case the Eye had been in inside the vault.

"I'm surprised they're giving up so much information so early on," Ruby commented, pretending not to know just how much *wasn't* being said. It wouldn't do her any good for Jaccob to figure out she knew more about the thing than either he or the CCPD did.

As she poured her guest a glass of wine, Ruby caught sight of her still-open web search about the thing. Damn. She had been so pleased to see Jaccob at her door unexpectedly, she hadn't thought to close either the tab or the computer. "I was just looking up what they were talking about," she lied, gesturing to her computer screen before he had a chance to notice and wonder. Stay ahead of the story—that was key to survival in entertainment as well as in relationships, apparently.

"Did you find out anything interesting?" he asked as he took his freshly poured tumbler of wine and looked back at the television.

"No." Truly, there hadn't been much on the internet she hadn't already known. And it just seemed like a better idea to play dumb on this particular subject. "You?" she asked, half-joking. "Any new and interesting developments since last night?"

Jaccob took a sip of his wine and shook his head. "Not really," he replied. "It's a magical thing nobody really knows much about—except everyone who knows anything about stuff like this is terrified that someone has it."

Ruby nodded. Good. That was good. She was pleased to hear she seemed to have more information on the Eye than the people who were trying to track it down.

"And no one has any idea who might have stolen it?" she asked, trying to make the question sound as idle as possible.

Jaccob frowned and shook his head. "From what I've been told so far," he replied, taking another sip of wine and reaching for a cracker, "which I'll admit isn't much, this thing has a whole lot of power in it that nobody really understands. The people who know about these kinds of things say it's dangerous. They tell me it doesn't matter who has it, because even the most well-intended, careful, studied magic user isn't going to be able to control this thing. The best-case scenario seems to be that the wizard or whatever blows himself up trying to figure out how to use it and leaves a hole in the ground large enough for the police to locate what's left of the jewel."

"Ouch," Ruby said, trying to hide her discomfort at the thought of being nothing more than a crater beneath her Regency Heights Mansion. There had been no mention in Loki's note of a possibility the thing might explode. Then again, there was every chance that whoever had shared this idea with Jaccob had been talking out of his or her ass. Knowing Jaccob's disdain for all things magical, he was inclined to believe the worst. And if the CCPD was really so terrified of the Eye falling in to the wrong hands, it would certainly behoove them to make him believe it.

"Yeah," Jaccob affirmed, reclining a little in his seat and resting his arm along the back of the sofa in a gesture that reminded Ruby of the way a teenager might surreptitiously put his arm around his date at the movies.

Pretending not to notice his boyish tactic, Ruby scooted closer and reclined a bit as well, resting her back against the curve of his arm and calling no attention to it whatsoever. "So we just have to hope the police find it before whoever stole it has a chance to use it." Ruby took a sip of wine and thought carefully about her next question. She couldn't appear to know too much—neither about the Eye of Africa nor about magic in general. But she wanted—she *needed* to know if the police seemed to have any idea how its magic might be accessed.

"Um," Ruby began, feigning confusion as she looked sideways at Jaccob, "don't those kinds of things usually have—" She paused and furrowed her brow. "—I don't know, *spells* on them, or something to keep people from using them if they're not supposed to?"

Jaccob took another sip from his glass and nodded his head. "I think so," he answered. "But I'm really not the guy to ask. I don't know a damned thing about this kind of stuff, and the police didn't say anything to me about it, probably because they know I don't like magic and they could tell me all about it and it wouldn't matter. It's not my job to know that stuff. I just catch the bad guys."

Ruby managed an almost girlish giggle at his assertion. How odd he was so straightforward about that. It was honestly a little bit adorable how cut-and-dry the world seemed to him. Magic was never a good idea, technology was as good or as bad as the people wielding it, and Stardust's job was to catch the bad guys. She spared a moment's thought for what it might be like to have an outlook so lacking in nuance. "I'm just trying to make you feel better," she lied, unable as she did to control the grin that had crept to her face at knowing his total lack of suspicion toward her. "Because maybe if it has some kind of spell on it then maybe the guys who stole it haven't managed to use it yet." She patted him gently once on his knee, and left her hand resting there for a moment before withdrawing it again. She noticed a tension in him at her touch, and forced a blush to her cheeks in response. There was nothing to be gained by being completely transparent in her intentions; if he needed her to be a bit coy about things, she could manage that for a time.

Jaccob swallowed hard and turned his body a little to face her. Ruby was surprised the movement wasn't one of retreat. The television news had moved on to a story about a series of break-ins that they were positing may or may not be connected to the theft of the Eye of Africa. Ruby knew, of course, that they weren't, although there remained the possibility that the Blights might be behind some or all of the mayhem without her having known about it. She knew they were working some agenda for Loki while she had them here, and she hadn't been bothered to give a damn as to what it was. So there was every chance this series of break-ins *was* related to the theft of the Eye, even if only indirectly.

"You know," Jaccob said, changing the subject as he inclined his head toward the television, "I mean it when I say you shouldn't be leaving your doors unlocked. With so much crime in the city, I just don't think it's safe."

"And I mean it," she replied, smiling wryly, "when I say I'm not worried. Who's going to bother me fifty stories up?" She raised her eyebrows and took a sip from her wine. "With Stardust right across the way?"

"I've been in this city for a long time," he answered, "and I can honestly tell you I have no idea." He smiled and shook his head. "But I know that stranger things have happened than a bad guy with the ability to scale buildings, or willing to drop in from a helicopter, or who can fly under his own power. Even the fiftieth floor isn't safe from the worst of the city, Ruby, and I'm not always home. If you're not going to put locks on the doors, will you at least let me install some sort of alarm system up here for you?"

Ruby shook her head and frowned. "Oh, no," she answered firmly. "I only just got all of the workmen out of here. I've finally got a little peace and quiet. The last thing I'm about to do is invite a bunch more strange men to drill holes in my walls and bother me all hours of the day."

Jaccob shook his head and chuckled, moving his hand from where it had been resting on the back of the sofa to her shoulder. "No, I mean, let me do it," he clarified.

"Yourself?" she asked dubiously.

He nodded. "You know, Starcom was a startup. I used to do all this stuff myself. And I don't think I've forgotten how."

"Oh, I'm sure you haven't," Ruby affirmed. "I can't imagine you trust many people with the Stardust suit. Clearly, that's the kind of thing you'd want to do for yourself."

"Exactly," Jaccob replied, grinning and waggling his eyebrows. "And you've got our security in the rest of the building, so it wouldn't be hard for me to come in here and add a discrete system just for the penthouse wired in to the emergency power we've already installed."

"And you'd do this yourself?" she asked him dubiously. "Just you? With no help?"

"Sure. It could be fun. It might take a few days," he qualified, "with me doing everything single-handedly, but I could do it no problem."

Ruby frowned playfully.

"I think I'll get you a personal alarm, too," he added. "A panic button so you can call me from anywhere if there's an emergency."

"And is this a service you offer to all of your top-dollar clients?" she teased. Ruby knew, of course, that there were special alarms and custom systems already in existence connected directly to Stardust. It had been one of those "special client" security measures that had almost foiled her plans to get away with the Eye of Africa. As much as Jaccob's ostensible concern for her safety seemed promising, Ruby knew there was every chance he was just trying to sell her another fifty grand worth of security equipment. But, then again, he *could* have been flirting. And she wanted to know.

Jaccob shook his head and smiled. "Free of charge," he insisted. "Friends and neighbors discount. And, I can promise you this is the only such offer I have ever made."

Ruby felt a blush come to her cheeks that she chose not to even attempt to stifle. So he was flirting. Good. This was very, very good. She narrowed her eyes and grinned. "I'll think about it," she said. And she would have to think, hard. On the one hand, there was something positively delightful about the thought of Jaccob rolling up his sleeves and putting in hours of work to wire up her penthouse to assure her safety. But on the other hand, any thoughts of alarms or surveillance in her private space made her shudder. And there was no explaining to Jaccob that the place was magically protected. Although the strength of the wards she'd managed to put in were paltry in comparison to what she had in her work space, there was still a layer of magical insulation about the whole building, one she meant to shore up firmly once she had the full power of the Eye of Africa at her command.

And she certainly couldn't tell him she'd given over the forty-sixth floor to Loki. The god, she was sure, had his own layers of magical protection—wards that would likely extend beyond his own little corner of the building. She couldn't see his magic at the moment; without her powers, she could barely see magic she herself was casting. But she knew Loki. She knew him very well, and she was sure that any space he claimed as his own would be magically prepared for whatever purpose he might want to put it to. So even though there was no evidence he'd so much as set foot in her building, Ruby was sure the space was well-prepared and ready for the day he decided to make use of it.

She really didn't need a Stardust alarm. But she liked the idea of being able to summon him any time of the night or day. *That* could be fun. She winked at Jaccob over her glass of wine.

"Will you at least agree to a panic button?" he asked, scooting a little closer, his arm now unabashedly draped across her shoulders.

Ruby frowned, unsure as to exactly what he was describing.

"It can look like an ordinary piece of jewelry if you want it to," he said, clearly aware she wasn't sure what he was talking about. "But it'll have a little transmitter in it. You press the button or flip the switch, or rip open the clasp—Chuck has one that works like that—and it activates a beacon and lets me know you need me."

Ruby took a deep breath. She had to admit to herself she enjoyed being offered the level of personal protection tech that it sounded like he had only previously arranged for his immediate family. That was lovely. But she wasn't sure she was ready to bring a homing beacon along with her everywhere that would summon Stardust double-quick were it to be improperly handled. It would do for now, she guessed, to accept the idea. She could manage the logistics of the thing after she had it.

"I like diamonds," she half-kidded, "and I like you. So I suppose I'd be agreeable to a little bracelet, or a brooch, that would bring you to my aid should I ever find myself in need of rescuing."

She thought back for a moment to the episode with the alien that had left her with her powers augmented. That night, she'd been freed by some no-name quasi-super who she'd never heard of, before or since. It had irked her at the time that none of Cobalt City's A-list had come after her. Having a device on her person that meant Stardust would drop everything and come to her aid certainly meant she was moving up in the world.

"I'll get right to work on that," Jaccob said, bringing his wine glass around to clink against hers.

Ruby smiled as she leaned in closer. It was strange, sitting on the sofa, drinking wine, and watching the news with Jaccob. There was something pleasingly domestic about the whole thing, and Ruby was a bit surprised she wasn't at all disgusted with herself for liking it. She was looking up at Jaccob and wondering what in the hell was going on in her head when she saw him blanch suddenly. His body grew stiff, he withdrew his arm from around her, and he sat bolt upright on the sofa.

Ruby's first inclination was to wonder if he'd been shot. His eyes were wide and his hands were shaking as he stared straight ahead at the story now running on the evening news. Blast those damnable gossips claiming to be journalists! There, as big as life on Ruby's 4k TV, was Elizabeth Stevens. The news anchor was going on about how, "once again, she was spotted flying solo at a charity event." They went on to mention "sources close to the noted philanthropist" who "would neither confirm nor deny that Cobalt City's most notable power couple had split."

Ruby was scrambling to find the remote control, nearly spilling her wine as her first grab at the thing missed and knocked it to the floor. She was practically on the floor herself by the time she managed to get hold of it and shut the television off. Before the picture blinked out, Ruby found herself pleased to have recognized Discontent in the background of the picture the newscast had splitting the screen with the co-anchor reading the story. It was good to know her bidding was still being done.

But seeing it on television was decidedly *not* good for the mood in the room. "I'm sorry," Ruby offered with genuine sadness. "I wish you hadn't seen that."

Jaccob nodded. He finished the last of the wine in his glass and frowned. "Yeah," he replied, "me too. But the news was bound to get ahold of it some time. I'm actually surprised it's taken them this long."

"Still," Ruby answered, resisting the urge to reach out to him. There was something in his bearing that told her touching him right now was a bad idea. And even though she was without any magical ability to tell his mood, her finely honed people skills were enough to guide her. "You shouldn't have to see your personal life broadcast to the public."

Jaccob nodded. "In a lot of ways, I'm used to it. But this split with Elizabeth, this is all new territory."

Ruby nodded. She didn't like the idea of talking about Jaccob's marriage, or his wife, but there was something that felt powerful in the way he seemed to be opening up. She decided she wouldn't be the one to change the subject.

"I'm sorry," she said again.

Jaccob shook his head and stood up, setting his empty wine glass down on the coffee table beside the tray of crackers. "I should be going," he said.

Ruby set her glass down beside his and stood to face him. "Okay," she answered softly, trying not to sound overly disappointed. She had to remember she was playing a long game here, and if Jaccob needed space to process things right now, then she'd give him that space. She would continue to play patient and supportive. It might be terribly frustrating today, but in time, she was sure, it would pay off. "I'll talk to you soon," she said tentatively as she walked him to the door.

Jaccob nodded somberly. "I'm seeing my kids tomorrow."

"Good," she commented. And it was good. Mike Stevens had just had a very promising meeting with Goblin Records Artist Development, and there was absolutely no doubt in Ruby's mind he would want to talk about little else. Jaccob would spend all day tomorrow hearing about her and thinking about her, and she didn't have to do anything but sit back and let his son sing her praises. That was fantastic timing. Her smile in that moment was genuine, even if it wasn't so supportive and magnanimous as she hoped Jaccob would presume.

"I'll call you," he said, although it seemed he was struggling with the idea.

She nodded, trying to keep her smile up as she bade him farewell. Ruby closed the door behind him as he reached for his StarBoard to head back across the narrow expanse to his own penthouse.

As she made her way back across the sitting room, she glowered at the reflective blackness of the powered-down television. That had been a setback, but how serious a setback remained to be seen. Still, she was frustrated and, if she was being completely honest with herself, a little bit sad. She shook her fist at the news anchors, even though they were no longer visible on the overlarge screen. As her gaze shifted to her laptop, still sitting where she'd set it when Jaccob had arrived, she set her jaw.

Moments like this one made her all the more determined to crack the secrets of the Eye of Africa. With magic like that, she needn't care that Elizabeth Stevens existed. She'd have Jaccob, and whatever else she wanted, just as soon as she had the magic of the Eye. She was bent over the back of the sofa, reaching for the machine, when she heard another knock on the glass. When she turned her head toward the sound, she was surprised to see Jaccob once again standing at her door. She had no idea what he was doing there, but rushed across the room—as quickly as she could while maintaining decorum—and pulled open the door.

Jaccob had an odd look on his face: something between senti-mental and remorseful, if Ruby had to guess. Her magic would have told her precisely, but her perception was likely close enough. "I'll call you Monday morning," he said. His voice was firm, convicted; it wasn't at all the noncommittal tone he'd taken just a moment ago.

Ruby smiled. "I'll look forward to it."

"Good," Jaccob replied. He surprised her then. Leaning into the doorway where she stood, he kissed her. Lightly, barely, he let his lips touch hers before he stepped back and bid her farewell again.

Ruby tried to appear neither too shocked nor too thrilled. She stood in the doorway and watched him fly home on his StarBoard, grinning as sweetly as she could. She waved at him on his balcony before stepping back inside her penthouse.

Glass walls meant any excessive celebration would likely be noticed, and jumping up and down like a giddy schoolgirl really wasn't her style. But as she crossed back to where her laptop and her research awaited, she wore a very self-satisfied grin.

CHAPTER
NINE

Knowing Jaccob would be spending all day Sunday with his adult children gave Ruby the perfect opportunity to go back to the house and do some more work on cracking the wards around the Eye. He'd already said he would call her on Monday morning, which meant there was no chance she'd miss him trying to reach her if she spent all day Sunday in her basement with no cell reception.

She left early, trying to time her drive across town so the church crowd would be sitting *in church* and not on the road at the same time she was. With the top down and the radio on, Ruby couldn't help but smile as she cruised through the city streets. It was a warm June morning, she was on her way to put her hands back on the most powerful magical item she had ever encountered, and every time she turned the station, her car's radio seemed to be playing a song that was making her money. She felt charmed.

There was rain in the forecast, so Ruby took the moment to put the roof back on her car in the driveway. On her way to the door, she used her business-only Starphone to make a call to the line on the forty-seventh floor she knew the Blights would answer. She and Doubt had already had the conversation that any calls coming in on that line after hours or on the weekend would need to be answered. She needed the Blights at the house today. There was research to be done if she was ever going to get to the heart of the power of the Eye, and she greatly preferred the idea of having them be the ones to do it. It wasn't that she was averse to research; she actually rather enjoyed delving into the whys and the hows of the magic she accessed. If she didn't, she wouldn't have amassed nearly as large an arcane library as she had.

Technically, Ruby had three libraries in her mansion in Regency Heights. Her large library was a social space, its walls lined with shelves housing everything from the classics to the latest issues of *Rolling Stone*. She often entertained artists, clients, and potential business partners there. Her private library was adjacent to her bedroom and sitting room and housed a more curated collection of favorites. Books about music and history, some more easily obtained volumes of magical understanding, and more than one unauthorized biography of Stardust could be found within. It was a rare occasion when anyone was invited into that room. And her secret library was just that: a secret. It was in her basement, adjacent to but not in communication with her ritual space. Before today, no one else had been allowed in.

But today she needed the help. There were still things she had yet to try that she knew might get her closer to unlocking the power of the Eye, and spending half the day up to her eyebrows in books didn't feel like a profitable use of her time. Then again, if there was something in her collection that could lead her to getting to the right thing faster, it felt like a waste of time not to have someone looking. The Blights were technically in her service, which meant they wouldn't be able to use any knowledge gained in her library against her—a fact she'd checked through multiple sources before trusting them with any of her magical knowledge. And besides, it was high time she got them off the forty-seventh floor and into hiding someplace else. The studios were starting to get some regular use, and she wasn't sure how long their cover as a new band in development was going to fly. Better she move them out to the house where they'd be better hidden.

Satisfied they were on their way over, Ruby made her way inside and went immediately to work with the Eye. She would find a way into this thing today or die trying.

It seemed to be waiting for her when she arrived. Surrounded by a circle she'd cast around it, laying on a square of crimson silk atop a mound of pink and gray salt in the center of the prepared space, the Eye was almost visibly pulsing with power. She'd left it the way she had in hopes the magic she'd cast would contain the power of the thing. Knowing intimately how this additional layer of containment operated, she'd posited, would be enough to allow her, once inside of it, to finally touch the magic of the Eye. Once she had a more experiential understanding of the flavor of magic attached to the mysterious item, she would be better able to tailor her attempts at gaining full access to it.

It was a visceral experience reaching for it then. The air within the circle seemed to crackle with static electricity. Her fingers tingled as she gingerly brushed them against the metallic sheath encasing the opal. The magic was heady when she had the Eye in her grasp. She hadn't feared it—hadn't been concerned the thing might harm or overwhelm her upon contact—a decision which, on hindsight, had perhaps not been the most prudent approach.

Ruby had never been struck by lightning, nor had she ever stuck her finger in a light socket, but she guessed the feeling overtaking her as she grabbed hold of the opal itself must be akin to that experience. Her hair stood on end and her breath caught in her throat. Her chest was tight, and her eyes suddenly felt twice their normal size, as though they no longer fit in their sockets or beneath their lids. She felt a cry leave her throat, but no sound escaped her lips. It was at the same time exhilarating and terrifying. She knew she must be touching magic more powerful than any she had ever encountered. There was nothing in her experience nor in her knowledge base to have prepared her for this. Intense sensations came at her; the feelings overwhelmed her as her land lay across the gem.

Ruby wasn't sure if there was actual light flickering, flecks of magic being thrown in the air, or whether she was perhaps hallucinating. She was sure the thrumming sound causing her head to pound was a combination of the blood rushing through her ears and the presence of magic disrupting the air around her. She was trembling, her heart was pounding, and she had trouble keeping on her feet.

It took an unusual amount of care for Ruby to come to her knees before the Eye. It wasn't a preferred position of hers, but she had so little control over her body at the moment she was pleased enough not to have collapsed entirely. Whatever she had done here had been, by several measures, successful. But Ruby wasn't convinced it was a success she was prepared for.

That was the thing about dallying with magic you didn't know enough about—it was dangerous. Ruby had known that. She had in her possession an item far more powerful than anything she had ever dealt with previously. And she knew there was danger in trifling with magics that weren't your own, particularly when the magics were contained within items powerful enough to have frightened custodians for generations.

Ruby was not frightened. That was not an emotion native to her, and she found herself unencumbered by fear even as the edges of her consciousness closed in around her. If this thing was about to kill her, then she had gone out in her prime. But her danger sense had always been as keen as her musical ear. She realized in that moment that as uncomfortable as she was, she sensed no real peril when handling the gem. The moment felt not unlike the first time she'd taken her car to its top speed on the freeway. Whatever was happening to her body may have been foreign, uninvited, and almost wholly unpleasant, but somewhere deep in her core, she felt in control.

It was odd, she figured, as she knelt there on the floor of her sanctuary, stray grains of salt digging painfully into her bare knees as her body convulsed, that she felt in control and unafraid. But that was the thing with magic—it didn't always make sense at first. She was determined to make sense of it. Her mind swirled as she willed her fingers to close around the opal, drawing it out of the salt and out of the circle. She had no idea what the result of that action would be, but she knew this was the best chance she had to connect to the Eye on her own terms—while it was already connected to her.

She realized, as the room began to spin and she felt the surety she was about to faint, that perhaps that hadn't been the best idea.

When Ruby awoke, she had no idea what time it was. She had no idea whether hours or minutes had passed. And she had no idea what had caused her to black out.

It hadn't been sleep; she was sure of that. There had been times in her history of using very powerful magic when the rites and rituals had drained her. There was nothing like magical drain. It was a bone-level exhaustion that could take days to recover from. But this had not been that. Ruby knew from the moment she awoke that whatever had knocked her out was thoroughly unfamiliar, and she was wary of trying to move too fast. And although she was displeased by the indignity of finding herself prostrate on her sanctuary floor, having no concept of what the hell was going on, she thought better of trying to scramble to her feet.

Ruby sat up slowly, still clutching the Eye in her right hand, and made the concerted effort she found necessary to draw in a deep breath. She felt strange, her head at the same time foggy and light. It was, the best she could tell, analogous to the feeling of a buzz diminishing as a hangover loomed following an evening of too much wine. And yet, she became vaguely aware as she got slowly to her feet, this sensation was entirely the inverse.

The more she moved about, the better she felt. Her mind settled into a state not unlike the heady rush of a third glass of champagne after closing a million-dollar deal. It was blissful. It was orgasmic. And it took Ruby a moment of reveling in it to be able to catch a normal breath and emerge for a moment from her sanctuary.

She didn't want to leave. Neither did she wish to lay down the Eye at this moment of marvelous rapture (for which she was certain its magic was responsible), nor did she wish to bring such a powerful item out from the protection of the earth, salt, and lead that shielded it from the world at large. The Eye could easily be a beacon if brought out into normal space, leading anyone who knew how to look directly to its location, and to her. Ruby knew there was every chance the CCPD had gotten their act together and had magic-using experts working with them in trying to locate the gem. And that was without even considering the possibility of one of the city's many magically aware superheroes getting involved, which they inevitably would if they hadn't already. Knowing also that there was a young woman somewhere in this town who could commune with spirits was a serious additional concern. None of the spirits in this town owed Ruby any fealty, and she was sure they could detect the magical energy of the Eye without difficulty, which meant she ought to be doubly careful.

But she needed to check in with reality. She needed to know what time it was, what day it was even. She had literally no clue how long she had been out cold. She needed to eat something and to drink something, to empty her bladder, and to check her phone for messages. Just because Jaccob was going to be out of touch while with his kids all day didn't mean there was no chance of messages coming in. Maybe he was unlikely to have reached out to her, but she still had business to conduct. And even if it was still Sunday, her business needed some minding.

She also needed to check in with the Blights. The longer she had been out, the more time they'd had to do the research she'd asked them to do. Now that she had most certainly touched the power of the Eye, she was that much more anxious to find out anything and everything she could about how its magic might be used. Ruby knew she was several stages away from truly being able to fully harness the power in the gem. But she was absolutely sure she'd just made some incredible progress. Whatever confluence of magics had caused this breakthrough, it had been a breakthrough all the same, and Ruby was positively itching to exploit it.

As difficult as she occasionally found prudence to be, Ruby allowed it to win out for the moment. She resisted the urge to slip the Eye into her pocket before heading upstairs. She carefully replaced it on the pallet of silk and salt within her cast circle, wiped her sweaty palms against her navy-blue cotton skirt, and left the room before she could change her mind.

Ruby gave full credit to the warm buzz left over from her contact with the Eye for the fact she didn't immediately erupt in a litany of swear words upon reaching the top of her basement stairs. The Blights were not in the library. They were in the kitchen. Doubt was rifling through the cabinets, Plague was standing beside Fire, who was toying with the stove. Pestilence was sitting alone at the zinc-topped breakfast bar trying not to touch anything, while Ruin and Decay sat at the small table by the balcony doors helping themselves to the fruit in the decorative bowl. Ruby hadn't ever been sure whether the fruit in that bowl was real or wax, so seeing it gobbled up by her otherworldly house guests was, to say the least, a peculiar sight.

"What the hell is going on in here?" Ruby asked the group of them, her voice oddly pleasant despite her words.

Doubt poked her head out of the pantry cabinet and frowned. "We got hungry," she declared.

Ruby rolled her eyes. She honestly hadn't thought about that. Truly, she hadn't had any inkling the Blights actually *ate*. She had sent them to stay on the forty-seventh floor without means of sustenance, and this was the first she was hearing of this particular complaint. She hadn't really spared a thought for their corporeal needs since they'd been in her custody. They were thought-made-flesh (or so it had been explained to her), but Loki had not passed along any care and feeding instructions when he'd sent them to do her bidding. She wasn't sure just who to be mad at for this one, so she let it go. Better not to sully the euphoria from the Eye by caring that her minions were eating food the household staff would have to deal with replacing.

"Just don't burn the house down," she said to the bunch of them, concentrating her gaze on Fire, who was doing things to the stove that Ruby had to admit she didn't understand. She was fantastic in a lot of rooms. The boardroom, the recording studio, the concert hall, the legislature, the bedroom—these were places her talents could be applied to an end she found beneficial. The kitchen was not among them. Whatever the Blights were doing in her kitchen was beyond her expertise, and she decided it would be in her best interest not to give a damn.

And anyway, the thing that mattered was what they had done in her library. Ruby glanced at the clock on the wall, and was surprised to find it was mid-afternoon. Knowing the Blights were cooking reminded her she should probably eat something herself. She crossed to her narrow, silver refrigerator as she asked, "Have you found anything?" She pulled open the refrigerator doors and brought out a small ceramic bowl full of raspberries. When she stepped back from the refrigerator, she found the group of them all pointing her toward a book she had somehow failed to notice sitting on the small table near the stairs she'd come up.

It was an old book, leather bound with embossing that had once been gold leaf but was now just a series of unintelligible indentations. Ruby wasn't sure what the book was, but she was sure it hadn't ever been written in English. There was a slip of modern-looking white paper marking a page near its middle. Her business line Starphone sat in its charging cradle on the same small table, and she spared a glance at the screen as she took a seat on an adjacent stool and flipped open the book. There were no emails, no text messages, and no missed calls—no alerts at all. This was good, she figured. No one was looking for her, and no one was waiting for her to return their call. What that meant in practical terms was she could dive headfirst into this book and not worry that business concerns were going to need her attention. Careful to touch the book with only her left hand and the raspberries solely with her right, she eased open the aged volume, slowly turning to the page that had been marked.

She had been right that the book wasn't in English. Her original presumption was that the tome would be in Latin, as most of her older books tended to be. The older the book, and the more arcane the knowledge, the more likely it was to have been printed in a dead language. The volume was printed on paper, and easily identifiable as having been put together using movable type, but Ruby was finding it difficult to discern exactly what the language was. It could have been Old English, or Cornish, or German; it was clearly neither Latin nor French nor modern Italian. The characters told her it wasn't Greek nor any language using Arabic, Cyrillic, Hebrew, or Asian-appearing characters. There were hieroglyphics on a few of the pages, but they seemed to be there as illustrations rather than anything intended to be read as text.

None of that mattered, though—not really—as Ruby had no means to read any of it. She frowned pointedly at the book as she popped a handful of raspberries into her mouth. When her powers had been intact, even before they had been augmented by her contact with the glittering alien, she'd had a supernatural aptitude for discerning the meaning behind words on any printed page. Not so these days.

Hieroglyphics, she figured, did put the focus in near to the right part of the world to give her information about the Eye of Africa. Knowing what she did about the history of written language and of printed books, and with her limited but growing understanding of the stories of King Solomon, the Queen of Sheba, and ancient developments in that part of the world, there was every chance that what the

Blights had uncovered was honestly pertinent to her current quest. Of course, there was really no way to tell without being able to read the book. Surely one or more of the Blights, magical entities that they were, had a way to read or otherwise decipher the text; otherwise how would they have known to point out this passage in the first place?

"Which one of you can read this thing?" she asked, not bothering to look up from the book and the bowl of raspberries.

"Discontent could probably read it word for word," Pestilence answered, getting up from his seat at the counter and crossing to stand closer, but not too close, to Ruby.

"All right," she answered, the thrall of the Eye still affecting her enough to keep her voice sweeter than it would have been ordinarily, "but since Discontent isn't here, and surely it was one of you who came across this passage and decided it was relevant to my interests, I would like to know which of you made that determination and precisely what precipitated it, please." It was clear when she looked around the room that the Blights were surprised by the ultra-pleasant tenor of her question.

Ruby herself was equally surprised. The effect of the Eye had barely diminished in the few minutes she'd been apart from it. Considering it was beneath earth, salt, and lead, and surrounded both by its native ward (which she was sure she hadn't managed to crack) as well as the circle she had cast herself, the fact that its magic was still with her was a very interesting point of data. She was pleased, to be sure, although cautiously so. It seemed she had somehow managed to take some of the magic of the Eye into herself, but she knew the experience she'd had was an accidental one. And she also knew, somehow deep in her gut where the magic in her had always lain, she had barely scratched the surface of what the object was capable of. And if this experience had been the equivalent of sticking a proverbial toe into the ocean of the magic of the Eye of Africa, then she was already aching to dive into its deep end.

"It was me," Doubt answered. She set a box of something Ruby didn't recognize from the pantry onto the kitchen counter and crossed to stand between her mistress and Pestilence. "I can't read it all," she confessed, "only the things written or printed with doubt in the mind of the creator."

Ruby nodded. So that's how it worked—each of the Blights could understand any text that somehow related to their own existence. Maybe.

"So why do you say Discontent would probably be able to read all of it?" she asked.

"Because everyone who had a hand in the book may have affected it," Pestilence answered. "If the author felt discontented by the unsolvable mysteries, or the typesetter was unhappy with his working conditions, or the man who made the paper, or who bound the book—"

Ruby nodded. "So, basically any book printed around the time this one was has a good chance of being readable by Discontent," she surmised.

A chorus of nods answered her.

"But because this was printed in the Guttenberg era by devout Christians," Doubt chimed in, "there was a lot of doubt as to the validity of the contents. Even though it was written as a book of arcane history, it was actually illegal for books of this type to be viewed by anyone outside of the clergy. At least—that seems to be the case according to the internet."

Ruby frowned. She hadn't remembered giving the Blights the Wi-Fi password at the studio, and she knew she hadn't given them the one for the house.

"The internet?" she asked. Not only was the Wi-Fi question in play, but she couldn't help but find it odd that a bunch of timeless, ageless, magical thoughts-made-flesh had somehow mastered the art of the search engine.

"One of the janitors left his Starphone in the studio space," Fire answered, pulling the familiar device from one of her pockets. "And we had a lot of time on our hands. We figured out how to use it."

Ruby's mouth fell open, but she wasn't displeased. An industrious bunch they were, and that suited her just fine. They were in her service, after all, and as long as they owed her fealty, she took no issue at all with their cleverness. It might even serve her well in the long run.

"All right," Ruby conceded, happy enough with the answer and more than anxious to get back to the central topic at hand. "So, based on what you were able to find on the internet," she began the sentence she'd interrupted anew, hoping to spur the conversation back to where it had been.

"This book you have," Doubt answered, picking up the volume carefully and examining the marked page, "was printed in order to keep awareness of certain kinds of magic available to those who might encounter someone trying to use it. It's practically a witch hunting manual. Only the flavor of the magic it deals with is decidedly African. It's framed as being pagan knowledge from the Old Testament, and it reads as disgustingly anti-Semitic in places. But this thing was printed a few hundred years before the discovery of the Rosetta Stone, meaning the prints of the hieroglyphs were absolutely indiscernible. In fact, I'm not sure they were aware it was a real written language. It's weird. The commentary seems half terrified and half completely dismissive. It's like they're saying these old gods and these old mysteries aren't actually real and therefore aren't really worth knowing about, but just in case they are real, then bishops and cardinals and the like should know how to deal with them. It's all filtered through Gnosticism, too, so it's really an ugly Christian mess of commentary. But when it gets down to the source material, the stuff that all the commentary is warning these clergymen of... well, that might lead in the direction of the Eye of Africa. I can't be sure." She shook her head as she stared down at the text. "But this could lead us to something. It's the best we have, anyway."

Ruby started in on another handful of raspberries and nodded. "Can you get this in front of Discontent?" she asked.

"We can do that," Pestilence assured her.

"Without interrupting what he's already up to?" Ruby asked as follow-up. The last thing she wanted at this point was to interrupt the good work being done keeping Elizabeth Stevens away from her husband. Keeping that up was second only to figuring out the secrets of the Eye, and she didn't want to let one cause become detrimental to the other, unless it was absolutely necessary. And at this point, she wasn't convinced it was.

"Yeah," Pestilence answered casually. "Shouldn't be a problem."

"It might take a day or two," Doubt interjected, "and I can't tell you how long it's going to take Discontent to make sense of it. I can't even promise Discontent *can* make sense of it, only that it's your best chance."

"All right," Ruby affirmed, looking around the room and then back into her now-empty bowl of berries. "Make that happen. I can afford to be patient as long as it means Discontent isn't interrupted, so take whatever time you need. But don't dawdle." She stood up and regarded the Blights.

They were all facing her and wearing the same looks of determination she recognized from the day of the vault heist. This was going to get done and it was going to get done well, she was sure of it.

She gave the lot of them a firm nod before heading back down the stairs to spend more hands-on time with the Eye. As she departed, she could hear the group of them stirring about her kitchen again and it occurred to her to call back a reminder. "And don't burn down the house!"

CHAPTER
TEN

Whatever she had done with that circle and that pile of salt to give her access to the power of the Eye, Ruby was now convinced it had been the right thing. She had continued to feel connected to it throughout several trips upstairs for food, drink, bathroom visits, and to check that the Blights hadn't done anything destructive to her house. She'd spent the rest of the day and well into the night meditating with it, handling it, and trying to feel out what it was leading her to do.

She had dealt with magical items before. Even though nothing she had handled up to this point had been nearly as powerful as the Eye of Africa, in her experience, items of this variety all behaved in a similar manner. Once she had made this near-accidental connection to it, she was confident she needed only follow its lead to in order to connect to it fully. Magical items *wanted* to exert their power. Being inanimate, the Eye's only means by which to do such a thing was in the hands of someone who was willing to channel it. Now that she had begun to tap into its power, Ruby was sure the Eye would lead her farther down the path to wielding it—if she could only figure out how it wanted her to do so.

By the time she finally retired to bed late Sunday evening, Ruby was sure she was making progress. She had reached a point where she could feel the Eye without having it physically touching her. When she concentrated, she could feel it surge, feel its power begin to brush against the empty place in her existence where her own power had once lay. That was a distinct victory. She hadn't wanted to stop. She would have stayed up all night working with the Eye, she had *planned* to stay up all night working with the Eye, but an interesting episode sometime after midnight had made her think better of it.

There was a moment, between chants, as she'd gotten up to walk off kinks in her knees from sitting lotus-style on the salt-tiled floor and rub a sore spot in her shoulder before continuing, when she became aware of a familiar yet unexpected feeling. Drain. She was feeling drained. The fatigue she was experiencing wasn't just the ordinary tiredness a person might expect from concentrating on a mental puzzle all day. This fatigue was of the variety she recognized from her days of testing her innate power. It had been months since she had felt the aching in the places where her magic had dwelt, but she knew the feeling. It was as distinct from ordinary fatigue as a sneeze was from a cough. And it was present.

True magical drain could only mean one thing—her own magical potential had been contacted by her work with the Eye. And this was wonderful. This was singularly thrilling. There could have been no better indication she was on the right track. But she also knew her magical muscles were, to say the least, weak. Her abilities, whether lying dormant or altogether missing, were atrophied with disuse. Overextending herself now could easily lead to the kind of magical burnout she had only ever read about. Ruby knew she could not afford a setback as dire as that. Truly, she could afford no setbacks at all. Just as someone planning to run long distances does well by conquering shorter distances first, Ruby chose to take her leave of the Eye and the magical space and rest until the drained feeling had past.

She awoke Monday morning to a pair of joy-inducing realizations: the fatigue had faded, and she could still feel the power of the

Eye. She was almost giddy as she raced through her morning ablutions. Her fingers were literally trembling with excitement as she snatched her personal Starphone from its charger and fired off emails to her assistant and to Jaccob claiming illness. She'd learned long ago that a migraine, be it real or concocted, was enough to get her out of just about any obligation. She had no qualms at all about lying to her business associates; the day-to-day operation of the company would go on just fine without her. Anything that truly needed her attention could likely wait until tomorrow. She also knew both her office assistant, Bridget, and her building manager, Arsho, wouldn't hesitate to call her in case of any legitimate emergencies, no matter what ailment had caused her absence.

Jaccob, on the other hand, she wasn't thrilled to be lying to. Upon reflection, she found that sudden attack of conscience oddly alarming. She'd had no compunction about lying to lovers in the past, and she and Jaccob didn't even qualify for that title. Yet she found herself strangely beholden to some concept she had of doing this thing—whatever it was they were doing—"right." Other than the fact that she'd used one of the Blights to get his wife out of the way, and the fact that she'd been somewhat less than forthcoming about her history with magic, she'd been basically honest with Jaccob up to this point. Come to think of it, without magical influence to exert, she'd been an awful lot more honest with Jaccob than she ever had with anyone she'd ever been involved with. She had been closer to completely honest with Jaccob Stevens than she ever had with any person for any reason. Lying to him now, bald-faced *lying* to him, just seemed wrong.

And that was not a feeling Ruby Killingsworth was used to. Still, she had her priorities, and the Eye of Africa was the most pressing. What Jaccob didn't know wasn't going to hurt her. He would be fine. And it had never caused her trouble in romantic pursuits in the past to leave a man wanting more. Being too available was never a good idea. So she was content enough to send him a quick text apologizing for not being in town like she said she'd be and heading downstairs to her sanctuary to make further progress with the Eye.

She had no idea whether the Blights were still in the house or not. And she decided she really didn't give a damn. They had their task, they had the book, and they had a clear understanding of what was expected of them. Where they had chosen to spend last night really had no bearing on her plans. Loki had sent them to do her bidding, and so far they had done so satisfactorily. She would trust them to do what they said they were going to do and keep her focus on making forward progress with the Eye.

It was scarcely an hour into the morning, and she was sure her decision had been the right one. The stirring she felt immediately in her magical center upon first contact with the Eye in the morning had been better than any jolt from caffeine she had ever experienced, making the fact that she'd skipped this morning's usual two cups of coffee altogether immaterial.

And when, several hours later, the sting of drain eked its way into the edges of her consciousness again; she put down the jewel and went back upstairs. She was being unusually patient with herself, uncharacteristically cautious. But the introduction of the feeling of magical potential back into her being was too precious a thing to be handled in haste or without due care. Plus, another bowl of raspberries sounded pretty good right about now.

Ruby opened the door from the basement stairs into the kitchen to find Plague and Pestilence sitting with Ruin and Decay at the breakfast bar, eating what she could only guess was cereal from her formal silver serving bowls. The carafe of milk was out on the counter, as was a pile of spoons of differing sizes. Ruby had no idea where they might have gotten cereal—she was pretty sure her staff wouldn't have gone against her interdiction against carbs not contained in bar mixers. But then again, maybe the Blights had gone shopping. She had no idea where they might have gotten any money, but there was every chance on the nights they weren't doing things for her they'd gone out and gotten jobs or robbed a bank or something. They were on loan from Loki, so the two sources of income seemed equally plausible.

She was just about to begin admonishing them against using silver serving pieces as cereal bowls when she noticed a large package sitting on the table by the terrace doors. It was a cherry wood tray with a floral arrangement on it, all wrapped up in cellophane and tied with a bow at the top.

"That came for you," Plague said, pointing at the package.

"Did you touch it?" she asked, crossing the room to further examine it. She was sure that Fire, Ruin, and Decay were able to control whether or not they had an effect on the things they touched; she liked to think that such power of restraint also extended to Plague, but she remembered the day the Blights had arrived at her penthouse—when she'd been warned she should go and wash her hands after touching the note Plague had handed her. She figured it was better to be safe than sick. It was one thing to spend a morning skiving off work under the guise of illness, it was yet another thing to actually fall ill. The latter was something she wanted absolutely no part of.

"Nah," Plague answered, shaking his head a little as he lifted another spoonful of whatever it was in the bowl to his mouth. "Fire and Doubt caught the delivery man when they were on their way out this morning."

Ruby nodded. It was good to hear the two Blights had headed out already. She could only hope they had taken the book with them and were on their way to connect with Discontent. It would be nice to get some answers.

Ruby crossed the room quickly to get a closer look at the tray. As she untied the ribbon and pulled away the cellophane wrapping, she saw there was more to this tray than a floral arrangement. The flowers were beautiful—white roses with sprigs of fragrant lavender interspersed throughout the ample bouquet. But the tray was covered with a selection of other small gifts as well. There was a one-pound bag of Italian roast coffee with the Schrodinger's Cup logo on the front, two large bars of 70% dark chocolate, and a bottle of very nice burgundy. There was a tiny card in a purple envelope peeking out from the back side of the flower arrangement; Ruby plucked it carefully from its flimsy holder.

She slid the card from its envelope and opened it. It was a tightly folded three-panel thing made from handmade paper that smelled faintly of the lavender from the arrangement. Ruby couldn't help but smile when she recognized the handwriting as Jaccob's. One of the things she found most endearing about him was his penchant for handwritten notes. This particular quirk in a man who ran a technology company so large his logo was on the back of nearly every electronic communication device in town was particularly adorable.

"Dear Ruby," the little card read, "I am so sorry to hear you're under the weather. I understand these headaches can be brutal. My assistant assures me you likely have a proper pharmaceutical remedy, but a quick search of the internet suggests certain easily procured items might also be helpful in easing your discomfort. Please accept my gifts of fragrant lavender, caffeine, red wine, and dark chocolate in hopes of helping you feel better. And if these things prove to be no help in improving your condition, then I trust you will find enjoyment in them once you have recovered. Feel better, Jaccob."

Ruby was beaming as she held the little card to her chest. This was an unexpected and wonderful surprise. She couldn't imagine a more delightful side effect of her feigned illness than this very personal and very thoughtful gift from her would-be beau. Maybe she'd have to fake a headache more often. Future headaches were a matter for another day, however. Today, she would be satisfied with the progress his lovely gift signified… and with having one of the delicious-looking chocolate bars for lunch. Whether her migraine was real or imaginary, dark chocolate could go a long way toward improving her afternoon.

Spurred on by chocolate and the thrill of having received Jaccob's gift, Ruby spent the rest of Monday afternoon making remarkable progress. She could use the Eye, focus power through it—or, rather, focus its power through her. She was able to feel it and sense it and tune into it even when she was no longer touching it. It was clear she was channeling power—that the power wasn't yet hers. But it was still an excellent development in her quest to regain her power, a giant step in the right direction. She might not have power of her own, but there was power she could *use*, and that was a marked improvement over her former condition.

By the end of the day, she had been confident enough in her use of the item, and in her mastery of the little magic she had gained access to, that she was able to bring it out of her sanctuary and onto the main floor of her house. And by the time the sun had set, she had enough confidence in her ability to interact with the thing that she decided to head back to the penthouse. Granted, she did so with the Eye securely inside of an earth-filled lead box she had long ago cast a ward upon. On top of those precautions, she'd only been willing to make the trip inside of her similarly shielded town car, but she had gone home.

It had been her intention to move into the Ruby Tower full time as soon as her apartment was ready. The result of that decision was that her favorite items of wardrobe, décor, and personal comfort had been relocated to the penthouse weeks ago. It wasn't that her rooms in the Regency Heights mansion were at all *un*comfortable, just that she had already begun to feel more at home in the high-rise downtown.

And, of course, Stardust did not live across the street from her house in Regency Heights. She very likely wouldn't see him tonight. But he'd know she was home. She fired off a quick text from the car letting him know how much she appreciated his very thoughtful gift. He'd see her lights on—she'd make sure to leave them burning late into the night. He'd probably think about coming over; he probably wouldn't actually stop by.

But he'd be thinking about her, like he'd been thinking about her today.

And that was enough to satisfy her for now.

CHAPTER
ELEVEN

Ruby had originally been against the idea of building a helipad on top of her tower. She'd wanted more of an art deco feel to the roofline—graduated tiers leading to an antenna—along the lines of the Chrysler or Empire State building. But when Arsho had explained the break they would get on their insurance premium by putting in the helipad (something about the ability to evacuate people off the roof in case of a fire or some such—truly she'd stopped listening after the dollar figure), she'd made the practical choice and agreed to it. The building was still exquisite, even with its more squared-off top, and she was saving almost a million dollars a year on insuring it. Ruby wasn't often one to go in for compromise, but that was one she could get behind.

The only time anyone had ever landed on the thing had been when the Fire Marshal had come to inspect it. There were times when Ruby had all but forgotten it was there. So when she'd gotten a frantic phone call from Arsho telling her that Marine One was incoming with the President of the United States aboard, it took a moment for that to register. She'd made that call to Prather's office trying to get ahold of Loki. And when it had come out that the President wasn't currently on intimate terms with his immortal benefactor, she'd thought that would be the end of it.

She hadn't dreamed the President would so much as try to call her back, never mind showing up on her rooftop. Even with her powers intact, Ruby wouldn't have been certain she could assert her will over an avatar of Loki, and these days she knew she had no magical will to assert. So she hadn't considered any relationship with Mr. President to be in the cards.

But, she figured, as she watched the famous helicopter descend toward her building's roof, apparently her overture to Prather had made some sort of impression. With or without the aid of magic, she was about to have to deal with him.

She wasn't altogether sure at first how she was going to play this. Lyle Prather was an ass. And he was a moron. He'd only ever gotten anywhere in life thanks to Loki's influence. And as much as Ruby didn't mind using the god herself when it suited her purposes, she drew a firm distinction between using Loki and Loki using her. The latter was never going to happen. But that was Prather's entire *raison d'etre*. Still, he was the President of the United States and he was paying her a call. She supposed the least she could do was meet him on the helipad.

But then she changed her mind. The helipad was windy, and having a giant rotor-driven machine landing on it was only going to make it more so. It wouldn't do to entertain a sitting President and the avatar of an immortal with her hair all askew. She fired off a text to Arsho instructing them to have Prather brought to her private office—the one in the residence, on the fiftieth floor, with the view of the river. Arsho answered instantly that they were already on the roof and trying to placate some very perturbed members of the United States Secret Service.

Ruby, who had no time for caring about the squabbles of the nation's chief executive and his government-issued minders, rode her private elevator up to her penthouse and stationed herself behind her rococo desk to wait and see if Prather was going to show up. She knew there was every chance his security detail would overpower him and strap him back in the helicopter for a tantrum-filled trip back to D.C., but if he made it into her office, she'd talk to him.

Ruby took a moment to check her email while she waited; Jaccob had taken to sending her pictures of puppies or kittens or baby pandas he randomly found in the internet, and if she didn't go through them regularly, they clogged her inbox to the point of exasperation. She was still laughing at one of these unsolicited examples of cuteness when Prather came through her office door.

He spun around immediately and shut it behind him, turning the tumbler to the lock suspiciously, as though he were on the run from the law. Of course, if he'd slipped his Secret Service detail between here and the roof, she supposed technically he was.

"What's the matter, Prather," she called to him from behind her desk, "afraid of police brutality?"

Prather's eyes got wide as he took a step away from the door. He shot one nervous glance behind him and then looked back at Ruby.

"You know that doesn't happen to rich white guys, right?" she teased.

The President shook his head as he continued toward Ruby's desk and took a seat across from her. The closer he got, the more obvious his distress became.

He looked like hell. For a fellow who was the acknowledged most powerful person in the world, who had gotten everything he'd ever wanted out of life, he seemed awfully miserable to Ruby. His skin was so pale and clammy that if Ruby hadn't known better, she'd have guessed he'd had a run-in with Plague on his way into the office. Something was dreadfully wrong, and she did not want to hear about it. But she had a very distinct feeling she was about to.

Prather bent over then, collapsing at the middle with his head in his hands. If he was going to cry right now, Ruby was going to throw him out. She had no time for such inappropriate displays of emotion, even from the leader of the free world.

"He won't talk to me," Lyle whimpered. "He won't answer when I call."

Ruby leaned back in her chair and crossed her arms over her chest. The "he" Prather was speaking of had to be Loki. Who else would he be so upset over losing touch with? And why else would Ruby be the one he was unloading on? The fact that Prather had been a some-time avatar of the god wasn't public knowledge. She guessed there was a very limited subset of people who knew, and an even more limited number who had ever interacted with Loki themselves.

As the President of the United States sat before her, whining like a preschooler in her baroque parlor chair, Ruby began to wonder if maybe she was alone in that regard.

"You do understand how this whole 'avatar' thing works right? You're in *his* service, Prather," she reminded the President, "not the other way around. He is an immortal god, which more than trumps your temporary elevation to most powerful public servant. Maybe he's just reminding you which one is boss."

"But he used to—" Prather stammered. "—he was always there. Why won't he come to me now? He got me here. And I need him. Why isn't he here when I need him?"

"Because he doesn't like being summoned." Ruby rolled her eyes and shook her head. "Will you listen to yourself, Prather? You're beginning to sound like those pathetic evangelicals you had to court during the election. *Oh, why hast my god forsaken me?!*" she mocked. "It's pitiful. And it's unbecoming of the office. You want to know why Loki isn't returning your calls? Here's my best guess: you're a little high-profile these days, Mister President. You're sticking out like the proverbial sore thumb. I'd guess the last thing Loki might want is for word to get out that the acknowledged most powerful mortal on the planet is bound to his service. He'll call you when he needs you," she assured him, "and not a moment before. Until then, you get to be the President. So go out there and be the god-damned President. Pun intended."

"But—" Prather began to challenge her.

"Did I stutter?" Ruby snapped.

"But I don't know how to be the President," he whined. "I don't know what the hell I'm doing! I thought he'd be here, I thought he'd help me."

Ruby rolled her eyes. This really was one of the most pathetic displays of humanity she'd ever seen in her life. Here he was—the President of the United States, throwing a tantrum in her office like a scolded child.

"Just do what you've been doing," she counseled with a shrug. "Smile and wave, go on tour. Enjoy your fame. Hell," she added, " pretend you're one of the Young Dudes. I can have them play a show for you if you want. You'd get to stand on stage with them and everything."

The idea of a White House concert had come to her not long after she'd spoken to Prather on the telephone. She wasn't sure whether seeing her talent associated with the current administration would be altogether beneficial, but she was sure if they were going to do such a thing, sooner was better than later. Having a show at the White House this early in the Prather administration left the artists better than three years in which to turn around and denounce the man. If it was going to happen, now was the time. She'd wanted to run the idea by Loki first, just to make sure, but if Loki and Prather weren't on the best of terms at the moment, she figured the god couldn't likely care less if she exploited his avatar for a little publicity.

"Do you think they'd let me sing?" Prather asked, his voice suddenly hopeful as he sat up straight in the chair for the first time since he'd come in.

For the dozenth time in so many minutes, Ruby rolled her eyes. "Don't press your luck."

Prather's whole bearing wilted. He looked back up at her with an expression that reminded Ruby very much of one of the puppy pictures Jaccob had emailed her. It was pitiful.

"Maybe for the finale," she allowed, "but not with a microphone."

The President shrugged, but seemed a bit more chipper than he had a minute ago.

"Now," Ruby addressed him firmly as she stood from her seat, "shall I walk you out, or will the Secret Service pounce on me? Normally I'd go in for that sort of thing, but I'm seeing someone."

"Yeah," Prather replied. "I heard about that."

"Congratulations," Ruby snarked. "It seems you own a television."

"They won't hurt you," he promised.

Ruby inclined her head in a gesture that told him in no uncertain terms she wasn't sure she believed him, and that he had better be correct. Knowing what he did about her, and about her relationship to Loki, she was sure he understood.

It was fortunate for all involved that Prather's detail didn't seem to mind her in the slightest when her office doors opened and the two of them passed through them. Ruby had to stop for a moment to admire the way Prather had managed to pull himself together. In the few moments it had taken them to cross from one room into another, he'd gone from a blubbering wreck to his wholly recognizable, pompous, puffed-up self. Sometimes it was easy to forget Prather had gotten his start in infotainment, but his ability to turn this façade on and off was a dead giveaway. He might be a downright lousy president, but this was one trait Ruby could point to that made him one hell of a good politician.

They spoke in generalizations and pleasantries all the way out of the penthouse, through the glass doors to the terrace, and up the stairs to the helipad, Prather rattling on about how he was excited to work with her on a concert, and Ruby gushing about what an honor it was to be invited to the White House. Anybody who had ever met either one of them would surely have been able to tell it was all total bull. But it didn't matter. The feigned politeness was enough to keep the Secret Service from appearing to give a damn about Ruby's being in such proximity to the President.

She walked Prather and his entourage all the way onto the heli-pad, where she found Arsho standing, almost at attention, staring at the shiny black Sikorsky sitting there. "You wanna walk up and touch it?" Ruby whispered in her employee's ear, just as she and Prather parted company. The rotors were beginning to spin, and the President and his detail were moving quickly so as to get aboard before the rotor wash became too unpleasant. "I bet Prather would let you touch it," she added.

Arsho, who had started mightily at the first comment in their ear, had finally managed to get ahold of themself. "No, ma'am, Miss Killingsworth," Arsho answered, very obviously trying not to appear too rattled by their boss's surprise words in their ear.

Ruby laughed out loud at her employee. She had never in her life met anyone more consummately professional than Arsho Barsamian. Ruby didn't like people, she didn't care for most of humanity in the slightest, but she had a soft spot for Arsho for some reason. Which was a damned good thing, she reasoned, since it had been Arsho's good intentions that had fouled up her ritual last Christmas and cost her her powers to begin with. Still, her building manager was good with money, even better with tenants, and worth every damned dime Ruby paid them.

And she'd have her magic back soon enough. Arsho hadn't meant to do her any harm, nor had they any idea they had. No, they could be forgiven soon enough, and for now it was best for all involved not to dwell on past mistakes.

Ruby elected to stay on the helipad to watch Marine One's depar-ture. She hadn't ever seen a helicopter come or go from her building before, and she realized she enjoyed the thought of the President of the United States popping by like this, although she would have much preferred the person holding that office to be someone other than the man who currently occupied it. The wind was almost as bad as she'd feared, but she figured there was no harm in her hair being mussed *after* a presidential visit. She'd just go down to her rooms and fix it before getting back to work for the day.

Marine One was still nearby, clearly visible over the afternoon skyline, when Arsho's phone began to buzz. They looked at it quickly before excusing themself and dashing away. Once again, Ruby was glad it wasn't her job to deal with whatever it was that had her building's manager running at top speed from the rooftop.

Ruby still had her gaze fixed on Marine One as it continued its trip over Cobalt City when she heard a familiar rumbling behind her. She smoothed her hair almost frantically, still watching the sky in the distance until she recognized Stardust was indeed coming in for a landing just to her left. She hoped she'd done enough to repair whatever damage the presidential helicopter had done to her appearance.

Ruby smiled as she turned to face her guest. Even with her hair not at its best, she'd much rather be entertaining Stardust than Prather.

"Was that—?" Stardust asked her, his voice a peculiar mix of wonder and annoyance.

Ruby couldn't tell whether he was more impressed or confused. Either way, at this point in their association, she liked that she had him guessing.

"It was," she affirmed, folding her hands at her waist and inclining her head toward the ever-shrinking dot in the sky that was Marine One on its return trip to Washington.

Stardust frowned distinctly—it was clearly a frown of consternation, and the most severe she'd ever seen the hero look. "Huh," he replied after a moment. "My capital really has slipped."

"What on earth are you talking about?" Ruby asked him pointedly. She knew he'd had struggles with the new administration, but she couldn't fathom why seeing Prather in town would cause him to say such a thing.

"It's just that I used to be warned ahead of time when someone was planning to be in city airspace—" he explained, gesturing to the suit he wore. "—for flight path reasons."

Ruby nodded. "Ah, I see," she said. "Well, don't take this one as any part of a pattern. I have a feeling this afternoon's visit was a bit spur of the moment."

Stardust seemed taken aback. He crossed his arms over his chest and studied her. "So, what?" he asked. "Prather just stopped by for coffee?"

Ruby's lip quirked as she realized perhaps the hero's interest in her meeting was something other than political. "Jealous?" she half-asked, half-accused.

His eyes got wide then, and Ruby was sure she'd been on to something with that line of thinking. "Concerned," he answered after a moment.

Without her powers to aid her, Ruby was at a loss to know exactly what Jaccob Stevens was thinking inside that armored suit. But his eyes told her he was walking a thin line between friendly and flirting, and he hadn't decided which side of it he wanted to come down on.

She resolved to do her best to help make up his mind in her favor. "Well, you have nothing to be concerned about," she assured him, reaching down to take hold of his gloved hand as she started toward the terrace stairs. "He had a little business to discuss with me, is all. As it turns out, he's a friend of a friend." Ruby hoped that would be adequate explanation, because there was no way she was about to explain anything further. She had very little practice making up a lie without magic to reinforce belief in it, and she really didn't want to have to do that with Jaccob.

"I don't believe you," Stardust said as he followed her down the curving metal stairs that led from the helipad to Ruby's private terrace. Just as Ruby's head began to spin trying to formulate a response, he added, "Prather doesn't have friends."

Ruby smiled. He'd been making comment on the President's character and not on her story. That was just fine, then. She could roll with that. She allowed herself a tiny laugh as she led him, his hand still clasped in hers, to sit on the terrace sofa.

"How about," she posed as the two of them took a seat, "he's a one-time partner to an old acquaintance of mine."

Stardust looked over at her and smiled. "Now that I'll believe," he allowed.

Ruby smiled back. Good. Truly, that was probably the best she could have done in describing the current nature of the tangle of relationships between herself, Loki, and Prather. It was enough that Jaccob wasn't pressing her for details.

"And, it seems," Ruby offered, moving on from her relationship with Prather to the ostensible reason for his visit. Best to control the conversation at this point, if she wanted to avoid unwelcome questions. "The poor bastard just isn't as popular as he'd hoped to be by this point in his presidency, and he wants my help to remedy that situation."

"And how's that supposed to work?" Stardust asked her dubiously.

"Heavens, Jaccob," she said, breaking what she knew was an interdiction against using his given name while he was in the Stardust suit. "Sometimes you make it sound as though you live under a rock instead of in that big glass tower over there. There is nothing that raises social capital higher and faster than getting into bed with pop stars. Figuratively," she assured him when his body tensed up at the metaphor. Even in the Stardust suit, Jaccob Stevens could be a precious cinnamon roll. "And there's nothing that makes a President more popular than if he looks like a man of the people."

"Prather is not a man of the people," Stardust countered. "I'm not sure he's ever actually spoken to 'the people.'"

Ruby shrugged. "That hardly matters," she replied. "We're talking grand public gestures, not sincere heart-to-heart discourse. A concert for inner city kids on the White House lawn featuring the Young Dudes."

"And you're going to do this for him?" Stardust asked.

"Why wouldn't I?" Ruby countered. "It'll have my artists' faces all over the news. There is nothing I like better than media exposure I don't have to pay for."

"Because the Young Dudes need so much additional publicity?"

Ruby smiled and shook her head with humor. As brilliant a technician and savvy a businessman as Jaccob Stevens might be, her charming neighbor clearly knew nothing about the way her business worked. "No, of course they don't," she affirmed. "But all of the artists I'm going to put on the bill in front of them do. I could probably even get Mike on that stage."

"He told me that was going well," Stardust said. "But I can't believe he'd be ready to play The White House any time soon."

Ruby shrugged. "I'm sure we could pick something he's working on and dial it up to be a single," she said. "It'll take some work on his part, but I think it might be doable. I'll talk to development and see if they can get it in motion. We've barely started planning this thing— haven't even picked a date yet. If we can have a single ready to drop in time for the day of the show, then I'll do it. Nothing like leaving the public salivating for more from an up-and-comer."

Stardust nodded once, slowly. Ruby could tell he was considering her words carefully.

"What is it?" she asked.

"Normally," he answered, "I'd be thrilled at the idea of my son playing a show at The White House. But I'm not sure how I feel about him being associated with *this* White House."

"There's no such thing as bad publicity," Ruby assured him. "And I can't imagine a downside to having the President of the United States beholden to me, even if that president is Lyle Prather. When a man with that kind of influence shows up on my roof unannounced asking for my help, I'm not going to say no."

"Better your roof than mine," Stardust said. "President or no, I don't think I'd have agreed to help Prather if he got on his knees and begged."

"Of course you would," she argued, rolling her eyes. "You're *Stardust*, remember? Big damn hero. If Prather was trapped in a fire and yelling for help, you'd swoop in and save him. I know you would." Ruby shrugged her shoulders and smirked. "Think of this as the public relations equivalent of that."

"Hrmph," Stardust sounded, obviously consternated at her point. "You don't mind helping to redeem the public image of someone like that? It is a little different from not letting him die horribly—which I would likely debate the merits of before saving him, by the way."

Ruby couldn't help but chuckle at Stardust's unvarnished honesty on the matter. "I suppose it is," she conceded. "But the truth is, I'm not really doing it for him. I'm doing it for me. I'm doing it for my company. When someone has that much power to make my business interests blossom, I cannot very well say no, even if that someone is a bloviating tick. If Prather is going to make my fortunes improve, then sign me up for a rousing chorus of 'Hail to the Chief.'"

"The conflict of interest doesn't bother you?" Stardust asked her plainly.

Ruby shrugged. "I try not to think too hard about that," she answered him wryly. "The fact is: it may be ethically ambiguous, but as it turns out, it's perfectly legal. And if I'm not willing to exploit that fact, then Prather is just going to go out and find someone who will. I have a fiduciary duty to my shareholders and my employees to do the best I possibly can by this business. So I'm going to see to that, even if it means I have to suffer the company of the dubiously elected leader of the free world."

CHAPTER
TWELVE

Ruby had been right to presume she wouldn't see Jaccob again on Monday night, but she'd also been right in guessing that he would know she was home. He'd sent her a text between the time she'd put out the lights on the fiftieth floor and when she'd put out the lights in her bedroom on the forty-eighth, telling her it had been nice to see her, that he was glad she was feeling better, and would see her soon. That had led to a very self-satisfied night's sleep.

She'd placed the Eye of Africa into the table at her bedside, in a drawer she'd had specially built with lead lining beneath the lacquer. She'd wrapped it in a cloth stitched with salt tiles, too. She wasn't sure just which magical precautions would keep the item from becoming a beacon, so she decided to throw everything she had at it. Ruby knew the wards on her penthouse were solid—they'd taken her weeks to spin and were being anchored in place by a number of foci hiding in plain sight around the apartment. But she also knew that these wards had been spun without the added weight of her own magical abilities behind them. She wasn't altogether sure that an item with as much inherent power as the Eye of Africa would be fully and properly masked by the wards as they were at the moment.

There was an appreciable difference in the power Ruby could feel radiating from the Eye when it was encased in lead and wrapped in salt, a difference that was palpable even when she was right beside it. By this she was sure she had done the right thing in storing it overnight with additional masking. She figured she'd spend the weekend spinning new wards on the penthouse using the power of the Eye to augment it, but until then, her stop-gap solution would do just fine.

And until then, she'd have to figure out how to conduct business as usual in her office on the forty-seventh floor while the Eye of Africa sat, practically calling to her, in a drawer in her bedroom on the forty-eighth. She was forced to hide her thrill during a particularly onerous meeting early in her day on Tuesday, when she realized she could still feel the thrumming of magic from the Eye resonating within her. She felt a connection to its power even though the physical item was shielded from her both physically and magically.

This was indeed, excellent progress.

She'd made what she needed to of that meeting, and was about to head upstairs for a bite to eat and a quick moment's recharge in the presence of the Eye when the door to her office opened unexpectedly. She was about to give Bridget or Arsho (whichever one of them had decided they were suddenly welcome to barge into her office) a stern piece of her mind when she felt her face flush.

Her caller was not an employee. Ruby couldn't help but smile as she swiveled in her Aeron chair and gestured with a wave for her caller to come further into the room.

"Well hello, neighbor," she said, trying not to show just how happy she was to see Jaccob Stevens standing in her office.

"I hope you don't mind," Jaccob said sheepishly, crossing the wide expanse of custom Persian carpet between Ruby's door and her desk. "I don't have an appointment."

Ruby quirked her lip. His contrition at this was clearly sincere, and she couldn't help herself but to find it endearing. He knew exactly what it meant to be barged in on in the middle of a busy work day, and he was clearly unsure of whether his visit to her office was a welcome interruption. She decided to let him in on a secret. "You don't need an appointment, Jaccob," she assured him. "My receptionist would have made you wait if I was in a meeting, but, as you may or may not have noticed, I have a standing directive to my security and my personal staff that you're welcome to be anywhere in the building any time you want."

Jaccob's eyes got wide; this was clearly a surprise to him. Ruby found it odd that he had perhaps thought her security was lax enough just to have let anyone through without an appointment. "Thank you," Jaccob said, obviously impressed.

"Well, I wouldn't even have this building if it wasn't for you, Jaccob," she replied. It had been Jaccob Stevens's neighborhood revitalization efforts that had paved the way for the development of the Ruby Tower in the first place, so it wasn't at all a stretch for her to be making such a claim. "The least I could do is welcome you into it." Ruby watched as a slight flush rose to Jaccob's cheeks. She smiled and pretended not to notice.

"How's your morning going?" he asked her. It was an obvious tactic to change the subject, but Ruby didn't mind going along with it. He could be so adorably awkward sometimes, and she liked the idea that every once in a while she could let him feel like he was getting away with something.

"Well it was a little bit awful until about a minute ago," she replied.

"Yeah?" he asked, sliding his hands into the pockets of his trousers. He was dressed smartly in navy chinos and a brown tweed jacket, with a white button-down shirt and subtly patterned tie; she was sure he'd come over straight from his own office. And she was equally sure he hadn't come across the sky to get here. The more she thought about the fact he'd just walked through three separate lobbies, past her receptionist, and through her door, the happier she got. It was a remarkable development in their interpersonal relationship, and she wasn't going to let it go without being acknowledged. "Rough morning?" he asked her then.

Ruby nodded. "Just the usual," she replied. "Someone wants one thing, someone else wants another, meetings that drone on forever and feel like they won't ever get anything accomplished no matter how much longer you're at the table."

"Oh boy," Jaccob said, "do I know that feeling. And what had you in this familiar predicament this morning?"

Ruby opened her mouth to answer, but stopped herself. He hadn't come here to talk business, had he? She thought a circuitous answer might be better than the actual story. "It's boring," she insisted, "insurance *stuff*." She made as ghastly a face as she could. Hopefully that would be enough to derail this talk of business and get on to more pleasant topics of conversation.

"You can tell me, you know. I run a big business, too," he reminded her. "I know what it's like to need someone to vent to."

"All right," she conceded. She really hadn't ever had anyone to tell her professional woes to, and if Jaccob wanted to hear about it—to commiserate with someone whose professional life was as similar to his own as one could get—she didn't mind telling him. It wasn't as though it was any trade secret or anything. "Metalcholy wants to use the Goblin Town Rollergirls in their next video, and the insurance company doesn't want to let them," she explained. "There's something about high-value artists and tens of thousands of dollars' worth of production equipment in the vicinity of a bunch of aggressive women on roller skates that just doesn't sit well with them."

"I can see where they're coming from," Jaccob allowed.

Ruby frowned. "You're not a heavy metal band," she countered. "I think I've got them talked into it. As long as there's a perimeter between the Rollergirls and the grip equipment, we use prop instruments when the girls are on set, and absolutely no musicians on skates, it looks like they're going to sign off on it."

"Nicely done," Jaccob congratulated. "I'm impressed. That sounds like one hell of a negotiation."

Ruby smiled. She had, of course, chosen not to mention the fact that she was sure the residual magic from the Eye of Africa she was able to access had been part of garnering the insurer's cooperation. Her magic, particularly her skill with mental manipulation, had always been a great asset in her business dealings. She'd managed to remain successful in the months since the loss of her powers, but knowing that today's victory had been at least in part due to her use of a little magic—even though that magic was borrowed—made the whole thing extra special. But Jaccob didn't like magic and he didn't know, nor could he ever be allowed to suspect, she had the Eye of Africa in her possession. It was enough for him to be impressed by her skills as a brilliant and persuasive businesswoman.

"All in a day's work," she replied casually as she rose from her desk and walked around to lean on the far side. "Now, you didn't come all the way up here to listen to me complain about the woes of keeping a metal band insured. So tell me: to what to I owe this unexpected pleasure?"

Jaccob stuffed his hands back into his pockets and averted his gaze for a moment. Even after these weeks of their association, it still struck Ruby how shy he could be sometimes. As a CEO or as Stardust, Jaccob was one of the most self-assured and assertive people she'd ever met. But one-on-one in a personal situation, he could be adorably demure. He shrugged his shoulders and lifted his head to look back at her, but his gaze instead settled on something on the desk behind her. "What is that?" he asked, taking his left hand from his pocket and pointing.

"What is what?" Ruby asked, feigning ignorance as she scooted ever so slightly to her left in a vain attempt to block his view of the thing she was sure he'd spotted.

Jaccob took a step closer and reached around Ruby, bringing forth the item in question. "This!" Jaccob declared, holding the little plastic figure up for her inspection. It was a figure of Stardust. Made from LEGO and painted in his signature gold super suit trim, Jaccob had to have known they had made these things. But from the way he examined the one in his hand, Ruby had to wonder if maybe he'd never seen one in person before.

She felt her cheeks flush, but tried to play it cool. "You don't want me to explain that," she claimed, but not with enough force to have any magic behind it. She wasn't altogether sure how much of the magic of the Eye she still had access to at this point, and she was already feeling the gentle nudge of drain. This was neither the time nor the place to push it. She'd use her many mundane skills to keep what control she could of this conversation.

"Yes, I do," Jaccob countered, examining the little toy further.

Ruby sighed. Pursing her lips and trying not to blush more, she conceded. "Promise me you're not going to laugh and point?" She'd teased herself enough over this thing, she didn't need to hear teasing from anyone else, least of all Jaccob.

"Promise," Jaccob agreed lightly, momentarily shifting his gaze from the tiny Stardust in his hand to the blushing woman beside him. "Tell me."

Ruby nodded. "I think about you sometimes, when I'm here stuck behind my desk. And it makes me smile. And I want to see you. But this is new, and we're not exactly out in the open. So having a picture of you in my office could lead to questions from people who come in here. Questions," she emphasized, "that don't have answers. But I thought a little toy figure of the superhero next door who also happens to be the man whose neighborhood redevelopment plans let me have this office in the first place—" Ruby paused and shrugged. "I thought the worst it would seem is quirky."

"I think it's cute," Jaccob said, holding up the Stardust figure, but looking through it to where Ruby was trying not to erupt in nervous laughter.

"I am not cute!" Ruby countered, spitting out the word "cute" as though he'd called her something far more dastardly, like "communist" or "cheap."

"I think you're cute," Jaccob told her plainly, reaching around her again and replacing the little LEGO Stardust where he'd found him.

"Well, I think you're cute," Ruby said back, still framing the words as though they were an accusation.

"Actually," Jaccob began again, grinning at her as she maintained her playful scowl at having been called "cute," "that's kind of what I came to talk to you about." He gestured to the figurine he'd just set back on the desk behind her.

"Merchandising?" Ruby asked, now wearing a genuine frown. "That's not a department I would have guessed you had problems with."

Jaccob practically threw his head back with laughter. "No, no. Not about merchandising, no," he clarified. "About pictures in offices, that sort of thing."

"I'm listening," Ruby said, crossing her arms over her chest as she raised her eyebrows in anticipation of whatever he was about to say next.

"Look," Jaccob began with a slow shake of his head. He took a deep breath and seemed in that moment to have found something very interesting in pattern of the carpet. "We've been at this for a few weeks now, and I know it's not easy. And you've been really patient in putting up with me. But I think it's time—" He paused and looked up at Ruby for a moment before shrugging his shoulders. "We've got to stop this sneaking around," he finally declared.

Ruby's breath caught in her chest. She had not seen this coming. She was sure she'd been doing everything right. Jaccob's deciding to call it off had not been at all on her radar. She tried to remain calm, tried to remind herself that she was getting close to unlocking the secrets of the Eye. She'd have all the power she wanted very soon, including power over Jaccob Stevens. It took every ounce of self-discipline she had not to reach deep in to her being and pull out what magical leavings were there to try and derail his train of thought. She could do it. She was almost sure of it. But in doing so, she would risk using up the last tendrils of magic that kept her connected to the power of the Eye, and possibly sever her ties to it permanently. She was playing a long game, she firmly reminded herself. She would make it through this setback and go at this whole thing anew once she had the magic she sought.

"If that's what you want," she managed to say in a tone so calm she surprised herself.

Jaccob stood up straighter and frowned for a moment. A stunned expression jumped to his face then, and he took Ruby by her shoulders, shaking his head rapidly. "No, no, no," he insisted. "Not—" His tongue seemed tied and Ruby had no idea what was going on. "I didn't mean—" He let go of her shoulders and put his head in his hands for a moment before meeting her eyes again. "That came out wrong. What I meant was that I want to take you out."

"Out?" Ruby asked. Well, wasn't this a delightful development? Her whole body began to relax as she uncrossed her arms. A smile once again tugged at the corners of her mouth. So he wasn't calling things off, he was stepping things up. Ruby tried not to let it show on her face just how thrilled she was at this.

"Yeah," Jaccob affirmed. "Out. In public. Out somewhere people will see us. I think it's time to stop hiding—to stop sneaking. I want you to let me take you out."

"All right," Ruby agreed easily. "What'd you have in mind?"

"Dinner," he answered plainly. "Tonight. We'll go to Tessien's. We'll sit at the Chef's table, and we won't care who sees us coming or going. Oh!" He changed gears suddenly. "Or if you'd prefer a *real* coming out, you could let me take you to Icons."

Ruby laughed out loud at the thought of that. Just the idea of showing up at the superhero-themed restaurant on the arm of the city's best-known superhero was overwhelming. "That sounds lovely. Tessien's sounds lovely," she amended, wanting to make sure he'd been joking about going to Icons. Although this was Jaccob—it was entirely possible he could have meant it. He had walked through the front door of the building, talked his way past two separate receptionists, and come into her office in full view of anyone who might have been around. If this had been a signal he was ready to go public with their relationship, Ruby couldn't imagine any place more public than Icons.

"But can we do it tomorrow?" she asked, remembering that, no matter the plan, tonight was no good. Jaccob always seemed to want to see her on the nights she was already booked. "I have a box at the Pops. They're playing tonight. It's the Tribute to Stage and Screen concert, and we're recording the whole thing for a live album. I have to be there. You could come with me, unless that's more in public than you're ready to for—it is going to be crowded."

"No," Jaccob replied. "I think that could be fun."

Ruby couldn't help herself but to smile broadly.

"What time is curtain?" he asked.

"Seven."

"I'll pick you up at six."

"Like a real date?"

"Like a real date," Jaccob affirmed.

"Black tie."

He nodded. "I would have presumed as much," he answered.

Ruby nodded. Of course he knew that. This man was a billionaire several times over. As much as he might bum around his condo in cargo shorts and faded comic book t-shirts, he knew what to wear to Symphony Hall.

"And maybe we'll get some dinner afterwards," Ruby suggested.

"Someplace that's *not* Icons."

Jaccob laughed at that as he reached for her hand. He brought her fingers to his lips for a feather-light kiss before letting go. "That will be great," he assured her. "I'll see you tonight."

CHAPTER
THIRTEEN

Jaccob Stevens' personal presentation might occasionally have
reverted to his awkward and nerdy youth, but he knew how to
court a lady in style. He'd had his car brought to Ruby's private tower
entrance promptly at six o'clock and had gotten out himself to ring
the buzzer. When she'd invited him up, he'd declined, preferring to
wait in the lobby with the doorman (who Ruby was sure was posting
about it on social media in real time). The way he'd looked at her as
she stepped from the elevator in her floor-length red silk gown made
every moment she'd spent lacing herself into her corset more than
worth it. She loved it when a man looked at her that way—it made
her feel powerful like very little else could. And she especially loved
it when a man she meant to conquer looked at her that way. All was
going as well as she'd hoped it might.

As they stepped through the heavy iron door and onto the sidewalk, Ruby couldn't help but enjoy the attention of onlookers as they
recognized the couple leaving the Ruby Tower. This was their first
night out in public together, and she reveled in every bit of attention
they were drawing. Jaccob held her hand on the short walk from the
tower to the car and smiled to the few passers-by as he watched her
get into the limo. He seemed to be just as pleased to be out with her as
she was to be out with him. This was all very good.

Jaccob got in behind her and settled into the seat across from hers. "You've mentioned you're a fan of scotch," he said, gesturing to a decanter in a keeper beside him, "but I don't know your feelings about champagne." It was then that Ruby noticed a bottle set to chill in a cooler built in to the seat beside Jaccob.

"I am decidedly in favor," she answered.

Jaccob smiled then. He carefully withdrew the already-uncorked bottle from its cooler, pouring two glasses full and handing one over to Ruby before he replaced it.

"To new things," Jaccob toasted, leaning in to clink his glass against hers as the car began to move.

"I'll drink to that," Ruby responded, tipping her glass toward his before enjoying her first sips of the dry bubbly as she settled in for their ride to the concert hall.

"And along those lines," Jaccob said then, setting his glass into a keeper to his left and reaching into his coat pocket, "I want you to have this." He withdrew a hinged box from his pocket and presented it to her.

Ruby didn't bother trying to hide the delight in her expression as she reached out with her gloved hand to take the box from him. "Jaccob, you shouldn't have," she said, turning to set her glass aside.

Jaccob shook his head. "Actually, I should have gotten this to you a while ago," he replied. "But I had to be sure it was perfect before I gave it to you. I tinkered with it forever before I decided it was ready."

"Are you telling me you made this?" she asked, prying open the box to reveal a delicate-looking silver bangle inset with diamonds.

"I had a proper jeweler set the stones," he admitted, "but other-wise, yes. Getting the circuits all working properly at that size was a bigger challenge than I'd anticipated."

"So this is—?"

"That panic button I told you I wanted you to carry."

"I was expecting something—" Ruby paused as she withdrew the pretty bracelet from its box.

"Something a little more functional-looking?" he asked, finishing her sentence for her.

Ruby nodded.

Jaccob smiled again, reaching out to take the bracelet from her. "I knew better than to think you'd keep something purely practical on you," he said. "And besides, diamonds go with everything."

"That they do." Ruby held out her right hand, presenting her wrist as he carefully undid the delicate clasp and pulled open the hinge.

Jaccob placed the bracelet on her wrist and clasped it shut. "Good," he said, admiring the bracelet on Ruby's tiny wrist as she held it in front of her face. "I got the fit right."

"It's perfect."

"The clasp there," he said, "is for any time you want to take it off. Like, for instance, if you want to wear it with gloves. And as much as I'd really prefer you not to keep it off for long, I acknowledge you might not be comfortable sleeping in it—and at the very least you're going to want to change wrists every now and again. So use the clasp when you want to take it off for benign reasons. The circuit doesn't connect there, so it doesn't affect anything. But if you look on the other side, you'll see the hinge is very delicate. You should be able to pull it open no problem. Should you break the hinge by pulling it open, or by yanking the bracelet off without opening the clasp—or should anyone handle you so roughly as to cause it to break—it stops transmitting. I have a receiver, here—" He showed her a pip on the side of his fancy Stardust wristwatch-looking-device. "All this does is monitor that your bracelet is intact. The moment it's not getting the all-clear, I can switch on a tracker and find you."

Ruby wasn't sure how she felt about Jaccob's being able to track and find her anytime, anywhere. But she did know that she was delighted that not only had he made the effort to create such an involved system for keeping her safe, but he'd even bothered to inlay the thing with diamonds. She'd likely quiz him as to the tracking technology later. For now, she thought better of any line of questioning that might make her sound ungrateful. She could feign renewed curiosity later. For now, she decided to be nothing short of demonstrably thrilled.

"I love it," she said.

"Good. I'm glad. I knew you wouldn't wear it if you didn't."

Ruby picked up her glass again. "You're very perceptive, and you have very good taste in jewelry. And also champagne," she added, raising her glass a bit before taking another sip.

Jaccob shrugged as he lifted his glass as well. "I'm hoping I haven't just shot myself in the foot," he joked. "I don't know how long I'm going to be able to keep this up."

"You don't have to keep giving me diamonds, Jaccob," she said. "And maybe next time, I can be the one to spring for the champagne."

"We're not even at the concert yet, and you're already talking about next time?"

"Let's just say I'm optimistic."

"Then so am I," he said back. He offered his glass again, and she tipped hers to clink the rims again.

They spent the rest of the ride chatting jovially and drinking champagne. Ruby was careful not to ask too many direct questions, but did her best to get what information she could out of Jaccob as to what was going on with the CCPD's investigation into the break-in at the occult vault. He didn't have a lot of information, but it sounded to Ruby that it was because the police didn't either. This was all good news.

She'd turned on the intercom to let the driver know how to get to the back door of the concert hall when Jaccob switched it off again. He'd said he would take her out in public, and he intended to do just that. He had the limo pull right up to the front of the building, beneath the marquee, and had the driver let them out on the red carpet that had been put down for the occasion.

So this was what Jaccob meant when he'd said "out in public." He insisted on using the main entrance to the concert hall, even though they had every right to use the stage door. A crowd was bustling about on the sidewalk, dozens of people in their finery queueing at will-call and waiting for others in their party. Ruby could hear the mutters of her name and Jaccob's as they moved through the crowd and into the building.

Flashbulbs were clicking and Starphones emerging from evening bags left and right to capture images of the famous hero and the media mogul as they made their way through the atrium lobby of the Liberty concert hall. Jaccob didn't seem to mind a bit. Either he was thoroughly accustomed to being surreptitiously photographed or he was all but completely oblivious. Ruby wouldn't have put money on either one, and truly she didn't care which was true. She was content to feign shyness at having her picture taken and to keep her eyes on Jaccob—pretending to be more hesitant than she was and seeming to defer to his attitude about things. He seemed content to keep his hand on the small of Ruby's back as she led them through the series of lobbies toward the stairs to her box.

Jaccob smiled politely at the crowds as they passed, and directed the occasional nod or wave to those who called out to him.

"You're popular," Ruby said softly as they started up the gold-carpeted stairs toward her box seats.

"You scared yet?" he asked. He was smiling, but Ruby had a very strong impression he wasn't entirely joking. She was sure he probably had a few real concerns that his life in the public eye would be a little much for her. That had likely been in part to blame for his surprise at her having treated a second night out as a given.

But she'd been backstage with The Young Dudes, and had cut her teeth in the music business on a ghastly but profitable mall tour with Cassidy Sweet. The attention Stardust was getting was much less frenzied and much more respectable than that usually directed at teenage pop stars; this was nothing she couldn't handle.

She turned her head to wink at him from her place on the stair above him. "No," she answered plainly. Ruby reached behind her and took Jaccob's hand for the rest of the trip up the stairs.

A maître d' was waiting for them at the top, a tray of champagne on a small table to his left, and the curtains to the box standing open to his right.

"More champagne?" Jaccob asked, gesturing to the bubbling flutes on the table as Ruby passed through the curtain and into the box.

"He'll bring it to us," she answered, taking Jaccob's arm and inclining her head toward the fellow holding open the tasseled curtain.

Jaccob covered her hand with his own and followed her through the curtain and into the semi-circular box, pausing for a moment to take in the view of the stage and the theatre. The Liberty had been recently renovated, largely to undo some questionable "updates" from the 1970s, and had been styled with a manner of opulence that made it seem older than it actually was. To Jaccob's left, an intricately carved proscenium cornice surrounded the magnificent gold velvet curtain that pooled heavily on the planks of the mammoth concert hall stage. Across and beneath him, the other box seats were filling with patrons sipping champagne in their finery and settling in for the performance. And to his right, the mezzanine of the main balcony lay just a few meters away, hanging in the sky just below the top boxes. People were milling about, finding their seats and making idle conversation. Jaccob heard a stranger call his name, and as he had done in the lobby, he acknowledged her with a wave.

All of a sudden, his hand went slack on hers, and in a moment, it fell away entirely. He took a step back, dislodging her hand from his arm as an almost stricken expression passed over his features. Startled by his sudden change in demeanor, she looked up at him, searching his expression for what had caused this upset. His mouth had fallen open and there was a panic in his eyes that Ruby wouldn't have guessed the man behind the mask of Stardust was even capable of.

"What is it?" she whispered, turning to look in the same direction as he was. But she realized even as she asked that she knew. She could see what he saw, and so she knew.

There in the second row of the mezzanine, standing up to converse with a group of shabbily dressed women, stood a statuesque blond woman in a simple silk gown who Ruby would have recognized anywhere. Of all the things she'd guessed might happen tonight, running into Elizabeth Stevens hadn't been one of them.

Ruby reached out and squeezed Jaccob's hand. "You can leave out the back," she told him, "the way I told you we could have come in. Just have your car pull into the alley. Your driver can pull right up to the stage door."

Jaccob nodded, turning on his heel to head quickly back through the now-drawn curtain and out of view of the theatre. But he stopped short. His hand was still on the curtain when he turned around and looked back at Ruby.

She was doing everything she could to keep the disappointment off her face—she didn't want him to be completely soured on the idea of being out in public with her. If aiding his easy retreat from an unexpected sighting of his wife was the thing she needed to do to ensure that, then aid it she would.

But Jaccob shook his head. "No," he said decisively after a moment. Jaccob turned and took a broad step back into the center of the seating area. He looked back at Elizabeth, who it appeared had spotted him but was trying not to stare, and waved; he waved at her just the same as he had waved at any of the random strangers who'd called out "Stardust" in the lobby.

And when he turned back to Ruby, his jaw was set. "She's the one who walked out on me." He reached out and took both of Ruby's hands in his. "She's the one who left. I'm not the one who caused this, and I'm not about to start running and hiding every time she and I wind up in the same place at the same time. I have nothing to be ashamed of," he asserted. "She left me more than two months ago, and I have every right to be out at the Pops with a lady of my choosing."

Ruby smiled up at him. She had decided against trying to bring along the Eye of Africa for the night, as she wasn't entirely confident in her ability to shield it from detection when out in the open. But the fact of the matter was this episode couldn't have gone better if she had.

"If you're sure," she said, squeezing both of his hands before turning to head to her seat.

Jaccob nodded. "I'm sure." But instead of following her, he gripped her hands tighter and pulled her toward him until the two of them were standing scandalously close together. "If you're okay with being out with me," he said quietly, "then I'm happy to be out with you."

Ruby nodded, meeting his gaze as she moved her hands to his waist. "I'm more than okay," she assured him. "I'm honored to be here."

Jaccob placed his hand on her cheek, tilting her face upward before leaning in to find her lips with his.

Ruby pressed herself into the kiss, wrapping her arms around his waist and seeing to it that they lingered there long enough for not only Elizabeth Stevens to see, but for even the slowest social media photographer to retrieve their Starphone and snap a picture. The kiss was sweet and lovely, and Ruby felt her face flushing pink as she finally stepped away from him. That had been unexpected and marvelous. The degree to which that moment had been a victory was more than Ruby was even ready to analyze in the moment.

Jaccob had kissed her—had *really* kissed her. *In public.* And this had not been the tentative brushing of his lips against hers that she remembered from the other night. This had been a real, honest-to-gods kiss and it had been given in a box seat at the Pops in front of an audience who, she was sure, was at this moment already making the surreptitious photos they'd snapped go viral online. This had been both a private statement—a stepping up of the intensity of kisses between them—and a very, very public one.

As the house lights blinked and Ruby moved to settle into her seat for the concert, she could not have been happier with the state of her world. The power of the Eye of Africa was reawakening the magic within her. And Jaccob Stevens had just kissed her in the face of his wife. There was almost no way this night could possibly get better.

C H A P T E R
FOURTEEN

Ruby's perfect night out at the Pops had grown slightly less than perfect during the opening movement of the second act. The musicians were just getting into the medley of selections from little-known musicals of the 1930s when Jaccob seemed to panic at something having to do with his wristwatch. He shook his head and frowned at the thing. Ruby knew it was much more than the designer wristwatch it appeared to be—he'd already shown her where the receiver to her own bracelet was attached. There was probably some crisis somewhere that required Stardust.

Either that, or Elizabeth Stevens still carried her own panic button and had triggered it just to spoil Ruby's night.

Jaccob leaned over in his seat and whispered in Ruby's ear. "Excuse me for a moment," he implored.

Ruby turned her head and nodded. "Everything all right?" she asked.

Jaccob was shaking his head as he stood and he shrugged his shoulders in reply. "I don't know," he admitted. "I'll be right back."

Ruby nodded again and did what she could to turn her attention back to the performance. The musicians were good, and the selections were interestingly arranged. This record would have no trouble selling. She tried to concentrate on facts and figures related to sales of albums that cost this little to produce, and on the percentage of the people in tonight's audience who might otherwise pass but who would be tempted to buy the record as a souvenir of the night they saw Stardust kiss a woman who wasn't his wife—and absolutely *not* on the fact that Jaccob had gotten up and left the box.

He was back in the box right around the time the movement was over. The audience had just begun to applaud; the conductor was turning on his podium to bow when Jaccob slid back into his seat with a sour expression on his face.

"Let me guess," Ruby whispered. She was still clapping politely, but the gloves she had worn meant the sound was deadened to the point of making the action all but pointless. "The city needs you?" She tried not to sound too annoyed or too disappointed. But she was both. She'd said before that she knew who he was and what he did, and that she absolutely understood there would be times he would be called away from her. But that didn't mean she had to like it.

"Yeah," he answered curtly. "I'm sorry, but—"

"No, no," Ruby countered, remembering that taking the high road on matters of Stardust had been a successful tactic up until this point. She knew she really ought to keep from souring things on a night when everything had gone so brilliantly. "Go and take care of things," she insisted, turning to pat him lightly on his knee as the applause was ending. The conductor was lifting his baton to begin the next movement as she continued. "Slip out the back. I meant it when I said you can have your car pull up to the stage door. My security people are down there, you won't have any trouble getting through."

"Okay," Jaccob agreed with a nod before once again standing from his seat. "I'll call you later."

"You'd better," Ruby mouthed playfully before blowing him a kiss and waving goodbye.

As soon as he was through the curtain, Ruby reached into her satin clutch and turned on her Starphone. She couldn't pull it out up here; the light would be bright enough to advertise to the rest of the auditorium that she'd been on her phone in the middle of the concert. But it was easy enough for her to fire off a text message to the number the Blights had given her for their recovered phone. "I don't know where Stardust is going," it read, "Please find out and be sure it makes the news."

People would see that Jaccob had left before the end of the concert. It needed to be clear as day it had been an emergency. "Make it a bigger deal than it is if you need to," she added, just to be sure. As long as everyone in town heard that Stardust had saved the city tonight, then they wouldn't be questioning why he'd left the Pops alone. And that, as far as Ruby Killingsworth was concerned, was absolutely necessary.

The rest of the Pops had been lovely, even without Jaccob there to enjoy it alongside her. Ruby could only hope that whatever had called Stardust into service during the concert would turn out to be high-profile enough to make the news. And if it hadn't been a big enough deal to begin with, the Blights should have been able to do enough to make it so. Not that she cared so much what the gossips would be saying; whether or not the photos went viral, that kiss in the box had been progress. And progress was a good thing.

She'd stayed for a few minutes of the onstage reception when the concert had ended, but very quickly the questions about Jaccob and his whereabouts had become grating. So after checking with the engineers that the recording had gone swimmingly, she'd called her car to the stage door and made a quiet exit. One calming snifter of brandy in the back of the car later, and she was back in her penthouse with the Eye of Africa. Tonight had been the first time she'd been so far from the jewel since she'd begun to connect to its power, and she felt a visceral difference in herself as a result.

It wasn't so much that she'd noticed herself diminished or her burgeoning power reduced while she was away; it was more that returning to her nightstand, unfolding the salt-lined cloth, and laying her eyes on the gem had invigorated and energized her to an unexpected degree. Returning to the presence of the Eye had acted on Ruby like a bump of pure cocaine. She'd been tired when she'd gotten home, not completely exhausted, but tired enough that she'd planned to get changed for bed and turn in for the night. Merely peeking in on the Eye where it sat in her drawer had been enough to give her a second wind.

She'd opened up the floor-to-ceiling bedroom windows and gone into her closet to change out of her gown, figuring she'd stay up for a while and work with the Eye. Surely she was accessing its magic unconsciously if just the sight of it was having an effect on her. And it had been a very encouraging development to have realized that some part of its power had stayed with her even as she'd been across town for hours. Maybe she would be able to see some real progress tonight.

Ruby was confident enough in the power she felt courtesy of the Eye that she was at least sure she could use it to reinforce the wards on the penthouse. That was a reasonable size job for the rest of the night. It would give her a chance to consciously and intentionally apply the magic of the thing in a rite of her own and, as long as the ritual proved successful, set the stage for further magic in the days to come.

She'd only just gotten out of her gown and corset and was beginning the rather tedious process of unpinning the complicated coif of her hair when she recognized a sound coming through her open windows. That was certainly a way to derail her plans, but she couldn't bring herself to mind. Her plans would keep. She slipped a black silk dressing gown on over her lace underthings and headed back into the bedroom.

As she made her way across the carpet, it was easy to spot Stardust through her open windows. He was flying past her penthouse at an unusually slow clip, with his head turned directly toward her building. And even at this distance, and even with his helmet visor down, Ruby had no trouble at all making out his chagrined expression when he realized he'd been caught peeping. She waved coyly at him. It seemed the acknowledgement caused him to abandon any premise he may have been holding to that he happened to be there by chance. Stardust stopped his tentative forward motion and hovered there, eight or ten meters outside Ruby's open windows, and gave her a tiny salute. Ruby shook her head and chuckled. Sometimes Jaccob Stevens, even when done up as Stardust, could be painfully adorable.

She gestured upward, hoping he would understand her invitation to meet her upstairs at the terrace.

Stardust nodded. With a brief firing of rockets in his boots, he was gone from Ruby's view, and she scrambled to slip her marabou slides onto her stocking feet and push her bedside drawer closed before heading upstairs to meet him. When she reached the terrace door two floors up, Jaccob was waiting for her just on the other side.

She grinned, but shook her head as she slid the door open. "You know you could have let yourself in," she scolded gently as he came through the door, pulling the Stardust helmet off as he did. Ruby took the helmet from his hands and set it on the nearby bar.

"I'll start letting myself in over here," he countered, beginning to fiddle with a series of switches on his robotic suit, "when you install a lock on that door and give me a key."

Ruby smirked, impressed at his unexpected trickiness. "Well, aren't you full of surprises," she teased. She meant to only be remarking on his clever angle at trying to get her to install a lock, but the comment happened to come right as the Stardust suit removed itself—automatically and mechanically—from Jaccob's person and folded itself neatly into the shape of a small suitcase on her floor. Jaccob was left standing before her in his undershirt, stocking feet, and tuxedo pants. She wasn't about to ask him what had become of the rest of his eveningwear. She gaped a little at the technological wonder she'd just witnessed.

But it was only a moment before the suit had lost its charm and she turned her attention back to the half-dressed superhero standing before her. "Come in," she encouraged, stepping away from the neatly folded robotic suit and farther into her sitting room. "Can I get you anything? I could make you tea, or we could open a bottle of wine—"

"Scotch?" he interrupted.

Ruby turned to him and smiled. "A man after my own heart." She gestured for him to have a seat on the sofa as she moved to the side table where she kept the decanter and glasses. "And a good call on the tea, by the way," she added. "I'm rubbish in the kitchen."

Jaccob laughed out loud at that.

Ruby looked back at him sheepishly. He probably thought she was kidding. "Pouring a glass of scotch, though, that I can handle."

"Neat," he told her, before she had the chance to ask him about ice.

"Splash of water?" she asked, holding up a tiny beaker with a dropper rested against its side. "You'll find the flavor really opens up with a few drops."

Jaccob nodded. "I'll trust your judgment," he answered.

Ruby quickly poured two glasses of the dark amber liquid from the cut-glass decanter and then carefully deposited three drops of water into each one. She walked the few steps to where Jaccob was standing behind the sofa and handed him a glass. He took a long sniff of the scotch and then a tentative sip. "This is good," he told her. "What is it?"

Ruby shrugged. "I honestly don't remember," she admitted, taking a sip from her own glass and gesturing for him to have a seat. "It's one from the Whisky Society. They're all catalog numbers with bizarre poetic descriptions. I stopped trying to remember what the names are ages ago. The building manager keeps a log, though. I can ask."

"It's not a big deal," Jaccob conceded, taking a seat on the nearest chair. It was a square thing, oddly modern in the original sense of the word. It could have come out of some Bauhaus museum. And Jaccob wore his surprise all over his face when it turned out to be far more comfortable than it looked. He took another sip from his glass and looked up at her.

"So tell me what tonight was about," she encouraged, walking around the back of the chair. "Anything interesting?" She'd learned pretty quickly that Jaccob appreciated being asked what had gone on in Stardust's world, and Ruby wasn't about to let an opportunity for him to regale her pass them by. She was moving to take a seat on the chair across from his when she noticed he suddenly seemed tense— an affectation that hadn't been present up to this point. She was about to ask him what the trouble was when she felt the left lapel of her dressing gown slide down her arm, exposing her bare shoulder and the top of her lace brassiere. "Is this bothering you?" she asked. "I can go get dressed if you—"

"No," he interrupted, shaking his head and lowering his gaze to the swirling liquid in his glass. "No. I'm just trying to be a gentleman. I'm trying not to stare."

Ruby felt the unexpected warmth of a blush rising to her cheeks. She was used to being looked at only when and how she wanted to be looked at. It hadn't occurred to her when she'd run upstairs to let him in that she was doing so in racy lingerie and a dressing gown—she was just happy to have him drop by.

And it hadn't occurred to her, because she hadn't let herself think too hard about it, that he'd be so shy about seeing her in any state of undress. It was funny, now that she thought about it a little, that wrapped in a dressing gown, wearing a balconette, bikini briefs, a garter belt and stockings, she was at least as covered up as she'd been in her swimsuit when he'd first come to call on her that afternoon on the terrace. Perhaps it was the sheer lace that had him flustered, or maybe it was just the fact that there was an understanding that swimsuits were made to be seen and lingerie, in theory, was not. Either way, he was being awfully demure, and she found it oddly charming.

But the truth was, now that she was thinking about it, she was a little bit self-conscious. The last woman he'd seen in such a state of undress had undoubtedly been his tall, svelte wife. She could only hope he liked what he was seeing. She hadn't put on lacy underpinnings tonight with the thought anyone might see them, but she was glad in this moment that she had. It was all she could do to exude confidence and offer to be accommodating.

Ruby found herself averting her eyes—staring into her own glass as though the scotch inside was suddenly much more interesting than it actually was. "I'll go change," she said, getting to her feet as she set her glass down a nearby end table. The offer was as much to assuage her own self-consciousness as it was to counter any awkwardness Jaccob might have been feeling. But she would never *ever* have told him that.

"No." Jaccob stood as well, his glass set hastily beside hers on the table. "I mean it." But he didn't manage to say anything more. He was standing now directly in front of her; they were inches apart. He sucked in a tense breath as he regarded her, his jaw slack and his eyes unblinking.

Ruby let the silence stand for a moment. Looking back at him expectantly, she stayed still and waited for him to decide what came next.

"I don't know what I'm doing," he sighed with a self-deprecating shake of his head. "It's been a long time… since—" He shrugged his shoulders as his gaze once again left Ruby's face.

"Jaccob," she addressed him quietly, reaching out and taking both of his hands. "We're not in any hurry here. You don't have to do anything you don't want to do. We can just sit here, have a drink, and then say goodnight."

Jaccob squeezed her hands. "But if I want—?" he began to ask, drawing her closer.

Ruby let go of his hands and ran her splayed fingers over his chest. The contact caused him to shiver, but he didn't back away.

"Anything you want," she assured him, leaning in to softly kiss his neck. "Whatever you want. And that includes when we stop." Ruby moved her hands from Jaccob's chest to his face, stroking his soft beard with her thumbs.

"You know it's not you, right?" he asked her, suddenly much more serious than he'd been just a moment ago.

Ruby nodded. Even though she had known that, it was still good to hear. Maybe he wasn't quite ready to go to bed with her, but it seemed as though he was at least ready to *talk* about going to bed with her. It was the least she could do to hear him out.

"It's just that I was married for a long time," he continued. Ruby had to suppress any expression of the glee she felt at his having used the past tense. "I haven't been with anyone else. I was faithful. All those years—" His voice trailed off and he pursed his lips for a moment.

Her magic would have let her in on what he was feeling in that moment, but she hadn't managed to figure out the particulars of using the Eye for such things, and there was something about the potential gravity of this moment that made her think better of having a try. Without it, Ruby had to be content using her mundane sensitivities. And those were telling her that Jaccob was having a moment of anger at his wife. All the better that she let him have it. She nodded again.

"I know," she affirmed. "It's all right. Whatever you're feeling about any of this, it's all right."

Tentatively, Jaccob placed his hands on her waist, bending his face to kiss her.

Ruby was careful not to return the kiss too fiercely. It was clear he still had some hesitation, and she didn't want to push too hard and spoil things. She knew she could seduce him then. It wouldn't even be any work. She could quicken her kisses, press her breasts against him firmly, and allow her hands to wander just so, and he'd be putty in her hands.

Men were easy like that. They were wired that way. Once a man was being handled with a particular finesse, all qualms and questions, all doubts and hesitations, anything at all that might be on his mind would vanish with the rush of blood from his brain to other regions. Even without magic to aid her, Ruby knew she could have him. But without magic, she knew she'd have no way to mitigate the morning-after regret he was likely to have if they rushed into things before he was ready. As much as she was sure the power of the Eye of Africa would be up to such a task, this was far too delicate a thing to trust to a power with which she was not yet intimately familiar. This was not an occasion for experiments. As frustrating as it was to hold back, Ruby knew patience would net her better long-term gain.

"That's nice," she whispered as their lips parted.

Jaccob dared to bring his hands forward, to where the belt on her dressing gown was coming loose. He slid his hands inside of it, bringing them to rest at the same spot on her waist they had been, only this time pressed into bare skin instead of thick silk.

Ruby delighted in the way his fingertips pressed into her sides and in the warmth of his palms against her as he bent his head to kiss her again.

Slowly, and fully prepared to stop if so prompted, she tugged his shirt tail from his trousers as his kiss grew more excited. She ran her hands over the rippled muscles of his back, careful to return his fervor but not to be the one to move things along. It was oddly titillating to Ruby to have to be so patient and submissive. If she were being completely honest with herself, it was driving her a little crazy. It certainly wasn't her usual approach, but as she felt Jaccob's hands sliding slowly up her sides until his thumbs found the curve of her breasts, she could tell it was working. She found it an interesting mental exercise—encouraging him without taking the lead—and she was having to keep her head about her in a way she preferred not to in these kinds of circumstances.

After a moment, Jaccob stopped kissing her. He stepped back, his breath ragged, his hands now on her hips, where his fingers had found the lace at the top of her garter belt. She let go of him then, letting her hands drop to her sides as she looked at him expectantly. "I," he said after a moment, his breath coming almost in gasps, "think you may have left the windows open downstairs."

"Maybe," she answered coyly, understanding now that he was making an excuse to head toward the bedroom. If he needed an excuse, then she was happy to let him have one.

"Do you think—?" he asked, a tiny blush rising to his cheeks as he momentarily averted his gaze from hers. "—we should go and check? I mean… it really isn't safe to—"

"Yes." Ruby's firm affirmation cut him off. "Let's go to the bedroom, and shut the windows."

CHAPTER
FIFTEEN

t had not been the best sex of her life. In fact, if she thought hard about it, it probably didn't rate in the top 100. But as Ruby lay awake in the dim light of her opulent bedroom, she nonetheless felt thoroughly satisfied. She had gone to bed with Stardust, and that was thrilling, even if the actual act had left something to be desired.

Breaking in widowers and divorcés had never been her favorite pastime, but in this case, she was more than willing to put in the work. Jaccob had been a careful lover, timid at first, and even after he'd seemed to relax a bit, his tastes had seemed almost painfully vanilla. Still, he'd been tender with her, thoughtful, and *my* but did he have stamina!

He was sleeping now, rolled onto his side facing her with the thin gray of the bamboo sheet covering him to just above his waist, the plush down comforters having been long ago relegated to the floor at the foot of the bed. He'd been strangely needy when things were done, and she'd accommodated him as best she could, waiting until he had drifted off to extricate herself from his embrace.

Glancing at the clock, it was nearly two a.m. She knew she should be trying to get some sleep. But she was antsy. Emotionally satisfied, but physically less so, she lay in her bed and watched the lights of the city as they flickered in the distance, her fingers positively twitching to touch the Eye of Africa again. It had given her a buzz of sorts when she'd lay her hand on it earlier, perhaps doing so again would be enough to get her past the mild level of frustration she was still feeling and allow her to get some sleep. Her alarm would be going off at eight no matter what, and she had a nine a.m. meeting with a band, no member of which had ever been terribly pleasant to deal with before noon. Her morning would be made better by a strong pot of French Roast and a few decent hours of sleep.

The difficulty lay, of course, in the very real possibility of getting caught. More than once since she'd disentangled her limbs from those of her guest, he'd reached for her in his sleep and found purchase on her body once more. There was every chance he could wake up, even slightly, roll over, and catch her with it. That was a risk she wasn't ready to take, even though he almost certainly wouldn't recognize the Eye of Africa for what it was. The local news was still following the case almost nightly, and from what Ruby could tell, the CCPD hadn't made a lot of progress.

Even with all the news coverage, there had been no photographs released of the Eye itself, only of the case it had been in before Decay had dispatched it in the alley. Stardust *might* have been shown a picture that hadn't been released to the public, but an added bonus to Ruby's decision to express interest in All Things Stardust was that he'd been rather loose-lipped about the whole investigation. Seeing as he hadn't mentioned any such photograph, Ruby could be reasonably confident that none were available.

Still, if Jaccob were to roll over and catch her fondling some gem in her drawer, the least he'd do was ask questions. And she didn't want to answer questions. She wanted to touch the Eye.

Ruby rolled over and looked loosely at Jaccob. He was sound asleep. She was sure. His breaths were deep and even, his eyes were shut, and there wasn't even the slightest sign of a twitch in his muscles. It might not be safe to take the Eye from its hiding place, but sliding the drawer open a few inches and reaching her hand beneath the salt blanket for a moment shouldn't be a problem. And if that wasn't enough, there was always the cold shower.

Ruby rolled again to the edge of the bed. Perched on her left side, she reached with her right hand toward the silver knob protruding from the nightstand drawer. Gently, so the rollers on the track would make as little sound as possible, she pulled the little drawer ajar before turning her head on her pillow to be sure Jaccob hadn't been disturbed. He was still. Ruby took a deep breath. Good. That was good. Just one brush of her fingers against the Eye of Africa and maybe she'd be able to settle in to sleep. She slid her fingers beneath the salt-tiled fabric covering the magical item.

It was a rush not unlike the orgasm the evening had so far been lacking. But rather than satiate her, it energized her. There was no way she was getting to sleep now. There was magic in her, and she needed to use it. She was aching with the totem's energy; she needed to move, she needed to engage.

Ruby looked over again at Jaccob. He was sound asleep. She slung her legs over the side of the bed and rose slowly. She crept across the plush carpets to where her dressing gown had been flung over a chair. She wrapped herself in the semi-sheer silk before reaching down and pulling the comforter from its resting place on the floor to occupy the space she'd just vacated on her side of the bed. There was a chance Jaccob would reach for her again in his sleep; she was gambling that finding *something* in her place would be less likely to wake him than finding nothing at all.

Satisfied that she'd done all she could do, she tiptoed out of the bedroom and across the hall into her music room. The magic of the Eye seemed to follow her, wafting into her awareness like the scent from a candle as she slid open the door to the marble-floored conservatory. She'd left the drawer cracked on purpose—hoping to maximize access to the magic without risking exposing the artifact to her guest's curious eyes—and the connection she felt to it even as she walked away was truly stirring. That was good.

She'd had magic to do tonight—an agenda that had been interrupted by an unexpected, albeit welcome, visit from Stardust. Perhaps getting a bit of her intended work done would exorcise enough of the wildness she was feeling to allow her a few hours rest before her day began. And if there was arcane work to be done in the penthouse, it needed to begin in the most sacred space the high-rise had on offer.

Ruby guessed most people would find it odd that the CEO of an entertainment conglomerate would consider her music room to be private space. Most people in her position would likely have put such a thing in a more social place in their home. But Ruby Killingsworth was not *most people*. Her music room was a precious place, second only to the prepared magical space beneath her mansion in the pantheon of what she guarded.

It wasn't widely known among her peers and associates that Ruby was capable of making music herself. She'd mostly been able to keep it secret that she'd started out in the business as a singer/songwriter.

She'd been a bit of a prodigy, to be honest. But she'd learned very quickly that the life of a performer just wasn't for her. Plenty of them were wealthy enough to be comfortable, but a scant few made enough money to keep up their lifestyle as their careers waned; a pop artist's career was bound to wane eventually. Add to that the way performers were owned, managed, and *handled* by the labels, and Ruby decided rather quickly that she preferred life on the corporate side of the music business.

She'd come to work for Goblin Records straight out of high school. As an intern, she'd all but completely taken over Cassidy Sweet's wildly successful multinational tour of shopping malls. Only a few years later, having orchestrated one of the greatest sales coups in the conglomerate's history, Ruby found herself suddenly occupying an office that read "Junior Vice President" on the door. Her climb up the ladder to CEO hadn't taken long after that.

Of course, magic had played no small part in her elevation from intern to mogul in record time. And these days, her musical abilities were second only to her magical ones on the list of precious, secret things. Her music room, on the private level of her residence, across the hall from her bedroom, was effectively a shrine to the relationship between music and magic and the success she'd found. Magical items and cloaked foci hid in plain sight, sharing shelf space with her music books and posing as objets d'arte placed about on occasional tables under the guise of decoration.

This room was the center of her magical presence in the penthouse, and it was the anchor point for the wards she'd spun to protect the place. She'd meant to spend tonight reinforcing those wards with the power of the Eye of Africa when Jaccob had shown up with other plans. Now that he was duly sated and sound asleep, she decided it was worth giving her intended task a try.

Worst case scenario, the Eye wouldn't cooperate with her attempts to channel and focus its power, and she'd wind up once again affected by drain. Seeing as it was nearly two in the morning, and she had every reason to want to be tired right now (not to mention several hours ahead of her during which it would be perfectly reasonable to sleep it off), she felt like she had very little to lose in the attempt.

But first, she needed to get the feel of the Eye. Making use of a focus, especially one as powerful as the Eye of Africa, for the first time was a massive undertaking. There was a learning curve to all magic, one that grew steeper the more powerful it was. Using it to shore up magical security without having tested her mastery of it was unlikely to end well. As deeply as she could feel its magic at the moment, the Eye wasn't fully hers to command. She was sure she could channel it, but she needed to feel what it was like to use and control this power before she tried to put it to use.

Ruby crossed slowly but deliberately to her piano. There was a book of music already on the stand, she opened it to a favorite song and took a seat on the bench. Inhaling deeply, focused on the feeling of this new magic and how it felt within her body, she placed her fingers over the key signature at the top of the piece, and shut her eyes. The music played then, the notes sounding flawlessly in Ruby's head as she passed her fingers over the notes on the page before her.

The song was perfect, finding its tempo as the speed of her hand waxed and waned along the staff. The music was coming from her bones, reverberating outward enough to rattle the lid to the piano's keyboard. She concentrated then, reining in the magic as best she could to control the volume—there would be too much to explain were the sound to wake Jaccob.

With a flick of her wrist, the music left the page. Sounding in her ears and reverberating down to her bones, the staff and its notes whirled about the room, visible all around when she opened her eyes. Ruby danced beneath herself, spinning and swaying as the ebb and flow of the stirring melody moved her, all the while careful not to let the song become audible past her own ears.

Her arms moved wildly now, conducting the phantom piano in frenzied crescendo as the music swirled about the room—visible staffs spiraling around her and filling the space from floor to ceiling. The sound became a tumult, magically sustaining notes and blending chords one into the next. Ruby was finding it harder and harder to control the tempo and the volume. She grounded herself, digging her feet into the floor as though in attempt to anchor a tug-of-war and strained her arms against the force of the music in her head and in her sights as it tried to carry her off. The notes were glowing, somehow ink-black and yet incandescent in the otherwise darkened room. Her heart was pounding, filling her ears with a percussion so discordant against the lights from the notes and the sounds in her ears that it made her nauseous.

It took all the strength she had; as though she were pulling against the power of a freight train, she silenced the music in her body. With a flick of her wrists, she returned the staffs to their place on the page. Ruby lurched toward the piano and slammed the book shut where it remained on the stand.

Her heart was still pounding, and she was decidedly short of breath. Her silk dressing gown clung to her skin in places, and her knees were about to give beneath her. It wasn't drain—not altogether— although there was an edge to how she felt that could certainly be attributed to that. This was fatigue. This was her body's inability to channel a power this intense without consequence.

She had been right to presume the magic of the Eye of Africa was far more powerful than any she'd encountered before. She could use it. She could access it now; she could channel it and direct it and use it for her own purposes. But her body wasn't used to being a vessel for power of this magnitude. If she meant to attempt a ritual that would imbue her with its power permanently, she would need to spend more time with it. She needed to further attune herself, to acclimate her body to the presence of energy like this.

She hadn't even begun to suss out what a ritual of this magnitude might look like, but experience told her it would be much longer and more involved than using the Eye to play a little music. If she were to succeed in binding the item's magic to herself, she would need to be conditioned to using it well enough to survive the experience. Ruby Killingsworth had never been an "or die trying" type of individual, and she wasn't about to start with this. Like any endeavor that required endurance, it would take training to work up to the ability to keep control over the item's magic for long enough to complete a ritual as involved as she was sure this would need to be.

But she'd had quite enough for tonight. As her heartrate returned to normal and she began to catch her breath again, Ruby felt as thought she'd just run a marathon. Or, rather, she felt as though she *imagined* she would were she to have just run a marathon. In truth, she'd never run anywhere in her life. But the metaphor stood in her head. She'd need to work up to a puissant ritual, but right now she needed to sleep.

With aching arms and on wobbly legs, she made her way back to the bedroom. She slid her sweat-dampened wrap off her shoulders and wadded it up before using it to blot away the excess moisture from her skin. She ducked into her closet and threw on a lace shift before tiptoeing back to the far side of the room and slipping back into bed beside Jaccob.

She pulled the comforter up over herself, delighting in the feel of the cool fabric on her still-fevered skin. She'd be able to sleep now, she was sure. Carefully, Ruby rolled onto her side and reached into the drawer to re-cover the Eye with its protective fabric. She'd still be connected to the magic, even through the protective layers she'd provided it, but the thrumming of the thing would be muted enough in the sealed drawer to allow her to sleep as soundly as her exhausted body was demanding.

A klaxon sounded suddenly then, breaking through the silence of the bedroom and nearly causing Ruby to fall off the edge of the bed. She barely had the presence of mind to slam the drawer shut as she sat bolt upright and searched for the source of the noise. She tried to access the magic of the Eye again; was that the cause of the alarm? Was someone trying to access it? Was it fighting back against being put away now that it had been taken out and used?

Ruby felt herself beginning to panic. Suddenly the lead lined drawer, clay box, and salt tiled cloth seemed woefully inadequate. Something might be going terribly wrong and she had no idea what it was or what she could do about it. For the moment she had to put those concerns aside. Before she was able to take on any magical investigations, she was going to have to handle the man beside her. Explaining away some stray alarm sounds to the person who had literally designed the alarm systems in this building was going to be quite a feat. She could only hope it had been a while since he'd heard the sound of the alarms he'd wired into this building and could perhaps mistake whatever this was for one of his.

She had only just begun to even consider the possibility that the sound actually *was* one of the building's alarms when Jaccob squirmed in the bed and groaned. She was sitting up, with the sheet tucked under her arms and an expression on her face that she hoped wasn't too panicked.

Jaccob rolled onto his side facing away from her and reached out for something on the far night stand.

It was his wristwatch. Or, rather, it was the device Jaccob wore that passed for a wristwatch but was actually a lot of things connected to Stardust. Had that thing been what had made all that noise? He sat up in bed, the device in his hand, and fiddled with its tiny screen before turning his head and looking at Ruby woefully.

"Sorry about this," he said, holding up the device. The claxon had stopped as soon as he'd laid his hand on the thing. And he seemed nonplussed, if a little sullen, about the alarm. What he didn't seem was at all *alarmed* by it, so Ruby figured his gadget had been what had caused the terrible racket and that maybe she'd be able to get her heart to stop pounding in a minute.

"You could have warned me," she said to him, "I about jumped out of my skin."

"Sorry," Jaccob said again, scooting over in the bed until he was able to lean in and kiss her cheek. "I didn't think about it. I'm so used to it—" His voice trailed off and Ruby could tell he wasn't sure what to say next. He'd probably never had to tell a woman about his insanely loud Stardust alarm before because he'd only ever been with one woman before now—and she probably pre-dated the wristwatch thing.

"It's very loud," Ruby commented, trying to sound as jovial as possible as she tried to shake the nauseated feeling of the adrenaline leaving her system. She was already exhausted. She was trying her best to look on the bright side—she was sure once this wore off, she'd have no trouble falling asleep.

"Yeah," Jaccob affirmed, still sounding a little embarrassed, "I can be a really sound sleeper. So—"

"So when the city needs Stardust, he doesn't have the option of a snooze button?" Ruby reached over and put her hand on Jaccob's knee as he nodded.

"Yeah," he replied. "Look, Ruby, I'm really sorry, but—"

"But you have to go," she surmised, interrupting him before he could finish the thought.

He nodded again, stifling a yawn as he reached over and patted her hand where it lay on his leg.

"Jaccob," she addressed him then, finding it somewhere in her to smile, "I'm not mad. I'm a little disappointed, but I'm not upset."

He leaned over and kissed her again before scooting to sit on the edge of the bed. After strapping the watch-like device back onto his left arm, he retrieved his shorts from the floor and pulled them on as he stood. Jaccob pulled on his trousers next, finding them in a lump not far from where his shorts had been. He then spent a moment looking around the room as though he were a bit perplexed.

"Over there," Ruby said, pointing to a chair on the far side of the room that was somehow where his undershirt had come to rest.

"Thanks," Jaccob said back, crossing the room to the chair she had indicated and throwing his shirt over his head. "I really am sorry about this."

Ruby shrugged as she moved to recline against her pillows. "Don't apologize," she insisted. "It's not your fault." She took a deep breath as Jaccob walked back to the head of the bed and bent down, kissing Ruby gently on her forehead before turning to leave.

"Good night," he said to her.

"Good night, Jaccob. When you catch those bad guys," she called after him as he reached the doorway, "I think I'm going to want a word with them." She was scowling playfully, and when Jaccob turned his head, he grinned back at her.

"That should be enough to strike fear into the hearts of anyone who would dare to break the law in the middle of the night," he joked, flashing her a smile over his shoulder before passing through the bedroom door and closing it softly behind him.

Ruby chuckled as she pulled the comforter up under her chin. She took a deep breath and sighed as she settled in to her pillows and blankets.

He had no idea.

The day would come when she'd fill him in, but there was a lot of work ahead before that could happen. There was much magic in her future. But first, she would sleep.

CHAPTER SIXTEEN

Getting out of bed the next morning hadn't been the chore Ruby had guessed it might be. Normally, functioning after less than five hours of sleep ended badly for her, and worse for anyone with whom she may have needed to conduct business. But the morning after the Pops, she'd rolled over in bed, slid open her drawer, and run her fingers over the Eye of Africa before so much as sitting up beneath the covers. That single action had done more to spur her to wakefulness than a whole pot of strong coffee ever had.

Not that she was planning to skip her morning coffee—quite the contrary. She threw on her black silk dressing gown, hastily discarded over a chair during the previous night's adventures, brushed her teeth, and darted upstairs to retrieve her first cup of the day before dressing. Her household staff had learned over the years that Ruby was not to be dealt with before she was properly caffeinated. It was no secret that Miss Killingsworth was not a morning person. The house manager at the mansion and the building manager who also handled the domestic staff for the penthouse were both well aware that new hires were to be told in no uncertain terms to avoid interacting with their employer before she left for work in the morning. This interdiction had come after many, many members of the household staff had been dismissed (and a few of them literally cursed) for inciting Ruby's ire before coffee. Both her temper and her penchant for revenge had become legendary in the music business, and those fearsome traits were never more prominent than when she was insufficiently caffeinated.

Her full pot of properly steeped French press coffee was on the counter where it belonged, her stark white ceramic mug and Goblin Records travel cup flanking it on either side. And there was not a soul in sight. Magic and coffee and not having to deal with other people—that was exactly how Ruby Killingsworth liked her mornings to go. She'd wondered when he'd left if Jaccob might be coming back, although she was pretty sure he wouldn't. They hadn't discussed it, and she wasn't sure that one episode of burgeoning carnal knowledge was enough to get him to change his opinion on when it would be appropriate to let himself into her apartment. It was probably for the best he hadn't come back.

She'd never gotten used to the idea of overnight company, always having preferred her gentlemen callers to take their leave as soon as it was polite. There was a niggling feeling in the back of Ruby's mind that this was likely not going to be the case with Jaccob; if his penchant for post-coital cuddling was any indication, she'd likely be awaking to find him still in her bed more often than not in the near future. She briefly entertained the notion of trying to steer things to his place—that way she could be the one to politely excuse herself in the middle of the night. But she thought better of it almost right away. His place was likely teeming with mementos of marriage and family and all that *stuff* he was still hung up on. And hangups never made for lessened inhibition. No, if she wanted the sex to get better, it would have to happen at her place.

She poured the delightfully aromatic dark liquid into the stark white ceramic mug and took a whiff. It was a small price to pay, she figured, for adding Stardust to her list of trophies. Having him in her bed overnight and dealing with him in the morning might not even be so bad, as long as the Eye of Africa was there to boost her mood even before coffee had the chance to.

The magic had certainly helped her mood immensely, and this day at the office had been a particularly trying one. Although meetings with the members of Metalcholy always bordered on ridiculous, this morning's had been extra laughable. Once again, she'd had to remind the heavy metal band's lead guitarist that it was off-brand and unacceptable for him to go about town in khakis and a polo shirt. And not for the first time, she'd threatened him with a personal stylist if he didn't go out and "at least buy some damned blue jeans." She didn't have a problem with heavy metal music appealing to all types, nor with the fact that Sturg was a math nerd who liked to work out his guitar chords on a slide rule. But she wasn't sure how the hard-core base of fans that kept the band lucrative would appreciate being let in on that little bit of trivia. It was the least he could do to try and look the part of rebellious rocker. She was glad to be able to share the news that she'd won the fight with the insurance company—they'd be able to have the rollergirls in their next music video. She could deal with the band herself, but the rest of the details of that shoot were going to be managed somewhere far beneath her pay grade. She had neither the patience nor the energy these days to handle a misfit metal band, a crew of adequate size to shoot this thing, and twenty-odd degenerate women on roller skates.

Ruby happily passed that buck right down the hill to her underlings. Sometimes it was good to be the boss. Sure, when issues like the one with the insurance company couldn't be resolved by her staff, they would eventually end up on her desk. But there were layers and layers of personnel between her and most of the problems the label experienced, and she liked those layers. She paid some of those layers very, very well to handle things like roller skating metal heads for her. So when her receptionist, Bridget, knocked on her door to let her know there was another band in her outer office, she wasn't sure what to think about it.

She didn't have another band on her schedule today. "What band are you talking about, Bridget?" she asked, trying not to get too cross with her friendly, white-haired receptionist. Bridget had been the face of the Goblin Records' outer office for several years prior to Ruby's having taken over. And if a career in multimillion-dollar entertainment had taught her anything up to that point, it was that it did no one any good to fix what wasn't broken. Her personal assistant she brought with her to the position, but the receptionist kept her job, and Ruby had no plans to run her off. Bridget was kind, grandmotherly, patient, pleasant, and soft spoken; she was everything Ruby was not. And she was everything the gatekeeper to the inner workings of an entertainment empire needed to be. Ruby couldn't be gruff with her, even if she did need more coffee.

"The one you've had in the studio all this last month," Bridget answered. "The odd ducks. Oh—" Bridget frowned and shook her head.

Ruby was frowning, too. She was pretty sure whoever was in her lobby had no business being there. It was either a prank being pulled by artists in her stable (to what end she could not guess) or it was some musical act who, in hopes of getting a meeting with the head of the label, had talked their way past security and was now pestering Bridget into thinking Ruby actually wanted to see them. She had half a mind to call the police and have them escorted out in handcuffs.

"What did they say they were called?" Bridget asked herself out loud.

"It doesn't matter what they call themselves," Ruby began to tell her. But before she was able to instruct Bridget to call security, the older woman looked back up as the answer obviously came to mind.

"The Blights," Bridget told her boss. "I knew it was some sort of a name with tribulations in it. But I couldn't remember. I guess it's the old age. But that's it. The Blights are here to see you."

Ruby was suddenly very glad of her uncharacteristic hesitation at calling the police on trespassers. She had forgotten that the dismissal she'd given the Blights when they'd first come into her service had included the directive "record an album or something." She wondered if they really had been making music all that time.

But that was a question for another day. If they had come all the way back down here from Regency Heights, then there had to be a reason. "Oh, yes," Ruby replied, playing off her earlier suspicion. "The Blights. They are an odd bunch, but they might be on to something. Send them in, Bridget."

"Right away, ma'am," the older woman replied, turning and shuffling back to the outer office to let the Blights in. Ruby sat back in her chair for a moment and appreciated that the band of Tulpas had asked Bridget to let them in rather than make any attempt to trick, lie, or otherwise sneak their way past the office staff. That was a little unexpected coming from a group of magical beings on loan from Loki, but it was a pleasant surprise to say the least.

As the group of them ambled into her office, it gave Ruby a moment's pause wondering how someone who had been around the music business as long as Bridget had could possibly have taken them for a band. But then she stopped to consider the conversation she'd just had with Sturg Ramstehl of Metalcholy about not making his way through the world dressed like the father of an Ivy League dudebro and decided she already knew the answer.

"Shut the door," she instructed Fire, as the orange-haired young woman brought up the rear of the group filing into her office. Once the door was securely closed, Ruby pressed a little button on the underside of her desk. It was a modified version of the "recording" light buttons they used in the studios, and part of the security system Starcom Security had installed for her before she moved her offices into the Ruby Tower. A light would come on in her outer office and another at the reception desk that said in no uncertain terms that Miss Killingsworth was not to be disturbed for any reason. As long as that light was burning, she and the Blights wouldn't be bothered.

She also flipped the switch that activated both the Faraday cage and the active sound interference mechanisms she'd had built into this office. Corporate espionage and creative thievery were real problems in the entertainment business, and Ruby wanted to make sure no one could listen in on her meetings with artists. The intellectual property discussed in this office could literally be worth billions, and so she'd had every information security measure that Starcom had to offer installed.

It was helpful to know no one could listen in on her talks with the Blights, either. Just in case anyone suspected her of malfeasance— which she was sure no one did at the moment—it was better to be safe than sorry on matters such as this. She indicated to her group of visitors that they should have a seat on the white leather sofa and chairs to her right. She'd learned a long time ago that bands liked to "chill" when they were being creative, and having something approximating a living room in her office helped with that. Seating for ten that didn't involve the conference table across the room apparently came in handy for more than just self-involved pop singers.

The Blights settled in without a word to each other or to Ruby. Fire, Doubt, and Pestilence took up residence on the sofa, Ruin and Decay made themselves comfortable in the overstuffed chairs, while Plague plopped down lotus-style on the floor in front of the glass coffee table and began picking through the bowl of hard candy and lozenges that Ruby kept for singers. She frowned down at him as she crossed to sit in the high-backed armchair that faced the table and couch. It was a throne-like art nouveau piece that shouldn't have gone with the rest of the décor in Ruby's ultra-modern office, but somehow fit in perfectly. The Blights had guessed correctly that this chair was reserved for the boss, and that no one had better so much as think about sitting in it. Cody, the most clueless of the Young Dudes, had almost made the mistake of claiming it when they'd come in to hear about the first-week sales of their sophomore album, but it had taken only a single raised eyebrow from Ruby to stave off that bad decision.

Good thing, too. The Young Dudes had made her a lot of money—were *still* making her a lot of money. It would be a pity to have to kill one of them.

"So, what do you have to tell me?" Ruby asked before she was even fully in her seat. She surveyed the group of them together and frowned. "Did you know that she thinks you're a band?"

"We've been in a recording studio every day for the past two months," Doubt reminded her. "Of course she thinks we're a band."

Ruby rolled her eyes as she settled farther back into her chair. "You'll have to let me hear what you've got," she drawled, the sarcasm as clear in her voice as the Blights had ever heard it. "But we're not here to talk about music right now, are we?" she asked with an abrupt change in tone. "You wouldn't be here in the middle of the day if you didn't have something to tell me. So tell." She crossed her legs and leaned lightly against the back of the chair, her arms regally draped over the velvet cushioned armrests. "You spoke with Discontent." The group of them nodded. "And?"

"Your ritual isn't in that book we found," Pestilence told her.

"My ritual?" Ruby asked. She wasn't sure she had ever mentioned the word "ritual" in front of the Blights; in fact, she was pretty sure she hadn't ever actually said it out loud in relation to the Eye of Africa. That made any reference they made to a ritual highly suspect. Knowing for herself she would need to perform some feat of ritual magic in order to take on the power of the Eye was one thing, having it be common knowledge all of the sudden was something else altogether. She narrowed her eyes and waited for her answer.

"Yeah," Fire answered, fidgeting in her seat. "The book talks about a ritual. It talks about The Queen of Sheba and how she was a witch who refused to properly submit to King Solomon, maybe, and how she had this thing that we're pretty sure is The Eye of Africa and that there's rumored to be some ritual that she created with it that could give someone ultimate power or whatever. But the book is really bible-y, and it's mostly a lot of Satan-this and witchcraft-that, and you really don't want anyone to know about this, so how about they maybe ought to avoid the Old Testament—"

"If we had a Jewish or a Muslim source," Doubt chimed in, "then we might have a better chance at getting information. Maybe."

"But there is one thing that we got that might be worth investigating," Plague said.

Ruby perked up a bit. She had been afraid that the book they'd found might be too churchy, but that was sadly the price to pay for having books that dated back to the invention of the printing press. Christianity had the market cornered on the written word for a whole lot of years, and any codex of a certain age was inevitably going to be tainted by liturgical concerns.

"What's that?" she asked. They hadn't come here en masse to tell her they had nothing.

"It refers to some scrolls. Jewish scrolls," Fire elaborated, turning to look at Doubt beside her on the sofa.

"There might be some information on some scrolls," Doubt conceded.

"Oh, but let me guess," Ruby said back, "they're under the Smithsonian? Or the British Museum? Or they're being held in some top-secret location in Jerusalem because only the holiest of holinesses or whatever can look on them or they're afraid of terrorists? Or something?"

Ruby rolled her eyes again. She had a passing familiarity with religion, and she was reasonably well versed in a number of traditions. But she'd never had any affinity for faiths, especially the big, monotheistic ones. And her last experience having anything at all to do with religions had left a very, very bad taste in her mouth. If she absolutely had to pick one of them to have to deal with in this instance, she supposed she should at least be pleased it was Judaism; they were the least crazy about most things, and she had at least a modicum of respect for their mystical traditions.

"It's across town," Ruin said plainly.

"I'm sorry, what?" Ruby replied, sitting up straighter in her chair. An intrigued frown descended involuntarily onto her face. "It's where?"

"It's part of a touring exhibit," Plague chimed in.

"And that exhibit is where?" Ruby quizzed. She wasn't so much wanting details right now, but knowing there was an ancient document that hadn't been tampered with by Catholicism that referred to the Eye of Africa and might have some information for her as to how she could go about getting its power—and knowing *exactly* where she might find such a thing—well, those were important matters.

"At the Cultural History Museum," Fire told her with a shrug.

"They're thousands of years old," Doubt asserted. "And they're in Aramaic. Even if they are the same scrolls the book mentions, which there's actually no guarantee that they are—"

"Discontent said the name the book calls the scrolls and the name the anthropologists at the museum think belongs to the scrolls is the same name," Decay piped up for the first time today.

"And how did Discontent know what the anthropologists say is the name that belongs to them?" Ruby asked. If she hadn't so much as known these scrolls existed, much less that they were being studied in a museum in her own city, she had to wonder how it was that one of the Blights could have known so much about it.

"Mrs. Stevens sits on the board," Ruin answered. "Discontent has been around the scrolls already because of hanging around with your boyfriend's wife."

Ruby winced and then chuckled. The idea of a woman her age and in her position having someone in her life referred to as a "boyfriend" seemed quite preposterous, and the idea of billionaire superhero Jaccob Stevens having that title applied to him more so.

"Of course she's on the board," Ruby groaned. A few years back, Elizabeth Stevens had quit her job working in the upper echelon of Starcom to be a full-time philanthropist. It was no surprise at all to hear she was on the board of the Cultural History Museum. "So the scrolls we need," she began again, shifting back to the topic at hand, "they're in some vault at the Cultural History Museum. We can handle that, right? The last vault we broke into was in a goddamned police station. A museum can't be any harder, can it?"

"Not in a vault," Doubt declared flatly.

Ruby frowned. "I'm not following."

Doubt shrugged and continued. "The scrolls," she said, "they're not in a vault. They're out on exhibit. They're in some glass cases out in the open where people can *ooh* and *ahh* and be impressed by the ancient Aramaic calligraphy or whatever."

"So they're just out in the open?" Ruby asked. Her mind was spinning. "We can just go and look at them?"

"Yeah," Fire affirmed.

"And that makes them harder to steal," Doubt pointed out. "They're in view of the public all day long and patrolled by actual security guards all night. It'd be easier if they were in a vault."

The gears in Ruby's head were turning. Could it really be this easy? She leaned forward in her chair and rested her elbows on her knees. "Maybe we don't need to steal anything," she suggested quietly.

"I beg your pardon?" Plague asked, his mouth full of candy.

Ruby shrugged. "What if we don't need to steal the scrolls?" she asked rhetorically. "If they're out on exhibit and the whole public can have a look, then that means *we* can have a look. And if we can look at them, and we can read them, then there's every chance we can learn either A: what's left of the scrolls doesn't have the information we need and we're back to square one or, B: that I can perform this ritual they describe based on just having read the scrolls and having them physically present isn't necessary. Now, there's always the chance that it turns out the magic is in the scrolls, and I'm going to need them in my hands to get what I want out of them, in which case we're going to have to figure out how to steal them anyway. But if they're really just out in the open and publicly accessible, then I think our best move is to go to the museum and see." She was met with a chorus of nods from the Blights.

"Worst case scenario," she continued, "we've had a chance to case the joint, which will be helpful if we wind up having to steal the scrolls."

More nods. Even Doubt seemed to be on board with the plan. This was an interesting and promising development. Ruby had been sure there would be some way to concoct a ritual to absorb the power of the Eye into herself, but she hadn't even begun to imagine there would be one already in existence. The idea that there was such a rite, and that it purportedly originated with the creator of the object was almost too good to be true. She could only hope there was enough information in those scrolls to allow her to successfully replicate it.

And there was only one way to find out.

CHAPTER
SEVENTEEN

The Cobalt City Museum of Cultural History was one of those buildings that could not have been mistaken for anything other than a museum. It was a too-large stone and glass building erected in the waning years of the nineteenth century, when building large museums was in vogue. All along the East Coast, these mammoth museums had sprung up, many of them almost identical to this one. In typical fashion, the museum sported a large rotunda in the front and a pair of two-story wings stretching from each side with small rooms off either end, forming a misshapen letter H. It sat across the street from the Cobalt City central library, a building of similar design erected in the same era. There was a bus stop directly in front of the museum that had been there since the "bus" was a rail cart pulled by a team of horses. Traffic in the area was always snarled, and there was painfully inadequate parking available.

The museum's ticket booth was housed in a temporary building out front with the Starcom Foundation logo emblazoned prominently on both sides. Ruby made her driver circle the block until she saw the Blights assembled in front of the blue-black structure. She had made sure they had the money for their own tickets; she wasn't about to let on that they were all there together. And she wasn't about to be the one waiting. She was surprised, but pleased all the same, to see

Discontent out front with the others. It would be good to have that resource available, although there was every chance that Ruin and Decay would have the power to read the aging, crumbling scrolls.

That was the thing with Ruin and Decay—everything came under their purview eventually. And these scrolls were thousands of years old. The photos Ruby had been able to bring up on her phone seemed to show they were in pretty rough condition. That meant that between the understandings of Ruin and Decay, what writing was left visible should be readily decipherable. And even if it wasn't readable by either of them, even if it wasn't readable by the combined powers of all the Blights put together, that was hardly the end of the world.

Ruby had become attuned enough to the Eye of Africa in the days it had taken her to plan this little museum excursion that she had been tempted to bring it along. She'd grown relatively confident she would be able to shield its presence, or at least the level of its power, from prying eyes were she to bring it out in public. The only real danger she saw was that she still wasn't sure how the spirits who spoke to this alleged young superhero Jaccob seemed to be counting on to help with the case figured in to things. Her best guess was that storing the Eye in a natural earth box was probably enough to keep them out. Ruby was no expert on spirits, but her understanding was they couldn't penetrate solid earth. The likelihood was that they would know there was *something* afoot—between the earthen box and the magical ward she'd cast around it—but they wouldn't be able to figure out what or why. Ruby still held that out as an option for a subsequent trip if she and the Blights weren't able to decipher the scrolls today.

The Scrolls of Solomon, as they had been christened by the marketing geniuses who'd sent them on world tour, were being housed in the West Back Room of the museum. The space had originally been intended to house an exhibit on Cobalt City's superheroes, but the library across the street had opened first and claimed that exhibit as its own. The feud between the two cultural institutions lasted to this day. But the net result was that the museum had an empty exhibit space that over the years had played host to everything from King Tut's golden sandals to the props used to make some of Hollywood's least successful science fiction franchises. Today it housed the Scrolls of Solomon.

The special exhibit required its own ticket, over and above the admission price to the museum. Ruby didn't give a damn about the money—an extra hundred or so bucks at this point literally did not matter. But the added security of a separate queue, complete with fraying velvet ropes, carpet runners that may have once been red, and the vest-clad, lanyard-wearing, terribly chipper elderly docent (who took her job way too seriously) really did. The banners and dramatic up-lighting, the bizarre theme music being piped through blown speakers, and the giant placards banning everything from backpacks to selfie sticks were all too much. The prohibitions against photography were particularly bothersome. She'd had a thought that maybe getting photos of the scrolls would come in handy.

Ruby had never liked it when the same rules applied to her as to everyone else. Most of the time, wealth, power, privilege, and fame had done enough to keep that from happening. But she knew better than trying to play any of that to her advantage any place where Elizabeth Stevens had considerable influence. Today she was doing all she could do to fly under the radar. But she still didn't like being treated like the proletariat. Having to show her ticket to the attendant at the exhibit entrance was annoying. For a moment, Ruby wished she *had* brought along the Eye of Africa, because without its presence, she couldn't be completely sure the little curse she'd whispered at the woman was going to do the trick. She decided to ask Plague to help her out before they left.

It took a few minutes for the group of them to all make it into the exhibit space together. There was a limit on the number of people the museum was allowing in to see the scrolls at one time. Ruby had picked a day and time for this visit when she thought the place would be at its least crowded, but she hadn't figured on the entire sixth grade from Cabot Academy being there on a field trip. Luckily, Ruin and Decay were at least a head taller than the average sixth grader and they were able to get a look even when the crowd was thick around the Scrolls.

The Scrolls of Solomon were laid out in sequence in a series of a shy-dozen credenzas arranged in a horseshoe around three sides of the square room. The cases had glass tops and a series of buttons along the edge. Each button activated one of the recessed drawers in the cabinet, bringing out on view for a minute before automatically recessing back into the dark, climate controlled cubby where it was kept. There were four segments to a credenza, some of them impossibly small, and only one drawer could be out at a time.

This was going to take hours. Fortunately, Ruin and Decay had already gotten to work. She had bought each of the Blights a burner phone and insisted they return the custodian's Starphone to where they had found it. The twins each had theirs secreted in their hand and were reading the text into them as best they could. Hopefully the recordings would be enough to begin decoding the ritual of the Eye. Discontent was angling for a spot just behind them and appeared prepared to do as they were doing.

But then what looked like a genuine smile came across Discontent's face, and they stepped away from the exhibit with a mildly excited wave. It seemed *off* to see Discontent smiling; it just felt wrong somehow. The smile itself was a little bit wrong, too, betraying the fact that its wearer didn't have much experience with smiling and wasn't quite sure how it was supposed to go.

Ruby's own smile grew similarly strained when she followed Discontent's path with her eyes and realized what had caused this strangely pleasant greeting to begin with.

Elizabeth Stevens had just walked into the room. If Ruby had to make a list of all the people in the whole entire world who she did not want to run into while she was trying to get work done, Elizabeth Stevens would be at the top of it. In fact, she may have been the totality of it. But she was here, and there was nothing that could be done about it. Fortunately, Discontent seemed to be managing her, and there was a distinct possibility Ruby could get out of here without ever being seen by her lover's wife.

But she really did want to have a look at the Scrolls of Solomon with her own eyes. She was terribly curious as to what reaction this stirring from the Eye of Africa she could feel possessing her might have to the viewing or the hearing of the words of its ritual. Between the sea of children and the woman in the back of the room, it seemed as though she might not get that chance today.

As frustrating as that was, Ruby had to remind herself the museum would still be here tomorrow. The exhibit wasn't scheduled to leave until sometime in the fall, so making a strategic retreat today would be a setback, but not a disaster. Still, she was sorely tempted to ask Plague to wander over to that side of the room for an introduction. The only thing that stopped her from doing that was the notion that, were Elizabeth Stevens were to come down with monkey pox or Ebola or something of the like, Jaccob would wind up having his kids around more often, and that would get in the way of their growing relationship.

Ruby wondered, almost idly, if maybe Pestilence could get a mouse to run up her rival's skirt or a hornet to sting her. That would be almost as good as monkey pox. She'd pulled her Starphone from her purse to send him a message when she felt a tap on her shoulder.

Ruby felt her whole body start. Her shoulders tensed and her mouth fixed itself into a snarl. Nobody but *nobody* touched Ruby Killingsworth without her consent. She was quivering with rage as she turned slowly to face her assailant, who was speaking softly to her.

"Excuse me, ma'am," a young docent in her green vest and sensible shoes addressed her. "But there are no photos allowed in here."

Ruby narrowed her eyes at the young woman. She could feel the magic rising to match her anger as she replied to the stranger. "I know that," she said back with an air of calm in her voice edged with just enough authority she could tell the other woman was already feeling small. "And I wasn't taking a picture, I was sending a message. And now I'm finished."

"Well, we don't allow pictures," the young woman repeated, as though she hadn't heard a word Ruby had said in reply.

Ruby shook her head and stepped away. She hadn't ever met the young docent's gaze throughout this exchange, instead keeping her gaze cast in the direction of Fire and Plague, who were hanging near the door, ready to make a distraction happen if necessary. Assuring Ruin and Decay adequate access to the scrolls was paramount, and the two near the door were only along to create mayhem if needed in furtherance of that goal. Plague knew exactly what she needed from him at that moment, as he was rushing to her side while Fire stood clearly poised to do some harm if called upon. Ruby was going to hate it when she had to return these Blights to Loki; this level of service from magically active beings was awfully hard to come by. There was definitely something to be said for borrowing minions from a God.

"Is there something wrong, Miss Killingsworth?" Plague asked as he approached, with the urgency of a bodyguard ready to call in SWAT. She and Plague exchanged a look that told the Blight everything he needed to know. He stopped and stood between the two women like a night club bouncer who saw a fight ready to break out.

"This horribly mistaken, egregiously underpaid person in ugly shoes—" she replied, her face deadpan, her voice as cool as if she were describing the color of the floor. "—thought incorrectly that I was in violation of the museum's no photography rule—when what I was actually doing was sending an email with billions of dollars' worth of implications. And in her misplaced zeal to enforce the rules to which she is bound, she chose to put her hands on me without my consent."

Plague nodded. He was standing straighter and looking quite official as he reached into his pocket and withdrew the phone she had gotten him. "Are you going to want to press charges?" he asked.

Ruby's lip quirked and her eyebrow rose a little. That was the perfect response. The docent seemed horrified and about ready to defend herself when Ruby answered him. "No, no, hardly worth it to clog up the court system when there was no real harm done."

The docent let out a sigh of relief as Plague nodded. "If that will be all then, ma'am?" he asked.

Ruby nodded. "You're dismissed, thank you."

Plague nodded and moved to put the phone back into his pocket as he began to walk away. He brushed his shoulder against the docent and mumbled a soft, "Excuse me," as he went.

The docent, clearly still horrified, just nodded and stepped back. Ruby wasn't sure whether it had been the mention of billions of dollars or the threat of arrest that had gotten to the woman, but either way, she'd been gotten to. That particular peon would almost certainly never put her hands on a strange woman in a Manu Julian dress again.

Plague strode with purpose back to his earlier position beside Fire, who it seemed had watched the whole episode while suppressing a giggle. Somehow, Plague looked a little less sickly at the moment. Ruby had to wonder if whatever he had done to adversely affect the offending young woman had taken some of the visible sickness away from him for a time.

She really had no idea how exactly the Blights worked.

She knew they were each the embodiment of the force after which they were named. And she had some idea, having worked with them for a couple of months now, that they were each endowed with powers connected to their root. They were each both the cause and the effect. It had been explained to her, though, that their genesis was as the effect. What she hadn't managed to figure out yet was the mechanism by which they could become the cause. She didn't know if it diminished them in any way. If Plague was at his core the net result of humanity's collective fear of plague and suffering from plague, then was his giving plague to someone on her request diminishing to him in any way? Were their powers finite? Was there the possibility for any of them to exceed the limits of their own existence and somehow work themselves out of being? She should probably find that out.

As it was, she was confident enough in humanity's constant obsession with the things that powered the Blights she was sure they weren't going anywhere while in her custody. If breaking into that vault at the CCPD hadn't done anything to damage Decay, then any of them had plenty enough power for her purposes.

The idea of giving that presumptuous docent something terrible and miserable had lifted her spirits enough that even the presence of Elizabeth Stevens wasn't going to get her down. And her mood had been even further boosted by having spotted Doubt making her way closer to where Discontent had the other woman engaged in conversation. Doubt's primary job during the operation today was to make sure the docents and security staff didn't notice what was going on with Ruin and Decay, but having her put a little energy into making sure that Mrs. Stevens didn't realize Ruby was in the room was a quite a relief. Ruby hadn't seen Elizabeth out again since that night at the Pops, and she really preferred to avoid a confrontation if at all possible.

She heard a buzzing sound coming from her purse and allowed herself to smirk as she pulled her Starphone from her bag again. She had guessed the message would be from Pestilence, letting her know he had gotten her order. But instead she found a message from Jaccob. He had made dinner reservations at Tessien's and was checking that she would be available to join him. They'd been getting together for dinner most nights since the night of the Pops concert, and it was becoming more and more routine for him to wind up staying over— for at least part of the night.

Stardust had been awfully busy of late, and as many as half the nights he'd spent with her, he was called away on some super-errand or another in the middle of the night. Ruby had wondered, but hadn't yet bothered to ask, how much of that business had to do with the Blights and whatever work Loki had them up to while they were in town. It didn't matter. She actually preferred it when he left in the middle of the night.

Ruby liked Jaccob. She liked him a lot. And when they were both awake, she genuinely enjoyed his company in a way she did with very few people. But he had a tendency to be clingy in his sleep; it was an affectation she neither enjoyed nor appreciated. She'd gotten better over the weeks at wriggling out of his embrace after he'd fallen asleep, but the sex had improved enough in that time that it usually left her quite tuckered, so waiting for him to pass out so she could get comfortable was annoying. Adding the fact that he would almost always curl up with her again if he awoke in the middle of the night, and her sleep was suffering more than she would have liked to admit. So the nights when he was called away were not so much a problem for her. The fact that Jaccob just saw her lack of moping at his taking leave at odd hours as her being supportive and agreeable was just icing on the proverbial cake.

She texted Jaccob back immediately, agreeing to dinner and adding a wicked double entendre at the end of the message so he understood she had intentions for after dinner as well. He texted her back a smiley face emoji and Ruby couldn't help but laugh out loud. Never before in her life had she known a man his age who communicated via emoji, much less the CEO of an international tech firm. Her laughter rang out a little louder in the marble-walled, dome-ceilinged room than she meant it to, and Elizabeth Stevens looked straight up at her. The tall woman frowned, and Ruby pretended not to have seen her there. Out of the corner of her eye, she saw Elizabeth shake her head and turn her attention back to whatever conversation she'd been engaged in with Doubt and the others.

Pestilence caught her gaze then and gave Ruby a stern nod, at which moment she surreptitiously turned her attention back to Jaccob's wife. Her gaze arrived just as a large black fly, and then another, and then another began to swarm around Elizabeth's face. Ruby was able to contain her laughter, but only just, as the three flies quickly became a swarm of a dozen or more. For minutes, no matter how she swatted and flailed, the flies enveloped Elizabeth's whole head until she covered her face with her hands and ran from the room, the flies in hot pursuit. Ruby wasn't sure how long Pestilence would be able to keep the swarm going—yet another bit about the powers of the Blights that she really ought to learn more about—but even if they dispersed the moment they were out of his sight, that had been lovely.

And as an added bonus: the bizarre incident of the flies swarming Mrs. Stevens had taken the attention of all in the room away from where Ruin and Decay were still at work reading from the scrolls. Ruby had to keep from laughing too loud, and she covered her mouth as though she were shocked rather than amused at the scene. But she was most certainly amused. In fact, she found the whole thing quite hilarious. It was enough to keep her laughing until Ruin and Decay gave her the signal that they had finished their task.

Flies swarming around the head of Elizabeth Stevens, a reservation for the chef's table at Tessien's with Jaccob, and the words to the ritual that could permanently endow her with the power of the Eye of Africa—this had been a very, very good day.

CHAPTER
EIGHTEEN

There was perhaps nothing in the life of a magic user more tedious than preparing for a ritual. And the ritual from the Scrolls of Solomon was more exacting than most. It made sense; a ritual to access something as powerful as the magic anchored in the Eye of Africa needed to be protected. No one but the most studied, most prepared, and most fastidious custodian of the item should be able to access its power.

But the work was nonetheless taxing and difficult.

The preparation was made all the more taxing and difficult by everything else on Ruby's schedule. Not only was her relationship with Jaccob getting more and more serious and taking up larger and larger chucks of her time, but she was still responsible for the day-to-day operation of Goblin Records. There were things she could blow off and let slide, and there were things she could delegate. Often she was able to assign a task to surrogates who were pleased and honored to be assigned a task directly by Ruby herself. She could trust her underlings, at least the ones she'd hired personally, so she wasn't too worried about giving them work she might ordinarily have done herself.

She also knew there was no small amount of talk among her staff about her relationship with Jaccob Stevens. And if they wanted to think these "chances to prove themselves" were acts of benevolence coming from a woman who was suddenly happy, she was going to let them go right ahead and think that. All the better to have their cooperation in giving her as much free time as possible.

There remained, however, the frustrating matter of things she could not delegate. When certain pieces of her business needed her attention, she had to give them her attention. There was still the ongoing battle with the insurance company over the Metalcholy shoot. The second day of production on the damned video, two of the rollergirls had been doing what they do, and one of them had wound up taking out a lighting instrument. This was, of course, *exactly* the kind of thing the insurance men had been nervous about in the first place. She'd wound up running all over town *herself* to see to it the deductible got paid and production stayed on schedule, which had cost her almost an entire day.

And the next day she'd spent consumed with development meetings. Normally, she'd have found a way to blow those off when she had something else she'd rather be doing. In fact, she'd oftentimes sent an assignee in her stead for reasons far less pressing than preparing for a ritual. But this month's slate of developing artists included Mike Stevens. She couldn't miss that one. Jaccob had mentioned that Mike seemed pleased with the trajectory he was on, but he wasn't really into sharing details. Ruby, of course, had promised to spy on the young musician for his father. But she knew she couldn't be seen playing favorites. If she was going to be in one of the development meetings, she'd have to take all of them.

They had at least been good meetings; she was encouraged by the growth of the Goblin Records stable. It was very likely that most, if not all, of them were going to make her a great deal of money. And she was more than pleased to learn that Mike Stevens was actually a very talented musician. It would have been no fun to have had to tell Jaccob otherwise. That one had been a particularly good meeting.

She'd happily make good on her offer to include him in the White House concert lineup.

It had been a good day of meetings, but Ruby would rather have spent the day preparing for the ritual. Prather's concert she could practically arrange in her sleep, but the Ritual of the Scrolls was a different animal altogether. There was a lot to be done in order to prepare for a ritual of this magnitude, and the first thing she absolutely needed to do was to find a way to understand it.

She had sent the Blights back into the studio on the forty-seventh floor to work on the recordings Ruin and Decay had made at the museum. Both of them had managed a reasonably thorough job of reading the Scrolls. Apparently the parchment had been through enough of both the requisite stressors to make them accessible to the twin Blights. Ruin and Decay had merged their recordings via the state-of-the-art audio suite in the Goblin Records digital studio, and had set to recreating the text, both in the original Phoenician writing and in a transliterated form more readily accessible for reading aloud. It had taken days for them to finish this process, but in the meantime, Ruby had been sent the raw audio from the museum to listen to. She'd loaded the tracks onto her private Starphone and had done her level best to listen to them between meetings. But after Jaccob had picked up her phone and accidentally caused it to start playing, prompting a panicked explanation of why a dead language was playing from her device, she'd decided to delete the recordings and wait for the Blights to finish their work.

For once, she was glad for Prather. He had been all but pestering her since their first meeting in her office, and he'd invited her to meet him at the White House ostensibly to discuss the upcoming concert. So what if it was Loki he really wanted to talk about, and so what if she had absolutely nothing to tell him? The photo ops would be priceless. Prather's personal cadre of White House photographers had done an admirable job of making even his despicable face look good in pictures; her impeccable makeup and smart summer suit would likely photograph extremely well. And if not, she'd surely have veto power over the shots by virtue of the fact that the President was begging her favor. At the very least, fielding his calls and planning her visit to Washington was helping to distract her from how slowly her progress toward regaining her powers was going.

She didn't need powers to assert her will over Prather. For that she had *leverage*, which she'd found throughout her life to be nearly as useful as magic for handling such concerns.

She'd given some thought to what Jaccob had said about not wanting to be associated with this administration. This *regime* as he'd called it. But it had been easy to dismiss his concerns. Surely he meant well, but there was a lot of information he didn't have. If he knew just how beholden the sitting President would be to her when this was all said and done, he'd understand. At least that's what she kept telling herself. Because, deep down, there was still a fear that maybe he wouldn't.

Jaccob was a Good Guy—a little too good sometimes if Ruby stopped to think about it. And maybe having the President, or anyone else in power, feeling like they owed you something wasn't something he'd be interested in. That was certainly a possibility. After all, the man had been saving Cobalt City for going on two decades, and she couldn't think of a time when he'd called in any of the favors the city owed him for that.

He was a good guy. And a Good Guy. And occasionally, it got to be a little much. He hadn't given her too much grief about her trip to Washington, but he hadn't asked her how it had gone, either. Maybe he'd have wanted to talk more about it over dinner. But maybe not—they tended to steer clear of contentious topics when they were out together. Their relationship had an ease to it, and Ruby credited that in part to their choosing to avoid talking about anything that might lead to a quarrel.

Whether Jaccob might have wanted to talk about her afternoon in D.C., Ruby decided she was better served canceling their plans in order to stay home and work on the ritual. Claiming she'd come back from her meeting swamped with new concerns over preparations for the White House concert, she'd politely made her excuses. Jaccob had tempered his obvious disappointment with characteristic understanding. That was certainly a perk of her lover having no clue about the entertainment business—between that and his natural tendency toward honesty and steadfast belief in the goodness of others, he always took her word on things like that. She'd spent the evening on her balcony, working with the first pieces of the transliteration the Blights had presented her with.

It was a chore to figure out just how much she could say at a time—too much and she might call forth magic she wasn't yet equipped to deal with. And a failure of a ritual of this magnitude could very well corrupt the magic forever and shut down the possibility of her ever succeeding, making this whole undertaking for naught. Ruby wanted to make damned sure that wasn't going to happen. But she had to get her mouth around these words.

Ruby had always been gifted with languages. She'd done her fair share of operatic study in French, Italian, and German until she had decided, in her teens, that opera wasn't her calling. As good as she'd been at hitting high notes and pronouncing foreign lyrics, she had never really enjoyed it, save for the applause and the impressed looks from her audience. And no opera singer had ever made anyone's list of the Top however-many Richest People. These days Ruby was on several of those lists. As an entertainment CEO, she'd used her penchant for languages to recruit and develop pop and rock artists from around the globe. These days she used her talents to make money.

And to make magic.

The magic in the Scrolls of Solomon was some of the most powerful she'd ever dealt with. Ruby had suspected as much from the outset, but she'd been sure of it as soon as the first syllables had crossed her tongue. Her usual practice when needing to rehearse the words of a ritual was to read them silently, in order, dozens of times. She would speak one phrase aloud with each read-thru, careful as she did to skip around in the passage so as to avoid unintentionally saying too many magic-wielding words in a row. And tonight, on the first time through, when she'd spoken the first lines of the rite, she had immediately felt the force of its power.

An hour into the process and she was tingling with it. Even in fits and starts of out-of-order phrases this magic was affecting Ruby hardily. It felt like the best wine buzz she'd ever had, topped off with a bump of coke and the additional ecstasy from the sudden start of a long-forgotten favorite song. She was blissful as she stood on her terrace, practically dancing in the summer breeze as the ancient words spun round and round in her head. It was unusually warm for Cobalt City, with the July nights well into the 70s. In her white linen lounge pants and sleeveless silk blouse, she cavorted with the winds, laughing and dancing as a few words at a time sprung from her lips in an ever-improving Phoenician.

She was amid a twirl she might normally have thought a bit ridiculous when she registered the familiar sound of rockets in the distance. She stopped her dancing and chanting as she dashed to the glass railing of the terrace and searched the skies for the source of the rumbling. It was only a moment before she spotted Stardust in the distance. He was coming in from the west and would have to pass her building to get home. Ruby waited until she was sure he would see her to smile and wave in his direction.

Stardust waved back immediately, diverting his course to land on her balcony instead of his own. Ruby was positively beaming as he came in for his landing. She doubted he (or maybe anyone save Loki) had ever seen her smiling so brightly. She moved to embrace him immediately. She may not have been in the mood to abide his

goodness or to make polite conversation, but with the magic enthrall-
ing her entire body, there was something else she was definitely in the
mood for. If Stardust was looking to have a good time tonight, then he
had certainly landed in the right place.

"Hey there, hero," Ruby greeted him, pressing her middle into
his and grasping his armored gauntlets so tightly she wondered if he
could feel it through the metal of his suit.

"Hello yourself," Stardust answered, flipping up the visor on his
helmet.

"So did you save the city?" she whispered, drawing her face closer
to his and feeling a tad bereft his lips were still out of reach inside his
helmet.

Stardust chuckled. "Alas, no," he said, inclining his head toward
her as he wrapped his arms around her waist. "False alarm."

"Oh, that's too bad," Ruby said back, adding an obviously flirty
pout to her words.

"Oh, yes," Stardust concurred, playing along, "I'm terribly disappointed, and in need of some consolation."

Ruby's eyebrows raised at the comment. This was the most forward Jaccob had ever been with her, and she was intrigued by his sudden brazenness. Equally intriguing were all the places her magically
enhanced imagination was taking her. She'd never really considered
sex in the Stardust suit before, and now it was all she could manage
to think about. The tension in Ruby's fingers increased as she gripped
the arms of Stardust's suit, her fantasies suddenly spinning madly to a
point she was having trouble concentrating on the present.

"Teach me to fly," she whispered suddenly, unable to control the
urge to say what was on her mind. She had only accessed a fraction
of the magic of the Eye of Africa, but she was quaking with it—mad-
deningly aroused, daring, and needful. Ruby didn't know if this was a
state native to the Eye or some wildness within herself somehow being
magnified, but whatever it was, it felt good. There was no drug, no

cocktail, no prior magic that had ever felt like this, and she was going to keep chasing this dragon until she had it by the tail.

Stardust was looking at her; he seemed intrigued. And there was a mischief in his eyes Ruby wasn't sure she'd seen before. What she was sure of was that she liked it. There was no way to know if he was being caught up in her magic or if this was just some natural manifestation of the progression of their relationship coupled with residual adrenaline from having *not* saved the city. But whatever its origin, when Ruby's feet left the ground, she was giddy with it. It was not a feeling she was used to. It was a unique joy that came, she supposed, from the coupling of powerful and overwhelming magic with the company of someone she was genuinely fond of. Ruby wasn't in the habit of liking other people, and the utter foreign-ness of this feeling only served to add to the enjoyment of the moment.

Stardust had her around her waist. His grip was firm beneath her ribs, and she held tightly to his arms around his biceps. As they rose higher and higher above the deck of the terrace, Ruby was stunned by the level of trust she felt. She knew he wouldn't let her fall. Although they were a mere few meters off the marble of the terrace, Ruby was acutely aware of the fact that a moment's journey to her right would put them fifty stories above the bustle of downtown. It was a thrilling realization, and Ruby's whole body shuddered with the danger of it, even though her rational brain was sure she was completely safe.

Ruby couldn't help herself but to grin up at Stardust as they rose higher and began to move to her left. She guessed he was planning to take them up the half-story and land them on the helipad.

But he paused after a moment. He looked down at Ruby, then his eyes darted to Starcom Tower before landing back on her face. If he was thinking about inviting her over—about flying her to his place to ravish her in his own surroundings—that was an idea she could get behind.

"What are you thinking?" she asked him softly, making sure her tone was equal parts eagerness and intrigue.

"I want to show you the city," he said.

Not exactly what she'd been hoping for, but nothing she couldn't go along with. "I've seen the city," she replied.

Stardust shook his head. "Not the way I see it." He pulled her closer, wrapping one arm snugly around her waist and letting go with the other. He made a series of gestures with his free hand and then looked down and waggled his eyebrows at Ruby. She had no idea what was going on. That situation was remedied in moments, however, when she recognized a sound coming from the direction of Starcom Tower, growing ever louder as it approached.

It was that StarBoard gizmo Jaccob had been tinkering with the first time he'd come over. The hovering platform had clearly been upgraded since that day. It looked sleeker, more put-together, and less likely to sputter out than the original had. With a metallic powder-coated finish and making much less noise than Ruby remembered, she actually couldn't be sure if this was the same StarBoard, or a new-and-improved model based on the earlier engineering. Either way, when it stopped in front of her and Stardust gestured for her to climb aboard, Ruby saw no reason not to. With Stardust's arm firmly around her waist, she stepped across thin air and onto the shining disc. She kept one hand on his arm while she took hold of the handlebars with the other, surprised at how solid the thing felt beneath her. She'd expected it to give a little when she stepped aboard, but the device had compensated for her weight instantly, without so much as a wobble.

Ruby had ridden a skateboard once. Once. In seventh grade, she'd entertained the notion of becoming what the kids in her school referred to as a "skater chick" because the "skater boys" in the grade above hers were by and large the most attractive in her sphere. This reminded her a lot of that. The board was similar in size and shape to the skateboard she'd tried, and it moved with her as she leaned and bobbled, getting her bearings on the hovering craft like she would on a set of too-loose skate trucks. But she wasn't worried. Stardust had her. He wouldn't let her fall.

Once Ruby was standing solidly on the StarBoard's platform, he moved to hover directly behind her, making sure to take her left hand in his before letting go of her waist with his right. He reached for her right hand then, taking hold of it where it gripped the StarBoard's silver handlebars before he began to ease the two of them forward. It took Ruby a moment to acclimate to the change; moving about on the StarBoard was not the same as standing still upon it. But very soon, she was able to relax and trust that she wasn't going to fall. The learning curve on the board was easy, and by the time Stardust steered them away from the building, Ruby was far more excited than she was nervous.

He flew her over the balcony railing and once around the Ruby Tower. Her building looked gorgeous from up here; the spire lit up in red, and the art-deco style windows glowing softly with the emergency lights. Even the stripe of darkness that was the forty-sixth floor seemed to work with the aesthetic. If they went no place else tonight, Ruby would be forever grateful for the chance to see her own exquisite building from such an exceptional angle.

"This is amazing!" she called out.

The sound of Jaccob's laughter met her ears before he answered. "I'm just getting started!"

Ruby caught herself actually *giggling* at the thought. Giggling! She wasn't sure she'd ever truly giggled before in her life. But then again, she'd also never flown before with the benefit of neither airplane nor helicopter. Perhaps the two were connected.

CHAPTER
NINETEEN

Keeping a tight hold on Ruby's hands, Stardust steered them away from the gleaming towers of Starcom Center and farther into the heart of downtown. Ruby had always enjoyed the view of the city's lights from above, but there was something particularly awe-inspiring about seeing it from this height and in this way. They flew across the city, admired the marquee lights of the theatre district, then followed the river along its length as it snaked through the city to the coast. By the time they reached the shore, Ruby was comfortable enough with the StarBoard that when Stardust asked if she'd like to fly faster, she didn't hesitate before shouting "Yes!" in reply.

He swooped them upward, taking them higher and higher into the sky as they ventured farther and farther offshore.

Ruby's gaze was forced upward as they rose, flying so quickly out over the ocean until the brightness of the stars all but completely eclipsed the glow from the city behind them. The feeling was electric, indescribable, the speed and the stars and the magic combining to make Ruby's head spin. It was hypnotic, the way the stars streaked and danced before her eyes, affected as her experience was by the heady magic that hadn't even begun to dim despite her distance from the object that had birthed it. She hadn't felt this way in ages. She hadn't felt this magical and unsinkable since…

Since the night she'd lost her powers to begin with. It had been more than six months ago now; half a year she'd gone without any magic to call her own. It had happened during her Christmas party— the night she was introducing her opulent new building to the City's cultural elite. She had set up a piece of ritual magic the likes of which she was pretty well convinced had never been attempted. The ritual had been targeting belief, using iconography from every faith Ruby knew or guessed could be in the room that night. Had she succeeded in her machinations, Ruby would have gained influence over all the evening's guests, even the supernaturally powered ones. The ritual would have given her the kind of influence that can only be attained by the use of dark magic.

But Arsho, her oddly yet wrongly perceptive building manager, had somehow been insulated thanks to the practice of a faith Ruby hadn't thought to include. They had realized something—although they hadn't been aware of exactly what—had been targeting the guests. And Arsho, in a misguided attempt at helping things, had interrupted the ritual, going so far as to pull the fire alarm so sprinklers put out the candles that were helping to anchor the magic.

It had been the worst night of Ruby's life, and a hardscrabble journey back to some semblance of wellness ever since. She did her best not to think about that, and instead to revel in the ecstasy of the return of that feeling of brilliance and release this moment was bringing. She was feeling magic in every cell of her body, and it felt divine. She was well on her way to possessing this unequaled power for herself and that, coupled with the incredible sensation of flight, was enough to keep her spirits up.

"Close your eyes," Stardust said into her ear as he slowed them to a stop. They were sky high and far out to sea, and she had no idea what he had in store for her next.

Ruby giggled again, but nodded her head as she complied with his request. She held her breath as she felt herself being slowly spun in place.

"Open them," he said when they were still.

Ruby was sure Stardust could feel her gasp when she caught sight of the city in the distance.

They were at least a kilometer up in the sky, and probably twice that distance out to sea. Cobalt City shone on the horizon, the dim industry of the shoreline fading upward into the twinkling of the vibrant downtown just beyond. It was beautiful.

"Wow," was all Ruby could come up with to say.

"I told you," Stardust said back, but without a hint of mocking in his voice.

"That you did," she replied. He had certainly been right when he'd said she hadn't seen the city like this before. Ruby shook her head at the magnificence of her adopted home. It was certainly breathtaking—a glittering metropolis filled with people who'd brought her fame and fortune. Far to the left of the scene, almost lost on the horizon within the amalgam of lights from downtown, Ruby could just make out the spires of hers and Jaccob's buildings. Their whole section of downtown, christened Starcom Center after the building that had inspired the neighborhood's ongoing renewal, was heavily under construction, the blinking warning lights atop the giant cranes adding a sequined-like quality to the whole area.

"That's our city," she declared.

Stardust nodded. "That it is."

"Thank you for showing me this."

"My pleasure."

Ruby was so enthralled by the whole thing she wasn't sure what to say next. It was the first time in her life she could recall having been utterly speechless. She was lost in the moment, in the mere sensation of being half a mile in the sky, far out past the harbor and hovering over the Atlantic. She had no idea how, but she was decidedly lacking any of the fear she was sure she ought to be feeling. She was so lost in these feelings, in fact, she didn't even notice when she began to shake.

"You all right?" Stardust asked, sidling up behind her and wrapping both arms around her middle.

Ruby shrugged. "It's cold up here," she answered honestly. It *was* cold. The altitude change had seen the temperature drop several degrees at least, and Ruby had been dressed for the warm summer evening. That could possibly have been the thing responsible for her trembling. She knew it could just as easily be the magic causing her quaking, but she couldn't very well tell Stardust about that.

He started at her words. "Oh," he said, "I'm sorry about that. I forget I'm climate controlled in the suit. Come on, let's scrub some altitude." With his arms still wrapped around her waist, he brought them quickly downward, until the air around Ruby once again felt like warm, Massachusetts summer.

She shivered again, this time almost certainly more from the magic than the ambient temperature.

"I have an idea," Stardust said then, clearly under the impression she was still chilly. He flew them scarcely two stories above the ground, where the night air was still warm and pleasant, back across the water and into the city.

He took them higher as they began to pass through town—high enough to ensure they'd miss the tops of the buildings they passed over, but not again so high as to give Ruby a chill. They sped through town, Stardust steering them both by the StarBoard's handlebars, until they arrived on the far side of the river in Quayside. He set them down on the roof of a building Ruby was surprised to discover had picnic tables on it. Tables on the roof of a business seemed like a rather odd choice to Ruby on the surface, but in a town full of superheroes, perhaps it wasn't even that rare. She was seeing the city from a whole new perspective tonight; it could be she was only surprised because it was her first foray onto rooftops.

He brought them in for a landing gently and kept hold of Ruby's hands to help her down off the StarBoard. "I'll be right back," he said once she was safely debarked. He gestured for her to have a seat at one of the tables before dashing off.

Ruby saw him wave a miniature salute at a pair of young women sitting at the farthest table before stepping off the edge of the roof and dropping to the ground below. She looked down at the bench in front of her—at least it looked clean. She had real trepidation about sitting on outdoor furniture in white pants. But standing around looking awkward wasn't going to do her any better.

She shrugged and lowered herself gingerly onto the nearest of the seats, flashing as polite a smile as she could in the direction of the occupants of the far table. The two young women looked almost immediately uncomfortable, and Ruby couldn't help but wonder what Stardust had inadvertently flown her into the middle of. She settled, facing away from the table and toward the direction in which Jaccob had left, and pulled out her Starphone in hopes she could look busy enough not to be forced into socializing.

She'd barely launched her email when Stardust returned, a pair of paper cups in his hands, and a wax paper sack dangling from a hidden hook on the arm of his suit. "Here," he said, handing Ruby one of the cups as he settled himself onto the bench beside her.

She thought about making some flirtatious, half-impressed comment about how surprised she was his gauntlets could be so gentle as to handle a pair of flimsy paper cups, but almost immediately thought better of it. He'd been far too gentle with her in the beginning—an affectation she had worked hard to remedy—she didn't want to make him think of regressing. Instead, she just smiled and took a sip.

"Hot cocoa?" she quizzed, cocking her head to the side and hoping her frown would read as playful.

Stardust nodded.

"Is there a flask in there?" she asked as follow-up, pointing her finger up and down at the Stardust suit. Ruby had never known any grown adult to drink hot cocoa on its own, but had on occasion seen it used as the base for a cocktail. Granted, that sort of thing usually happened in wintertime, but still.

Stardust shook his head. "Nah," he answered blithely with a shrug as he set down his cup and the bag. "It's just that it's way too late to drink coffee, and this place never has decaf."

Ruby couldn't help herself but to laugh out loud. Jaccob was a Good Guy; Good Guys drink hot cocoa at midnight in July, apparently. She shrugged her shoulders and had another sip. She couldn't believe herself, doing something so damned wholesome, and enjoying the company of some*one* so damned wholesome. It wasn't like her at all. In fact, if she really drilled down on it, it wasn't like her to even abide the company of anyone so unfalteringly good.

But, then again, she rarely could abide the company of anyone. Ruby had never had many friends. For a time, there had been a precious inner circle, but they had run into the kind of problems Ruby figured inevitable when groups of heartless, flexibly scrupulous people ganged up. The series of betrayals would have been funny if they hadn't been so tragic. Ruby had made sure, as she always did, that she was the last one standing. Since then, the only company she'd really enjoyed for any stretch was Loki's. He was an evil bastard, but he was at least honest about it. And she could be honest with him, too. With him, there was no playing like she was some mundane genius or polite businesslady. Loki knew what she was, and they could have a laugh anyway. Even though the majority of their dealings had been adversarial—or perhaps because of it—the god had been just about the only person whose company she didn't on some level detest for the last several years.

Until Jaccob.

Ruby had started this whole trifling for sport. She'd been going after the feeling of conquest and the social capital that came with seducing Cobalt City's marquee superhero and most famously married man. It had been an ambition at first, which had become a game—a dalliance. The fact that she had started to give a damn was unwelcome proof that she could still surprise herself. But as she sat there, on the roof of a donut shop, drinking hot cocoa with a man who was trying his best to lick powdered sugar off his mechanized super suit, she realized it had definitely morphed into something altogether unfamiliar.

She wouldn't so much have contended that she had *feelings* for Jaccob. Ruby wasn't entirely convinced she fully possessed the capability for feelings at all. But this challenge, once met and conquered, had steered her in a wholly unknown direction. It felt dangerous and exciting, this new adventure in romance, and Ruby felt more and more titillated the deeper into it she got. Perhaps it felt so temptingly treacherous because she hadn't a planned endgame for their association; there was no plan left to execute at all. The only end she'd had in mind had been getting Jaccob in her life. She'd never stopped to think about what she was going to do once she had him. Sitting on top of a donut place drinking hot cocoa certainly would never have come to mind.

"I didn't know what kind of donuts you like," Stardust said, pulling the contents of the bag out one-by-one and placing them onto napkins he'd spread out on the yellow-lacquered picnic table, "so I got us a bunch."

Ruby stifled a chuckle into her hot cocoa. She shrugged and tried to smile. It was a sweet gesture, buying a sack full of donuts so she could have her pick. It was the kind of thing she would usually associate with an over-eager employee, deriding them for their obsequiousness if she caught wind. But somehow coming from Jaccob, the gesture seemed sincere, and not at all despicable. It may have been the lingering magic making her unusually amiable, but Ruby had no inclination to belittle his overzealous donut acquisition.

"You're adorable, Jaccob," she told him, not bothering to hide the amusement in her voice, "but I don't eat carbs."

Stardust crossed his arms over his chest and studied her carefully. "You ate lumpia," he said, "and croquettes."

"When?"

"At Durian!"

"Well," she replied, a flush rising to her cheeks, "first dates don't count."

Jaccob started. He turned his attention from the buffet of donuts he'd been laying out and sat down beside Ruby on the bench. "So you figured that out?" he asked her sheepishly.

"Figured what out?" she asked, glancing at him sidelong over her cup of hot cocoa.

"You figured out that was a date," he answered.

"Actually," she said, reaching out to pat him on his armor-suited knee, "I wasn't completely sure about it until you confirmed it just now."

Jaccob chuckled. "Oops," he commented. "I guess I'm not much a man of mystery."

Ruby shrugged. "That's part of your charm, Jaccob," she told him. "You may be some big damned hero, but you lack pretension. That's not something I encounter very often in my business. It may keep you from being as shady as you might be in romantic dealings, but I promise it's an endearing quality." Ruby smiled again, wondering what had come over her to cause her to say that.

She wasn't nearly the exponent of honesty and forthrightness she'd just made herself out to be. In fact, earnestness and transparency were hardly qualities she admired in anyone, much less ones she'd bothered to cultivate in herself. She tended to enjoy such sincerity and goodness only in an adversary; it made them predictable and therefore easily defeated, be that on the field of combat or at the negotiating table. But in a comrade, she wasn't so fond of such sincere goodness. This left her thinking as she sipped her too-sweet hot cocoa.

She'd never seen Jaccob as a comrade. He wasn't a colleague nor a teammate. He wasn't even an ally she'd coaxed and courted to her side, although she had to admit that having Stardust all but at her beck and call was a benefit of this whole endeavor. He was, rather than a partner or a comrade, a conquest. Ruby had had her share of romantic conquests before, but there was something *greater than* about what was going on with Jaccob. The whole exercise in seducing him had begun as a way to increase her public influence. She'd looked for the person in the world from whose association she could possibly gain the most, and she'd seduced him. It was as simple as that. He was a trophy to be won, and now that she had him in her possession, she was free to flaunt him out in the world the way she would a Grammy or an Oscar.

So why was it, now that she had him, she was so concerned with his happiness? She'd surely never given a damn about the feelings of her lovers in the past. She supposed it might have something to do with the fact that he was the single most wealthy and influential individual in Cobalt City, and perhaps the country, maybe even the world—Avatars of Immortals notwithstanding. But then again, it was more likely just the high she was still feeling from the intense magic the Eye of Africa had impressed upon her before he'd happened by the roof of her building tonight.

Yes. That was most likely it.

Because it couldn't be any other thing.

CHAPTER
TWENTY

O nce Stardust had polished off the sack full of donuts, and Ruby had indicated she was quite finished with her hot cocoa (as much as she was planning to drink of it, anyway) he'd offered to take her home. With a wink and a simper, she'd given him a better idea. She wanted more time in the sky.

Stardust seemed more than happy to oblige her.

Flying with him was exhilarating. He was willing to let her do as much on her own as she dared to. They'd flown side-by-side for a while, Stardust holding her left hand while she used her right to steer the StarBoard. When she'd insisted, he'd even let go entirely, letting her try to fly solo but all the while making sure she felt just as safe alone in the sky as she had in his arms mere inches above her balcony.

Upon reflection, she realized she'd been far less prudent than she ought to have been high above the streets of Cobalt City. Nobody's perfect; even Stardust makes mistakes. And although had anything happened, Jaccob surely would never have forgiven himself, that wouldn't have made the fall to her death any easier. Next time, she reasoned, she'd keep hold of his hand.

And there would be a next time. She was sure of that.

The luscious amalgam of the adrenaline from flying and the soul-level tingling brought on by her renewed proximity to the Eye of Africa had made for what might have been the best sex of Ruby's life. It had certainly been the best with Jaccob. Granted, that wasn't saying much. He'd been a timid, although tender lover in the beginning—patient and generous, but lacking imagination. It had taken him a little time to come out of his shell in the bedroom, and then a little *more* time for Ruby to be honest enough about her predilections to be satisfied. His taste had veered so far toward the vanilla that she'd been a little bit afraid of scaring him.

But between the connection she'd felt from him all night while they flew, and the fantastic feelings of magic and excitement that had her whole body buzzing, she'd decided to let down a little more of her guard.

Gods, that had been a good decision.

And an easy one, come to think of it. Jaccob was making lots of things easy that she'd always imagined to be difficult. The most difficult thing about her whole association with Jaccob was having to come to terms with the fact that a genuinely good, decent, caring person had taken a real shine to her. Plenty of men (and a good number of women) had come under her thrall in the past, but they'd all been under her magical influence. The few others she'd let herself get close to over the years had all been out to use her in some way. And Jaccob was neither. It was foreign territory, this mutual-respect-and-attraction thing, but it was exciting to explore. Setting her sights on having Jaccob Stevens for her own had been a very good decision indeed.

Getting into bed with Stardust had turned out to be very rewarding.

Getting into bed with Lyle Prather (proverbially speaking) was proving to be something else altogether. He was getting on her very last nerve. She'd promised him an update on the concert at the White House, but had yet to give it to him merely out of spite. The plans were going along swimmingly; the show would be happening in a week and so far, things had come together without a hitch, save for the fact that Prather had been calling Ruby's office relentlessly looking for his update. She'd never been so glad in her life for not having given someone her personal number.

Poor Bridget was the one having to field all these calls. Ruby was pretty sure her receptionist hadn't voted for Prather, but there seemed to be no convincing the woman that a call from the sitting President of the United States wasn't a priority. That resulted in Ruby's getting multiple messages from Bridget each day telling her Prather had called and wanted her to call him back.

She tried to take pleasure in the fact that the man who'd recently risen to the position touted "leader of the free world" had reached the point of practically begging for her attention, but the man himself was a gnat. Ruby couldn't help but find him annoying. If she hadn't already been in hock to Loki for the loan of the Blights, she might have requested his assistance with his jilted avatar. But as it was, she thought it best to leave the god out of the whole mess until she'd secured the power of the Eye of Africa to herself for good. She would need the Blights' help to get that accomplished, and she didn't want to risk irking Loki into taking them back just as she was on the cusp of making it happen.

Because it would be *just like him* to do something like that. Just like it was entirely in character that he appeared to have not so much as stepped foot in the eleven-million-dollar penthouse she'd offered him. She'd been down to check on the place a few times, once having considered berthing the Blights there. But the flat was inappropriately furnished for living. She'd left it empty, but for the few icons and fetishes she'd had brought in to allow Loki to occupy the space. An entire floor of the newest, chicest, most sought-after address in the city stood unadorned save for a scattering of ceremonial items. And so far the troublesome god had failed to show. Because Loki was being Loki.

If he had done this to anyone else, Ruby would have found it amusing. Being on the receiving end of his tricks had never been her favorite. But she supposed a scheme that cost her only in dollars was as friendly as the god was likely to get, and she could live with that. What was a bit of real estate compared to a friendship with a deity?

She wondered, though, how that friendship might be tested when he found out about her collusion with Prather. He'd been understanding about shrewd business decisions in her past, and it even seemed like he'd forgiven her for the kerfuffle in Bayreuth. But rendering aid to a potentially disgraced Avatar in his hour of need might be over the line. Ruby was suddenly second guessing her long-running policy of not giving a damn. Choosing not to stick her nose into the business of gods and monsters that didn't directly concern her had served her well in the past, but not knowing how this all worked nor how Loki was likely to react were he to discover her colluding with Prather was causing her a smattering of dismay. She supposed this was one of those times when it would serve her better to ask forgiveness than permission.

Jaccob had made it pretty clear that he detested magic, and even more abundantly clear that he despised Prather. She couldn't imagine how he might feel about Loki. Ruby knew she was playing a possibly dangerous game, putting herself in the middle of this triangle, but she'd never been one to shy away from danger before, and she wasn't about to start now—not when she was right on the verge of getting everything she wanted. But still she was aware she'd need to tread lightly in the coming weeks. Once she had the magic of the Eye for her own, everything would be easier. For now, she needed to take special care to keep her relationships intact; with no magic to assist her and no supernatural means to repair any accidental damage done, she had only herself to rely on to keep the peace where Loki, Prather, and Jaccob were concerned.

After the White House concert, she could wash her hands of Prather if it suited her. She'd have gotten everything out of him that she needed by then. And if that meant both Loki and Jaccob were happier with her for having done so, then all the better. The President was already becoming a real thorn in her side, and one she only tolerated because of his connections to Loki. Even then, she might have blown him off already had it not been for his ability to create free publicity. This concert at the White House would be more than enough to satisfy her need for the national stage at the moment, and she'd already decided she'd sit the rest of this current political climate out.

Things at the national level were becoming too divisive. The whole country, it seemed, had taken a side. And the two sides absolutely *hated* each other. Ruby didn't care much which side was right, only that she had artists on both sides of the divide. As long as Goblin Records as a whole kept from stating a clear position, she'd continue to have customers on both sides of the political divide.

She'd stand beside Prather today, loudly denounce him the next time he did something publicly asinine, and then wash her hands of anything that so much as smacked of politics until well after the next election. It would be better for everyone this way. Loki surely wouldn't ask her for favors where the President was concerned—to hear Prather talk, the two weren't even on speaking terms at the moment. And Jaccob would surely be glad to hear her declare that she'd given Prather his very last chance to be a decent human being and that she was through dealing with him. Yes, that little strategy would work out nicely on all fronts.

But they had to get through this concert first.

The decision to hold the spectacle on the North Lawn had been Ruby's alone. Her insistence that she be able to come and go from the White House via helicopter precluded having crowds amass on the much larger South Lawn. The only access via chopper was to the Ellipse off the South Lawn, and they couldn't well be trying to land in the middle of a crowd of spectators. But Ruby had fought with the D.C. traffic on her prior visit to the White House, and she was not about to do that again. The concert would be on the North Lawn, she'd declared flatly, or there wouldn't be a concert.

The Secret Service had objected rather strongly to this plan. *Security concerns*, they'd insisted; the North Lawn faced out to Pennsylvania Avenue, and any events held there would be visible to the uninvited public. This, it had been explained most emphatically by the security liaison, was unacceptable. But Ruby knew she'd have Prather on her side were this quarrel to go to the mat, and she knew he'd rather compromise the security of the concert than have Ruby pull the plug on it altogether. She'd won that fight easily.

The more difficult conflict to resolve had been the one with Jaccob over whether or not he'd be accompanying her to the show. He despised Prather, detested the man both personally and politically. Getting him to agree to being seen in public beside someone he abhorred so voraciously had been an argument she almost hadn't won. Ruby had never missed her magic more than in the most heated of their exchanges about the White House concert. She'd never come close to losing an argument before, and she'd had no idea how to deal with it. Had he not capitulated eventually, she feared she'd have gone quite mad with the experience. Fortunately for all involved, she'd finally won him over.

Or, rather, her angle of attack had won him over. She'd never had any compunction about using whatever leverage she had to get a person to come around to her way of thinking, and her relationship with Jaccob Stevens, although unique in a number of ways, was no exception to this. All it took to finally get him to agree was to remind him of his son's part in the whole thing.

Not only would Mike Stevens be included in the concert lineup, his first single "If Tomorrow," would open the show. And he was also invited to join the all-star cast on stage for the Young Dudes' grand finale—she'd even given him a solo. The song would be recorded live, pushed through production immediately, and released as an exclusive online single the next day. Being able to be present for both his son's debut performance as a professional rock musician, as well as the recording of his first released single, was enough to talk Jaccob into coming along. He did warn her he was likely to curse the name of the sitting President with every breath, a behavior that Ruby asked only that he please refrain from in the vicinity of a live microphone.

Jaccob, whose public blunders had almost never been of the verbal variety, had laughed at her admonition, but had promised to try his best.

The flight from Cobalt City to Washington took scarcely longer than an hour and a half, time that Ruby and Jaccob spent on her Gulfstream's leather sofa debating the merits of various brands of private and corporate jets. She'd chosen to fly down alone with Jaccob in the smaller plane, rather than join the artists on Goblin Records' triple-seven jet liner. The performers had to get to D.C. early for rehearsals and press appearances and things Ruby didn't care to bother with. She had people she paid handsomely to handle those sorts of details these days, and she would much rather spend her morning lounging comfortably in her penthouse than crammed aboard an airliner with her underlings.

She'd also much rather be able to go straight to the show without having to deal with managing concert preparations. She'd learned over the time she'd been at the head of the company that even the most qualified professionals tended to defer to her when she was present. And while advantageous in the vein of seeing to it that her vision was always executed correctly, it often led to her being asked to micromanage situations wherein she just didn't give a damn.

And this was one of those times when she just didn't give a damn.

The White House concert would happen just fine without her there to give orders at rehearsal. She was more than happy to let the people she hired handle things. All the better not to run her stockings nor muss her coif before the cameras rolled. She'd been sure to give the supervising director the instruction to get plenty of "candid" shots of her with Jaccob. And she'd given very explicit orders to the video editor to include the most adorable of them in the final cut. She wanted to make sure she looked her absolute best for national television.

Which is why it irked her so much that she'd inconveniently forgotten the problem of rotor wash. Ruby had been the one who insisted on traveling to the White House from the airport aboard a helicopter. Spending one more instant in Washington D.C. traffic was absolutely not on her agenda. What she hadn't bargained on when she'd made this proclamation was that the only helicopter permitted to land at the White House was the Sikorsky Prather had used to visit her in a few months prior. And although the President had agreed to her request to arrive aboard the craft without hesitation, travel aboard a military-grade helicopter owned by the government posed its own set of problems. Unlike with her own aircraft and pilot, she had no control over whether the craft's engines were running as she approached. She was most dismayed to discover that they were.

Not normally one to break into a run under any circumstances, Ruby dashed on her platform heels through the rotor wash and into the cabin of the chopper.

"Damn," she said aloud, when she a glimpse of her reflection in the shaded window beside her seat.

"What's the matter?" Jaccob asked as he settled in beside her. Ruby rolled her eyes at him as she worked to un-pin what was left of her up-do and began combing through her tousled mane with her fingers.

"That'll teach me to have my hair done for television," she replied tersely. "Or to rely on another person's helicopter—one or the other."

Jaccob chuckled as he leaned back and fastened his seatbelt. "You look fine," he told her when she had the last of the pins out.

She was examining her reflection more closely and her frown surely made it obvious that she felt otherwise. "I do not want to look *fine*," she snapped. "I wanted to look good. I wanted to look all done up and put together and camera ready. Fine is not going to work for me today. I'm going to have to find one of our stylists backstage and get him to do something about this, only I didn't build enough time into the schedule to do that. So now it's leave my hair all loose and slovenly, or risk throwing off a multi-network broadcast schedule to get it fixed."

"I like it down," he told her then. His tone was unexpected, softer than she thought she'd be able to hear over the cabin noise as the chopper lifted off toward the White House. "It's unexpected," he added, "refreshing."

Ruby took a deep breath and turned her attention back to her reflection. She did look nice with her hair down—younger, maybe, although she wouldn't dare go as far as "youthful." Why hadn't she noticed before that her long tresses seemed to take some of the heft out of her too-round cheeks? She so rarely looked at herself with her hair loose, but Jaccob saw her like this almost daily. If this was the way he preferred her, she couldn't blame him. Perhaps it was a bit young and a mite unprofessional, but she decided she liked this look—at least enough not to throw off the whole day's schedule to change it.

"If you like it," she said, "then I'll leave it." There was no reason not to let him think she was doing it for his benefit.

Jaccob leaned over and kissed her cheek.

And Ruby started to wonder who the hell she was becoming. Never before in her life had she let anyone she was romantically involved with influence how she presented herself, especially not a man. She'd always dressed, coiffed, and groomed herself by her own preferences alone. The very idea that she'd just agreed to wear her hair loose in public even in the tiniest part because Jaccob Stevens had said he liked it caused her a disturbing amount of consternation. But she had far greater things to concern herself with today then how come she'd suddenly put such stock in someone else's opinion of how she wore her hair.

She'd have adequate time for introspection later. For now, she needed to put the self-consciousness and self-examination away and concentrate on the day's business. She had more than enough on her plate without succumbing to an existential crisis on the way to the White House.

CHAPTER
TWENTY-ONE

For the rest of the ride to the White House, Jaccob had insisted on holding Ruby's hand. Hand holding was an activity she'd heretofore eschewed, but Jaccob had somehow made it palatable. It was yet another piece of this relationship that was puzzling to Ruby; just one more thing to add to the pile of questions she'd have to face once she had the time and the energy for self-reflection. And she had already established that now was not that time.

She'd let go of him when they'd landed on the South Lawn, to pull out her business phone. She texted Prather in rather firm language to tell his pilot to turn the damned engines off before she got out of the helicopter. She'd managed to comb through her locks well enough after taking her hair down, but there was no way her loose mane was going to survive another bout with winds of that velocity—at least not in a way she'd find acceptable for public consumption.

She hadn't told Jaccob what she was doing with her phone out, but rather had just gestured for him to wait before disembarking the craft. When the rotors shut off, she flashed her most self-satisfied grin before standing and heading for the exit.

Jaccob chuckled. He'd always said he was a fan of her nerve, and she always appreciated it when he seemed impressed. He shook his head in obvious amusement, but followed her off the craft.

Ruby could tell as they started across the lawn that Jaccob and Prather were purposely avoiding each other. As they made their way across the Ellipse and into the building, they each stood as far to Ruby's respective sides as they could while still able to converse. Not that it mattered; nobody was saying anything. Ruby honestly figured that was for the best. The two men had a long history of animosity between them, and she honestly wasn't sure which one was more annoyed at having to be within ten feet of the other.

Not that she had the bandwidth to mind. She had bigger fish to fry today than the fact that her lover and this politician she was using for her own gain didn't care to be around each other. She let Prather and his Secret Service bodyguards lead the way, and she held Jaccob's hand as the two of them followed close behind. She wanted to be sure that, in the conflict between the two men who currently flanked her, everyone knew whose side she was on. They passed through some series of halls and passageways Ruby vaguely recognized from her last visit to the White House before coming to the staging area for performers and crew.

Ruby was careful not to trip on the yards of electrical cable and television monitor setups that had been crammed into the corridor. It wasn't so much an ideal setup, but the Secret Service had only been so willing to have the White House cluttered up with her equipment and personnel. At least the crew seemed to be coping. Ruby did her best to ignore the chaos and keep walking out toward the stage. It didn't so much matter what the backstage was looking like at the moment. She trusted her crew to have things under control. What really mattered was the state of things where the audience and the cameras could see.

When they exited the building onto the North Lawn, Ruby was plenty pleased at the state of the setup, but a little surprised at the size of the crowd. She'd known that there would be a large audience, but with the stage, lights, camera platforms, and boxes for secure/VIP seating, the number of people they'd invited hardly seemed to fit. The invites had been Prather's call—or, rather, his issue to manage. She was sure the Secret Service was none too thrilled at the density of the crowd.

But that wasn't really Ruby's problem. If the White House security staff had to deal with inner city children and special invited guests all crammed onto the lawn like sardines behind a fancy fence, she gave not one sliver of a damn. The more the merrier, as far as she was concerned. The larger the crowd of underprivileged youth in front of the stage, the more generous she looked for throwing this concert in the first place. And the footage.... Ruby couldn't help but to grin at the thought of how magnificent it was going to look on video that the place was packed to overflowing. It was always a risk with an outdoor venue that the audience would have more spreading-out room than was ideal if you really wanted to capture the size of the crowd in a shot from the stage. Having them packed in so tightly meant one less thing she had to worry about.

But it was also giving Prather a perfectly captive audience.

Yuck.

Jaccob spotted Mike in the wings as Prather took the stage to kick off the show. Apparently they'd arrived just in time. Ruby deemed this a best-case scenario; the only thing she hated more than being tardy to this kind of thing was being made to wait. She knew the concert wouldn't have started without her; the President needed to speak before the music began, and the only way she'd gotten dispensation to ride aboard his helicopter was to agree that he would be waiting on the lawn for her arrival. Technically, the Sikorsky wasn't supposed to be flying guests of the President without himself aboard as well, but civilian guests aboard the presidential helicopter was hardly the first irregular order of business out of this administration. Executive escorts notwithstanding, she had been prepared to wait backstage for a few minutes before things got started. The fact that everyone had their acts together well enough to have Prather walk on stage all but immediately spoke volumes about the control the stage manager had over the event.

That fellow would be getting a bonus, and soon.

"Hey, kid," Jaccob said to his son, pulling out his Starphone to take a selfie with the stage in the background. "Picture with your old man before you go on?"

"You know," Ruby called as she crossed to where the two of them were standing. "There is veritable legion of photographers and videographers here today. Any one of them would be happy to take your photo."

"But then I wouldn't have it in my pocket," Jaccob countered with a wink in her direction.

Ruby shook her head and held out her hand. "Then at least let me take it," she suggested. "I'll make sure you're both in focus."

Jaccob chuckled but handed the device over.

As she took hold of it, Ruby couldn't help but notice the look on Mike's face; it told her he wasn't used to his father handing over his phone so readily. That was good to know. Taking a few steps back for framing purposes, she switched the Starphone's camera out of selfie mode and then pointed it at the two men. "Smile," she instructed. The two of them did as she asked and she snapped the picture. Checking quickly that the captured image was as adorable as she'd hoped it would be, she closed the distance again and returned the phone to its owner. Jaccob checked the picture himself before locking the screen and putting it away.

"Thanks, sweetheart," he said, leaning in to kiss Ruby on the cheek as he slid his phone into his jacket pocket.

She smiled back, but much of her attention was still on Mike. She found it odd enough herself when Jaccob insisted on using pet names for her; she was sure it must have sounded completely bizarre to his son. Normally Ruby wouldn't have given a damn if Mike was shaken by hearing his father use a term of endearment toward a woman who wasn't his mother, or by seeing him kiss her so unabashedly.

But today Mike Stevens wasn't just her lover's son. He was also an artist in her stable making his international debut, and she was not about to let some eccentricity of their personal situation rattle him right before he took the stage. She did what she could to take charge of the situation and immediately shifted gears.

"You ready?" she asked Mike, turning to look him in the eye and assuring that her tone was all business. She wasn't sure how much of the magic of the Eye she was carrying with her today, and she had no idea whether she was able to assert any supernatural influence over him at all. But with or without magic, she was still his employer, and that had to count for something.

"Yes, ma'am, Ms. Killingsworth," he replied, nodding rapidly as he fidgeted with his guitar.

"You're tuned?" she asked, gesturing to the instrument that hung from around his neck by a black and silver leather strap.

Mike nodded again.

"Warmed up?" she asked.

More nodding. "Yes ma'am," he answered again. "I'm ready."

"Good." Ruby took him by the shoulders then and looked him squarely in the eye. "Now," she said firmly, making sure she had his full attention. "You're going to go out there, and this is going to feel like nothing else you've ever done. There are going to be cameras in your face, videographers moving around all over the place with grips trailing cable behind them. There'll be lights in your face and crowd noises that make whatever you thought you heard through the monitor during your sound check all but moot. You've got your earpiece," she reminded him, gesturing to the tiny monitor he wore in his right ear. "Trust it. The house sound doesn't matter—all right? What matters is what's going into the system. And if at any time this starts to feel overwhelming or uncomfortable, just turn your head. I'm stage left for a reason."

She'd been coming into the studio sporadically over the past few weeks as Mike had been recording the album version of the song he was about to perform. She'd had the vocal booth set up just so, with the engineers through a window off to the singer's left. "I'm right where I've been all week. If you need reassurance, you can look over at me the same as you've been doing in the studio. I'll be right where you expect me to be."

"Okay." Mike nodded, and Ruby could tell he was processing her words carefully. This was a thing she often did with new artists when she put them in front of a large audience for the first time. She wondered, though, if Mike would take this as his being given some sort of special treatment on account of the fact she was sleeping with his father. That wasn't a presumption that would inspire confidence, and she needed Mike to have all the confidence he could going into today's performance.

"I wouldn't have you out there today if you weren't ready," she told him. Now go," she said, gesturing to center stage, where Prather had finished his opening remarks and was waving to the crowd amidst a mass of cheers. "Kick ass."

"Yes, ma'am." Mike was smiling as he gave her one last nod and then turned to head on stage. The backup band was getting themselves into place as Mike moved toward his mark behind the microphone stand, waving at the crowd as he went.

Ruby reached out her hand to Jaccob, who took it and followed her to stand in the first wing.

"That was one hell of a pep talk," he said in her ear as the band began to play.

"I meant it," she replied. "He's really good. Listen."

Mike hadn't even gotten into the first chorus before Ruby knew for certain she was right to have chosen him as the lead-off artist for this show. And by the time the bridge was ending and the song was modulating, she was sure they had a hit on their hands. She turned her head for a moment to look at Jaccob. He was beaming. She liked that look on him a lot. Smiling almost as widely herself, she leaned her head against his shoulder for a moment.

Jaccob turned briefly to smile in her direction before looking back to where Mike was performing.

It was clear to Ruby that the applause when the song was over was more than Mike had been prepared for. He stood for a moment, appearing dumbfounded, before taking his bow. He swung his guitar around behind him to wave to the crowd as he bounded off stage toward where Ruby and his father were waiting just off stage.

"Incredible job, son!" Jaccob exclaimed, intercepting Mike with a hug as soon as he hit the wings.

"You could have stayed out there longer," Ruby added. "They're still cheering for you."

Mike stepped out of his father's embrace and shrugged. "The stage manager told me to take one bow and get off stage," he shared.

Ruby nodded. Good for that stage manager making sure to manage the time they'd be stuck in this political cesspit. And good on Mike for following directions even under such extraordinary circumstances.

"Well, you were fantastic," she told him. "Now Jaccob," she said, turning her attention to the man she'd come with. "We should get to our seats. We can't just stand backstage for the whole concert. Mike, you go back to the green room and enjoy yourself. We'll see you again before the finale."

Mike nodded and headed off in the direction of the backstage lounge.

Ruby had always made a point to take good care of her artists backstage—she was sure he'd be comfortable there until the finale.

As for her own seats, the comfort level remained to be seen. But she had made sure going in that the stage left VIP box where hers and Jaccob's seats were reserved was shared only with celebrity guests and noted philanthropists. So at least she could be assured of her relative social comfort. The politicians were to be seated stage right; Prather and his cronies had a box to themselves, which seemed to suit everyone just fine. Ruby spent the next two performances wondering if she had the power within her to set it on fire.

Not that she would. No matter how despicable the political detritus sitting on the other side of the venue, she'd never sabotage her own event like that. But still, it was fun to fantasize. For years she'd toyed with the idea of being able to curse liars so their trousers really would combust. Never had she wished for that power more than she had in the time she'd spent dealing with Prather. But today would be the end of it. Unless Loki approached her personally for something having to do with this despicable buffoon of a man, she had no intentions of so much as speaking to him again.

And today wasn't about him, anyway. Ruby was sure, though, that he absolutely thought it was. The whole angle she'd taken with him in the first place was that hosting this concert for disadvantaged children would be good for his image and approval rating. But as far as Ruby was concerned, it only mattered that it would be good for her company's bottom line.

And the concert was fantastic. There was something about privileged rock stars playing for poor children from rough, inner-city neighborhoods that made the energy of a live show just that little bit better. Maybe it was a "there but for the grace" thing. Ruby didn't know, but what she did know was that today's show had been even more spectacular than she'd been expecting. She could practically hear the stock price going up.

All of the artists had been well received. That was another thing about performing for the underprivileged—they had no real expectations and were usually happy with whatever they were given. Mika Sparkles and the Topiary Twins had been particularly popular. Ruby made sure to email her online sales division to raise the prices of both acts' available downloads before close of business. There was no reason not to maximize the profit margin. If the accusations of greed started flying too loudly, she'd just turn around and find a way to get everyone who'd been invited to the concert a code to download it for free. Although, with the number of smartphones she was seeing in the audience, she hardly thought it would be an issue. For a group touting itself to be among the underprivileged, there was an awful lot of cutting edge technology in their pockets.

Not that Ruby gave a damn, not really. Whatever poor people did with their money wasn't really any of her business. The only reason all of these Starphones were on her radar at all was she was concerned about audience video making it onto social media before the official video debuted and ruining her cross-platform ratings. Just before heading backstage for the finale, she shot off an email to her legal department instructing them to serve firm but polite cease-and-desist orders on any video more than fifteen seconds long that featured the stage or the artists. That might have been holding the reins a little tight, but it was better than allowing some enterprising kid in the audience to live stream her entire show on his advertiser-sponsored WebTube channel and make money on the production before she did.

It was nice to have a little business to do during the concert. Jaccob was a little enraptured, it seemed. She'd known he'd spent his youth failing to gain entrée into what was generally considered the "cool" crowd. Sitting in the grandstand with rock stars and celebutantes seemed to have put him in some sort of nerd nirvana. It helped his mood, too, that everyone in their box had been at least somewhat critical of Prather since his election. The stage left VIP box was a veritable who's who of people Prather would rather not have let in. They were all there to support the artists. It had been Ruby's idea to have some Prather opponents in the audience to reinforce the fact that today's show wasn't about political grandstanding, but about coming together for the country.

Or some such.

She'd let her PR people handle the exact wording of the anti-political message. What mattered to Ruby was she had a place at this concert where she wouldn't be surrounded by political sycophants and Presidential yes men. It made for a reasonably pleasant afternoon. The music and the company would have been enough to assure some enjoyment, but watching Prather squirm at the presence of some of his most outspoken opponents made it outright fun.

She snagged Jaccob by the elbow as the Young Dudes took the stage to uproarious applause. They were the last regular act—the headliners, as it were. They were scheduled to play an abbreviated set of their greatest hits before being joined on stage by the rest of the lineup (and Prather himself, at his own insistence) for the big live-recorded finale.

And Ruby meant to be aboard a helicopter on her way back to Cobalt City within moments of the final chords. She had no desire to be around for any of the business of breaking down, nor had she any interest in holding the hands of fragile artists wanting reassurance their performance had gone as the boss had wanted it to.

Plus, she needed to be back in her office to watch the rough cut of the video on a proper-size screen, and she wanted to be there in time to see it as soon as it was ready. Her agenda meant they would be backstage to watch the end of the show. Ruby preferred the sound from the stage deck, anyway—it wasn't nearly as loud as out in front of the speakers, and there was something about being closer to the unamplified instruments Ruby had always found more satisfying than hearing music through speakers.

Mike had come to stand beside them to listen to the last of "Girly Girl," a tune he'd confided in Ruby he wasn't altogether fond of and that he was therefore fascinated by its near unequaled success. Ruby hadn't wanted to go into the dynamics of teen pop and recording for the lowest common denominator, but she'd been happy to let Mike know he was being managed by the Artist Division and not by the

Pop Division and therefore wouldn't be asked to compromise his musicianship to cater to a wider audience. Today's concert notwithstanding, that was.

The finale was being billed online as "The Young Dudes and Friends," and so the musical style was straight out of their playbook. Ruby didn't actually like the song herself, but she understood its mass appeal and marketability. Prather had demanded to hear a preview and he, to absolutely no one's surprise, had loved it. Ruby had agreed to let him on stage to sing along partly because she enjoyed having the leverage of being able to take that privilege away from him if he got too annoying. But mostly she had agreed to let him on stage for the finale to ensure she wouldn't be stuck dealing with him when the concert was finished. By the time Prather was off the stage and finished rubbing elbows with all the rock stars, Ruby and Jaccob would be safely ensconced aboard a helicopter far enough off the ground as to not be asked to stand beside the President for a photo op.

A few charmingly candid pictures of her with Jaccob at the concert was one thing; forcing a smile while being herded into posed group shots for some interminable period wasn't on her agenda for the afternoon. She and Jaccob stood, hand in hand, in the first wing as the finale music started. Jaccob patted Mike on the shoulder as he went to step onto the stage, stumbling as Lyle Prather pushed past him, bounding onto the stage and waving at the crowd as the opening strains of the song rang out.

Mike looked back at his dad and Ruby and rolled his eyes at the antics of the buffoon who was supposed to be a statesman. The three had a brief laugh before Mike turned his attention back to the show and continued onto the stage.

He'd barely taken a step past the curtain when Ruby suddenly felt all the air being sucked out of her lungs. There was a sound—louder maybe than anything she'd ever heard—and yet for a moment she wondered if she was able to hear at all. Somehow she knew there had been an explosion. Her eyes went to the stage. Where Hunter had been standing, shaking hands with the kids in the front row, there was now a crater in the apron of the stage.

Ruby's eyes darted back and forth. Were all the boys still on stage? She counted four; shouldn't there be five? Which one was missing?

Her hearing was coming back, she knew because there were screams from everywhere.

CHAPTER
TWENTY-TWO

Jaccob grabbed hold of Ruby's arm as a second explosion sounded. He yanked her to stand just in front of him as he pulled Mike backward with his other hand. "Stay close!" Jaccob yelled, loud enough to be sure he was audible over the noises of chaos from the stage and panicked cries from the crowd. He stripped off his jacket in a motion so fluid and practiced that Ruby was surprised she didn't recognize it, before tapping a switch on each wrist and wrapping his arms around Ruby and Mike.

"What are those?" she asked.

"StarBands," he answered curtly. "Short range force field emitters. As long as you're close we should all be safe."

She looked down for a moment at the diamond bangle on her wrist, wondering for a moment if her own bracelet had any hidden powers like this. But she didn't have time to let herself wonder. There were screams from all sides and more sounds of explosives going off in the crowd. Jaccob had her covered, and for now that was enough.

"We've got to get out of here," Ruby insisted as a third, or was it a fourth, explosion sounded. Shrapnel flew in their direction, shards of metal and bits of cable making the StarBands' field sizzle as they bounced off it and back toward the stage.

Jaccob nodded. "Any idea of the way?" he asked.

Ruby shook her head. "No!" She'd been shown the way from the helicopter to the stage. And she'd been fielding questions and answering emails the whole way. Before today, she'd only been here once, and then she hadn't been paying rapt attention either. She could no more find her way back to the South Lawn than she could fly them home herself.

"I do," a voice called out from behind them.

Ruby rolled her eyes as she turned to face the source of the sound.

It was Prather. He was crouched in a ball on the stage deck behind them, trembling in fear with his hands covering his head. He must have dove between their legs when the first explosion happened. And she'd thought he was pathetic before.

"I know the way out," he insisted. "And with me along, they'll let you through—they'll have to!"

Ruby clenched her jaw. The obnoxious moron had a point. Security in the White House was intense under any circumstances; she could only imagine how tightly locked down the place would be in the midst of a violent attack.

"All right," Ruby allowed, stepping closer to Jaccob and gesturing for Prather to stand. She was sure the field from the StarBands had kept that barrage of shrapnel from hitting the President just now. Jaccob's vigilance and constant state of preparedness had probably just saved the man's life—at the very least, he owed them an escape. "Get up!" she insisted when she saw he hadn't. "Go!"

Prather nodded. He scrambled to his feet and gestured for Ruby and the others to follow him as he took off away from the stage. He led them down the stairs and onto the lawn, through the security cordon, and into the building.

There were Secret Service men behind them, chasing after the group as Prather led them through a maze of corridors. Ruby was vaguely aware that a few of them had tried to stop Prather's progress. They were calling out to him from all sides, but were being largely ignored.

Jaccob had positioned himself so the StarBands' force fields had the group of them completely surrounded. The few Secret Service men who tried to get in front of them had been unceremoniously zapped down by the StarBands.

Ruby wouldn't have guessed that Prather, as portly and out of shape as he was, would be able to move as fast as he was moving through the halls. He led them past the tangle of cable and grip equipment, around a corner, through a door and into a room Ruby was only vaguely able to process was the Oval Office before they were across it and back out the other side. They dashed out onto a covered walkway, down the sidewalk and onto another lawn.

It was quieter back here, wide-open and devoid of people. Ruby much preferred this to the cacophony of panic on the North Lawn, and she felt even better when she saw Marine One in the distance. They rushed, although no longer running full-out, across the South Lawn and into the Ellipse. The Marines on guard duty seemed more than a little shocked at the group of them as they dashed across the grass and scrambled up the stairs aboard the helicopter.

"We're under attack!" Prather yelled to the group of Marines. "Go! Take off! Now! That's an order from your Commander in Chief!"

Two things had Ruby amazed in that moment: the fact that the Marines on duty with the helicopter seemed somehow unaware of the explosions going off just on the other side of the building, and the fact that Prather had suddenly begun to sound presidential. As she buckled herself into one of the chopper's cushy armchairs, she wondered if maybe the helicopter's crew had mistaken the sounds of the explosions for part of the show. It was honestly better if they did. If the Marines aboard the chopper knew the White House was under bombardment, they might have some hesitation in letting the President be airborne above it.

She wasn't sure how much the helicopter's crew had believed Prather when he'd told them they were under attack, but Ruby was convinced by the swiftness of their preparations for liftoff they had taken his assertion—that they were getting an order from their Commander in Chief—to heart. Ruby could not have cared an iota less what their motivations were, but when Prather asked her to give the pilot the destination via the intercom, she had no problems directing him to the airport where her Gulfstream was waiting. She pulled out her phone to text her assistant, but saw she already had a message letting her know her pilot had been alerted they were inbound. The jet would be ready for takeoff as soon as possible.

Sometimes Ruby wondered if she paid her personal staff too much, but times like this were proof positive there was no such thing.

Mike was sitting across from her and had pulled out his phone. "Was there live coverage of this thing?" he asked as the rotor noise grew greater, and they began to lift off the turf of the White House South Lawn.

Ruby nodded. "Some," she replied. "All of the regular Press Corps were allowed to roll on whatever they wanted, as long as they agreed to pay licensing for any music that made it into their broadcast. Why?"

Mike shook his head. Holding out his phone so Ruby could see the screen, he answered. "I have six missed calls from my mom."

"Send her a text before you lose signal," Ruby told him. She'd known from the trip in that Starphones didn't always have the best coverage at altitude. She had the right gear aboard her own aircraft to make that inconsequential, but Marine One was either lacking the requisite technology, or they had it turned off. Either way, no one would be making a call until they reached the airport. "Once we're back on the plane, you can use my office to call her. It's quiet back there, she'll be able to hear you. Text your sister, too. Call her after your mom if you think you should—if your mom ever lets you off the phone. Tell them your dad was there. Make sure they know you're safe and unharmed."

Mike nodded, turning back to his phone.

The rest of the trip to the airport was spent in silence. The lot of them were likely shell shocked. But Ruby had bigger things to worry about than her feelings on the matter of having almost been blown to pieces. She had no idea whether or not all five Young Dudes were even alive at the moment. Hunter had been right in the path of that first blast, and there was every chance he'd been killed by it. And what the hell was she going to do about that?

There would have to be public vigils, probably a tribute album, some kind of memorial scholarship or charity fund of some such, and she'd have to be oh-ever-so sensitive about finding his replacement. Or maybe there wouldn't be a replacement; she could probably make do with only four Young Dudes. Some of the most famous bands in history had only four members. She couldn't decide whether a nation-wide casting and talent search or a solemn declaration that Hunter's place would always be his own would test better with audiences. She'd have to get her social media team on that presently.

Of course, there was still a chance he'd survived the bombing. That option was clearly the better one. No matter how much insurance the label had on the kid, no single payout would ever match the Young Dudes' chief heartthrob's future earnings. That held especially true now that he had been injured while performing a free concert for inner-city kids. There'd be photo ops and interviews, some kind of touching tribute for the families who had lost loved ones in today's bombings—and Ruby was sure there had been fatalities, even if Hunter wasn't one of them. And then there'd be the inspirational follow-up album and the epic, world-wide comeback tour. She'd have to get her writing team on a stirring solo for Hunter to lead off the live show.

She'd have them write a version for the others to sing if Hunter wouldn't be there to do it himself.

It was all very troubling, as was the stinging sensation she was experiencing from what must have been a million tiny cuts on her face from whatever microscopic shrapnel had managed to make contact before Jaccob had activated his StarBands. Even the magic in her felt off-kilter. She was still feeling it; she hadn't lost her connection to the power of the Eye of Africa, but there was something Not Right about the magic in her orbit at the moment.

As she sat still, watching out the window as the familiar sights of the D.C. Mall grew tinier and tinier in the distance, she tried to center herself. She had hoped to be able to shake the icky feeling that had come over her right before the explosions had started and had stuck with her ever since. But nothing she tried seemed to be doing any good.

As the helicopter was still ascending, she had thought to ascribe the unpleasant feeling to an adrenaline spike. But she knew that experience well, and this was not that. This was something else altogether. This was a magical bad feeling.

Those had been magical explosions.

She realized she'd known it all along. Her reaction in the moment, before Jaccob had activated his StarBands, hadn't been to flee. Her instinct had been to fight. And in the entire history of her life, she had only had that response when the threat was a magical one. And she hadn't had that reaction at all in the months since she'd lost her powers. When a threat had come at them the night they'd stolen the Eye, she'd been keen to get the hell out of there and let the Blights handle it on their own; that hadn't been even close to her MO before her powers had been stymied.

But now that she had some subset of borrowed power and a full-on connection to magical energy, she was bristling to fight back at whatever had been behind the attack. Better that she hadn't had the chance, she knew. Jaccob still didn't know she'd ever had magic, much less that she had some use of it now. And he had no inkling she was spending nearly every moment they weren't together working with a stolen magical artifact to get her full powers back. Jaccob hated magic, she knew that. And she also knew, from the times he'd come to her needing to unload the woes of being Stardust, that the authorities still didn't have any leads on the Eye nor any idea as to who might have stolen it. There was no way she was about to spill those particular beans.

She wasn't sure whether or not Stardust would be involved in the investigation of the White House bombing. Prather's cabinet had brought Archon in to be in charge of Superhero Affairs, but there hadn't seemed to be much movement in the direction of including the super-powered in the doings of the administration. If they meant to make a policy move in that direction, Stardust would be a good hero to start with. A man whose powers stemmed from technology and not anything inherently superhuman could be just the right person to grease the proverbial wheels. Jaccob hated this administration, and he hated Prather personally. But he'd rescued the man, and he'd been present for an attack that had done real harm to some of the nation's most vulnerable. He could very well be talked into aiding in the investigation down the road.

If it came to that, she might have to find a way to tell him what she knew.

She could only hope whoever was doing the initial investigation would be able to figure out the magic component for themselves before it came to that. Or maybe she wouldn't have to tell. Maybe, and she wasn't sure at the moment, but maybe she didn't actually give a damn. She wanted the culprits caught and identified mostly because it would keep the story alive and playing in the news, and every story about today's show was, on some level, a story about her company and her artists. Free publicity was her favorite kind.

But on the other hand, the list of people who likely wanted Prather dead was as long as her arm. And the attack had almost certainly been aimed at him. The explosions started at the moment he took the stage; that couldn't have been a coincidence. What difference did it make which one of his enemies had been behind this afternoon's attacks? Someone had tried to end a terrible human being, and Ruby didn't really give a damn who that was.

Ruby cared a hell of a lot more about how much work this whole mess was about to cause her than she did about bringing the bombers to justice. She was still trying to decide how much she was going to let herself engage with the FBI and the Secret Service and whoever else was going to be all up in her face with their investigation when the helicopter began to descend.

Ruby was at the edge of her seat when Marine One came in for a landing just a few dozen yards from where her Gulfstream was already warming up on the tarmac. She was more anxious than she might have been willing to admit to get the hell off of Prather's aircraft and back aboard her own. Not for nothing, she'd have access to the internet and a bottle of cognac aboard the Gulfstream.

But more than that, she didn't like the energy of this flight, and she didn't like being in such close quarters with Lyle Prather. A miasma of decay followed the man around, and it was wholly unpleasant to be so near to him. She wondered if it had always been that way, or if it was an artifact of whatever had caused the spiral of madness she'd seen him descending into ever since he'd been elected to the highest office in the land. And she wondered, too, if it was something that had always been there, if perhaps her new connection to ancient, foreign magic that had let her in on it.

Whatever it was that put her in touch with the rotten-feeling energy that seemed to be following Prather around, Ruby was in a hurry to be rid of it. As soon as the helicopter had touched down, she was out of her seat. She waited by the door for the Marine in charge to open it and fold out the stairs, but she didn't stand on protocol once they were deployed. She dashed down the stairs, sending a look over her shoulder to both Jaccob and Mike that said clearly they would do well to join her post-haste. She wouldn't actually leave her lover and one of her artists behind at the airport, but it wouldn't do to let them think it was okay to dawdle, either. The sooner they were the hell out of D.C. airspace, the better.

Ruby didn't look back again as she dashed across the tarmac toward her waiting aircraft's extended boarding stairs. She was already approaching the cabinet where her liquor was secured when Mike came clambering up the stairs with Jaccob close behind.

"The office is in the back," she told Mike, gesturing with the ice tongs toward the rear of the aircraft. "You'll have cell service while we're on the ground, so call your mother now. And explain to her immediately that you're okay and on a plane leaving Washington. Then make sure she knows you're about to lose signal. Wait until the Wi-Fi comes up at ten thousand feet and then call her back from the VOIP phone on my desk."

Mike nodded as he darted through the cabin in the direction she'd indicated. Ruby could only hope he'd understood all of that. The last thing she figured she wanted right now was a freaked out and motherly Elizabeth Stevens showing up at Starcom Tower looking for her son. It was better for all involved if Mike could talk her down from any designs she might have on coming in to the city now. If he could placate her concerns while they were still en route, then Ruby could be reasonably sure she wouldn't have to deal with Mrs. Stevens coming into her sphere.

Ruby had a glass of cognac in her hand as she moved to greet Jaccob at the door. She handed the glass to him and took hold of the door mechanism; no need to wait for the copilot to come back and do something she could do herself. If her getting the door shut on her own meant they'd be getting off the ground even a moment earlier, then she'd be damned if she didn't do it.

To her surprise, she just about shut the thing in the President's face.

"What the hell do you think you're doing?" she demanded.

"I'm going with you!" Prather replied.

"The hell you're not!"

"But… but I got you out of there," he said. "I showed you the way, let you use my helicopter!"

"Yes," Ruby allowed, "and we're very grateful. Now you're going to get back on that helicopter and go back where we just came from."

"But it's dangerous!"

"You don't say!" Ruby mocked.

"Someone tried to blow up the White House!" Prather reminded them, as though somehow they might have forgotten.

"That they did," Ruby agreed. "And it's your White House. You're the president. So get back aboard that fancy helicopter, you pusillanimous cretin, and go run the country!"

The steward had come aft from the jumpseat at the sound of his boss's yelling, and Ruby gestured for him to pull the stairs in. She threw her hands up in exasperation as she charged away from the door and into the plane's main cabin. She wondered for a passing moment what her mild-mannered steward might think about slamming a door in the face of the President of the United States, but her wonder didn't last. It didn't matter; she'd learned over the course of this era without her powers that those in her employ who had signed magically binding contracts were still bound by them. That steward had no more choice in whether to close the door when she told him to than her driver had in keeping secret whatever went on in her car. Having magically bound employees had proven useful time and again, so although she'd had to be a little extra gentle with them in the months since she'd lost her powers (for fear of losing one and having no power with which to bind his replacement), it had been worth it to assure complete devotion in her personal staff. And it paid off when she needed the door shut in the face of the blubbering leader of the free world.

Mike had already headed into the back office when Ruby made it into the cabin and settled herself on the sofa beside Jaccob. She had to stop herself from laughing when she saw he'd already fastened the seatbelt on the overstuffed leather sofa snugly around his hips. With everything they had just been through—with everything they had just witnessed—with the full and clear understanding they had only just gotten out with their lives, still Jaccob was going to follow the rules. Seatbelts fastened for takeoff.

Ruby didn't bother with hers. She placed her hand on his knee as the aircraft started to roll. She'd told the pilot she wanted to be off the ground as soon as possible; she was glad he'd taken her request to heart. Depending on what the Secret Service learned in the next several minutes about the origin and nature of the attack on the White House, there was a chance they would shut down all nearby airspace. That order almost certainly wouldn't come while the President was still airborne aboard Marine One, so as far as Ruby was concerned, they had about as many minutes as it would take him to return to the South Lawn to get the hell off the ground and as close to out of D.C. airspace as possible.

Jaccob looked up at her and shook his head, placing his hand over hers where it rested on his knee. "How are you?" he asked quietly.

Ruby shook her head. "I suppose I've been better," she said. "I can't remember the last time I ran like that; I'm woefully out of shape. Honestly, I'm not sure I ever have run like that. And I certainly haven't ever run like that in heels."

"Yeah," Jaccob allowed, "I guess I didn't think about that."

Ruby smiled at him. The plane had begun to accelerate; they'd be off the ground soon. This was the best news she could think of under the circumstances.

"Still, ruined pumps or twisted ankles notwithstanding, it beats the alternative." She leaned in and caught his eyes as the plane's front wheels lifted off the ground. "Thank you for saving my life," she whispered.

Jaccob smiled, lifting her hand to kiss it before leaning back against the soft leather of the airplane's sofa.

"You're welcome," he replied.

It was always strange for Ruby when he said that. "You're welcome" coming from Jaccob wasn't the rote response it was when most people used it. When Jaccob told someone they were welcome, he sounded like he really meant it—like the recipient of the sentiment was truly welcome to whatever it was they were discussing. That level of sincerity could be unnerving. In most people, it was a real put-off. But in Jaccob, it was somehow endearing.

It was one of the many mysteries Ruby was wrestling with about this whole undertaking. She found most people with this much goodness in them to be unpleasant company, but here she was quite fond of the quintessential good guy.

Life could be ironic like that.

CHAPTER
TWENTY-THREE

They spent the first half-hour or so of the flight back to Cobalt City in silence. Mike hadn't ever come forward to join the others in the main cabin, electing instead to remain in Ruby's back office for the duration. She wasn't sure whether he was still talking to his mother and sister or whether he'd just thought to give her and Jaccob some privacy. Not that she cared. She was actually a little bit grateful for the chance not to be "on" for one of her employees at the moment. She was feeling felt more than a little bit shaken and needed to pull herself together before being the boss again.

She could only guess Jaccob felt similarly. The longer the silence stood, the more she wondered when he'd be getting up to head aft and check on Mike. But he never stirred. She presumed he needed a moment, too. Maybe he needed to gather his thoughts before having to be the wise father or the upbeat superhero. Either way, Ruby was glad to be solely in his company. It was an odd and foreign feeling, being so comfortable in the presence of another person. Before today, she'd have guessed she'd be happier alone at a time like this. But somehow Jaccob's presence, even his silent, apprehensive presence, was strangely soothing.

But as the time went on, and his demeanor didn't appear to signal improvement, she began to get concerned. Reticence wasn't usually his style; this afternoon had clearly affected him more than she'd figured at first. He'd had it in him to save her life and Mike's, but since then, it had seemed like he was positively shrinking.

Jaccob had finished his first glass of cognac and had silently accepted a second, but hadn't had more than a sip before he'd set the snifter down and laid his head against Ruby's shoulder. She'd let that be for a while, for once not minding being a source of another's comfort. Normally she didn't cotton to being clung to like this, but seeing as they'd all nearly been blown to a million pieces, she was willing to offer him some temporary measure of grace. She was content to let him lay his head on her shoulder, to put her arm around him, and to marvel at the fact this whole thing was happening.

"How are you doing?" she asked him after a time, punctuating her question with a chaste kiss to his temple and a squeeze of his shoulder. The silence had begun to drive her crazy, and she was reaching the point where she was genuinely concerned for his mental state.

Another oddity of her relationship with Jaccob was this bizarre level of caring about how another person felt. Sometime between her having sent Discontent to get Elizabeth Stevens out of the picture and this afternoon's frightening developments, she'd apparently started to give a damn. It left a bad taste in her mouth, but facts were facts and there was no use in denying them. At the very least, she could be reasonably certain Jaccob wouldn't use her sudden-onset concern against her.

He sat up and picked up his mostly full glass of cognac. "I... I don't know," he answered. "I've never regretted rescuing anybody before."

"You think you regret it?"

"Yes." He looked at her then, his jaw clenched and his hands balled into fists in his lap. "What does that make me?" he asked.

"Human," Ruby answered gently. "You saved a man because that's what you do. The fact that you saved a despicable man is secondary—it's hardly even relevant. In the moment, you reacted like you would any other time, the same as if any other random citizen had been in harm's way. Only this time, the person you saved wasn't a random citizen at all; he was a very prominent, hateful buffoon."

"I didn't even do it on purpose!" Jaccob exclaimed, knocking back a pronounced sip of his drink.

"I know."

"Why did it have to happen like that?" he groaned. "Why did he have to be standing there?"

"Dumb luck," Ruby said. It was her best guess.

"Does it make me less of a hero that I wish he hadn't been?" Jaccob asked then. "That I wish I hadn't saved him?"

Ruby shrugged. "You'll want to think that one through to its logical conclusion," she said after a pause. "If he hadn't been right there, the Secret Service would have saved his life instead of you. Meanwhile, the three of us might never have found our way through to the South Lawn, or we might not have been allowed out. You, Mike, and me might still be stuck there, in a crashed White House, with Prather's thugs and what's left of the Young Dudes. No, I think it's for the best that things happened like they did. You saved the President while saving your son and—"

She paused for a moment, wondering just how she ought to refer to herself in this situation. "Girlfriend" seemed a bit stilted—she was over forty, and Jaccob was older still; something about referring to them in terms of "boyfriend" and "girlfriend" just sounded silly. But "friend" didn't come close to accurate, and she wasn't sure how Jaccob would cotton to it if she decided to use the word "lover." Fortunately, she found she didn't have to solve that problem, as Jaccob chimed in before the pause could grow awkward.

"But I saved *this* president," he sighed. "This despicable, loathsome, hate-mongering danger to our country. He's irredeemable, Ruby. I hate him. I hate him so much that I almost missed my son's big moment because he was going to be there."

"I think we'd all agree we're glad you changed your mind on that one," she said.

Jaccob shrugged. "He's really good," he said quietly. "Mike—he's really got a lot of talent."

"Yes, he does," Ruby agreed. "And he's smart, and he takes direction, and he works hard. He's got a very bright future in this business."

Jaccob reached out and took Ruby's hand again. "Then it was worth it, I guess," he said.

"Dealing with Prather?" she surmised, "saving his life?"

"Dealing with him, being photographed with him, saving him, even."

Ruby nodded. "I think everybody's aware of your opinion of the man," she encouraged.

"But now I've saved his life," Jaccob countered. "Everyone's going to know I saved his life. They're going to think I wanted to—that I did it on purpose, that I planned—"

"No one is ever going to accuse you of planning to save Prather," she assured him. "Because that would imply you were aware there was the possibility of an attack. Which you weren't. Which you couldn't have been. You wouldn't have let your son within a hundred miles the White House if you'd known an attack was imminent. So don't think anyone will be under the impression you were standing by just to save Prather's life. You were there to see your son on stage. Period."

She shook her head. Keeping hold of Jaccob's hand on her right, with her left she reached out and pulled open the top drawer of a nearby end table. She fumbled around in the drawer for a moment before pulling forth a small black remote control from inside it.

"What's that?" Jaccob asked.

Ruby grinned, clicking the button that brought a screen at the front of the cabin to life. "Let's see how the story's developing," she suggested. "If anyone is trying to take the 'Stardust loves Prather' angle—which I cannot believe anyone would, because it just doesn't sound credible, and they'd come off looking like a jackass—but if you think there's a chance one of these yellow journalists or another is trying to sell that bill of goods, then we should know as soon as possible. We should be prepared. If we know before we land that someone is making claims as to your motivations during the attack, then we should be ready to speak to that. You can have a statement ready. Something like: 'I'm thankful I was there to keep my son safe; knowing that other lives were saved as a result of my actions is an added blessing.' Something like that."

"Wow," Jaccob said, "you're good at that. I'm afraid I'm rather lacking in public relations savvy."

"You don't say?" Ruby chuckled. She had figured as much from the near debacle that had come out of Stardust's choosing to avoid politics when Prather had first come to power, no matter how many of his super-allies were engaged in active resistance. She was sure it was that refusal to engage that had him worried for his image now. If he'd been as vocally opposed to the Prather regime as most of his fellows, then there'd be little to no doubt his having saved Prather today had happened purely by accident.

Jaccob chuckled at her commentary. "Yeah," he allowed, "I guess that one's a little obvious."

"A little," Ruby agreed with a smirk. "But don't you worry, darling. You're in good hands. PR happens to be my strong suit."

"You don't say?" Jaccob half-mocked, winking at her.

Ruby winked back. "I'm just saying you don't need to worry about message and branding and such if you don't want to. Stick with me and I'll do as much of that as you want me to."

Jaccob chuckled and inclined his head in her direction before turning his attention to the television.

Ruby punched the digits to tune into 24-hour news.

It was no surprise the featured story was the White House

bombing. There had been plenty of news media invited to the event, plus the entire White House Press Corps had been allowed in. Anyone else might have been astonished at the level of gore currently on the screen, but Ruby understood the need to compete for viewers when an event was as saturated with coverage as this one was. She had no problem with the gruesome live shots.

There was chaos and carnage as far as the eye could see. In-studio reporters tried their best to narrate the shaky and occasionally distorted pictures coming in from their cameras still on the North Lawn. They were reporting the number of dead and wounded, with updates every couple of minutes. Ruby was pleased to hear that medevac helicopters had already been dispatched to the White House, and triage was being set up by the Secret Service with the support of the Marine Corps on the scene. She let herself wonder for a minute whether Prather might have a hard time landing in the midst of all that, but she decided she honestly didn't care. Whatever inconvenience this whole episode was for that abominable louse was fine with her. It was an attack against him that had caused his whole thing.

And if he hadn't been a horrible, despicable, slimy piece of trash, then today's attack would never have happened. If he was bothered by its aftermath blocking his travel path or disturbing the peace of his opulent government residence, then he ought to be thankful it wasn't a whole lot worse. A bit of inconvenience surely beat being blown to a million pieces.

There were two reporting segments in particular that caught Ruby's attention as she sat on the sofa with Jaccob watching the coverage unfold over cognac. She knew he was interested in what they might be saying about Stardust; she cared about that part, but she was equally interested in what the news had to say about her people.

Every person on that stage when the explosions happened, save Prather himself, had been in her employ. If she was about to need some bereavement press releases drafted or a few job openings posted, the sooner she knew that the better. Those were the kinds of things that had to be crafted with care—not just any member of her PR team could be charged with such a sensitive assignment. She'd learned that somber fact the hard way early in her career when she'd inadvertently come off as callous and cold in her public response to the deaths of a few fans at a Cassidy Sweet show in a California mall. She resolved to handle any similar situations differently. So she turned up the volume when the story switched to the fate of the Young Dudes.

The picture on screen shifted to some footage from their performance this afternoon. Ruby couldn't help but to critique the aesthetic; the lights were a little too red for a daytime show, and she seriously wished Jordan hadn't worn that awful patterned shirt. She'd have to talk to Artist Management again about not letting the talent pick their own wardrobe. She'd been having that fight with the Young Dudes since their second album, and they always seemed to want to test their limits. Gods, she hated boy bands sometimes.

But it was their well-being, not their appearance, that had to matter most today. Ruby didn't hate boy bands enough to want to be rid of the one that had been her consistently highest revenue property for the past five years. Annoying and rebellious as they could be sometimes, the Young Dudes had made her heaps of money, and she was very concerned as to their ability to continue doing that.

The reporter in the studio read from a teleprompter that Hunter had been one of the first victims evacuated; he'd been alive the last anyone knew. So that was good news. She'd have to get Bridget or one of her artist managers to find out hospital details. The other Young Dudes were all being treated for minor injuries and were expected to be released within the hour. There was brief mention of Amani Kasabian and of Cate and Nicholas from Nicetime as being treated for injuries as well, but of everyone's injuries, Hunter's seemed the most concerning.

Ruby took a deep breath and another swallow of cognac. At least she wouldn't be losing more than one source of income.

Jaccob seemed to be in a state between completely miffed and mildly pleased that Stardust seemed to be a non-story.

"You know," Ruby said, looking back and forth between Jaccob and the television screen, "there's every chance the cameras were all pointed the other way. There's every chance no one even saw you help Prather."

"You don't think it'll come out?" he asked her dubiously.

Ruby took another drink and shrugged. "Probably not if we don't want it to," she said. "And even if it does get out that Prather left with us, he owes you pretty big right now. I'm sure we could talk him into telling the truth if he gets asked. You wanted to get us out of there. He knew the way. In exchange for his access and guidance, he got to take advantage of your shield technology until we were all clear of the danger."

"You think Prather would do that?" he asked dubiously.

Ruby sighed. "Like I said, he owes you, and he owes me. And with his history, and with his well-known attitude toward superheroes, he might. Not that it matters much. We know what really happened, and the cameras don't lie. So if there is footage of what happened, all it's going to show is you saving yourself and the people nearest you, and that lunatic poltroon diving for cover at your feet."

Ruby shrugged and took another sip from her drink; as far as she was concerned, the conversation was over. Either no one would ever know Jaccob had helped Prather at all, or everyone would hear from every quarter the full and unvarnished truth of the matter. The story switched then from the wounded entertainers to speculation about the perpetrators of the bombing. The story seemed to be set in the minds of the broadcasters that the attack had been orchestrated by Islamist terrorists.

They switched feeds again and re-ran part of a story from several months ago. Ruby had all but forgotten the fuss when nearly the entire complement of an internment camp for suspected terrorists had somehow vanished. News of that variety rarely crossed her radar at all. She preferred to keep her consumption of media curated to include only things that directly affected her empire, but that had been such a big story at the time that she distinctively remembered it having happened. She hadn't given it thought since. Thinking about it now, she was sure the news anchor was completely off-base.

They cut to a shot of a briefing room. Vice President Michaels stood beside whoever was taking the current turn as White House Press Secretary. The portly blonde man with an obvious spray-tan was declaring today's attack the work of rogue Islamists with an agenda against America.

She almost let the truth slip right then.

She was glad she managed to hold her tongue; there'd be an awfully lot of explaining to do if she were to have just blurted out what she knew in that moment. Jacob would want an explanation, and she wasn't in any way prepared to give him one. But those claims were entirely false and she knew it.

They hadn't been attacked by bombs, they'd been attacked by magic. Ruby knew that, and she was pretty sure anyone with two clues to rub together about explosives and forensic analysis knew that, too. The Secret Service had to know by now. And if they didn't, they would soon. There wouldn't be any devices found—no switches or powder, no fuses, wires, or intended projectiles. Whatever had exploded in the crowd today had been magical, not mechanical.

And it hadn't been Islamic magic.

Ruby had enough experience with magics of different origins that it was usually easy to identify the root of the power behind any mystical energy she encountered. Islamic magic had a very particular feel and flavor to it, and today's explosions were decidedly not of that origin. The energy behind this magic was not Islamic energy. It wasn't even pre-Islamic. And the more Ruby thought about it, the more she was convinced it wasn't even Middle Eastern.

Ruby had a definite suspicion as to where the magic behind these explosions had come from. She had a strong familiarity with the general flavor of the energy. And Ruby knew, in a way that not many people did, of someone who had both the power to affect an attack like this one and also a beef with Prather large enough to get them to act.

It was only a hunch, but it was a powerful one.

She'd have to look into it further after she got home.

CHAPTER
TWENTY-FOUR

There was only one way to verify Ruby's suspicion as to who had been behind this afternoon's attacks. When the car from the airport dropped her off at her building, she didn't even bother going up to her penthouse. Instead, she took the elevator only as far as her offices, then dashed across the lobby and to the public elevator bank.

She was sure she looked a mess, doubly sure when she caught the looks on the faces of the few passers-by who saw her in the lobby. She had literally forgotten it was the middle of the work day. Thankfully, she was alone in the elevator lobby when the car came. She'd have hated to have had to shoo unsuspecting employees or visitors out of the lift, but she'd have done it. Ruby used her thumb print to unlock the keypad allowing her access to the non-business floors of the building and punched the button for the forty-sixth floor.

She stepped off the elevator into the empty marble foyer of the penthouse beneath her office and crossed through the vestibule's arched entryway into the open great room of the opulent residence. The décor had been brought up and set out exactly to her specifications. This was good. This meant what she was here to do was actually going to be possible. It had taken some doing to get all the requisite items imported and delivered—she'd had to go so far a few times as having the crates mislabeled as fakes and knock-offs so that she could bring them into the country. It seemed multiple international governments took issue with illicit trafficking of antiquities, and some even had problems with legitimate purchases by private collectors outside their countries of origin.

But not a single one of them appeared to give a damn about cheap copies of those same antiquities. A few shoddily printed labels and a forged paper trail putting the true items elsewhere was all it had taken. Ruby wasn't surprised that no one in the customs office had been able to identify the genuine article when told they were looking at a fake. The best and the brightest never seemed to find their way into government service. That held especially true under the current administration.

The statuary and tapestries were all set out just so, as was the sparse-but-still-impressive oversized baroque furniture. But the furnishing, as perfectly suited to purpose as it was, wasn't enough to keep the place from feeling empty. Ruby's footfalls echoed loudly as she crossed into the center of the great room. It amazed her that after everything she'd been through today, her shoes still hadn't grown uncomfortable. That was part of the value in expensive shoes, she figured.

It occurred to her that perhaps she should have taken a moment to try and repair her appearance, but the conversation she'd come here to have seemed far more pressing than her hair or her face. She was sure she'd hear about how haggard she looked, but that was hardly the most important happening of the day, although she was well aware that allowing herself to be seen in such a disheveled state was nearly as rare an occasion as an attempt on the life of a world leader.

Either way, she needed to do what she needed to do, and she was far too anxious to shower and change before she did it. Ruby crossed swiftly to the switch on the wall and activated the mechanism to draw the curtains. Jaccob and Mike were next door, and it would do her no good were they to get a peek at the conversation she was about to have. She'd done a good enough job keeping the truth of this association from Jaccob thus far. Getting caught now would just be embarrassing. Letting him catch her at this because she'd left the curtains open would have been a rookie mistake. And Ruby Killingsworth did not make rookie mistakes.

"Loki!" she called out. "Loki!" She paced back across the mostly empty marble room. "Loki, will you please show up and talk to me? You know I'm not falling for the whole 'needs an avatar to manifest' business; I set up the fetishes in this place myself."

She looked around the room then, taking mental inventory of the anchors and icons she'd had brought in. Promising Loki a forty-sixth floor condo would have meant nothing if she hadn't prepared the space to allow him to actually show up there. She'd done the arranging herself once the attendant items had been delivered; she knew it was right. If Loki failed to show, it was by choice and not by necessity. Ruby shook her head. "Listen here, you magnificent bastard. I need to talk to you. Don't make me use a summoning ritual."

"Now, now, Ruby," Loki's voice sounded from behind her. "Threatening to take me by force? Tsk tsk. That isn't very becoming."

"I'm more interested in what you're *becoming*," Ruby snapped as she turned to get a look at him. He was lounging in a red and gold rococo chair she'd had brought in for exactly that purpose. The thing had practically screamed his name when she'd seen it in a castle in Saxony. When she'd gone to outfit this sanctuary, she'd had her office make that castle an offer they couldn't refuse. She was glad it had been delivered in time for this conversation. The god was splayed across it, one leg hanging over the arm rest and one hand stroking the intricate carves in the gilded frame.

"And what's that?" he asked.

"Self-destructive and batshit crazy," she answered plainly. "Did you or did you not attempt to assassinate you own avatar today?"

"You mean my ex-avatar?" Loki asked smugly.

Ruby's jaw dropped. That could explain Prather's erstwhile feelings of abandonment. "Well, that's news."

Loki shrugged, turning to sit properly in the chair and smiling. "I've got three new little darlings to make my way through in the mortal realm," he told her.

"Three?" Ruby wasn't sure she'd ever heard of one god having multiple avatars before. But then again, Loki always had been a rule-breaker.

Loki nodded.

"Well, aren't you a damned overachiever?" she asked. "And how very like you: to have made the sorry sonofabitch the presumptive leader of the free world and then abandoned him to his fate."

"Isn't it, though?" Loki mused. "What is it you tycoon types say? It was very 'on brand'?"

Ruby laughed. "Indeed."

"But to answer your question, I didn't try to blow him up. That was Muslim extremists. Or didn't you see the news?"

Ruby frowned and shook her head. "I didn't have to see the news," she said. "I saw the whole thing up close and personal."

Loki looked horrified. He stood abruptly and took two long strides in her direction. "Mjolnir!" he exclaimed. "Are you all right? You look all right."

Ruby nodded. She was glad, all the sudden, that it was rather dim in here—otherwise she was sure he'd have amended that to "you look like fresh hell."

"Date a superhero," she said. "It could save your life."

Loki closed the distance between them. He rested his hands on her shoulders and shook his head. "I'll keep that in mind," he snarled. He took a tiny step back and crossed his arms over his chest. "You thought it was me?"

Ruby nodded.

"Why?"

"Because it was magic," she replied frankly. "They're not saying that on the news. I don't know whether they haven't figured it out yet or they're just not telling the media, but it was magic. The story seems to be that radical Islamist terrorists snuck the components for IEDs into the event, put the bombs together on site, and tried to blow up the President. And no one's contradicting that. But the fact is, that is not what happened. Those explosions came from magic, and it wasn't Islamic magic."

"How can you be so sure?" he asked, turning away from her and walking toward the large picture window at the far side of the room. With a flick of his fingers, the velvet curtain drew out of his way, allowing Loki his first look at the view from his new penthouse. The sun was setting, and the sky over the water was a vibrant shade of red-orange. Ruby followed him to the window, glad at least that he'd chosen to pull open the curtains on a side of the building not facing Starcom Tower.

"Didn't you hear me?" she asked, "I was right there. If Jaccob hadn't been standing beside me, I'd have been blown to oblivion. I felt the magic. I could taste it. And it didn't taste like Islam. It tasted—" She paused as she turned from the view of the water to look at the god beside her. "A little like you."

"Hmmm," Loki purred, turning to lean his shoulder against the pane glass of the window. "You remember what I taste like."

Ruby quirked her eyebrow and smirked. "Now wouldn't you like to know if I remember it fondly?" she teased. "But I mean it. Magically speaking, it felt far closer to your work than anything with roots in Islam."

"Well, it wasn't me," Loki declared flatly, standing up to his full height and taking several steps back from the window.

"I had to ask," she said.

"Of course you did," he replied, his tone indicating both an affirmation and a dismissal. He'd paused to examine one of the icons Ruby had placed in the vestibule. It was a statue of him, half-scale and reasonably accurate, standing on a pedestal just tall enough for the god to look himself in the eye. "But if I were after Prather, I wouldn't do it in front of a crowd. And I sure as hell wouldn't do it in front of Stardust. For all his well-tempered pontificating on what a rotten human being Prather is, the man can't help but rescue anyone in range."

"For what it's worth, I believe you. I didn't really think it was you to begin with. It was just… sort of your flavor."

"You talking flavors and magic like this," Loki said, turning from the statue's gaze to Ruby's, "does that mean you have your powers back?"

Ruby shook her head and wrinkled her nose. "Not quite yet," she replied. "But I'm working on it—with the help of the Blights you sent me and, of course, the Eye of Africa."

At the mention of the item, Loki's eyes lit up. "You found it?" he asked, advancing on her position in a way that nearly anyone else would have found menacing.

"Mm-hmmm. I did."

"Do you have it with you right now?" he asked, the hunger and excitement clear in his voice.

Ruby shook her head. "It's locked up safe and tight at the moment," she answered. Ruby took a step closer to Loki and pressed her hands against his chest. "You want to touch it, don't you?"

Loki growled under his breath. "I wouldn't mind," he allowed.

Ruby nodded, grinning wickedly. "I think that can probably be arranged," she said. "Once the ritual is completed and I have my full power back, I don't see why I couldn't let you come by for a cuddle with the Eye. After all, I owe it to you that I even have the thing."

"You'd do well to remember that," he said.

"I promise. Now, to the magic that tried and failed to murder your former avatar and, by extension, yours truly this afternoon," she said, getting back to her point in asking him here in the first place.

"Any ideas?"

Loki shrugged and shook his head. He turned again to look out the window. "You know my style has been copied across cultures," he replied, tracing some sort of pattern on the glass of the window with the tip of his gloved finger. "Have you looked into Nazis? I hear they're making a comeback."

Ruby crossed to join him at the window. "I haven't looked into a damned thing," she replied, "nor do I intend to. I was curious because it felt like you might have been behind it even if you weren't personally responsible for making the place blow up. And if you had been the source of the explosion, then I was going to apologize for foiling your plan and offer to help you try again."

Loki was clearly taken aback a bit by that comment. He turned abruptly to face her. "You? Apologize to me?"

"For this, sure. If that had been the case."

Loki was visibly astounded. He was shaking his head as he turned to walk back into the center of the room. "You've been spending way too much time with a good guy, Ruby," he insisted. "I've never so much as heard of you apologizing for anything ever before in your life, certainly not for foiling one of my plans. I seem to recall you cackling with sadistic glee the last time you screwed me over."

"To my own ends, you're right. I certainly have no qualms about fouling up someone's plans in furtherance of my own agenda. None at all. But this... today—" She shook her head and sighed. "If saving the life of that pompous miscreant formerly in your employ had put a monkey wrench in some plan you had, then the least I could do was to offer my contrition and try to make amends. You don't fail often, Loki," she declared, as much to stroke his ego as to make her point. "Which was yet another reason I wasn't sure it was you—at least not directly. And I just wanted to make sure I hadn't inadvertently caused you problems."

"Well," he said, turning to face her. "It wasn't me. And the only problems you've caused are for your superhero boyfriend, who's going to go down in history as the man who saved America's most despicable president."

"He's aware," she chuckled. "And he's not real happy about it. The only consolation I can come up with is that the Vice President might actually be worse. He's just as evil, but with a working knowledge of how governing works. I'd be more afraid with him in the chair than with Prather, to be honest. But if you'd been the one trying to have the bloviating tick murdered this afternoon, no matter how incompetent a minion you might have sent, I wanted to say I would be perfectly willing to do what I could to facilitate you getting another shot."

"You need to watch yourself, dear," he said. "Good guy boyfriend is making you lose your edge. The next thing you know, you'll start braking for animals and making anonymous donations."

"Oh, how dare you" she accused, clearly mocking. "I would never do such a thing. And you know it."

"I don't know," he said back, "You're being awfully thoughtful and generous. It's not at all like you."

"Well maybe it's just the near-death experience," she posited.

Loki took a deep breath. "You're sure you're okay?" he asked.

Ruby frowned. "And you're showing an unusual degree of care and concern," she countered. That was the second time in the space of one conversation when he'd inquired as to her well-being. It was more than a bit out of character.

"I am fond of a scant few mortals," he declared flatly. "And among that paltry number there is only one who has been grated my favor, and only one who is in on the verge of unlocking the secrets of one of the most powerful magical items ever forged. So pardon me for giving a damn whether you live or die."

"Well, you're awfully sweet about it," she admitted. "And I have to say, it's nice knowing someone cares whether I live or die."

"You mean not counting the superhero boyfriend," he sassed.

Ruby rolled her eyes. "He's a good guy, remember?" she replied. "He even saved Prather. He cares if everybody lives or dies. It's not the same."

"Oh, but it is, isn't it? Let me guess," he said, taking a few steps closer. "He gave you that bracelet."

Ruby nodded. It was an easy guess. The bracelet was lovely, but it wasn't her usual taste. Loki had known her long enough to be able to make a guess like that. "It's a techie thing," she explained, holding out the bangle for him to inspect at will. "It's got a button on it I can push to summon Stardust at any time to any place."

"And you think he goes around giving those out to all the fair citizens?"

"No," she allowed, "I'm sure he doesn't. But I'm still glad you give a damn I wasn't blown to pieces today."

Loki spared her his most charming half-smile. "Just don't tell anyone," he insisted. "If word got out it could ruin my reputation."

"Or mine," she countered. "I'd just get called a liar because nobody would believe me."

"That's a thousand years of carefully curated public image," he declared.

Ruby dipped a curtsy in feigned reverence. "You surely have cultivated a brand. Nazis, huh?" she asked him then, once again getting back to her original point.

"You talked about my brand yourself," he replied. "You should know as well as I do how me and mine have been co-opted and borrowed and oddly translated by certain political factions over the years."

"True," she agreed. "But Nazis, Loki, really?"

"It was just a suggestion," he offered.

"Well, I suppose I don't really care," Ruby said. "As long as it wasn't you then I don't give a damn who it was trying to kill Prather this afternoon. The man's got more enemies than I have millions, and

I have neither the time nor the energy to figure out which one of them tried to forcibly scatter him across the White House lawn."

"Even though you were nearly scattered right alongside?" he asked.

Ruby quirked her lip into a grimace. "Lie down with dogs, wake up with fleas. Hang around with asses, and you may need to cover your own."

Loki shook his head as he closed the distance between them. "You always have had a way with words," he mused.

"It's one of my many gifts."

"Right up there behind humility."

"I never claimed to be humble, nor selfless nor generous. But I'm a good ally," she contended, stepping closer to Loki and making a point to look him in the eye. "And for as long as we're on the same side, I won't screw you over. You—tricky bastard that you are—might not be so trustworthy. But I trust you. I trust we are on the same side—the side that cares about keeping the Blights from being discovered in Cobalt City, and the side that cares about unlocking the magic of the Eye of Africa, and the side that could not care less about Lyle Prather and whoever it is that's trying to kill him."

"Agreed," Loki declared. "And I must say, I'm not used to being trusted. I find the concept... rather exhilarating."

Ruby grinned. "If you were going to screw me over on this one, it would have happened already," she informed him flatly. "The worst you're liable to do at this point is to try and steal the Eye of Africa after I've finished with it. And at that point, I'll have my powers back, so what do I care if you take the totem? I'll be finished with it!"

"You mean," Loki said back, an air of intrigue creeping into the edges of his voice. "That you'd be willing to just... give it to me?"

"After I have my powers back?" she clarified. "After I'm finished with it?" Ruby stepped forward and took the god by his hands. "I'm trying to get my powers back, Loki, not take over a dimension. That's more your kind of thing than mine. Me, I just want my life back. So once I have that—once I have all the power I'm currently missing, and I'm sure it's all really mine and not still some extension of the fetish through me—then I will be more than happy to pass it along."

"I'm glad we got over being enemies," Loki said, drawing her hands to his face and kissing her knuckles lightly. "We're so much better together."

"Cut from the same ginger cloth," Ruby commented. "The wickedness in me recognizes the wickedness in you. I respect an unapologetic agenda. And you respect unabashed ambition. Neither one of us would be any better off if the other fails, and the both of us have figured that out. Worthy adversaries though we may have been, it's far less fun trying to put down someone you admire and respect than it is to be smacking down all of the *other* worthless beings who deserve it more."

"Yes, it's true. We can do far more damage—or good, depending on your point of view—together than if we work at crossed purposes."

"Exactly," Ruby concurred. "You point me to a magical item and lend me out some help to get my hands on it, I use the thing to repair myself, and then when I've finished I'm more than happy to turn the item over to your custody. I know I'll be able to get it back if I need it. I know where to find you." Ruby turned her head from one side to the other to indicate the opulent condo she'd gifted him.

"That you do, my dear," he replied. "And I'm very pleased that you have it set up just so. I appreciate a place so prepared I can manifest without need of an avatar. Even with three of them, sometimes it's nice to take a gander at you mortals with my own eyes."

"I'm glad you like it," she said. "It's your place, do with it as you will. Only I will ask that you try very hard not to blow it up. I have a good insurance policy, and my agent is pretty good about not asking questions. Living with Stardust across the way means I actually have a rider for things going kaboom unexpectedly. But still, please remember I live two floors up, and I happen to like this building the way it is.

Having to rebuild would be a pain in the ass. And I'd just rather not."

"I promise," he said. "Nothing too incendiary at your precious address."

"Now," Ruby said, shifting gears, "speaking of my address and things going kaboom, I really should get upstairs and get a shower. I have this miasma of violence and peasants about me at the moment. I need to wash it off."

"I wasn't going to say anything," Loki teased, letting go of her hands as he quirked his lip in her direction, "seeing as how you nearly died today and all."

"It pleases me that you care more for my survival than my comportment," she said.

"Well, only because we're here," he replied. "No one's going to see us together."

"Oh, there you are, you pretentious dandy. Don't ever change."

"Wouldn't dream of it."

"Good." Ruby stepped past him as she started back toward the elevator. "I'll be seeing you," she said in parting.

"Maybe sooner than you think," he replied, stopping Ruby in her tracks with that statement.

She turned around slowly to face Loki, one eyebrow raised in an expression that told him she would appreciate an explanation.

"You know the Blights are on loan," he clarified. "I'm going to have to have them back."

"Soon," she replied firmly. "Just let me get through the ritual and have powers in my own right and I'll gladly turn them over."

"Well, you had best put a rush on it," he replied. "I know powerful rituals can't be hurried if you expect proper results, but the Blights aren't mine, and I don't know how long we can keep them here."

"I'm nearly there," she assured him. "You'll know when it's finished."

"I mean it, Ruby," he warned as she turned again to leave. "The time is going to come when they have to go back, and when that time comes, it won't matter whether you've completed your ritual or not."

"I appreciate the heads-up," she said. "I'll do my best to finish quickly."

"Not your MO, if I recall correctly," he called after her. "I seem to recall you like things drawn out 'til nearly morning."

Ruby rolled her eyes. Good on him for getting in a lascivious barb. "Good memory," she declared with a grin.

"Please tell me your superhero boyfriend at least has some stamina," he teased.

"Well, he's no god," she replied, "but we're working on it."

"Well look at you with a little project," he mocked. "Your patience and generosity are shockingly admirable."

"And your snark is familiar and comforting. Now," she called, still not bothering to turn and face him again. "Off with you. I need a shower and sleep. I'll be in touch."

"You've been warned," he called out again as Ruby pressed the button for the elevator. The doors opened immediately. As she stepped in and turned to press the button to take her down to her office, she spared a glance back at Loki.

He was already gone.

CHAPTER
TWENTY-FIVE

A quick dash across the Goblin Records lobby, an admonishing look from Bridget, and a brief ride up her private elevator later, Ruby could not believe the relief she felt as she stepped into her own apartment. She really did need to shower, and she was positively aching to run her fingers over the Eye of Africa after today's magical craziness.

She thought about grabbing a drink first, and decided there was no harm in taking the short walk to the bar in her sitting room as a chance to peer across the way and see if she could get a glimpse of what was going on in Starcom Tower. It wasn't peeping if he had the shades open, right? She strode across the elevator lobby and through the vestibule toward the veranda doors and adjacent bar.

And was thoroughly surprised to find Jaccob leaning against her sofa. They'd compromised on his proposal of a lock on her door. She'd let him do a little tinkering with the building's wiring—putting alarms on the doors and windows of her penthouse; he'd wired in hidden code boxes all about the place. The system recognized Ruby by voice and by retinal scan, so all she had to do to keep an alarm from sounding was to speak the proper disarm phrase. And she'd insisted Jaccob give himself a code. The system had been in place for weeks now, but this was the first time she was aware of him using it to let himself in.

She smiled when she saw him, unconsciously reaching up to smooth her hair. "Hi," she greeted, rushing to him and taking both of his hands in hers. She was a bit surprised at herself for being so pleased to see him, but it was hardly the biggest surprise of the day. "I wasn't expecting you," she said. "I wish you'd called me; I'd have come up if I knew you were waiting."

"It's okay," he said. "I just wanted to—" Jaccob paused and looked closely at her. "Where have you been?"

Ruby did her best to smile. She was sure she looked a mess, with her hair all askew, and having made no effort to repair her face after this afternoon's calamity. Loki hadn't made nearly the issue out of it she might have guessed he would, but still, keeping to this disheveled state for this long was wildly out of character. It was unsurprising that Jaccob, in his perpetual and endearing concern for her, had noticed. Ruby tensed all over; she couldn't very well tell Jaccob she'd been downstairs talking to Loki.

"I was in the office," she lied. "I was dealing with our video production problems." It wasn't a complete fabrication; he didn't have to know the work she was referring to had been done entirely via her phone while waiting for and riding on elevators. "The FBI is demanding we hand over all our footage. They think we may have caught the bombers on camera. And they've already filed an injunction to keep us from releasing anything we'd already made copies of. They're afraid it could hinder their investigation, or something."

Ruby rolled her eyes as she crossed to the table where she kept her scotch decanter. She'd have been satisfied with a gin rickey to have in the shower, but as long as she was pausing to discuss this ugly business, she was going to have a dram of scotch. She gestured to the glasses and waited for Jaccob to nod before setting two of them in front of her and pulling the stopper on the decanter.

She continued as she poured two glasses. "Meanwhile I have multiple networks that carved out room in their schedules for the debut of this music video. We're using captured audio from the rehearsal and trying to cut together some sort of moving retrospective, feel-good/ Americana type thing from our camera checks, backstage photos, and old concert footage, so we have something to put on the air. I've got engineers on their way here now to see if they can do anything with that rehearsal audio to make it worth releasing on StarTunes." Replacing the stopper, she said, "And I'm getting pressure from all sides to donate any profits from this whole thing to whatever charity is bound to pop up in support of the bombing victims. Some people are saying *I'm* supposed to set up a fund or something to help pay the medical expenses of anyone who was injured in the bombing. Like it's my fault they don't have insurance."

"They're inner-city kids, Ruby," Jaccob reminded her. "Technically, it's Prather's fault they don't have insurance."

"Well then, let him pay for it," Ruby snarled. "The fact is we did this concert for free." She crossed back toward Jaccob, handed him a glass, and gestured for him to sit, sinking into the sofa herself and taking a generous sip from her drink. "I was only willing to do a free show because I knew we'd make it up. Between the publicity value and the sales of the single, I thought we'd at least break even. Now, because some fascist asshole or another decided to blow the thing up, I'm set to be out a cool eight and a half million dollars, give or take. All I can do is hope the Young Dudes comeback tour will make up the shortfall."

"Comeback tour?" Jaccob asked.

Ruby nodded. It was a scheme she'd come up with on the plane, and she was getting set to move forward with whether or not Hunter made it through this ordeal. Getting the text message saying that the fan favorite Young Dude was likely to make a full recovery already had her planning and scheming. "I'm sure I sound completely heartless," she allowed, taking another sip from her glass. "But I have a lot of people's livelihoods riding on my ability to keep this company in the black. It's better for everyone if I don't get all caught up having feelings about all this and just do my damned job."

Jaccob took a sip from his glass and reached out a hand. "You could have died today, Ruby," he reminded her. "From where I sit, you're allowed to cope however you see fit."

"Thanks," she offered. "I appreciate that."

"Hey, it's the truth. And if running your business and staying focused on the things you do best is the way you're going to get through this, then I'm sure not going to judge you for it."

Ruby smiled at him over her glass. "That's because you're a better person than most," she replied.

Jaccob shook his head. "I'm such a great guy that I have serious regrets over saving the President's life, remember?" he said.

Ruby frowned. "Don't be too hard on yourself," she said. "I'm sure you're not the only one who's disappointed he survived this afternoon's attacks—the bombers themselves notwithstanding. The man's got plenty of enemies."

"And now who knows how many are my enemies, too?" he asked, half rhetorically.

"Listen," she consoled. "You did what you do and saved my life and your son's. Prather just happened to be standing right there. Someday, when the FBI releases the video, we'll leak the story to any sympathetic media we can find that you weren't there to save Prather at all. Because I know for a fact there were cameras backstage. I can't imagine we don't have footage of the moment you activated those force fields. Everyone will see you're grabbing hold of Mike and me and you don't even see that Prather is there. In fact," she added "won't it be grand if one of the camera men got a shot of Prather diving for the deck like the spineless coward he is? They'll see him throw himself at the ground behind Stardust and maybe even start to question the man's whole stance on superheroes. Prather's been calling out your whole ilk for how many years, but the minute he's in danger himself, he falls at Stardust's feet and practically begs to be rescued."

Ruby squeezed Jaccob's hand and took another sip from her glass. "They can only keep the footage out of the public eye for so long," she assured him. "And if they try to say there's something vital to national security or some such, then I happen to know a sympathetic judge or two who will grant me an injunction so I can at least view my own footage. I know we had a camera on Prather when he walked out on stage—we probably had half a dozen. Sooner or later we'll be able to prove you saved his life purely by accident."

Ruby smiled at Jaccob over her glass. The bit about a sympathetic judge was at best a half-truth, but she wasn't going to go into detail with Jaccob. The fact of the matter was that she'd done a little magic on the man years ago while he was still in private practice, and the effects had remained over the years he'd been climbing the judicial ladder. Having a member of the Circuit Court of Appeals in her thrall had been a nice card to have up her sleeve over the years; it was one she'd rarely had to play, but it was always nice to know it was there.

"But you said on the plane you thought it might never come out?"

"And that remains a possibility, especially now that we have the cover of claiming the FBI won't release the footage. But if it does come out, I'm telling you, you have a leg to stand on. Any footage we caught will just prove our point that you were in no way trying to help the President."

"I guess that's what I've come to," he said, sounding suddenly the most deflated he'd seemed all day. "I guess this is what I get for refusing to take a side when this all got started."

"It's not so bad," she said. "You saved a citizen. Because you're a hero. Nobody's going to hold the lives you save against you."

Jaccob shook his head and looked back at her over his glass. "I'm not a hero, Ruby," he said softly.

"Well, you sure look like one from over here," she said.

He shook his head more intently. "I'm not," he insisted. "I'm just a nerd in a hero suit. The heroes are my old teammates. They're banding together again—did you know that? They're mobilizing against this monster in the White House and his horrifying, xenophobic, wrong-headed agenda. And what did I do? Huh? The man who was once their leader? I went to a goddamn concert on his lawn. I'm not a hero. Maybe the suit's the hero. But me, I'm just—"

"A good man," Ruby finished his sentence before he had a chance to. "A human man who has questions and who hesitates. A man who keeps those he loves from danger, who's shown himself to be just as fallible and indecisive as the rest of us. That's certainly more heroic than most."

Jaccob looked up at her and tried to smile, but the expression didn't quite manifest.

"And you know it doesn't matter to me. I could not care less whether you decide to join this big anti-Prather super team, keep fighting crime just the way you always have, or, hell, dismantle the suit and sell it for scrap. That super stuff—the suit included—isn't the part of you that interests me. In fact," she added, quirking her lip as she made a point to catch his gaze. "I like you just fine wearing nothing at all. If you'd care to come downstairs with me, I can do my best to prove it."

That time, Jaccob's smile went all the way to his eyes. "I wish I could, but I can't," he replied. "I have to go; the kids are over. Chuck's really taking this hard, and Mike's more shaken than I think I've ever seen him."

"Can you blame them?" Ruby finished her scotch and then smiled over at Jaccob. "It's been a pretty terrible day," she reminded him, as though there were some way he might have forgotten.

"They want me to take them away for a while," he told her, averting his eyes as though he was ashamed of what he'd said. "They asked if we could take the boat out—just weigh anchor in the middle of the ocean and do nothing for a week or two."

Refilling her glass, Ruby said, "Well, this is surely the time of year to do that. The seas should be calm and the weather's likely to cooperate."

"You don't mind?" he asked, sounding more than a little surprised.

"Mind?" she repeated. "Why would I mind?"

"Because you were standing right there today," he answered. "Because you could have been killed. And because we're—" He hesitated a moment before coming out with the word, "together." Jaccob shrugged as he drank the last of the scotch from his glass. "I was worried you'd be upset—that you'd feel like I'm abandoning you when you need me."

Ruby cut him off with a stern shake of her head. "First off," she began, "I've never needed anyone and I'm not about to start. So if you're under any delusions that that's the basis of this relationship, then I will beg you to reevaluate. Because I like you, a lot. And I like having you around. I *want* to keep you around. But I was perfectly capable of taking care of myself before we got together, and I'm perfectly capable of taking care of myself now. Plus, these are your kids, Jaccob. If anyone ever said you shouldn't put them first, then that person is an ass. The fact that something horrible happened and the first response from your adult children is to ask you to take them someplace where they can feel safe, well, I can't imagine a lot of parents have that kind of relationship with their twenty-somethings. It's damned remarkable, and there's no way I'd try to stop you from nurturing that."

"You're sure you'll be okay?" he asked, setting his glass down on the coffee table and scooting closer to her on the sofa.

Ruby couldn't tell whether he seemed more relieved or disappointed to hear she didn't mind him running off with his kids for a week or two. Truly, the idea that she could seem supportive of his relationship with his kids was a fantastic bonus, but the fact was his timing couldn't have been better.

She was very nearly ready to undertake the Ritual of the Scrolls.

The instructions were that she should begin atop the highest hill, and she figured the five-hundred-fifty or so feet above the city where her helipad lay would more than satisfy that requirement. But there was every chance the ritual would create some sort of spectacle up there—the kind that was sure to draw the attention of the romantically interested, perpetually concerned superhero across the way. Having him in the middle of the ocean with his kids for a week or two would give her just the window she needed to get through the ritual without his being at all the wiser.

"I promise." She put her glass on the end table, turned back to Jaccob then, and smiled. "The fact that your kids want to spend time with you is a good thing. I'll miss you," she offered, wondering if that would be enough to assuage his apparent disappointment in her assertion that she'd be fine without him. "But I'll be all right. And if I'm not, then I just have to pull this hinge apart." She shook the diamond bangle around her wrist before moving her hand to stroke his beard.

"And I'll come running," he replied. "Or *flying*, as it were."

"Then I'll be fine," she assured him, leaning in and kissing him sweetly. She didn't mind his leaving for a week or two. In fact, she was more than a little bit excited by the development. But she knew better than to let him go away without leaving him wanting more.

"You'll let me hear from you?" he asked, taking her hands in his as he moved to stand.

"You call me," she replied, standing with him and gesturing him toward the terrace door. "Interrupt my work day, please. I'm going to be underneath all this death and pain and whatever for the entire foreseeable future, and I would like nothing more than to have a bright spot every now and again."

Jaccob squeezed her hand and nodded. "I can do that," he agreed.

"Good," she said. "And can you do one more thing for me?"

"Anything," he replied, stopping his progress and pulling her closer.

Ruby grinned wickedly. If he was about to reconsider her earlier invitation to go downstairs to the bedroom, she'd make sure he knew it still stood. "Oh, *that* would be lovely." But it wasn't what she was about to ask. "But I thought you said the kids were waiting," she reminded him.

Jaccob made the most adorably pitiful face Ruby had ever seen a grown man wearing as he nodded in reply. "The kids are waiting," he affirmed.

"It'll be all right," she assured him. "I'll say very dirty things over the phone if you want me to."

Jaccob flushed a bright shade of pink and Ruby couldn't help but giggle. The precious naiveté of this man was downright entertaining at times. How anyone could have been married for over twenty years, fathered two children, raised them to adulthood, and yet still blush at the thought of a little phone sex just baffled her.

"What did you want me to do, exactly?"

Ruby's eyes went wide and her mouth fell slightly agape. This was the closest to double entendre she'd heard out of him, and she had to admit she liked it. "Now, now, Jaccob," she chided playfully. "Don't start teasing me when you know full and well you're not going to be able to stay and play."

Jaccob shrugged. "It's going to be a long two weeks," he sighed, stepping back and moving his hands to her shoulders.

Ruby nodded. "We'll get through it," she promised. "You're going to call and make my day every afternoon, remember?"

"That I'll do," he agreed again. "And I mean it, what was the other thing?"

"Make sure Mike takes his guitar with him," she said, her tone suddenly all business. Ruby knew from experience there was a chance not enough blood was in Jaccob's brain for his memory to be all it should. Speaking so firmly was a long-trusted tactic to get his frontal lobe engaged so he'd be more likely to remember what she was saying.

"He seems the type to work his feelings out in music. And if he's got something passionate in him, something he needs to get out about what went on today, I want him to be able to do that. I like the idea of him getting away with just his family. I think I'm going to suggest that to all my artists who were there this afternoon. Self-care is critical. And for most musicians, I find that includes the ability to make music out of whatever is ailing them. Let him know that if he has anything ready to share at the end of the trip, then I'll let him have whatever time in the studio he wants, and I'll put whichever producer in there with him he feels he works best with, and I'll give them whatever support they need to get that art out in the world."

Jaccob leaned in and kissed her again. It was a chaste kiss, as chaste as the first one he'd ever given her, but it was sincere. "Thank you," he said softly. "I'll tell him."

"Have a lovely trip, Jaccob," she said, starting again in the direction of the terrace. "Let me know when you're heading back toward port. I'll set up something special for when you get home."

"All right." They walked hand-in-hand to the terrace door where Jaccob stopped and shook his head. "I'm going to leave the StarBoard here," he said, turning to look back at Ruby. "I'll feel better with you having a way out of here if you need it."

Ruby frowned and shook her head. "Fifty stories up?" It was a conflict they'd had since the burgeoning beginning of their relationship. Jaccob always seemed to think she was in danger, and Ruby had met with variable degrees of success in convincing him she was perfectly safe. "With all the security I had put in when we built the place and all the extra security I let you put in, and the elevators and the stairs and the helipad?" she reminded him of the levels of mundane protection she had access to in the penthouse. If she'd thought he'd take at all kindly to the news that the place also had multiple levels of magical protection, she'd have told him that, too. And, not for the first time, she wished she thought he would.

The deeper she got into the use and the exploration of the Eye of Africa, and the closer she and Jaccob got, the more ardently she wished she could share her magical predilections with him. But she knew how he felt about all things arcane, and the last thing she wanted was to let him in on that part of her life before she was sure she had magic enough within her easy grasp to make him not care so much.

"Please," he implored, "Just keep it where you can get to it. Just to make me feel better?"

Ruby rolled her eyes. She shook her head as she relented, pulling Jaccob by the hand away from the glass-walled terrace and toward the door to the elevator lobby. If he couldn't fly the StarBoard back to his own building, he'd have to travel the old-fashioned way. "If it will make you feel better to know I have it, then I'll keep it."

"Good," Jaccob affirmed. "I know you don't have a lot of practice, but you've flown it before and I trust you could get across to my building. If anything comes around with intent to do you harm, then you yank open the switch on your bracelet and get the hell out of here, okay?"

Ruby heaved a patient sigh. Jaccob's habit of being protective ran the gamut between adorable and annoyingly paternalistic. This was one of the times it was skewing to the latter, but Ruby knew it also wasn't the time to pick a fight about it. "I can take care of myself," she assured him as they crossed the vestibule into the elevator lobby. "I've done it for my whole life and I can do it now." Jaccob opened his mouth to challenge her, but she cut him off before he had the chance. "But in case there's something new coming my way, in case this afternoon's attackers now have a target on me or on us, I will keep these tools at the ready. And I promise to call you if anything looks even remotely out of hand. But I doubt it will be necessary. So go. Have a good time. Enjoy your children. Let yourself relax. Call me when you can. And I'll see you when I get back."

"All right," Jaccob said, pressing the elevator button before leaning in to kiss Ruby again. "And thank you for humoring me."

Ruby laughed. She didn't mind that he knew what she'd been doing, as long as he didn't seem too bothered by it. It appeared he didn't mind. "You're just lucky you're cute," she said.

It was Jaccob's turn to laugh. "I'll call you tomorrow," he said, stepping onto the elevator.

Ruby winked. As the gilt doors began to slide shut, she called, "You'd better." Ruby waited in the elevator lobby until she saw by the indicator light it had reached the ground floor. She'd miss Jaccob while he was away, she was sure—particularly in those hours of the night when she'd begun to count on being able to roll over and find a man in her bed or send a text and have one at her door within moments. But lacking sex for a week or two would be worth it for the magic she would possess once she'd completed the Ritual of the Scrolls.

She'd even be able to tell him about her magic. Once she had the power to bend his will—to convince him her magic was nothing to be feared or bothered by—she'd be able to be honest with him.

Well, maybe not *completely* honest. There were plenty of things she was sure she wouldn't be sharing with him no matter how long their relationship lasted nor how powerful her control over him ever became. But it would be nice to be able to be more fully and unapologetically herself around him. She didn't enjoy having to keep so many secrets and having to censor herself around Jaccob.

She was pretty sure he was in love with her, or at least trending heavily in that direction. And she liked that. And she didn't like having all of this deception looming between them. She was also pretty sure he'd be hurt and disappointed to learn the depth and the breadth of what she'd been keeping from him, and that just wouldn't do.

That in and of itself was bizarre. She'd never cared about anybody else's feelings before. And had it not been for Jaccob's sweetness and devotion, she'd have probably found it altogether distasteful she cared about his. But there it was. She did care about Jaccob's feelings, and she didn't want to hurt him. It was more than just not wanting to damage this thing between them, too. At first, she'd been sure that was what was compelling her to keep her magical past as well as her supernatural ambitions from him. After all, she'd had an agenda where he was concerned and she hadn't wanted to do anything that might damage that.

But somehow that whole thing had melted into an actual concern for his feelings. Even without magic, she was sure now that a hurt—even one as big as her coming out a magically gifted—would be forgiven in time. She was surprised to discover that the idea of causing him any hurt in the first place was troubling her far more than was any direct effect that hurt might have on her relationship.

It was odd and it was out of character, but it was true.

Fortunately, the concern would be moot in short order. Once she had the magic back in her to keep that hurt from ever happening, they'd both sleep easier. And if getting to that point was going to mean going a couple of weeks without sex, then that was a price she was surely willing to pay.

CHAPTER
TWENTY-SIX

Ruby had spent the better part of several days doing nothing but preparing for the Ritual of the Scrolls. It was easy enough, it turned out, to be scarce around the office in the wake of having nearly been killed in a bombing. Normally she would have scoffed at being the object of someone's patience and understanding, but under the circumstances, she'd decided to use it to her advantage.

Jaccob had sent her the most adorable picture of himself in a captain's hat as he'd prepared to leave port with Mike and Chuck for what they'd decided would be a two-week sojourn to Bermuda aboard his yacht. With the photo, he'd sent a link so she could check his GPS coordinates in case she got worried he'd been out of touch too long. That had been very dear and thoughtful of him, she supposed. She was sure he would never have guessed she'd be using it to make damn near certain he was almost to Bermuda (and therefore as unlikely as was humanly possible to turn up on her veranda) in order to begin a powerful ritual.

Fifty-or-so stories up on her helipad was definitely going to be an adequate location. She'd had the Blights check and double check, and there was no mention anywhere of natural rock nor of earth nor of anything that pointed to the ritual having to take place in nature. It was only the height above sea level that seemed to be the determining factor, and Ruby was pretty sure the top of a skyscraper was the highest up this ritual would ever have been attempted. She had no idea whether greater height gave her greater chance of success, but what she did know was that with Stardust in Bermuda, being this high into the skyline meant she had little to no chance of interruption.

She picked a night when the forecast said the sky would be cloudless, giving her a clear view of the waxing moon, as had been called out by the ancient text as being critical to the success of the rite. A clear night, the highest point in the city, and a tunic of deepest blue stitched with horsehair. In the beginning, she hadn't been sure how she was going to go about getting that sewn without her magic. Even in Cobalt City, tailors had their limits. But then Doubt had mentioned that nowhere did the Scrolls say the garment had to be stitched *exclusively* with horsehair, just that the stitching was required, so the few stitches Ruby was able to add herself to the finished garment should be more than sufficient. She made sure to do the work on the tunic in the presence of the Eye; she was sure she'd have gotten some feeling from the object if she was doing something wrong.

Such a feeling had never come.

And so as the sun had set on the night in question, she had gone up to her helipad to begin the ritual. She would have her powers back, and soon. She was as excited as she was tense, and it took her a minute to center herself properly; magic like this was hard enough to keep in hand when you had your emotions fully in check. Losing control of herself, even a little, could prove an unmitigated disaster.

With the Eye of Africa clasped tightly in her right hand, and the Blights stationed dutifully behind her, Ruby lifted her face to the sky and began to speak the words she'd spent so many weeks memorizing. Her breaths felt shallow, even as the very first words escaped her lips.

As she spoke the words of the incantation, the helipad before her seemed to fade into nonexistence. She was somehow standing suspended in mid-air as before her appeared a seemingly endless tunnel of concentric vortexes.

She was terrified.

Ruby couldn't remember another time in her life when she'd been frightened by magic. But fear was surely the emotion she was experiencing as she hung there in space, looking ahead to nothingness and knowing she had to take a step.

Grasping the Eye as tightly as she was able, she began moving forward into the swirling emptiness that greeted her. She continued the incantation.

How long had she walked that it appeared she'd made no progress? Days? The swirling void around her neither progressed nor transformed, remaining a terrible monotony of garish light and all-consuming blackness. Were it not for the ever-increasing temperature of the Eye of Africa squeezed tightly within her fist, she'd have wondered if the ritual was fully engaged. A glance at her hand saw the jewel beginning to glow. Ruby continued her trek forward through the nothingness.

The air around her seemed hot and dry all of the sudden. What had been nothing but light and magic beneath her feet began to feel coarse and loose like sand. It was taking more and more effort to make every step. The exertion was taking her breath, making it harder and harder to speak the words of the rite as she struggled forward.

The Eye was shining now, blinding light escaping from between Ruby's clenched fingers. It was blistering hot against her palm, but she held fast. Dropping the instrument of magic would almost certainly disrupt the ritual; she'd keep hold of the Eye of Africa if it burned a hole clear through her palm.

She'd been warned there would be trials. She was prepared to be tested. If holding onto a white-hot stone was one of them, she'd gladly bear it.

The sand beneath her feet got deeper, coarser, and began to

materialize into dunes stretching out as far as Ruby could see. She'd passed to some other place on the Coil, she was sure of it. But where and when she was, or what rules of magic applied here, remained terrifyingly unknown. Was it even permissible to use the magic of the Eye to aid her in the trials of the Ritual?

Ruby had no idea.

A lifetime of experience with magical rites and rituals told her it was better not to try. No matter the difficulty she faced here in this place along the Coil, conquering it on her own, without the use of borrowed magic, was the best guarantor of success. It would be trying; it might be the most difficult ordeal Ruby had ever undertaken, but she would get through it on her own mettle.

It was her best chance.

She was making progress now—visible, discernable progress. The dunes in the distance grew closer and closer until an imposing mountain of sand filled her view. The Eye was leading her now, drawing her forward as though it were magnetized. Her hand rose in obedience to the magic overwhelming her and spurring her onward.

She began to climb.

The sand beneath her slipped and slid as she struggled upward, the hill crumbling under her weight with every step. The whole dune seemed to be collapsing beneath her, and yet the massive height of the thing remained unaffected. The steep face of the dune made it impossible to climb with only her legs. She tucked the white-hot Eye of Africa into her bodice, recoiling a little at the pain where it seared the flesh on contact.

With both hands, she continued to claw her way up the mountain of sand. The desert around her felt like an oven, the arid ether parching her lungs with every heaving breath as she battled her way toward the top. The sand was scorching hot—sharp granules infiltrating her velvet slippers and scoring the quick beneath her nails. Sweat dripped from every pore in her body, sizzling when it hit the gem tucked into her bodice, all of it evaporating almost immediately, too quickly to do any good in cooling her down.

But the Eye itself began to grow cold. At first, Ruby hadn't noticed. She'd been doing all she could to put the discomfort of the stone's heat out of her mind; it had taken her some time to become aware of its cooling. By the time she clambered onto the uneven summit of the dune, the gem had gone from feeling like a branding iron to an ice cube tucked in her bodice.

Ruby paused to catch her breath, aware suddenly that the air around her had also cooled. It was easier to breathe up here, although catching her breath after a climb that tough would still take minutes. And the Eye was still drawing her forward.

She hadn't been thinking when she'd tucked the gem into her bosom. She'd only meant to tuck it into her underthings as quickly as possible, but reaching across with her right hand in a hurry had landed the Eye of Africa squarely atop her heart. She felt it now, its chilled energy radiating out from her body as her pounding heart began to settle atop the mound of sand. Its obtrusive brightness had modulated into an otherworldly glow, and it thrummed with magic in time with her frenzied pulse.

A gust of wind blew her off balance. Oven-hot as the air below, it shifted the dune beneath her, knocking her to her knees. She lurched forward to catch herself as loose grains of hot sand pelted the exposed skin of her face and arms. The wind blew harder as Ruby struggled to get to her feet. The Eye was still compelling her forward, but the gusts were overpowering. Ruby inched forward on her hands and knees, her head pointed downward so as to keep the blowing sand out of her nose and mouth. It was difficult enough to breathe air this hot, the addition of the whirling particulate making it all but impossible.

And still she was all but gasping. Ruby Killingsworth had never been one to go in for physical fitness, and here on this dune she was paying for that decision in spades. Crawling across the shifting dune, her heart still pounding from the trek up the dune to the summit, she closed her eyes and tried her best just to follow where the Eye wanted to lead. She had to remember what she was doing here. She had to remember what was at stake. Her magic was on the line, and she'd be damned if she would be deterred at this point by a sandstorm and an ethereal desert.

She kept her eyes shut and redoubled her focus. The air was so thick with grit it wouldn't have been safe to open them; visibility was surely nil, besides. And yet she was as sure of where she was going as she had been when she'd first seen the dunes rising in the distance. Ruby continued forward, crawling through the shifting sands as the wind continued to buffet her from ahead.

She knew the summit of the dune wasn't wide. But she also knew the normal laws of the physical universe didn't necessarily apply in other parts of the Coil. As long as the Eye spurred her onward, she would continue forth. Forward and forward, she scrambled along on her hands and knees, straining to make progress against the heavy headwind.

She'd known it must be coming, but still it took Ruby by surprise when her hand reached out for the next spot of dune and landed downhill from where she'd expected. She shifted then, sure the headwind would work in her favor, trying to keep from falling down the far side of the dune.

Her effort was for naught. The wind shifted to swirl all around her as she felt herself begin to fall. Downward she went, tumbling end over end. For a full minute she fell—farther, she'd have guessed, than she'd climbed to begin with. Some time during her descent, the air had cleared. And it had cooled, the wind now blowing a mild temperature without its painful cargo aboard. Ruby was almost able to catch her breath. Her heart continued to pound in her chest, echoed by the glow and the resonance of the Eye of Africa where it sat in her bodice.

The fall ended abruptly. A landing from such a height should have been painful. It should have hurt rather a lot, but it didn't. Although the sudden deceleration was jarring, there was no real physical discomfort.

In fact, her landing was nothing short of a relief. The wind had stopped, having deposited her in a cool, dim room where she found it was safe to open her eyes.

The swirling sand had gone from her environment, but not so from her person. Streams of the coarse stuff emptied from the folds of her tunic as she got to her feet. Ruby ran her hands over her face, shaking loose the layer of caked sweat and sand that had formed on her forehead and temples. She continued to catch her breath as she took stock of this place where she'd landed.

It was a room, a chamber that would have been a circle had it not been for the corners. There was neither a visible door nor a window—no way for Ruby to discern how she'd gotten in nor how she would leave when the time came. The walls were carved in intricate shapes with every surface covered in brightly colored tiles laid in complex geometric patterns that made Ruby's already-throbbing head swim. Her eyes strained at first to adjust to the dimness of the place, but soon enough she was acclimated. The smell of balsam grazed her nostrils when she inhaled deeply, a pleasant sensation after the shallow, panting breaths she'd been forced to settle for on the dunes.

Ruby shivered as she stood in the center of the cavernous chamber. It was cold in here, and her skin was still slick with the last vestiges of sweat from the heat of the dunes. She reached into her tunic and withdrew the Eye of Africa from where she'd had it nestled. The last thing she wanted was an ice-cold thing against her skin in this already chilly room.

That had been the thing, apparently.

As she brought forth the jewel, its glow intensified, brightening in such a way that it seemed to bulge in her hand. For a moment, she actually feared it might shatter there on her palm. The glint from the gem became sun-bright, causing Ruby to squeeze her eyes shut in defense. When she opened them, she found she was not alone.

Before her stood a woman, or maybe she was a goddess. She was a good two heads taller than Ruby, and larger in every dimension. She was lithe and well-muscled with skin as dark as jet; she was quite honestly the most beautiful woman Ruby had ever seen. She was dressed in a garment of simple white, adorned in a veritable armor of lapis and opals cascading from a solid gold collar. She wore a gold headdress bejeweled in cut stones matching her sparkling tabard.

The woman's eyes were bright, glowing almost incandescently with the same intensity of the jewel in Ruby's hand. There was only one person this could possibly be. In a gesture of uncharacteristic humility, Ruby bowed her head and lowered herself to genuflect before her host. "Makeda," she said, her parched voice barely a whisper as she held the jewel up for the inspection of its original master.

Ruby dared lift her face. Makeda was considering her, standing back with a grim yet thoughtful look on her face. She brought her hands up to her chest, and made a gesture that looked to Ruby like wringing or rending. In a moment, she understood it. The Eye of Africa rose on its own from her flat palms and moved through the air toward its former owner.

Halfway to what Ruby guessed to be the totem's destination, it stopped. Makeda flared her fingers, and Ruby watched in awestruck horror as the Eye of Africa disintegrated in front of her.

She felt beaten, betrayed, wounded. She was ready to travel wherever in the Coil was necessary, to exact revenge against Loki for sending her on a torturous fool's errand. The ritual wasn't even over yet, and the Eye had been lost!

The ritual wasn't over yet.

Makeda gestured for Ruby to stand, not with a movement that Ruby altogether recognized, but somehow she understood. Whatever magic the Eye of Africa had imbued her with before tonight was with her still. It was that magic, she felt in her very bones, allowing her to communicate. And if the magic of the Eye persisted, then the Eye itself persisted. This was the thing that was supposed to be happening. This was all part of the rite.

"Without moving while living," Makeda's deep, resonant voice sounded then. "It moves when its head is cut off."

Ruby took in a deep breath. The smell of fir trees had become almost overpowering as she searched her brain for the answer to this riddle.

She'd known the riddles were coming. She'd read them and studied them and had the Blights do tireless research as to their content, possible translations, and proper answers. She would be tried during this rite, and these riddles were part of the trial.

"A tree," she replied. A breeze wafted through the chamber, sounding a hollow whistle as it passed over the carved columns flanking the chamber's corners.

Makeda nodded. Letting her hands back down to her sides, she spoke the next riddle. "Produced from the ground, man produces it," she began, "while its food is the fruit of the ground."

Damn these things were confusing! But if they were merely questions, they wouldn't be riddles. Ruby searched her brain for the answer. "A wick," she said, to which Makeda gave a nod. Ruby's nerves began to lessen; the violent spike of adrenaline from the moment she feared for the Eye's destruction was passing out of her system. She could do this. She knew she could.

There were nineteen riddles in all. Each was conveyed, she was sure, more by magic than any common language; still, Ruby was convinced there were some things lost in translation. Or perhaps it was merely the distance of time and not the difficulties of grammar and syntax that made the words so confounding to Ruby's ears. Still she replied. For each riddle, there was a prepared answer, and once she'd managed to focus herself, purge the adrenaline from her system, and engage her logical brain, she'd managed.

Years of training herself to recall facts and figures had made the memorization of the riddles and their responses easy enough to manage at her desk. But the challenge of answering cryptic queries from an imposing goddess in a room with no exit was nothing a person could adequately prepare for in the mortal region of the Coil. Eventually, she found her rhythm, answering Makeda's questions with certainty and calm.

When the riddles were through, Makeda inclined her head. Ruby did the same in return, and when she moved again to gaze back at her hostess, realized she was once again alone.

The ground trembled beneath her. At first it was a gentle rumble, but in the space of seconds, the tiles beneath her feet were shifting as fast as the sand had on the dune that had led her here. Ruby had been in an earthquake once, as a child on a family vacation to California. She remembered it well, how terrified she'd been then. This movement of the ground beneath her feet was wholly unlike that one had been.

She heard a loud crack, and then another. Searching for the source of the sound, she looked up just in time to see the ceiling cleave along its length and begin to crumble down around her. Before her, the floor tiles began to almost liquefy, pouring themselves down a tunnel that was opening beneath the floor like a sinkhole.

But it wasn't a sinkhole.

As chunks of stone and fragments of tile began to fall from above and shatter all around her, Ruby realized the tiles from the floor weren't being lost down the tunnel, but rather *building* it. This was the way out. It had to be. As the still-quaking chamber collapsed behind her, she dashed for the tunnel, cringing at the feeling of the sand still in her shoes but not daring to pause and dump it out. The chamber was imploding on her; she was sure of that now.

She ran farther and deeper into the relative safety of the tunnel, never slowing until she could no longer hear the tumbling of stone and shattering of tile. As the clamor of destruction faded, Ruby noticed a new sound behind her. She turned her head to see the Blights running in step behind her.

She hadn't known whether having them on the helipad would allow them to join her on her quest. They hadn't been present in the void, on the dunes, or in Makeda's chamber, but for some reason (which Ruby chose not to question), they were here with her now. Grateful for the help, she offered them a nod and gestured for them to follow before continuing deeper into the tunnel.

CHAPTER
TWENTY-SEVEN

The tunnel went on for what could have been a mile or more. Tiles from the chamber surrounded them on all sides at first, making the floor of the cylindrical tube tricky to navigate, but leaving no question in anyone's mind as to whether they were headed in the right direction. As they went, the tiles grew sparse, receding from the floor as it flattened to a reasonable walking surface of natural clay. The ceiling was next. The empty spaces swooped out from above and along the walls, giving the remaining tile pattern a tentacle-like quality as the colors spread farther and farther apart and eventually disappeared.

Ruby found herself then in a nondescript cavern, nothing but oddly rippled stone on all sides. The uneven floor and domed ceiling seemed to stretch out infinitely before and behind her, with no sign of the steep downhill she'd traversed on her way from Makeda's chamber. It was bright enough at this spot to see several meters in both directions, but with no visible source of light. Ruby leaned tentatively against the curved wall and set to dumping the remaining sand from her velvet slippers. She felt anxious, unsure, and unprepared.

Nowhere in the Scrolls of Solomon had she read mention of a cave. Then again, the Scrolls themselves had been rather vague on the experience of the ritual. Other than the riddles, there hadn't been much by way of detail. *Trials* they had said, *ordeals*. There hadn't been mention of desert sand, come to think of it.

Ruby leaned against the wall of the cavern, happy enough for the moment to have caught her breath and thankful she appeared to have a moment to collect her thoughts before moving forward. It was warm in here, too—pleasantly warm. Ruby felt comfortable for the first time since she'd left the roof of her building back in Cobalt City. But she was miffed as to what she might do next.

"Any ideas?" she asked the seven Blights as they milled around the cavern. "I don't remember anything in the Scrolls about a cave."

"Lava tube," Fire said back absently.

"Pardon?"

"You said 'cave,'" Fire replied. "And, I mean, it is a cave, I guess. But technically it's a lava tube."

Ruby frowned; she had no idea what the girl was talking about.

"Like, usually when you think of a cave it's like, a thing formed by water and erosion or whatever. But this is a lava tube. Definitely formed by hot magma."

"How can you tell?" Ruby asked. She wasn't sure whether this information was at all relevant, but still she was curious. "Lava starts fires. So it's kind of my thing."

"So it's a volcanic cave," Doubt chimed in. "So what?"

"Because volcanos make opals," Ruby realized. Her mouth fell open, and her heartrate jumped. Was that what this was? "I think—" she said after a moment. "I think we're in King Solomon's Mine."

"So, what?" Doubt asked. "We keep walking?"

Ruby nodded. "I think so." Ruby stood firmly and looked around at the Blights. She centered herself again, the way she had on the helipad before speaking the opening lines of the ritual. And she knew which way to go. She turned decisively and headed up the tunnel.

"You're aware you're headed back the way we came?" Discontent asked her.

"But it isn't," Ruby challenged. "The rules of the mortal realm don't work here. This is the way." She led them at a generous clip along the surprisingly flat tube. The light was lessening; whatever was causing it existed only in the area where they'd congregated. Ruby didn't bother to pause and wonder why or how that was the case.

"I don't think this is the way," Doubt contended.

"If Doubt is doubting something," Pestilence piped up.

"Exactly," Ruby affirmed, not bothering to slow her stride as the cavern got still darker. "Look at the walls."

"It's dark," Discontent griped.

Fire snapped, "Like that's ever stopped us." She drifted to the outside of the pack, raised her hand, and sighed. A tiny flame arose from each of her fingers, lighting the space just enough for all of them to see clearly the cavern's ridged stone walls and ceiling.

"If we were really just going back the way we'd come, we'd be well back into tiled walls by now," Ruby assured them. "We're going the right way."

The lava tube was long, twisting in places; it widened and narrowed unexpectedly, causing more than one episode of complaining as the Blights bumped into each other behind her. It was a tight space for eight people to navigate, but Ruby trusted her minions would find a way to work it out. She didn't have the mental energy to tend to their walking formation.

As they continued forward, Ruby shut her eyes against the darkness and tried to access the feeling she'd had before when the Eye had been shining in her grasp. What had it felt like searing her skin? What had it felt like ice cold and tucked into her bodice? What had it felt like to be blinded by the light escaping from between her fingers? And what had it been like to feel it leading her?

Ruby stumbled.

"Look, boss," Plague called out. "light!"

Ruby opened her eyes just as the group of them stepped into a pool of unexplained light not unlike the one they'd first encountered when they'd found themselves in the lava tube.

This part of the cavern seemed more finished, less natural than the place the earlier pool of light had shown them. In the center of this decidedly circular chamber stood a waist-high stone cauldron. It appeared to have been fashioned out of a stalagmite, which in and of itself seemed odd. There had been neither stalagmites nor stalactites along their path thus far. It occurred to Ruby also that this was the *end* of the lava tube. The strangely perfect circle they'd just stepped into was closed on all sides, save the small opening through which they'd entered.

"Wait!" Ruby called out as the Blights began to circle around the strange artifice. She didn't know where the word had come from, much less the feeling that had precipitated it, but she could only hope it had come from her attempted connection to the Eye. "We're not ready. We shouldn't be here. Don't move."

With that, she shut her eyes again and tried to feel what the Eye was leading her to do next. She lifted her hands to chest height, turning them palms-up as she drew in a slow and grounding breath. Slowly, gingerly, with no deliberation, she drifted back. Her feet shuffled silently across the smooth stone until she was sure she was outside the lighted circle.

Ruby felt her palms rise toward the ceiling, moving without volition as her head tilted upward in concert. Her heartrate was rising again, her breathing catching in her throat. When she opened her eyes, there was light spilling from her palms—it was as though the Eye were still in her possession. The ceiling shone with raw gems; crystals embedded in the rock of the cave had the light from her palms refracting in all directions. Tiny rainbows speckled the cavern walls as the jewels glittered in their rocky beds.

She did her best to ignore the light and the glow and the exquisite sight of the shimmering rainbows filling her view. She stared straight upward, concentrating her gaze on where the light from her two palms intersected. The point of light she'd found grew brighter and brighter, until it shone with all the intensity of the Eye when its light had burst through her fingers as she'd traversed the windy dunes. The light left her palms then, absorbed before her eyes by the gem at its nexus until the glow had gone from her entirely and was concentrated wholly in the stone.

The light modulated, changing in color and intensity as the crystals around it seemed to lose their ability to refract its beams. Eventually the brightness resolved itself into a diffuse glow, with the gem no longer putting off any light at all. A breeze blew through the cavern then; it was cool and fresh, and Ruby couldn't fathom from whence it might have come.

In the instant Ruby took to inhale the sweet, balsam-scented air that passed by her, the gem dropped from above and into her upturned palm. Ruby's heart was still racing, her breath still ragged, as she clutched the glowing gem to her chest. It was the Eye of Africa.

Or, rather, it would be.

Ruby knew then what she had to do next. She walked reverently back into the circle of light, this time not even considering a pause before she approached the cauldron at its center. She had the opal, but the totem was incomplete. She needed to finish its creation for herself. The cauldron was cool when she touched it; a solid mass of something metallic filled the bottom third of its bowl.

"Fire," Ruby directed, gesturing with her chin to the cauldron before her.

Fire stepped forward and nodded at Ruby. She dipped her hands into the bowl then, tensing her jaw as she pushed them through the solid metal, turning it as she did into a bright orange molten pool.

Ruby held her breath as she lowered the opal toward the cauldron's viscous contents. She was fully prepared for the liquid to burn; she braced herself for the inevitable pain and was taken aback when it failed to materialize. The slick metal was cool and refreshing against her hands as she passed the opal through the molten contents of the cauldron.

The metal collected itself upon the opal in just the configuration Ruby remembered from all previous dealings with the Eye. This was it. The totem was re-forming itself before her eyes. She could hear her name being called in the distance. Was this the sound of the magic of the gem being tied to her?

She heard it again.

No.

That wasn't right. The sound was discordant. It was all wrong. She shouldn't be hearing her name right now. Ruby's hands began to shake. Suddenly, she couldn't keep hold of the Eye. The cave was moving, swaying, wobbling, flashing in and out of existence maybe, as the sound of her name being called out from somewhere became louder and louder and closer. The circular chamber in which she stood began to crack and cleave, the solid stone walls crumbling into dust so fine it filled the air with clouds of grayish powder.

In an instant the walls were gone, and the air so thick with dust that Ruby could scarcely catch her breath. She doubled over, coughing and retching, losing her grip on the Eye as she was overcome. She fell to her knees then. Covering her nose and mouth with the sleeve of her tunic, she reached with her other arm back into the cauldron, rooting around in the ever-thickening metal to try and recapture the lost totem.

She heard her name again.

Ruby could no longer see the Blights. The room was too thick with powder for her to see more than a few inches. The liquid in the cauldron was quickly solidifying around her hand and she still hadn't found the Eye.

"Ruby!" She heard her name called again. This time, not only was she aware of the direction from which the sound had come, but she knew who was calling out to her.

"Loki!" she managed to shout.

The next thing she knew, the god was behind her. He had her by her elbow and was pulling her away from the cauldron just as its contents hardened entirely.

"What the hell are you doing?" she demanded. "The Eye was in there! It's lost! You've lost it!"

"We've got bigger things to worry about," he told her as he pulled her away from the crumbling lava chamber. He was forcing her to run faster than her fatigued legs wanted to move, but his grip on her arm told her she'd best keep up or else risk losing it.

She'd have asked him what the hell he was talking about, but she was still too overcome by the dust and silt in the air to say any further words.

"Where are the Blights?" he asked then.

"They are here!" a man's voice answered. The voice was thick with an accent Ruby didn't recognize, but the admonishment in the man's tone was as clear as day. "And now they go."

There was a sound like a train passing through the cavern, and the dust kicked up in all directions as Loki pulled Ruby ever faster through the cave.

"What's going on?" she managed to ask as the walls of the tube began to crumble in larger and larger chunks all around them.

"I told you the Blights weren't mine," he replied. "That was Mahakala, their caretaker—a Tibetan god from whom I borrowed those seven without asking."

"You lent me another god's minions without having asked him first?"

"Not his minions, precisely," Loki answered. "He doesn't wield them, he just… watches them. Thought it was an awful waste of so much power just to have them milling about like he did. And he has thousands! Look how long it took him to realize these seven had gone missing."

"Loki, I swear to you, I'll—"

"Swear at me later," he interrupted, still tugging her arm. "But now you need to run!"

"What the hell is happening?" she asked, still running at a quick clip and surprised her heaving breath was even allowing her to speak.

"He found the Blights and he came to get them. I was barely able to get here in time to warn you. And he's known as a wrathful deity for a reason; he ripped a hole in the fabric of this whole dimension—it's imploding on itself. If we don't get to some other place in the Coil immediately, we're likely to be destroyed right along with it!"

It was then Ruby noticed they were no longer running in a cloud of dust. The lava tube was looking less and less familiar as they went. They were running to an exit. They were running to a point where Loki was sure he could get them back through the Coil. Say what you would about Loki's wickedness: he was a good fellow to have on your side sometimes.

"Get ahead of me!" he shouted, as the sounds of cleaving and crumbling rocks grew steadily louder behind them.

Ruby did as she was asked, rending her arm from his grip and charging past him at a speed she managed to amaze herself with. Looking over her shoulder, Ruby could see Loki was keeping up, but his attention was still behind them. He was gesturing with both hands back into the cavern. Likely he'd cast some magic to slow the destruction of the dimension, or maybe just to shield them from it. But Ruby could tell she was already headed out of the doomed dimension when the ground softened beneath her feet. She could only wonder if she would be taking any magic with her.

She'd been *so close* to completing the ritual. She was sure of that based both on what she knew of the ritual from the text of the Scrolls and how she felt in her gut in the moment she'd immersed the opal in the molten silver of the cauldron. But close only counted in horseshoes and hand grenades; there was every chance she'd gained no magic at all from the experience.

But it was not for nothing that she was getting out with her life.

She could see a portal opening ahead, the dark sky of Cobalt City looming in the distance. It was a view she recognized. Loki must have come looking for her in her building and discovered her magic in process. That would explain how he'd managed to find her in the lava tube. This portal he'd opened was in almost an identical place to the one she'd opened at the beginning of the ritual. In a few short paces, she'd be home. Another brief glance over her shoulder to assure herself Loki was still behind her, and she charged forward through the open portal.

She was spun round in the turbulent air of the hastily constructed gateway between realms, shaken like a rag doll by the winds of the transition point, and lifted high into the sky by the portal's energy before being tossed to the ground. She landed half a story below. Flat on her back on her veranda, having missed the edge of the helipad by several feet, she was sure the pain from the hard landing was the only thing keeping her conscious.

Loki was out of the portal a moment later. Did it toss him about like it had done to her? Ruby's vision was getting blurry. She wasn't sure what she was seeing. Loki, dashing down the stairs in her direction—was he calling her name?

There was another sound. It was familiar… comforting. Ruby let her eyes shut and reveled in the sound of the Stardust suit approaching from out over the water. She must be hallucinating.

Loki had her hand now, he was patting her face and calling out her name again. But all she could hear was Stardust.

But Stardust was in Bermuda.

She must be hallucinating.

Loki told her to open her eyes.

And she did. She opened her eyes just in time to see she hadn't been hearing things. Loki's face told her she wasn't seeing things, either.

Stardust was clearing the last several meters between the edge of the veranda and where she lay on the paving stones, scrubbing considerable speed as he came closer.

Ruby was just able to watch him come in for a landing before her injuries got the best of her. She'd barely had the chance to wonder how he'd gotten there when she passed into unconsciousness.

CHAPTER
TWENTY-EIGHT

Waking up in the hospital had not been what Ruby had hoped for in that last minute she'd been aware of things on her veranda. But when she awoke and saw her reality, she wasn't exactly surprised. She felt like hell. She wasn't sure she'd ever felt so awful in her entire life.

There were dozens, hundreds of things she needed to be doing, but all she'd been able to do in those first few days was sleep. Those first few days, every time she was awake, she'd insisted on having an assistant on call. She'd been keen on managing things as best she could, even from her hospital bed, but every assistant Bridget or Arsho sent her seemed to be willing to do little more than read the cards on the ever-increasing flower arrangements that filled every available space in the room.

Jaccob had apparently been there the first day or two. The best she'd been able to piece together from what the nurses were telling her was he'd stuck around until everyone was sure she was going to pull through. After that, he'd gone back to Bermuda to see after his kids and his yacht; this was according to the card attached to the flowers he'd had sent over. It was a lovely arrangement, but it wasn't a bundle of Gold of Kinabalu orchids, either. The difference between the seduction and the breakup, she figured.

There was more to that message, enough to tell her that the breakup she feared when she'd first seen the flowers was already well underway. The questions were vague, and gentle for the most part. But she was sure based on what she read that their relationship was most likely over for good.

That had sent Ruby down a spiral of curiosity. Had a member of her staff read Jaccob's card when they were collecting those from fans and employees? Had they thought she felt dumped, sad, and lonely? Had they thought she'd only sent for them so she'd have company?

She could not have cared less about having company. What she cared about was *running* a company. Relationship questions could wait until she had the bandwidth.

Damage control had been her first priority. Enough of the fallout from the White House concert had been either handled or delegated in the days before she'd attempted the Ritual of the Scrolls that she hadn't been immediately worried about the status of those bits of business. It was her own status she was most concerned about.

Word on the street had it she'd fallen from her helipad onto her veranda. Apparently Arsho had bought the story so completely that they were already in the process of having an OSHA-approved safety railing installed. It was a cover story that made her sound clumsy and a little bit pathetic, but Ruby supposed things could be worse. There was no mention of magic nor of Loki in any of the news media, so at least she could be thankful for that. There were a lot of questions about what had happened she wasn't prepared to answer.

The visits from assistants had lasted less than a week. Ruby couldn't abide forced cheerfulness, and the staff she'd been sent by her office all seemed to have been hand-picked to deliver just that. She'd been able to take care of business from her Starphone ever since.

It was three days into the second week of her hospital stay when she'd gotten an honest-to-goodness visitor.

She'd told the desk no one was to be allowed in, but somehow she guessed they figured her directive didn't apply to *him*. Ruby had only just opened her eyes when she realized the person leaning on her door jamb wasn't one of the hospital denizens she was used to seeing.

The moment she made eye contact with Jaccob, she ardently wished she hadn't. There was a hard conversation in their future, and she had neither the energy for it nor for ignoring the proverbial elephant in this sterile, uncomfortable room between them.

Ruby closed her eyes again and counted to ten. There was every chance he hadn't come to talk. Maybe he'd just stopped by to ask after her condition—just to look in on her for a second. Maybe he wouldn't have come to her room at all if he'd known there was a chance she'd be awake. Closing her eyes again gave him the opportunity to retreat. If he was dreading their next conversation the way she was…

When she opened her eyes again, he'd stepped into the room farther. Apparently he wasn't going away. Ruby turned her head toward him and smiled as best she was able.

"I wasn't expecting to see you," she said softly as she fiddled with the bed's controls to make her more upright. If she was going to have it out with Jaccob, she wasn't going to do it lying flat on her back.

Jaccob shrugged. "I wasn't expecting to come," he admitted.

Ruby smiled sadly as she nodded.

"But hey," he said, his tone artificially light as he struggled to fake a smile. "I'm finally getting to see you without makeup on."

Ruby's gut knotted up. She knew he was trying to be cute, but all he'd done just then was to activate her most primordial defenses. She tried to play it off. She wasn't sure what he was doing here, but he was being pleasant for the moment, which was more than she had let herself hope for. She'd try to go along with the banter. "I told you I was hideous," she snarked, quirking her lip in the way she always did when she was only half kidding.

"I don't know," he countered, "I think you're looking pretty good right now, considering—"

"Considering," she repeated the qualifier. Truly she was sure she looked at least as bad as she felt. The hospital had let her assistants bring her clothes from home, so at least she was greeting him in her own aqua-colored silk peignoir set and not one of those ghastly cotton gowns. She'd also been able to wash her face and apply her usual anti-aging creams for the past several days now, but she was still sure her pallor was frightful. If she'd known she would have a gentleman caller, she'd have at least bitten her lips and pinched her cheeks a little to get some color. As it was, she just shrugged, happy enough he hadn't immediately agreed with her assessment of "ghastly."

"How are you doing?" he asked her then.

Ruby shut her eyes and took a deep breath. It was a more serious question, and his tone had changed. This was a clear departure of the small talk from a minute ago. "I'm not dead," she declared flatly. "But you didn't come here for small talk."

"That's not funny," he chastised. "You very well could have died up there. You *almost* died up there. "

"How did you even get there?" she asked. It was a question that had been on her mind since she'd first spotted him hovering above her balcony. "You were in Bermuda. That's what, a thousand miles away?"

"Closer to twelve hundred," Jaccob replied. "But I wasn't all the way there. I've been making some improvements to the suit. And I'd been out testing it. Chuck was on Skype with her mom, and Mike was doing stuff with his guitar, so I took the suit out to test some of the upgrades. Turns out it'll do every bit of Mach-point-five."

"Still, that's several hours away, isn't it?"

"Like I said," he answered. "I'd been headed north out over the ocean for a couple of hours already. I'd let the Coast Guard know where I was going to be flying, just in case. If the suit malfunctioned, I didn't want it to be over land, but I wanted to be within easy rescue. So I'd vectored in toward the coast and then I'd flown north, keeping just a few miles offshore. I was more than halfway to Cobalt City already when the alarm rang from your bracelet."

The bracelet!

"I set the bracelet alarm off." Ruby had dithered back and forth over whether or not to wear her gift from Stardust during the rite. Interesting things tended to happen to precious metals worn by a magic user through a ritual. But the Ritual of the Scrolls wasn't well known, and there was always a risk when adding anything to the pre-scribed regimen. There was also no indication of how technology at that level would behave in the midst of magic that powerful. At the very last minute, she'd decided against keeping the bracelet on her arm and had taken it off (rather roughly now that she thought about it) on her way out the door to go up to the helipad.

It occurred to her to be interested in the time that had elapsed between the bracelet sending its signal and the time Jaccob arrived on scene. Two hours wasn't nearly the amount of time she'd experienced on the other side of the Coil; there was a lot she wanted to analyze about the differences in time. But that was a question for another day.

Jaccob had already gone on. "You did," he affirmed. "But only for a blip. I wondered if it as a real emergency or just some kind of acci-dent, so I called you. I called your personal phone and then I called your business phone. I called through the alarm system and then I tried the house phone at Regency Heights. And when I couldn't reach you, I tapped into the cameras on my building and tried to turn them enough to see if I could get a look at your place. What little I saw was your doors standing open and your helipad apparently on fire. I couldn't get there fast enough. Even at top speed, that was two hours of personal hell."

"I'm sorry I scared you," she said, finding it odd just how much she meant it.

"You scared the hell out of me. And then to get there and see you like that—" He shook his head and took a deep breath. He ran his hands over his beard as he let it out, a gesture Ruby recognized as

Jaccob trying to keep his composure. "I thought I'd lost you," he said, casting his eyes down at the floor.

Ruby folded her hands in her lap and pursed her lips. Of all the outcomes of this whole adventure with the Eye of Africa, this was one she hadn't been able to foresee.

Jaccob looked back up at her after a moment and tried for a smile. "But you look like you're doing okay now. So tell me, please," he implored. "Answer my question. How are you?"

"The way it's been explained to me is that my body looks like it's been subject to sudden deceleration from high speed," she answered. "Or like I was caught in the blast radius of a giant bomb, a fact I find amusing in the most ironic way possible. I survive an actual bombing only to be nearly killed by my own plans gone sideways a short week later. They tell me there was some damage to pretty much every organ in my body. Lots of internal bleeding, I guess. But I'll live. Life won't be a whole lot of fun for a while, but I'll live."

"Good. I mean, not the part where things won't be any fun. But the rest of it, that's good."

"Better than the alternative," she allowed. "But, like I said, that's not what you came here to talk about."

Jaccob nodded his head and sighed. He pursed his lips and crossed his arms over his chest. "Magic?" he asked then, stepping farther into the room and lowering his voice as he did.

Ruby swallowed hard, finding suddenly she couldn't look at him anymore. She figured she might as well come clean, or at least somewhat clean. There wasn't a whole lot she could imagine confessing now that would make him think worse of her than he probably already did. There was no harm she could see in sharing. "I was born with powers," she explained. "Mental manipulation mostly, ability to persuade, some elemental manipulation, too—little stuff. But last year, when I went through what I went through with the alien, it left me with more powers—different. But then last winter, they just disappeared." She wasn't about to volunteer the how and why of when that had happened, and she hoped Jaccob wouldn't ask. "It was like having my arm cut off," she shared, suddenly able to look him in the eye again. "And I wanted them back. All of this, that's what all of this was about—getting my powers back."

"And Loki?" he asked dubiously.

Ruby sniffled, stifling a laugh at the ridiculousness of the truth she was about to reveal. "An old business associate," she answered. "Would you believe we have the same taste in composers?"

Jaccob laughed a little himself. "You are a fan of Wagner," he observed.

Ruby nodded, glad the mood was a bit lighter—even if only for a moment. Awkward silence fell between them, and then Jaccob spoke again. "Why couldn't you tell me any of this?" he asked, taking another step toward her.

"Jaccob," she countered dubiously. "Were we even ten minutes into drinks at Durian before you told me how much you detest magic?"

Jaccob's mouth fell open, but he did not speak.

Ruby went on. "Now why in the world would I come out and tell you something about myself that I already knew you hated, especially when it was a moot point? It didn't exist anymore, so there was no need to tell you the thing about myself I knew you were going to hate. I wanted you to *like* me."

"I did like you," he answered quietly, reaching for her hand where it lay on the blanket.

"Past tense," she observed, hearing herself sniffle but letting him keep hold of her hand.

Jaccob shook his head. "I don't know," he admitted, squeezing her hand before letting it go and beginning to pace alongside the bed. "Was this—" He looked back at her and shook his head. "Was any of this even real? Persuasion, manipulation. How much of this was that?"

Ruby could feel her lower lip beginning to tremble, and she took a moment to compose herself before answering. "Didn't you hear me?" she asked him. "I lost all my powers. You and I? This was just a run of the mill rebound."

Jaccob squeezed his eyes shut.

She had him there. But that's not what he'd meant for it to be and Ruby knew that.

"Ruby," he said, crossing back to stand beside the bed and taking her hand in his again. "You know I didn't—"

"I know," she interrupted him. "Your intentions were honorable. I think they still are. But you're confused and upset, and you don't know exactly what you're feeling or what you should do next."

Jaccob nodded his head. "Something like that."

"I understand. I know this is a lot to process."

"Yeah," Jaccob exhorted. He took a seat on the edge of her bed and looked her in the eye. "Was it worth it? All of this—what you went through—was it worth it? Did you get your power back?"

"I don't know," she answered. "Magic is a serious thing; it's not to be trifled with. I wouldn't dare try to use it with all the drugs they have me on."

Jaccob nodded, but he seemed slightly amazed. "That makes sense," he said.

"But it surprises you."

"Making sense isn't something I'm used to with magic," he answered sincerely, the first hint of a genuine smile coming to his face. "I'm having trouble reconciling the two."

Ruby smiled. "I like that I can still surprise you."

Jaccob smiled fully then, but after a moment his face fell. "Ruby, I—"

"Don't," she interrupted. "You don't have to say it. I know."

"It's just—" he began again.

"No, really," she insisted, cutting him off a second time. "I know." She took a deep breath and squeezed his hand in both of hers. "Look,

I have a feeling your wife's going to be getting in touch with you very soon, if she hasn't reached out already." Her voice was shaky, and her hands were, too. The part she wasn't telling him was how much she knew about that. The fact that Discontent had departed along with the other Blights almost surely meant Elizabeth Stevens would come to her senses and return home any day now.

Ruby had meant to have her full power restored and therefore the ability to keep Jaccob from wanting anything to do with Elizabeth before that happened. But with the way things had ended up, Ruby had no doubt Mrs. Stevens would be back home in short order.

"I don't know about that," he said, averting his eyes.

Ruby's eyebrows rose. It had been her perception before Discontent had shown up that Jaccob and Elizabeth Stevens had had a perfectly happy marriage. If that wasn't the case—if there was a chance they might stay split even after Discontent was out of the picture—then Ruby wanted to make sure she wasn't closing any doors.

"If that doesn't happen," she posed, "give me a call some time."

Jaccob stood up and then leaned down to kiss her lightly on the forehead. "I'll do that," he replied.

Ruby wasn't sure whether he was being polite or sincere.

"And Jaccob," she said, as he let go of her hand and took a step toward the door. "I promise. Even if my power has returned, I promise I'll never use magic on you." Even as she said it, she knew it was a lie. She knew because she was using her power to make him believe that. And she could tell by the genuine warmth of his expression that he did.

She felt bad using magic on him this way. But only a little. It had been his asking after the state of her powers that had caused her to consider a small test, and when she'd seen the opening, she'd taken it.

All was fair in love and war, after all.

EPILOGUE

She had no idea what time it was.

She was alone in her penthouse with the fabulous view. It was a breathtaking early fall night on the Massachusetts coast. The sunset had been a dazzling show of orange-red refracted through steel frames and glass facades. Now, in the darkness, the lights of the city twinkled and danced in exquisite color below and beneath her fiftieth story terrace. Ruby Killingsworth didn't see any of it; her eyes were pointed exclusively at the penthouse across the way.

Sometime after dark, after she'd shut off the television and turned out the lamp. Just as she'd resigned herself to pop a couple of Zolpidem and be done with this day, she'd noticed the lights on the Stevens residence. This was the thirteenth night since Elizabeth Stevens had come through the door, designer luggage in-hand, and been welcomed home by her husband. And it was the first night since then that Ruby Killingsworth had dared to open her shades. She didn't want to look at that. She had no interest in bearing witness to the newly rekindled Stevens marriage.

And yet she knew she'd have to. She'd doubtless run into them at some important function or another. After all, their son Mike was in her artist stable now. And she and the Stevenses ran in the same social circles, so she knew she would have to face them sooner or later.

Oh, what the hell? she'd thought. *I might as well get it out of my system.* And so slowly, under the cover of darkness, she'd slid open the glass doors leading from her sitting room onto the terrace. She'd tiptoed across the polished marble flagstones and settled herself on one of her cushioned chaises—the same one, she remembered, that she'd been reclining on when Jaccob had paid her that first visit on his StarBoard.

And she let herself stare. She gave herself permission to wallow. She forced herself to look—to get used to the sight of her former lover together with his wife. And when feelings of regret or of anger or of sadness came calling, she let them come. Best to exorcise all emotion now, she figured; better to appear unaffected when one day they met again.

She had no idea how long she'd been lying there when she became aware she wasn't alone. She could sense a presence behind her; someone was on her terrace. Her visitor had appeared suddenly and silently. Which meant there was no question in Ruby's mind who was there.

"This can't be healthy," Loki said aloud by way of announcing himself.

"Since when did you give a damn about my well-being?" she asked sharply, not so much as bothering to turn her head to acknowledge him.

"Now, now, Ruby," he chided, "don't go making me admit that I care."

Ruby sighed. She really was not in the mood to deal with Loki right now, but she had no idea how to tell a god to get the hell off her terrace. "How did you get here?"

"You set up my fetishes all over the forty-sixth floor," he reminded her. "And what's a couple of stories when you're immortal?"

Ruby rolled her eyes and let out a tense breath. *Of course* this would be the moment he finally decided to show up of his own accord.

It was just her luck. "Come here to rub salt in my wounds?" she asked, allowing just enough nastiness to seep into her voice that Loki would be sure to know she was thoroughly displeased with his intrusion into her personal crisis.

"No," he quipped lightly. "Kicking a person while she's down isn't really my style." He crossed the dark balcony and joined her on the chaise, sitting himself on its edge just behind her. "I've got to hand it to you, Ruby. You said you would do it and you did. That'll teach me to underestimate you. I really thought you wouldn't be able to pull it off. Brilliant move, using Discontent to get rid of the wife like that."

"Thank you." Ruby hated to admit it, but that bit of praise made her feel marginally better.

"Oh, you're welcome," he answered. "It really was inspired. You ought to be proud of yourself—you managed to bed America's least eligible man."

"That I did. And now it's done."

"Did you really think it had a future?" he asked plainly. "You know he's far too good for you."

Ruby turned her head just enough to catch his eyes and frowned. "Thanks," she groaned, her voice filled to teeming with angry sarcasm.

"I don't mean he's *better* than you," the god clarified, moving to lie beside her on the chaise. He spooned up behind her with his head propped on his bent arm so he could still see what she was looking at. "It's just that he's, you know, good. Full of goodness," he emphasized with a shudder. He really did have a distaste for the truly altruistic. "Truth and justice," he sneered. "Save the citizens!" He wrapped his arm around Ruby and squeezed. "That's not you, Ruby. Another month and you'd have been bored to tears with goodness. Another year, and you'd have been asking me to come and murder him in his sleep—if you lasted that long."

Ruby leaned back, settling into the god's embrace and letting herself enjoy, for the moment, the feeling of his arm around her. "You're probably right. But then," she asked, turning her gaze back to the goings-on across the way. "Why is that so damned hard to look at?"

She didn't expect an answer. And Loki had none to offer.

He held her quietly for a time. "They're not happy," he announced after a moment. "You can see that, right?"

Ruby shrugged.

Loki placed his hand on her shoulder and continued. "Look at her," he said. "She's not altogether sure she wants to be there. Only a few short weeks ago, she was so unhappy she felt the need to leave. And even though that feeling has passed, she'll spend the rest of her life wondering where it came from. And every time they argue, every time he irks her, every time she's the slightest bit put out with him, she'll wonder if coming back was the right thing to do. Oh, see there?" He pointed to the movement in the Stevenses' kitchen. "She won't let him get within ten feet of her. And he hasn't looked her in the eye one single time. She knows about you. It'll be a long time before she lets him touch her again. And when she finally does, she'll always wonder if he touched you the same way he's touching her. And storms forbid he ever wants to try anything new in bed."

Ruby let out a guffaw in spite of herself. She surely had taught the vanilla superhero a few things in that department.

"Does that make you feel better?" he asked in response to her sudden laughter.

Ruby shrugged. "A little," she allowed. "A bit of schadenfreude always helps my mood." Ruby curled up tighter on the chaise as she fell silent again. She was fighting the urge to let her breath heave in her chest. If she was going to cry about this again, it would not be happening in front of Loki.

Loki lay his head down beside hers. "Did you love him, Ruby?" he asked.

The question sounded odd to her ears. Not only did it seem entirely preposterous to be discussing *feelings* with the Norse god of mischief, but equally odd was the tone in his voice. For the first time in the history of their association, he seemed to be speaking with total, unqualified sincerity. Ruby squeezed her eyes shut in defiance of her building tears and answered him with equal honesty.

"I don't know," she whispered. "I was barely myself without my powers. So, whatever I felt—whatever *that* was—it wasn't altogether real. It wasn't complete, because I wasn't complete. So even if did love him, what does it matter when I wasn't myself?"

"You have your powers back now," he surmised.

Ruby nodded. "I have powers," she answered. "More and different than I've ever had. They're mine, I'm sure. Not granted or bestowed or borrowed. Mine. They sit in me the way my original powers did. But they're new. They're not the same as before, and I've only just begun to get to know them." She raised her left hand and brought it up in front of her face. And then it ignited. All at once, with no warning and no build-up, her fingers erupted in a blue-white flame. "Like this. I've never been able to do this before."

"Mmmmm," Loki sounded in her ear. He reached around and took her flaming hand in his, interlacing their fingers together as his own hand ignited in a purplish flame much like her bluish one.

Ruby stared for a moment, watching as the flames danced together against the pitch black of the night sky, enjoying the interplay of colors their joined hands had created. After a moment, suddenly fearful of being spotted by the neighbors, Ruby extinguished her flames. She grasped his hand tighter, and his fire flickered out in response. Then she leaned back into him and pulled his arm snugly around herself.

She'd likely regret this later—being so open with Loki, needing to be held. This moment would surely come back to bite her, but right now she couldn't be bothered to care. It felt good to have an arm around her, even if it was Loki's arm. "Do you want to stay tonight?" she asked him quietly. "I know I usually talk a dangerous game, but as you can see, I'm hardly in a position to take advantage."

He sidled up closer and kissed her lightly on the side of her neck. "You make a very tempting case," he said, moving his lips from her neck to her earlobe, where he nibbled a bit before going on. "But—and don't take this the wrong way—I still don't trust you."

Ruby chuckled. If she were Loki, she wouldn't trust her either. "No offense taken," she assured him, turning her head to give him better access to her neck, where his mouth was still doing delightfully wicked things. She wasn't going to beg him to stay, no matter how badly she wanted not to go to bed alone. But she wasn't going to tell him to stop, either.

"Would you let me tie your hands?" he asked. His voice sounded eager, hopeful even.

"If you'll let me choose the bindings," she countered. A little light bondage and sex with a god sounded like just the thing to pull her out of her torpor. She wondered if her new powers would work on a god. Either way, this line of discourse felt promising.

"Of course," he agreed.

Ruby took a deep breath and sighed. The idea of blowing off a little steam, coupled with the comfort of knowing she wouldn't be sleeping alone tonight, was enough to get her to take her eyes off the Stevenses next door. Ruby stood, still holding her visitor's hand, and looked down at where he lay on the chaise.

Loki grinned wickedly.

Ruby couldn't help but smile back as she tugged on his hand, inclining her head toward the door to her penthouse. "C'mon then," she invited, encouraging him to follow. "Let's go inside."

ABOUT THE AUTHOR

Amanda Cherry is a television actress, musical performer, roller derby official, and Star Wars nerd. She is a contributing writer and podcaster at www.Tosche-Station.net, and a prolific tweeter of tweets (@MandaTheGinger). Amanda serves as Chief Editorial Assistant for *Mad Scientist Journal* (www. MadScientistJournal.org) and blogs about writing and life at www.TheGingerVillain.com. She lives happily in the Seattle suburbs with her husband and son, three cats, and adorable dog. She enjoys documentary films, leggings-as-pants, and not having to go outside.

ABOUT THE COVER ARTIST

Lee Moyer's award-winning work is featured in many annuals and anthologies and has been exhibited at the Smithsonian Institution and galleries in NYC, LA, and London. He is best known for his theatrical and film art for Laurel & Hardy, Spider-Man, Tori Amos, Stephen King and "The Call of Cthulhu." In collaboration with Ray Bradbury, George RR Martin, and Neil Gaiman, Moyer designed and painted three literary calendars that raised six figures for charity. His "Elements of Illustration" and "Kickstarter White Paper" are widely read. His games "The Doom That Came to Atlantic City" and "Cursed Court" are available now.

83007180R00175

Made in the USA
San Bernardino, CA
20 July 2018

Belief, both in the shaman and his audience, is another important variable in the shamanic cure, according to Levi-Strauss:

> The efficacy of magic implies a belief in magic. The latter has three complementary aspects: first, the sorcerer's belief in the effectiveness of his techniques; second, the patient's or victim's belief in the sorcerer's power; and, finally, the faith and expectations of the group, which constantly act as a sort of gravitational field within which the relationship between sorcerer and bewitched is located and defined.[158]

This level of psychological commitment to the blues can be observed in the blues community. According to Keil, "The blues fan . . . is devoted to the genre as a whole and has no doubts as to its validity."[159] Spencer describes the involvement somewhat more poetically, "The whole being of the singer was engaged in a deeply spiritual expression and confession that left the 'blue' soul washed afresh at the blues altar."[160] At the start of a recognizable number a blues audience will burst into a mixture of applause mixed with shouts of encouragement like "sing it baby" or "play your heart out." Also, throughout the song when signature phrases are sung or played, or when a gesture associated with that performer is made, the audience will again signal their recognition with audible approval. Rarely is there studied or overt indifference displayed.[161]

Another close parallel between shamanism and the bluesman's role is the tendency for both the performer and the audience to become possessed by the material or experience trance-like states during the performance. The two earlier examples by Adam Gussow of experiences of unitary reality during improvisational interaction clearly have a quality of possession or trance. Eliade points to the importance of music in shamanic inductive practices: "Among the Ugrians shamanic ecstasy is less a trance than a 'state of inspiration'; the shaman sees and hears spirits; he is 'carried out of himself'. . . However, the basic experience is ecstatic, and the principal means of obtaining it is, as in other regions, magico-religious music."[162] Garon suggests that the influence of the blues can be thought of as like a possession or similar to a voo-

---

158 *Structural Anthropology*, p. 168.
159 *Urban Blues*, p. 160.
160 *Blues and Evil*, p. 39.
161 This is somewhat similar to the intensely vocal worshippers of the "Amen Corner" found in many fundamentalist churches, both black and white, in the South.
162 *Shamanism*, p. 223.

doo trance[163] and Little Whitt Wells even refers to the blues as a "trance music."[164] One can have little doubt about the hypnotic inductive influence of the blues when listening to a one-chord drone in the blues of Junior Kimbrough or John Lee Hooker.

Storr points out that it is not uncommon for musicians to describe feelings of being 'taken over' or 'possessed' during a performance,[165] but this tendency is intensified in the blues because of the strong emotional content in the blues. However, the observations of Cammerloher suggest that this possession may not be unique to the blues, or music, but may be a part of any artistic experience taken to sufficient depth:

> The artist does not choose his subject matter at all; the subject matter chooses him . . . It is quite simply the archetypes at work in time that rise up in him . . . They seize upon him, and he seizes upon them, clutches them, bites into them, and does not let them loose because they do not let him loose - until he has wrought them, acquired them, made them his possession, and shaped them into a work. It is like Jacob's wrestling with the angel; and often the hollow of the artist's thigh is thrown out of joint . . . The artist as creator is not conscious of all this. He has his

---

163 *Blues and the Poetic Spirit.*
164 Quoted in Herman, *Big Mo and Little Whitt*, p. 32.
165 *Music and the Mind.*

idea and that is enough . . . He seeks and finds, whether he knows it or not, the symbolic content of the work. Thus art becomes the symbolic forming of archetypes working in time.[166]

Neumann offers similar observations on the tendency towards possession in the creative process:

> It is part of the paradox inherent in what we have described as the unitary reality that, although it manifests itself in and through creative man, it cannot be 'known' by him. He does not grasp it, he is himself seized and possessed by it, and even when he helps to fashion and develop, with the full cooperation of his conscious mind, an experience which is intuitive or which gradually takes possession of him, the primary fact that he has been overwhelmed is always a significant element in the situation . . . It is precisely this state of being overwhelmed by emotion . . . which is the essential prerequisite for the process of unification and fulfillment that calls into being the totality of creative man and connects him with the unitary reality appearing within him . . . The Logos-principle of the artist, however strong it may be, is subordinate to the strength of his Eros-principle, which creates a third world in the form of art, whose essential nature is to embody features of the unitary reality, to be a copy of that reality or to bear witness to it.[167]

In the context of our discussion, the bluesman is not just the trance invoking shaman-performer; the bluesman also serves as a witness, a witness to unitary reality.

One of the things which both Cammerloher and Neumann seem to be addressing is the autonomy of the experience, wherein the artist is not so much the creator, but instead a mediator. Often during a possession or trance state the shaman becomes a mediator between the spirit world and the patient. Larry Neal, an African-American poet, makes similar observations about the role of the bluesman. He refers to the "ethos of the blues" as an "emotional archetype" which he terms the "blues spirit."[168] In Neal's view the "blues spirit" is mediated by the performer, who reflects upon and responds, via his music, to the realities of life.

---

166 *The Position of Art*, p. 445.
167 *The Place of Creation*, pp. 103ff.
168 Quoted in Spencer, *Blues and Evil*, p. 36.

However, the shaman must be initiated into the shamanic role before he is able to mediate the spirit world. Eliade describes the various processes of shamanic initiation, including: initiation through sickness or visions, apprenticeship to an elder shaman, ritualized journeys such as tree climbing or descent, or investment of shamanic power by spirits.[169] In the Navajo culture the sacred songs are first sung by the gods and then given to the medicine men to carry to the people. The following is an account presented by LeDell Jackson, of the crossroads initiation of his brother, bluesman Tommy Jackson. In Jackson's account it can be seen that there is a close parallel between these shamanic rituals and the ritual initiation at the crossroads associated with the blues:

> Now if Tom was living, he'd tell you. He said the reason he knowed so much, said he sold hisself to the devil. I asked him how. He said, 'If you want to learn how to play anything you want to play and learn how to make songs yourself, you take your guitar and you go to where a road crosses that way, where a crossroad is. Get there, be sure to get there just a little 'fore twelve o'clock that night so you'll know you'll be there. You have your guitar and be playing a piece sitting there by yourself . . . A big black man will walk up there and take your guitar, and he'll tune it. And then he'll play a piece and hand it back to you. That's the way I learned how to play anything I wanted.'[170]

In this description, in addition to the image of the conjurer and initiate, we also find the image of the pact with the Devil, an archetypal motif brought into full relief in Goethe's *Faust*. Another bluesman, Luther Trice, reported that he was told to go to the crossroads on nine consecutive nights to learn the blues from the devil, but ran away when he saw the devil, whom he described as, "a beastly figure that had balls of fire coming from his mouth and red-hot eyes."[171] Trice's initiatory experience has parallels to Odin's initiatory death on world tree, Yggdrasill, which lasted for nine nights. These parallels suggest that the initiatory experiences of the bluesmen are fundamentally archetypal in nature.

One of the enduring aspects of blues musicians is their relationship to their instruments. The term "easy rider," in the blues, refers to a sexual partner who did not create many problems. "Easy rider" is also a term widely applied by bluesmen to their instruments, especially the guitar. Oliver points out that, "the use of a term widely applied to a

---

169 *Shamanism.*
170 Quoted in Titon, *Early Downhome Blues*, p. 31.
171 Reported in Spencer, *Blues and Evil*, p. 30.

lover, showed a close, if subconscious, psychological relationship between singer and instrument."[172] The anthropomorphic idea exists in the blues that the instrument often has its own voice and something it wants to say. Often a bluesman, such as B.B. King or Rev. Gary Davis,[173] will call out "speak" or "talk" to his guitar before beginning an instrumental response to the lyrics just sung. The instrument becomes animated and the impression is created of a spirited dialogue between the instrument and the musician. Similarly, Eliade speaks of the "autonomy" attained by the instruments used in the magico-religious music of shamanistic practice.[174] It is almost as if the instrument of the bluesman can fulfill the function of the Other in the intersubjective dyad or that the instrument becomes a transitional object[175] for the performer. Willeford writes, "Many a blues performer has used the interaction between voice and instrument as a means of re-creating a world with others,"[176] again underscoring the blues experience as an example and experience of unitary reality.

Robin van Loben Sels, in investigating common characteristics of shamanic practice, identifies seven primary attributes which most shamans utilize in their shamanic role: gesture, mask, sound, silence, rhythm, respiration, and movement.[177] All of these attributes are consistently utilized by blues performers. The descriptions of shamanistic practice and explanations of shamanistic modes of healing seem to provide a compelling explanation for the appeal and psychological power of the blues and the bluesmen. Levi-Strauss summarizes the shamanic process in the following passage:

> It is a relationship between symbol and thing symbolized, or, to use the terminology of linguists, between sign and meaning. The shaman provides the sick woman with a language, by means of which unexpressed, and otherwise inexpressible, psychic states can be immediately expressed. And it is the transition to this verbal expression - at the

---

172 *Blues Fell This Morning*, p. 107.

173 An example of this dialogue is present in Davis' song, *Death Don't Have No Mercy*.

174 *Shamanism*, p. 180.

175 The transitional object is the term adopted by Donald Winnicott ("Transitional Objects and Transitional Phenomena." *International Journal of Psycho-Analysis*, vol. 34) to describe the infant's first "not-me" possession which is used under stress and in times of emotional separation from the primary love object.

176 *Abandonment, Wish, and Hope in the Blues*, p. 196.

177 *Shaman: A Differentiation of Image from Instinct*, Unpublished diploma dissertation.

same time making it possible to undergo in an ordered and intelligible form a real experience that would otherwise be chaotic and inexpressible - which induces the release of the physiological process, that is, the reorganization, in a favorable direction, of the process to which the sick woman is subjected.[178]

In like fashion, the blues artist, by willingly entering into the state of blues possession and by using his creative imagination to depict some aspect of the mundane, daily life that he and the listener can connect to, transforms that original experience, and creates a third thing which alters how the mundane stimulus for the song is perceived or experienced. In doing this, the listener is then also inducted into the process of transforming the mundane into something richer. The listener becomes the *soror mystica*[179] to the bluesman-adept. This is literally a depiction of the alchemical process by which the *prima materia* of daily life becomes the gold of unitary reality. This connection, this transportation into unitary reality, obscures subject-object distinctions in the experience among audience members and between the musician and the world, musician and audience, and musicians and their instruments.

178 *Structural Anthropology*, p. 198.
179 *Soror mystica* is a term from alchemy which refers to a female alchemist or assistant ("mystical sister" or "sister in the work") who is paired with a male alchemist.

6

Healing in the Blues

"The art of healing comes from nature."
—Paracelsus

Blues as Therapy

There can be little doubt about the healing power of music if we look across time periods and cultures as reflected in the following statements: "Music's the medicine of the mind;"[180] "The spirit will not descend without song;"[181] "Nothing unites the parts of man, his body and soul, as does music, which is a conjunction of the rational and irrational;"[182] and "Music finds the way to the soul."[183] Music has been associated with health and healing since antiquity.[184] Anthropological research has traced the origins of shamanistic practices including chants, drumming, and dance as far back as the middle Paleolithic period (about 300,000 to 30,000 years ago). Manuscripts from ancient civilizations such as Sumer, China, India, Greece, and Egypt describe the use of music as a therapeutic tool. The blues overtly maintains the archetypal link between healing and music that existed thousands of years ago in these ancient cultures, but which has been lost as an explicit intention in most other contemporary forms of music. The strong connection between healing and the blues can be detected in John Lee Hooker's choice of *The Healer* as the title to one of his recordings.

I won't dwell much on the parallels between the experience of music and the process of analytic therapy. Thomas Moore[185] and Mary Lynn Kittelson[186] have already well documented many of the important parallels and metaphors which exist in this area. I only deal briefly with this area, not because it lacks significance, but because the analogies in this area are not specific to the blues and can be generalized to most

180 John Logan (1744-88).
181 Old African dictum.
182 Boethius (480-524 A.D.).
183 Plato.
184 Rolla, *Your Inner Music*.
185 *Musical Therapy*.
186 *Sounding the Soul*.

forms of music. Instead, I will concentrate on how the blues, as a specific musical form, is therapeutic to the listener, the musician, and the collective culture.

There are some close parallels between the healing process of analytic therapy and the process of creating and experiencing music. However, a primary difference between the blues and analytic therapy lies in the intent. In analytic therapy an effort is made to avoid contaminating the patient with one's own unexamined or unmetabolized complexes. In practice this goal is, at best, only approximated and we recognize that both patient and analyst are mutually affected by the shared process. In the blues the intent is somewhat different and yet shares a similar quality of mutuality. The bluesman attempts to create a song that can express what the performer is feeling or has felt, but also to create a song that can move or affect the listener, otherwise the song is ineffective. Hence, the goal in the blues is to create a contagion, through the music, that is able to get inside the listener and evoke an emotional response to the song. It is likely that the music resonates with the listener because the listener has had a similar experience or because the song itself is of such a universal, archetypal nature that almost anyone would have the potential to respond out of the depths of the collective psyche. However, the song can also evoke a response because of the singer's capacity to create a feeling response in the listener via the psychological process of projection. This idea is consistent with a statement by bluesman Leonard "Baby Doo" Caston who says, "Blues is a sound . . . it's a feeling that a sound would put you into."[187] Storr also points out that the listener's response to a particular piece of music is governed by his subjective state of mind at the time and that some part of his reaction will be influenced by the projection of his own emotions rather than it being solely a direct consequence of the music.[188]

Garon agrees that it is primarily the psychological process of identification with the singer by which we derive our enjoyment of listening to the blues. Drawing on the work of psychoanalyst Roy Schafer, Garon indicates that the highest level of identification is "generative empathy" in which the subject, "feels what the object feels; and yet, above all, out of self-interest as well as interest in the object, he maintains his individuality at the same time."[189]

---

187 Quoted in Titon, *Early Downhome Blues*, p. XVI.
188 *Music and the Mind.*
189 *Blues and the Poetic Spirit*, p. 16.

Garon also draws a theory of aesthetic illusion from the work of psychoanalyst Ernst Kris who speculates that the unpleasant in art is experienced as pleasurable because the aesthetic illusion acts as a protective device. Kris says, "Pleasure is gained in freedom from guilt since it is not our own fantasy . . . The maintenance of the aesthetic illusion stimulates the rise of feelings which we might otherwise not permit ourselves, since they lead to our own personal conflicts. It allows in addition for intensities of reaction which, without this protection, many individuals are unwilling to admit to themselves."[190]

While I agree with Kris that part of the pleasure associated with the blues is a form of personal catharsis that must first be constellated by identification with the blues singer, I would also suggest that internalization (i.e., introjection) occurs in the listener based on modeling by the blues singer. Observing or listening to the bluesman wrestle with and survive his emotional life, his pains or trials, gives the listener courage to face his own inner pain by connecting with what is universal in each of us through interaction with another. I also propose that pleasure is derived from the blues exactly because it allows us to identify as fully as possible with feelings in the singer that we might otherwise exclude from our own awareness because of the pain involved. Like

190 Quoted in Garon, *Blues and the Poetic Spirit*, p. 17.

the mythological activities of Pan and Dionysus, the blues permits a movement towards healing and wholeness through an assimilation of material from our own shadow.

But perhaps we should examine more closely what it is within ourselves and our culture that needs the healing offered by the blues. Neumann says, "We have lost our sense of unitary reality, our experience of identity and of the sympathy of all things, and as a result we have fallen into solitude and isolation of a dead and empty cosmic space."[191] Elsewhere Neumann proposes the function of art is to remind us of and connect us to unitary reality: "When the numinous and overwhelmingly vital power of reality speaks to us in 'great art,' this always involves a change in ourselves and, simultaneously, a change in our world."[192] The blues helps restore our sense of unitary reality by its emphasis on the emotional life of the individual and the universal themes of human experience. In the blues, it is the music itself, the performer, and the audience, which provide the activating energy by which the archetypal field is constellated and unitary reality is experienced. The "sympathy of all things," to which Neumann refers, is present in the blues and the goal of the blues is becoming more sentient, rather than more conscious. Arthur Schopenhauer, a German philosopher, indicates that, "In the course of life . . . head and heart grow more and more apart; men are always separating more and more their subjective feeling from their objective knowledge."[193] The blues works to heal, or provide therapy for, the split that Schopenhauer is describing, making the knowledge of the heart more available to the knowledge of the intellect.

Neumann also describes the experience of unitary reality as, "the process whereby reality becomes transparent."[194] Based on Neumann's observations, we could consider the blues to be an active process or experience of becoming transparent so that the edges of experience are no longer so tightly bound by the merely personal and ego-attached. This is similar to the Meister Eckart's theology of attachment (*eigenschaft*) to the world via an ego-centered perspective which is transformed through a process *lassen* (meaning to "let go") and *abgescheidenheit* (meaning "detachment") so that a deeper connection with the god-head can be

---

191   *The Place of Creation*, p. 98.

192   *The Place of Creation*, p. 113.

193   Quoted in Storr, *Music and the Mind.*, p. 162. It seems likely that Schopenhauer is referring primarily to patterns in Western culture and the split which he is describing may not be applicable across all categories of race, class, gender, culture, or psychological typology.

194   *The Place of Creation*, p. 124.

experienced.[195] Neumann also indicates that: "This is the world [i.e., unitary reality] conjured up by ritual, religion, and art, and attachment to it invariably brings with it the renewal of polarized man through the profound emotion that sweeps his ego away from its fixed moorings in the conscious mind and the divided, 'fallen,' purely human world and regenerates it by contact with the great world of man's primordial origins."[196] Here Neumann is referring to the healing that is associated with a return to sacred time or primary experience, the *illud tempus*,[197] in which the sacred mythical origins are re-experienced. In like fashion, the blues has the potential to heal the illness that results from being too far removed from one's original state.

The blues facilitates a form of transformation, but not a transformation associated with insight. According to Neumann, "The archetypes are elements of the unitary reality. But they are invariably umbilical points of contact with it, as it were, since wherever the archetypal world forces its way into our life and exerts a determining influence upon it, we are - even if we do not know it - in touch with unitary reality."[198] As von Franz has pointed out, it is the archetype that heals and renews.[199] The power of the blues rests in its capacity to transform, at a deep archetypal level, an individual's feeling states; strengthening one's capacity to cope with oppression and suffering in life and increasing one's sense of connectedness and relatedness in life. However, with the blues, this process is most often occurring on the periphery of our consciousness, just out of our ego awareness. This idea is echoed in T.S. Eliot's observation about a, "music heard so deeply that it is not heard at all, but you are the music while it lasts."[200]

Jung's ideas about the transformation of libidinal energy help us understand one of the underlying healing mechanisms by which the symbolism of the blues operates within the individual, as well as the collective. In the blues, a certain amount of psychic energy (libido) is made available, both by the performer and the listener or audience. But as Jung points out, psychic development cannot occur by will alone;

---

195 Forman, "A Psychological Account of Meister Eckhart's Mystical Transformation." *Journal of Psychology and Christianity*, vol. 6, pp. 21ff. Meister Eckhart was a 14th century theologian, philosopher and mystic whose works have been seen as having parallels to certain ideas in Mahayana Buddhism.
196 *The Place of Creation*, p. 100.
197 Eliade, *The Sacred and the Profane*, p. 80.
198 *The Place of Creation*, p. 99.
199 *Interpretation of Fairy Tales*, p. 32.
200 Quoted in Skar, *Music and Analysis*, p. 389.

it requires the attraction of a symbol.[201] The blues presents a symbolic form which acts as a healing container for a shared ritual process, and as such is experienced on both a personal and collective level. The blues serves as the vehicle by which the instinct moves towards opportunities for emotional release, much like Jung's description of the Wachandi tribesman of Australia who, during a spring fertility ritual, thrust their spears into a ceremonial hole.[202] In this ritual, the spears and hole serve as the analogues for the male and female genitalia. Pointing to the important link between music, sound, and psychic energy, Kittelson says: "Sound is vibration and resonance. As such, it has a close affinity with psychic energy."[203] Kittelson also indicates that, "psychic energy, like a rich, musical piece, strikes and enters the ear in a moving simultaneity of levels."[204] As we can see, for both the performer and the audience, the blues serves as a vehicle to constellate, focus, and release libidinal energy among the participants.

Leonard Goines states that blues music serves the same function for blacks as psychotherapy does for whites.[205] He sees the blues as asking questions which allow the listener to see and understand the nature of his problem rather than proposing solutions, much like the analyst's role in depth psychology. This view is consistent with statements from bluesman Elmer Lee Thomas: "In my life I've been in positions where I've been lost and the music has comforted me. It's been my psychiatrist really,"[206] and an observation made by Memphis Slim: "When I have troubles, the only thing that helps me - I mean that's the only way to kind of ease my situation."[207]

One observer of the blues, Ernest Ansermetat, made the following comment in 1918: "The blues occurs when the Negro is sad, when he is far from his home, his mother, or his sweetheart. Then he thinks of a motif . . . and on the chosen motif, he plumbs the depths of his imagination. This makes his sadness pass away - it is the Blues."[208] Notice the similarities between Ansermetat's comment and the statement made in 1968 by bluesman turned preacher, Rev. Robert Wilkins:

---

201 "On Psychic Energy," *The Structure and Dynamics of the Psyche.* CW 8, par. 47.
202 "On Psychic Energy," par. 83.
203 *Sounding the Soul*, p. 43.
204 *Sounding the Soul*, p. 217.
205 Cited in Spencer, *Blues and Evil.*
206 Interviewed by Maureen Jung, "Acoustic Blues in Oakland." *Living Blues*, Issue 126, p. 39.
207 Quoted in Spencer, *Blues and Evil*, p. 39.
208 Quoted in Jones, *Blues People*, p. 175.

> In blues it's what you call a felt-inward feeling - of your
> own self . . . It's something that happened to you and cause
> you to become sorry . . . Then you compose the song to
> that feeling that you have. And then you would sing it and
> after you begin to sing it, then you become accustomed to
> it through psychology that 'most anybody could have the
> same feeling as you did. It's universal . . . Singing the blues
> helps relieve your natural soul.[209]

One could describe this process as an instance of Logos meeting Eros. Both authors identify a discordant feeling state as the initial impetus for creation in the blues. They also note that the act of creation and the use of imagination is used to transform a feeling state. Finn points to just such a transformative process as the root of Robert Johnson's blues mastery. He suggests that it was the death of Robert Johnson's young wife during childbirth, rather than a supernatural initiation at the crossroads, which served as a creative or initiatory crisis for Johnson and forced him to deal with his pain through the creation of art.[210]

Catharsis and Naming

There seem to be two important aspects to the transformative process in the blues; catharsis and naming. According to Keil, "Individual catharsis is still a *sine qua non* to successful [blues] performance."[211] The etymological background of the word "catharsis" is important to our understanding of the blues. Campbell indicates that, "The word 'catharsis' (Greek *katharsis*; from *kathairein*, 'to cleanse'), which in Aristotle's usage denotes the effect of tragedy as 'effecting through pity and terror a *katharsis* of these emotions,' was a term which referred in the Greek religious vocabulary to a spiritual transformation brought about by participation in a rite."[212]

The power and importance of naming autonomous psychic contents is apparent in the familiar fairy tales of Rumpelstiltskin and Rapunzel. Levi-Strauss identifies an analogous process existing in South American shamanistic healing songs: "the song constitutes a psychological manipulation of the sick organ, and it is precisely from this manipulation

---

209 Quoted in Titon, *Early Downhome Blues*, p. 32.
210 *The Bluesman.*
211 *Urban Blues*, p. 76.
212 *The Inner Reaches of Outer Space*, pp. 133ff.

that a cure is expected."[213] In the blues world, a similar naming and curing process is depicted by Keil:

> B.B. King, Bobby Bland, Jr. Parker, and Ray Charles are the incarnations of soul: they do transform the collective "mind" into representative activities. A good blues lyric is a representative anecdote, the distillation of a problem, the naming of a malaise . . . an urban blues lyric is also a representative antidote, ritually acted out, for the malady named. The naming-and-curing ceremony is a grand synecdoche (literally - from the Greek - 'a receiving together').[214]

Examples of the naming-and-curing process can also be heard in the following blues songs by Lil' Son Jackson and Clifford Gibson:

Gambler's Blues - Lil' Son Jackson

You know I once was a gambler boys but I bet my money wrong
Now I ain't got no money and all I got is gone.

You know I'm thru with gambling,
Some other hustler can have my room
Well now drinking may kill me, but gambling won't be my doom.

Well I gambled so long till I thought I would never change
Well I ain't gonna gamble no more, I swear I'm gonna save my change.

Whiskey Moan Blues - Clifford Gibson

I been drinkin and gamblin, bar'lhousin' all my days
But I have found someone to love me, I'm goin' to change my ways

I've always heard but now I know it's true
If you mistrust a good woman she'll turn her back on you

If your woman loves you she'll stand by you to the end
Nobody can steal your place, you can leave her with a bunch of men

If you got a jealous hearted woman, be careful what you do
'Cause there's always somebody, tell her lies on you

---

213 *Structural Anthropology*, p. 192.
214 *Urban Blues*, p. 181.

Whiskey has been my pleasure, good time places I've always found
But it seems so different now, since I have settled down

Shadow and Healing

Another critical aspect of the healing capacity of the blues is the salient presence of shadow material in the blues. The blues is an ongoing inter-active phenomenon which perpetually retrieves, reclaiming the aspect of the human condition which Jungians refer to as the shadow. Jung indicates that, "One does not become enlightened by imaging figures of light, but by making the darkness conscious."[215] The darkness of the blues embraces violence, sexual dysfunction, infidelity, addiction, mi-sogyny, pain, suffering, sadness, and grief. These experiences are raised up, not to glorify them, but to acknowledge the existence of these ex-periences in our lives. The blues performs the work of the "new ethic" discussed by Neumann, i.e., the redemption of that which is typically suppressed or repressed.[216] This view is consistent with Spencer's per-ception that "blues people sought wholeness that was attained through imperfection."[217] The embracement of the shadow by the blues is also consistent with the perspective offered by Garon, who says, "Part of the unique attractiveness of the blues is that it is through the blues singer that we are not only able to face our own despair, but can also demand an end to repression and insist on the erotization of everyday life. The blues singers present us with a vision not only of our unhappiness but of its conquest as well."[218] Garon also speculates that individuals who find the blues repulsive are repulsed because they have lost contact with their innermost needs and desires via repression. Extending Garon's line of thought we can also speculate that some individuals find the blues objectionable because the emotional content of the blues constel-lates their defenses against suffering.

The blues do not just heal on an individual level, but also a collec-tive level. Contemporary acoustic bluesman Corey Harris points out the commingling of individual and collective forces within his blues experience:

---

215 "The Philosophical Tree." *Alchemical Studies,* CW13, par. 335.
216 *Depth Psychology and a New Ethic.*
217 *Blues and Evil*, p. 70.
218 *Blues and the Poetic Spirit*, p. 84.

Well, it is African music that came from Africa and was pre-
served by the generations up until this time, an unbroken
stream . . . It just happened to grow up within the confines
of America and change . . . And I'm playing the music that
people in my family have really gotten off on for a long
time . . . And it helps to keep me sane. It's a great release
valve . . . A lot of good vibrations you can take in to change
your mood. Music has a real healing effect. That's the function it serves me.[219]

Garon points out the healing effect that the blues has had on the
African-American community:

The blues is the musical and poetic expression of work-
ing-class black Americans, and as such it has served and
continues to serve a specific function in a specific social
context . . . As the poetic voice of a people distinctively
victimized by the whole gamut of the repressive forces of
bourgeois/Christian civilization (economic exploitation,
political disenfranchisement, racism, etc.), the blues long
ago found itself in the service of human emancipation by
virtue of the particular manner in which it deals with such
[social] repression.[220]

Spencer also offers some observations of collective healing and the
blues: "Restoring wholeness and balance in the lives of the disinherited
was the work of the 'blues god,' as evidenced by the success the blues
has had in blurring the psychically unhealthy boundaries between the
sacred and the nonsacred."[221]

However, the blues does not just address oppression of blacks by
whites. The blues also addresses issues within the black community. In
songs like Hi Henry Brown's *Preacher Blues*, Son House's *Preaching the
Blues*, Bo Carter's *He Calls That Religion*, and Luke Jordan's *Church Bell
Blues*, both the preachers and their church followers were joked about
and disparaged for their moral hypocrisy and self-righteousness. In this
sense the bluesman became the therapist of the collective, illuminating
the cultural shadow of the black community. An example of this pattern is found in Washington Phillips' *Denomination Blues*: "*Preachers are
preachin' and think they're doing well but all they want is your money and
you can go to hell.*" Similar sentiments are reflected in the *Preacher Blues*
by Joe McCoy:

219 Interviewed by Ari Frede, A. "Words, Sound, Power: The Blues Vision of
     Corey Harris." *Living Blues*, Issue 126, pp. 27ff.
220 *Blues and the Poetic Spirit*, p. 2.
221 *Blues and Evil*, p. 73.

Some folks say a preacher won't steal,
but I caught three in my cornfield,
One had a yellow, one had a brown,
looked over the mill and one was getting down.
Now some folks say a preacher won't steal,
But he'll do more stealing than I got regular meals.
I went down to my house about half-past ten,
Looked on my bed where the preacher had been.
He will eat your chicken, he will eat your pie,
He will eat your wife out on the sly.
I been trying so hard, to save my life,
Just to keep that preacher from my wife.

Diggs points out that the transformative aspect of the blues is not restricted to the collective psyche of the African-American community, but includes the collective psyche of European-Americans as well:

> The blues are called the 'blues' because they satisfy the archetypal requirements and the specific cultural and historical necessities to function as the manifest blue or *unio mentalis* of the unconscious alchemy of race in America. The blues effects change in African-Americans and European-Americans as they have come to hold the psychology of black and white in literalized enactment of the alchemical nightmare of the dissociative Western mind in its move toward a union of opposites, or albedo, at the end of our age.[222]

As we can see from Diggs' statement, the blues can be seen as operating on both a collective and a personal level, acting on the collective psyche of all Americans as well as the individual psyche of the blues listener. In fact, the blues revivals of the 1960's and 1990's point to a need within the collective psyche for what the blues offers. Poet William Carlos Williams says, "It is difficult to get the news from poems, yet men die miserably every day for lack of what is found there."[223] The same thought also applies to the collective need to embrace and be embraced by the values reflected in the blues.

---

222 *Alchemy of the Blues*, p. 32.
223 From "Asphodel, That Greeny Flower."

Humor and Healing

In the blues, humor is used as one way of dealing with or transforming despair. An oft repeated line in many blues songs is *"laugh to keep from cryin."* However, the humor is often subtle and self-effacing, such as in Johnnie Temple's *Lead Pencil Blues (It Just Won't Write)*, an entendre about impotence. Other samples of humor in the blues follow:

Prison Wall Blues – Gus Cannon's Jug Stompers

> *When I leave these walls, I'll be runnin' dodgin' trees.*
> *You'll see the bottom o' my feet so many times*
> *You'll think I'm on my knees.*

Phonograph Blues - Robert Johnson

> *Beatrice I love my phonograph, but you broke my windin' chain*
> *And you taken my lovin' and you give it to yo' other man.*
>
> *And we played it on the sofa and we played 'side the wall*
> *But boys, my needles have got rusty and it will not play a-t'all.*

My Stove's In Good Condition - Lil Johnson

> *I've got a range in my kitchen, sho' bakes nice and brown*
> *All I need is some good daddy, who turns my damper down*
>
> *And my stove is automatic, you don't have to burn wood or coal*
> *You got to strike a match baby, and stick right in the hole*
>
> *And it's yas yas baby, my stove is all cleaned out*
> *I always keep it in good condition, you know what I'm talkin' about*
>
> *Mmmmm . . . my pot is boiling low*
> *If you can't keep it percolatin', Baby I swear you'll have to go*
>
> *I don't want no charcoal, if you can't bake my biscuits brown*
> *When my wood gets too hot, I swear you'll have to turn my damper down.*

Pussy Cat Blues - Jane Lucas

You can play with my pussy, but please don't dog it around
If you gonna mistreat her, no pussy will be found.

Clearly, sexuality plays an important role in humor and healing in the blues. However, sexuality wasn't the only topic dealt with humorously. In fact, an entire class of blues, usually referred to as hokum blues, was rather nonsensical and had a bouncier, ragtime feel. An example of a hokum song is Robert Johnson's *They're Red Hot*:

Hot tamales and they red hot, yes, she got 'em for sale
I got a girl, say she long and tall -
Sleeps in the kitchen with her feets in the hall
Hot tamales and they red hot, yes, she got 'em for sale, I mean -
Yes, she got 'em for sale, yeah.

Alchemical Blues

Turning to alchemy allows us to understand more fully the healing aspect of the blues. Some insights into the transformative aspect of the color blue can be gleaned from Jungian analyst James Hillman:

> The blue transit between black and white is like that sadness which emerges from despair as it proceeds towards reflection . . . the blue transition toward *albedo* . . . Blue protects white from innocence . . . The transit from black to white via blue implies that blue always brings black with it . . . Blue bears traces of the *mortificatio* into the whitening.[224]

We can see from Hillman's comments that the blue associated with the blues is a color of transitioning that forms a bridge between the *nigredo* or *mortificatio* and the *albedo*. The blues allows inner experience to move from one feeling state to another, a process of alchemical transformation.

According to Hillman, "It is the blue which deepens the idea of reflection beyond the single notion of mirroring, to the further notions of pondering, considering, meditating . . . the blue mood which sponsors reverie."[225] He continues by saying, "Once the black turns blue, dark-

224 "Alchemical Blue and the Unio Mentalis." *Spring*, vol. 57, pp. 133ff.
225 *Alchemical Blue*, p. 137.

ness can be penetrated (unlike the *nigredo* which absorbs all insights back into itself, compounding the darkness with negative introspections). The shift into blue allows air so that the *nigredo* can meditate itself."[226] Based on Hillman's description of the alchemical process, it is the "blue" tincture of the blues that allows the individual listening to the blues to reflect, acknowledge, and reclaim feelings and states that would otherwise be lost in the nigredo blackness of the unconscious.

In this same work, Hillman indicates that blue is the transition between the black *nigredo* and the white *albedo* which is the accomplishment of the *unio mentalis* or union of the soul and spirit (psyche and logos - perhaps also understood as the interpenetration of image and thought) which is prior to further union with the world (i.e., the *unus mundus*). Once again the transformative nature of the blues and the connection of the blues to unitary reality is emphasized.

When I am engaged in therapy, the blues become a way of resonating with the patient. On some level, in my listening reverie, my patients are always singing the blues. Things my patients say or the feeling in the room will often bring to mind different blues songs. The songs embedded in my patient's bluesy narratives will constellate a feeling I have had while listening to the blues. In this way I come to know that I am in the presence of the blues once again. It provides me a different way of entering their world, one that doesn't rely on conceptual language. I believe my experience is similar to that of Thomas Moore, who says, "What I wish to propose is musical therapy as distinct from music therapy . . . At its best it is a recognition of the value to soul of the art of music in all its variety . . . The psychotherapist as *musicus*, as musician, must have an ear for the temperament and harmony which resonate deep within the melodic (personal) events of life."[227]

---

226 *Alchemical Blue*, p. 139.
227 *Musical Therapy*, pp. 128ff.

Blues Personification

Perhaps the most important aspect of the blues, for the purpose of heal-ing, is the vivid, gripping capacity the blues has to personify a psycho-logical state and create an interaction or dialogue with that state. The lyric structure of blues songs frequently reflects the personifying nature of the psyche. Jung says, "The personification enables us to see the relative reality of the autonomous system, and not only makes assimi-lation possible but also depotentiates the daemonic forces of life."[228] Jung also emphasizes the reality of this interaction: "They [personifi-cations of the libido] manifest themselves as . . . personal agencies. In this form they are felt as actual experiences and are not figments of the imagination."[229] Elsewhere, Jung talks about "the meaning of the personification."[230]

Because the blues allows the externalization of these split off com-plexes through song, the blues can be thought of as a naturally occur-

228 "Commentary on the Secret of the Golden Flower." *Alchemical Studies*, CW13, par. 55.
229 *Symbols of Transformation*, CW5, par. 388.
230 "Individual Dream Symbolism in Relation to Alchemy." *Psychology and Alchemy*. CW12, par. 220.

ring form of active imagination. Skar indicates that there is a similar process at work in active imagination and GIM (Guided Affective Imagery with Music), a specific technique used in music therapy.[231] She indicates that the transcendent function is at work in both, bridging the gulf between consciousness and the unconscious. Like GIM, the blues utilizes the power of music to access imaginal states within the listener. However, in the blues, as opposed to jazz, classical, or pop music, the entire lyric structure, tone, and presentation is geared toward accessing, experiencing, and expressing universal affective states. I believe that it is this capacity to personify and develop an imaginal dialogue with a mood or state that gives the blues its unique healing capacities, just as the personification process does so powerfully in dreams.

It is the archetypal affective state referred to as the blues which is most likely to be personified in a blues song. In Robert Johnson's *Come On In My Kitchen*, he sings, "*Some other man got my woman, lonesome blues got me,*" personifying the blues as an entity holding him hostage. According to David Evans, "The phrase [lonesome blues got me] nevertheless literally refers to possession by a mood that seems to be represented as a spiritual force or being."[232] Elsewhere, Evans indicates that the blues are often represented as some sort of walking and talking supernatural being, not merely a 'feeling.'[233] Ma Rainey, in *Slave to the Blues*, is personifying the blues and appealing directly to this personification when she sings, "*Do you hear me screaming, you're going to take me to my grave.*" In many of these songs, the blues is taking an active role in creating disruption or disturbance in the singer's life, just as we experience the disruption caused by autonomous complexes in our daily lives:

Man Stealer Blues - Bessie Jackson

I went to bed last night and these blues wouldn't let me rest
'Cause I ain't used to sleeping by myself.

Oh blues, Oh blues, blues don't you see?
You are carryin' me down, blues you tryin' to kill poor me.

Now blues and trouble walk hand in hand - have mercy
I never had these blues, until my best friend loved my man.

---

231 *Music and Analysis.*
232 "Robert Johnson: Pact with the Devil." *Blues Revue,* Issue 21, p. 13.
233 "Robert Johnson: Pact with the Devil, Part 2." *Blues Revue,* Issue 22, pp. 12

Blues Leave Me Alone - James Lane

Blues, blues, blues, blues trying to driving me away from home
Man, the blues so bad, blues tried to follow me all day long
Blues, the blues won't let me take my rest
My mind is ramblin like wild geese out in the West
Well you my all day study, baby, you my midnight dreams
I love that woman better than anyone I've ever seen.
Blues won't you please leave me alone

Conversation With The Blues - Big Bill Broonzy

Oh blues, I wanna have a little talk with you
Yeah now blues, I wanna have a little talk with you
Ah you done cause me to lose my woman,
Ah blues I guess you're through

Oh blues, Big Bill wants to talk to you
Now I believe you've been drinkin' moonshine,
Blues cause you don't care what you do

Now looka here blues, I wanna talk to you
You been makin' me drinkin', gamblin', and stay out all night too
Now you got me to the place, I don't care what I do

Yeah now blues, I wanna have a little talk with you
Now I believe you've been drinkin' moonshine,
Blues cause you don't care what you do

Yeah now blues, why don't you give poor Bill a break?
Now why don't try to help me to live,
Instead of tryin' to break my neck?

Waking Blues - Otis Harris

Did you ever wake up with the blues and didn't have no place to go
An' you couldn't do nothin' but just walk from door to door?

Good morning Mister Blues, Mister Blues I come to talk with you
Mister Blues, I ain't doin' nothin' an' I would like to get a job with you.

Mister Blues - Lucius Hardy

Howdy, Mister Blues, where have you been so long?
I've been telling everybody that you were long gone.

Tell me, Mister Blues, how long did you come to stay?
Please go right now, you gonna drive my baby away.

Oh Mister Blues, as soon as you got in town
My baby told me she would leave, she was Texas bound.

Now look here, Mister Blues, I want you to leave my door
And when you go this time, I don't want you back no more.

Preaching Blues (Up Jumped the Devil) - Robert Johnson

'It's up this mornin, blues walkin' like a man
Worried blues give me your right hand.

And the blues fell mama's child and tore me all upside down
Travel on, poor Bob, just cain't turn you' round.

The blues is a low-down shakin' chill.
You ain't never had 'em, I hope you never will.

Well the blues is a low-down achin' old heart disease
Like consumption, killing me by degrees.

Rambling Blues - Ida Cox

Early this morning, the blues came walking in my room
I said, "Blues, please tell me what you are doing here so soon?"

They looked at me and smiled but they refused to say
Asked them again, then they turned and walked away.

"Blues oh, Blues, you know you've been here before
The last time you were here you made me cry and walk the floor.

Blues Trip Me This Morning - Tommy McClennan

The blues grabbed my leg this morning,
Tripped me, throwed me down.
Lord, I wouldn't hate it so bad
But the news done got all over town.

Good Morning Mr. Blues - Little Brother Montgomery

The first time I met the blues, I was walking down through the woods
He knocked at my house, and done me all the harm he could.

The blues got after me, and he run me from tree to tree
You should have heard me begging, Blues, Ohh, Blues don't murder me.

Oh good morning Blues, Blues I wonder, what are you doing here so soon?
Yes, you be with me in the morning, Blues, and every night
and every noon.

In reading through the lyrics presented above, it becomes clear that the blues is a psychic reality to these singers. There is not much differentiation between inner experience and outer experience, just as one would expect when a unitary reality field is constellated. The blues takes on shape and form, being experienced as smiling menacingly, knocking at the door, or "walking like a man." Like Hermes, the blues arrives and departs, or sometimes even moves into your house. The blues is wrestled with, just as Jacob wrestled with the angel of God.[234] The blues is conversed with, questioned, and appealed to. The blues even has the capacity to kill. However, what is clear from all of these examples, is the singer's deference to the power of the blues.

There appears to be an archetypal structure underlying these personifications. Spencer says that the blues is a personality, specifically the personality of the African trickster-god *Legba* and his African-American derivatives.[235] Spencer feels that it is *Legba* who best personifies the blues because of his duplicitous nature; being both malevolent and benevolent, disruptive and reconciliatory, profane and sacred. Meanwhile, Garon offers the African trickster god *Eshu* as the source for the

---

234 *Genesis,* Chapter 32.
235 *Blues and Evil.*

close association between the blues and the devil.[236] Support for the interpretations of Spencer and Garon emerges from the fact that various African gods, including *Legba* and *Eshu*, were often syncretized with the devil in Afro-Caribbean religions such as Haitian voodoo and Santeria. However, Evans disputes these interpretations based on his understanding of the references to the devil in the lyrics of Robert Johnson and Son House. Evans contends that the devil is the devil of Christian mythology, not a syncretized representation of *Legba* or *Eshu*. Elsewhere, Evans claims that the most common personification of the blues is a malevolent being or trickster whose character is similar to the devil's.[237] Spencer states that the mythological importance of the trickster is that the trickster is the revealer of the unacknowledged or unrecognized aspects human situation through his behavior. Thus, Spencer believes that the trickster illustrates how the blues singer reveals, "the sacred element of secular life by sanctioning the ordinary in all its contradiction and anomaly."[238] The diversity of opinion as to the archetypal background of the personification of the blues again points out to the coexistence of unitary reality with the blues. These interpretations of the blues point to the interconnectedness or multi-determined nature that is characteristic of unitary reality, a movement away from dichotomous, polar consciousness where something must be one thing or the other.

References to the devil and evil in the blues suggest that evil was perceived to be a reality that was morally and physically threatening. This is consistent with Jung's view of evil as a reality that cannot be relativised. For Jung, evil is a menacing and psychological reality in opposition to good, although maintaining that both are expressions of the paradoxical opposites contained within the archetypal image of the Godhead. The reality of evil, personified as the devil, can be heard in the following blues songs by Sonny Boy Williamson and Robert Johnson:

Deep Down in the Ground - John Lee "Sonny Boy" Williamson

You hear that rumbling deep down in the ground
Now it must be the devil, you know, turning my womens around

---

236 *Blues and the Poetic Spirit.*
237 *Big Road Blues: Tradition and Creativity in the Blues.*
238 *Blues and Evil*, p. 12.

Me and the Devil Blues - Robert Johnson

Early this mornin' when you knocked on my door
And I said "Hello, Satan, I believe it's time to go."

Me and the Devil was walkin' side by side
I'm goin' to beat my woman 'til I get satisfied.

She say you don't see why that you will dog me 'round
It must-a be that old evil spirit so deep down in the ground

You may bury my body down by the highway side
So my old evil spirit can catch a Greyhound bus and ride.

Death is another common personification in the blues world. The personification of death in songs provides a vehicle for expressing and working through grief following the death of a loved one but also provides a means of personalizing and interacting with a powerful force in life that can otherwise seem rather abstract and impersonal:

Death Room Blues - Blind Willie McTell

Tombstones is my pillow, cold grounds is my bed
The blue skies is my blanket, and the moonlight is my spread

Early one morning, death walked into my room
Oh well it took my dear mother, early one morning soon

She left me moanin' and cryin', moanin' like a turtledove
Death walked in and got my dear mother, and the only friend I loved

Mmmm . . . eehh . . .
Cryin' Lord have mercy, and she was the only friend I loved

Ever since my mother died and left me all alone
All my friends have forsake me, people I haven't even got no home

Mmmm . . . feel like moanin' and cryin'
Death walked in a got my mother,
And that was the only dear friend of mine

Death Don't Have No Mercy - Blind Gary Davis

Well he'll leave you standin and cryin in this land
Well death will leave you standin and cryin in this land
Well he'll come to your house and he won't stay long
You look in the bed and somebody will be gone
Death will leave you standin and cryin in this land

Oh, death always in a hurry in this land
Well he'll come to your house and he won't stay long
You look in the bed and your mother will be gone
Death always in a hurry in this land

Well he won't give you time to get ready in this land
Well he'll come to your house and he won't stay long
You look in the bed and somebody will be gone
Death won't give you time to get ready in this land
Death don't have no mercy in this land

Even inanimate objects became animated in the blues through personification. In the two following examples, trains become the personification of the subjectively experienced cruelty of abandonment by a lost love:

Big Four Blues - Leroy Carr

Big Four, Big Four, why would you be some mean?
Why, you the meanest ol' train that I ever seen.

You taken my baby away and left me standin' here
Well I ain't got no one to love, and I swear I can't go nowhere

---

Panama Limited - Georgia White

I've got the choo-choo blues, had 'em all night and day
'Cause the Panama Limited carried my man away

There goes that mean ol' train, leavin' for New Orleans
Lord I got the blues, I could almost scream

The Blues Narrative

Although the narrative of the blues is textually rather loose and free, there is an underlying structure that provides some ordering. Blues lyrics, especially country blues, usually fall directly into three-line, AAB stanzas; that is, the second line repeats, sometimes with slight variation, the words in the first, and the third line completes the thought or image, with a rhyme at the close. Many of the stanzas of a blues song cohere around a single theme or group of related ideas, for example around the desire for sex, and these stanzas would be linked associatively rather than linearly. Charters indicates that it is the repetition of the first line and the use of verses as thematic blocks rather than narrative units that gives the blues its unique character.[239]

Willeford (1985, p. 190) makes the statement that: "The verbal content of the blues is concerned with emotional situations implying stories that are usually not told explicitly; rather, the personal, subjective reactions of the singer or fictional persona are made the center of attention. That is, the blues, unlike the ballad, is non-narrative and often even anti-narrative in its suppression of the storyline."[240] Despite Willeford's assessment, I believe that the blues does possess a narrative form but the narrative line is more implied and the continuity is provided by the affective links in the song. Bluesman John Cephas, addressing the issue of narrative form in the blues, says: "Something happened in life to cause a guy to write about his life with the blues. It's all life stories in song. It's very profound, you know. It's actually telling a story, true-to-life stories from out of the black community."[241] Most often a blues song does not tell a story in a linear or complete way like a ballad does. Rather, it tells its story in snippets, in a non-linear, imagistic, associative manner. Therefore, blues songs are structured much like dreams and complexes. The blues song circumambulates around a theme or image, developing various facets or associational links, rather than trying to maintain a cohesive story line. Often a dream does not reveal its meaning until it is placed in the context of a series of dreams where it can be seen that there is an ongoing dialogue within which the narrative is embedded. Only by listening to the body of the blues can the larger story be heard, but it is a story that is both individual and collective. Even when the narrative of a song changes from performance to performance, as the singer is influenced creatively by his or her audience, it is

---

239 *Working on the Building.*
240 *Abandonment, Wish, and Hope in the Blues,* p. 190.
241 Quoted in Spencer, *Blues and Evil,* p. 46.

not that the narrative line is being lost; rather the narrative line is in an ongoing state of creative flux. The story is continually unfolding rather than remaining fixed and stagnant.

This blues pattern, in which the first two lines of a blues stanza develop a theme or image and the third line of the stanza is a response that results in a resolution or conclusion of that theme, is also typical of the "call and response" pattern found in African-American church services which takes place between the soloist and the choir.[242] Titon points out that blues songs also have structural similarities to the traditional oral sermon of the African-American church: "Formulaic composition and improvisation; repetition of small textural units in parallel form; ideas that cohere associatively instead of logically or chronologically; and an expressive tone of voice . . . to signify emotion."[243] Both instances result in a dialectic taking place within the song. In fact, there is a second level of dialectic, a double dialectic, taking place between the words being sung and the instrumental response (i.e., "breaks") which usually follows in the space immediately following the words just sung. This call and response interaction - between blues performers, between singer and audience, and between singer and instrument - conveys the intense dialectical nature of the blues and evokes the same depth of dialectical activity that is suggested by Neumann's concept of the "ego-Self axis,"[244] as well as conveying the idea of the co-creation of a narrative moment.

The narrative impulse is firmly embedded in the blues. Garon points out that the extensive utilization of the first-person presentation is one of the things which distinguishes the blues from other song forms. He goes on to characterize it as a "self-centered, high personalized" format in which the effects of everyday life are recounted within the context of the singer's reactions to them. What results is a unique level of personal presentation which intensifies the bond with the audience. In its personal approach to the subject matter it, "remains close to its instinctual sources, relatively unalienated, and unashamedly primitive."[245]

Perhaps the narrative impulse is so strong in the blues because, as Keil suggests, in the African-American community more power resides in the spoken word and the oral tradition than in the white communi-

---

242 Keil, *Urban Blues.*
243 *Early Downhome Blues,* p. 18.
244 For full explanation of the "ego-Self axis" see E. Neumann "Narcissism, Normal Self-Formation, and the Primary Relationship to the Mother." *Spring,* vol. 30.
245 Garon, *Blues and the Poetic Spirit,* p. 9.

ty.[246] Kittelson associates the oral tradition with the body, as opposed to the association between the written tradition and the mind: "The language of the oral tradition, of the fairy tales and myths, songs and poems, vibrates with the body, pulses with the heart."[247] The blues is an important part of this oral tradition, both individually and collectively. Coline Covington, Jungian analyst, indicates: "Our need to create stories is, of course, linked to our need and capacity to symbolize. Story-making is not only an interpretative act, it is also a symbolic process and, as such, carries within it the seeds for change."[248] Therefore, the blues may be seen as a way of creating a personal and collective narrative, or in more Jungian terms, a way of delineating an aspect of one's personal, as well as cultural, mythology. We've discussed some aspects of this mythology while exploring the archetypal underpinnings of the bluesman's role and now we can explore how this "living and lived myth"[249] evolves.

Psychoanalyst Roy Schafer discusses the importance of recognizing the orienting function of an individual's personal narrative in analytic therapy:

> Experience is not simply 'there in the mind' waiting to be found and retrieved by objective introspection. Different people tend to construct experiences of the same event differently, each for reasons of his or her own. Many of the reasons originate early in life and therefore give rise to primitive forms of emotional and cognitive experience, and these persist unconsciously and influentially into adult life ... I invoke the idea of narration precisely in connection with the inevitability of alternative descriptions. Using the term broadly, I designate as narration whatever qualifies as a telling or as the presenting of a version of an action ... Narrating, giving an account, presenting a version, developing a storyline, telling ... In this dialogic way, each analysis amounts in the end to retelling a life in the past and present - and as it may be in the future. A life is re-authored as it is co-authored.[250]

---

246 *Urban Blues.*
247 *Sounding the Soul,* p. 66.
248 "No Story, No Analysis?: The Role of Narrative in Interpretation." *Journal of Analytical Psychology,* vol. 40, no. 3, p. 406.
249 C.G. Jung, "The Psychology of the Child Archetype." *The Archetypes and the Collective Unconscious,* CW9i, par. 302.
250 *Retelling a Life,* pp. XIIIff.

Likewise, Covington speaks powerfully of the need for a narrative experience, and the healing which it provides, but also of the interactive aspect of the narrative process:

> The narrative form gives meaning and coherence to our experience . . . It is only the credible story that makes life bearable, it is, I think, more importantly, the act of meaningful story-making, which is only made possible through relationship, that gives us a sense of self and distinguishes us as creators of our own lives . . . It is by creating a narrative that we realize and express our need to internalize the other and to experience ourselves as internalized by an other in a meaningful way . . . it has a transmutative effect, that is, it produces psychic change.[251]

The interactive nature of the blues exchange is captured in the following comments by Keil who says:

> The blues tell a story to him [the blues fan] and every artist has a slightly different story to tell . . . For many Negros, life is one long sacrificial ritual. The blues artist, in telling his story, crystallizes and synthesizes not only his own experience but the experiences of his listeners. It is the intensity and conviction with which the story is spelled out, the fragments of experience pieced together, rather than the story itself which makes one bluesman better than another.[252]

Covington continues to amplify this emphasis on the interactive nature of the narrative construction, but also brings into focus the important function that remembering plays in the construction: "It is through the mutual act of remembering that the on-going construction of a narrative can occur. As a result of the interaction between them, requiring them both to enter into the story, the teller and the listener become introjected as participants in an internal dialogue between self and consciousness."[253]

Remembering and reconstructing are two important aspects of the narrative process - in the blues and elsewhere. Levi-Strauss indicates that "there is a kind of continuous reconstruction taking place in the mind of the listener to music or the listener to a mythical story."[254] For Julio Finn the remembering and reconstruction process of the blues serves as

---

251 *No Story, No Analysis*, pp. 407ff.
252 *Urban Blues*, pp. 160ff.
253 *No Story, No Analysis*, p. 415.
254 *Myth and Meaning.*, p. 49.

"the cultural memorial of slavery, a musical memoir commemorating the history of blacks in the United States."[255] Therefore, the blues is a part of the African-American cultural identity. Covington indicates that the construction of narrative is closely linked to identity formation, or the establishment of a sense of self. This implies a sense of history and continuity, and the story comes, "to serve as a form of transitional object combining factual and imaginal, internal and external realities, and reflects our desire to internalize one another."[256] The implication of Covington's remarks is that the development of a narrative contextualizes the individual within a culture. In the comments that follow, Spencer stresses the importance of the context for the ongoing creation of the blues narrative: "What makes blues singing authentic was not the ability to imitate the text and texture, both of which were relatively concrete, but learning these in the context where the reason the text and texture were as they were could be witnessed firsthand and explained by the 'old people' who knew."[257] Taken together, the underlying thrust of the observations by Covington and Spencer is the idea that the narrative process is essential to the creation of a context for the individual and the context is essential to the development of the narrative - a reciprocally influential process.

Part of the narrative process in the blues is the fluidity of the blues creative process. According to Titon, early blues singers rarely sang a song the same way twice. Most often the song was built up on a foundational stanza, which established the song's title and announced a basic situation.[258] It seems unlikely that the early bluesmen even desired to play a song exactly the same way twice, using the same lyrics and stanzas, because there was so much emphasis on their capacity to improvise lyrics to fit the local situation and mood. Often the lines and stanzas of the blues text move from one song to another with the musician fitting snatches of one song into another song where an associational link is formed. Admittedly, this at times leads to a reliance on certain stock phrases such as *"woke up this mornin', blues all around my bed"* which has found its way into dozens of blues songs. However, in some ways it works much like a recurring image in a dream: calling attention, increasing familiarity, reminding, and ultimately etching a particular image into one's awareness. However, it also leads to a certain decon-

---

255 *The Bluesman*, p. 230.
256 *No Story, No Analysis*, p. 405.
257 *Blues and Evil*, p. XXX.
258 *Early Downhome Blues*.

structive feel in which familiar words may reappear, reconstructed in a new musical context and amplifying a different situation or affect.

Some aspects of the blues format will remain the same but the lyrics are often fluid with little reliance on rules. This is one of the areas where the influence of the trickster can be felt most readily. The lyrics may vary from one performance to another or from one performer to another in order to reflect the idiosyncratic personality of the performer or variations in the performer's emotional state at the time of the performance. Performers covering another artist's song or a traditional arrangement will add flourishes to make it their own. Titon indicates that blues singers obtained their lyrics by borrowing and trying to memorize traditional stanzas from other singers which they mixed with idiosyncratic and improvised stanzas in most of their performances.[259] The idiosyncratic nature of the blues singer's style can be seen in the following description of Robert Johnson's recordings:

> Johnson's blues lyrics are extreme in their preoccupation with the interrelated themes of his relationship to the devil and sin, the state of his soul and his relationship to God; sorcery, both as a practitioner and victim; and death and the afterlife, including ghosts. If Johnson's lyrics are any reflection of his life and thoughts, he lived in a world of fear, suspicion, and nightmares. His other major themes are more conventional (for blues): travel/rambling and love/sex. In both, his actions are often described as compulsive.[260]

The blues narrative is constantly changing, being edited and commented upon, but always reflecting an aspect of the performer's and audience's immediate subjective narrative experience. Some lyrics may be added and old lyrics discarded or the speed and style of the instrumental portion may vary greatly. Examples of this aspect of the blues may be found in listening to multiple takes of the same song by a particular performer. For example, Jimi Hendrix, widely known as a rock musician, but not often recognized for his contribution to the blues, made two takes of a song *Voodoo Child* which were so different in content and feel that both were included on the same record. Another example is the variation in lyrics from the song *Smokestack Lightnin'* by Howlin' Wolf. Howlin' Wolf sings, "*Smokestack lightnin', shining just like gold,*" while Sam Chatman renders the line, "*Smokestack lightin', bell what shine like gold,*" and Lightning Hopkins sings it, "*Smokes like lightnin',*

---

259 *Early Downhome Blues.*
260 Evans, 1996a, *Robert Johnson: Pact with the Devil*, p. 12.

velvet shines like gold."[261] Clearly, the same image evoked differing associational material from these different bluesmen. A similar qualitative
difference can also be heard in two versions of *Chain Gang Blues*, both
recorded in the same era:

Chain Gang Blues - Ma Rainey

> *The judge found me guilty, the clerk he wrote it down*
> *Just a poor gal in trouble, I know I'm county road bound*
>
> *Many days of sorrow, many nights of woe*
> *And a ball and chain everywhere I go*
>
> *Chains on my feet, padlock on my hand*
> *It's all on account of stealing a woman's man*
>
> *It was early this morning that I had my trial*
> *Ninety days on the county road, and judge didn't even smile.*

Chain Gang Blues - Kokomo Arnold

> *Says the judge found me guilty, and the clerk he wrote it down*
> *Sheriff said, "Now I'm sorry buddy but, Lord, you chain gang bound.*
>
> *Says I didn't mean to kill her, but bloody murder was my crime*
> *Now I'm out here on the chain gang, Lord, just servin' my time.*
>
> *Says I got chains round my body, chains all down round my shoes*
> *Now that's the reason Cap'n hear me singing,*
> *Lord, these chain gang blues.*

In the next example, Eddie Boyd and Willie Dixon, in 1953, take one
line, *"Got me accused of forgery and I can't even write my name,"* from a
song, *Levee Camp Moan Blues*, by Texas Alexander, recorded in the late
1920's, and create an entirely different song around that one image:

Third Degree - Willie Dixon and Eddie Boyd

> *Got me accused of peepin and I can't see a thing.*
> *Got me accused of beggin and I can't even raise my hand.*

---

261 Cited in Willeford, *Abandonment, Wish, and Hope in the Blues*, p. 191.

Bad luck, bad luck, is killin me.
Well I just can't stand no more of this third degree

Got me got accused of murder, I ain't harmed a man.
Got me accused of forgery, I can't even write my name.
Bad luck, bad luck, is killin me.

Got me accused of taxes, I ain't even got a dime.
Got me accused of children and ain't narry a one of them was mine.
Bad luck, bad luck, is killin me.
I just can't stand no more of this third degree.

Often the lyrics of several songs will run together, not out of a conscious desire to create a medley, but because of an openness to shifts in the affective and associational links in the material. Blues lyrics often rely on the use of metaphor, allegory, double entendre, allusion, and ambiguity in much the same manner that is observed in dreaming. Because of the reliance on these devices the blues creates an atmosphere in which individual affective responsiveness is deepened.

Clearly, the use of, and comfort with, the imaginative process is essential to the development of the blues narrative. Garon says, "Here lies the revolutionary nature of the blues: through its fidelity to fantasy and desire, the blues generates an irreducible and, so to speak, habit-forming demand for freedom and what Rimbaud called 'true life'."[262] Similarly, Willeford says, "The blues shows with special clarity things of importance about the transformative workings of imagination - about imaginative transcendence - about the interrelationship between imagination and feeling."[263] Finally, Covington brings us back to the reason the imagination is so important to the narrative process in the first place: "The narrative process . . . creates an imaginative space within which the story itself becomes a transitional object which can be referred to and transformed over time."[264]

---

262 *Blues and the Poetic Spirit*, p. 54.
263 *Abandonment, Wish, and Hope in the Blues*, p. 175.
264 *No Story, No Analysis*, p. 414.

Paul Kugler's work on discourse helps us understand the archetypal basis of words and meaning in the blues. He proposes that just as there are visual images, that there are also sound images, or "acoustic images," which are related based on their phonetic similarities. He goes on to state that "the acoustic image is the crucial intersection between the external and the internal, between the literal and the metaphoric."[265] That is, the acoustic image encompasses both subjective experience and objective experience. One could say that the blues narrative emerges out of a particular set of archetypally based acoustic images.

However, the narrative of the blues is not just contained by the words used in the lyrics. Kittelson, citing linguistic analysis, indicates that only one percent of acoustic signals emitted by the human voice is of linguistic use and purpose.[266] The remaining ninety-nine percent of the meaning derived from the human voice comes from its sound, its vocal and phonic aspects. This is especially true in the blues. Most often it is not the words of the blues song which are most important, it is the sound created by the singer's voice. The bitterness of a love gone wrong, the gravelly weariness of many years on the road, the transitory relief of misery that accompanies a Friday night drunk can all be experienced through the singer's voice just as much, if not more, than through the words being used to convey these experiences. Most often this is paralleled instrumentally through the anguished sound of guitar strings being stretched to mimic a wail, the bent note of a harmonica, or the minor chords of the piano, which are used to mirror the discordance being expressed by the singer's words and voice.

One of the most important aspects of the narrative impulse in the blues is a process referred to as "signifying." Garon indicates that signifying is a form of indirection, a double-voicedness, a form of figurative-implicative speech, that serves as a way of saying one thing and meaning another.[267] Titon indicates that signifying in the blues embodies an African-American approach to the world: "Signifying involves wit, irony, indirection, masquerading, appropriating, encoding, and a host of other means toward obtaining one's ends through shrewdness rather than force. The epitome of signification is the trickster . . . Signifying is viewed as a historical as well as contemporary strategy among

265   *The Alchemy of Discourse*, p. 113.
266   *Sounding the Soul*, p. 104.
267   *Blues and the Poetic Spirit*.

African-Americans in the face of white hegemony. Blues is one of its products."[268]

According to Jones, the use of signification relates back to patterns of African language usage which, "aims at circumlocution rather than at exact definition. The direct statement is considered crude and unimaginative; the veiling of all contents in ever-changing paraphrases is considered the criterion of intelligence and personality."[269] This tradition continued with slaves who used signifying within their work songs to sing insults and comments about their overseers which they could not say outright and the practice continued among prisoners, sharecroppers, and even through the 1960's, where overt and institutionalized racial oppression still presided. Often insults in songs were directed toward inanimate objects, animals, or other persons in the community but the individuals singing or hearing the song knew whom the derision was directed toward, specifically white people in positions of authority or power. An example of this is *Mother Fuyer* by Dirty Red:

Monkey and the baboon playing Seven-Up,
Monkey win the money, scared to pick it up.
The monkey stumbled, the baboon fall,
Monkey grabbed the money an' he run like hell!

In this song the "monkey" is the black man and the "baboon" is the white man. Another example of signification is *.44 Blues* by Roosevelt Sykes:

Lord, I walked all night long with my .44 in my hand,
I was lookin' for my woman an' I found her with another man.

I wore my .44 so long, Lord, it made my shoulder sore,
After I do what I want to ain't goin' to wear my .44 no more.

Lord, and my baby said she heard that .44 whistle blow,
Well it sounds like the train ain't gonna blow that whistle no more.

Lord, I got a little cabin, and my cabin is Number 44,
When I wake up every morning the wolves scratches at my door.

In *.44 Blues* the "cabin" is a reference to his prison cell and the "wolves" scratching at the door are the prison guards. Sykes seems to enjoy linking the number on his cell, the caliber of his gun, and the

---

268 *Early Downhome Blues*, p. 274.
269 *Blues People*, p. 31.

number of the metaphoric train whose "whistle" is used to allude to the shooting of his girlfriend.

As Oliver puts it, "As a singer placed layer upon layer of meaning on a phrase he protected himself with a cloak of obscurities."[270] Oliver's interpretation of signifying is consistent with the statements of Memphis Slim who says, "Blues is kind of a revenge. You know you wanta say something . . . you wanta signifyin' like - that's the blues . . . We all fellers, we had a hard time in life an' like that, and things we couldn't say or do, so we sign it, I mean we sing . . . So it give him the blues, and he can't speak his mind. So he made a song of it, he sang it. Still, he was signifying and getting his revenge through songs."[271] Worth Long interprets the blues similarly, but with an emphasis on signification as a form of protest song:

> I see the blues as an eminent example of protest tradition within African-American song style. It's a question of how they felt they were able to express it, whether it was direct or indirect, hidden or just straight out . . . a lot of it was double entendre and hidden. When Jimmy Reed put out 'Big Boss Man' - man, now, everybody wanted to hear that. They understood it. He didn't have to say anything more. He's just philosophic; 'you ain't so big, you're tall.' So that's a freedom song as far as I'm concerned, and it is of course blues.[272]

However, not all signification was used as a means of addressing white oppression, it was also used to address other subjects, especially sexual issues, which would be frowned upon by repressive influences of Christianity and the Victorian era. The influence of signification can readily be experienced in songs involving entendre, such as:

Empty Bed Blues - Bessie Smith

Bought me a coffee grinder, got the best one I could find
So he could grind my coffee, 'cause he had a brand new grind.

He's a deep-sea diver with a stroke that can't go wrong.
He can reach the bottom 'cause his breath holds out so long.

He boiled my cabbage and made it awful hot
Then he put in the bacon and overflowed the pot.

---

270 *Blues Fell This Morning*, p. 323.
271 Quoted in Garon, *Blues and the Poetic Spirit*, p. 201.
272 Quoted in O'Neal, *I Once Was Lost But Now I'm Found*, p. 379.

I'm A King Bee - Slim Harpo

Well I'm a king bee, buzzing around your hive
Well I can make honey baby, let me come inside

I'm young and able to buzz all night long
Well when you hear me buzzin' baby, some stinging is going on

Well I'm a king bee, want you to be my queen
Together we can make honey, the world ever never seen

Well I'm a king bee, can buzz all night long
Well I can buzz better baby, when your man is gone

The extensive use of signification in the narrative process of the blues has created some confusion or misunderstanding in those attempting to interpret the blues. Blues historian Francis Davis indicates that, "Blues lyrics - so often misunderstood by literalist moralists, from the pulpit to the politically correct - must be understood as having evolved in a culture shaped by a prophetic tradition that entails interpreting the world metaphorically."[273] Similarly, Diggs indicates that: "Where the post-modern mind has created an oppositionalism, between the semiotic process of signification and the archetype of the truth, the blues, in its functional role as the *unio mentalis*, is able to unite them. In the blues, the veiling and denial are not at odds with the truth, they are ways to reveal it."[274] In fact, Spencer feels that the main aesthetic standard of the blues performance is indistinguishable from the ethic of telling the truth.[275] However, it would be important not to overidealize the capacity for metaphorical communication through the use of signification. It is clear from the lyrics of Sonny Boy Williamson's *Don't Start Me Talkin* that signification can also be used in a self-serving fashion to hide activities:

We'll I'm goin' down to Rosie's, stop in Fanny May's;
Gonna tell Fanny what I heard her boyfriend say.
Don't start me talkin'; I'll tell everything I know.
I'm gonna break up this signifyin', cause somebody got to go.

---

273 Quoted in D. Whiteis, "The History of the Blues." *Living Blues*, Issue 121, p. 111.
274 *Alchemy and the Blues*, pp. 38ff.
275 *Blues and Evil.*

Jack gave his wife two dollars to go downtown and get some market.
Gets out on the streets, Ol' George stopped her,
He knocked her down, and blackened her eye.
She gets back home, tell her husband a lie.
Don't start me talkin'; I'll tell everything I know.
I'm gonna break up this signifyin', cause somebody got to go.

She borrowed some money, go to the beauty shop.
He honked his horn, she begun to stop.
Said, "Take me, baby, around the block.
I'm goin' to the beauty shop, where I can get my hair a chop."
Don't start me talkin'; I'll tell everything I know.
I'm gonna break up this signifyin', cause somebody got to go.

7

Imagining the Blues

"The space of imagination is the space of freedom – a space
in which, in an entirely natural manner, boundaries are
crossed, space and time relativized, and possibilities we no
longer or do not yet have are made available to experience."

—Verena Kast

As we have seen in the preceding chapters, the theme of imagination
and creativity plays an important role in the blues and the blues performance. However, the blues listener can also adopt an imaginative and
creative relationship to the music of the blues. Psychoanalyst Stephen
Mitchell associates the development of psychopathology with a failure
of the imagination, causing: "a life stuck because old constraints fore-
close the possibility of new experiences, new states of mind."[276] In the
system of psychology developed by C.G. Jung, the imagination plays
a central role in cultivating a deeper relationship to the wellsprings of
one's psychological life. Jung was convinced that the connection between imagination and psychological wholeness was so important that
he developed a specific therapeutic process for cultivating an imaginative relationship with the unconscious images that appear to us in
dreams and fantasies. He referred to this technique as "active imagination" which he sometimes described as dreaming with one's eyes
open. The recent publication of Jung's *Red Book*[277], a distillation of his
own active imaginal processes, is a testament to his commitment to the
method.

The process of active imagination is intended to deepen the connection with images emerging from dreams or fantasy as a means of
opening up a dialogue with the unconscious aspects of one's psyche.[278]
Initially, this involves creating a quiet, undisturbed atmosphere, mov-

276 *Hope and Dread in Psychoanalysis*, p. 222.
277 *The Red Book: Liber Novus.*
278 An accessible introduction to the process of active imagination can be
found in *Inner Work* by Robert Johnson.

ing into a relaxed state, and concentrating on an image from a recent dream or fantasy while noting how the image shifts or changes as attention is focused on it. As familiarity with the process of active imagination increases, the engagement with the imagery increases. The person engaged in active imagination begins to adopt a particular stance with the images; confronting them, asking questions of the figures that appear, or claiming a position in regards to a specific issue. Ultimately, Jung saw this process as opening up a dialogue with one's deeper Self as well as generating new psychological positions in life. In contrast to other imaginative processes, like guided imagery for relaxation, the unfolding of an active imagination is always determined by the person doing the imagining, rather than being controlled or influenced by the analyst or therapist.

Often music, especially the blues, can reach emotional depths which words cannot address. A process similar to active imagination, which I'll refer to as imagining the blues, can be used to deepen the connection between the blues and one's interior life. The process would initially be the same as active imagination in terms of cultivating a quiet, relaxed state. But, instead of selecting an image from a dream or fantasy to contemplate, a particular blues song is selected for contemplation.

The initial step in imagining the blues is to become absorbed by the music - to be taken over by the rhythms, tones, and words - to be carried along by the music like a wave. As the experience deepens, reflections on the experience can emerge: imagining the environment the singer is singing about, remembering times in life when a feeling has arisen that is similar to the feeling expressed in the song, sensing a stirring in one's own body in response to a moan emanating from the singer, or becoming aware of moments of identification with a figure from the song who is the focus of the singer's love or anger. Like active imagination, the goal of imagining the blues is not to fix something or cause a bad feeling to go away. The goal is much broader – to cultivate and deepen a relationship to one's interior psychological and emotional life.

To better convey the process of blues imagining, I invite the reader to enter into imaginal engagement with *Cypress Grove Blues* by Skip James. In listening to *Cypress Grove Blues* you might quickly feel a downward pull from the descending guitar run which opens the song. The vocal line opens with, *"I'd rather be buried in some cypress grove than to have a contrary woman Lord I never can control."* Initially you might be drawn into an imagining of the feeling, texture, or smell of the cypress grove. Or perhaps the implicit image of a grave is evoked – calling you into an imaginal, but perhaps frightening, relationship to the dark, moist qualities of earthy containment or entombment. As your interior imagery and emotional response deepen, your thoughts and fantasies might turn to the contrary woman and what it is about her that makes her so difficult to deal with, or wondering what she may want from the singer. The song continues with, *"When your knee bones go to achin' and your body gettin' cold, you know, you're just gettin' ready, Honey, for some cypress grove."* Here you may feel the proximity of death closing in, particularly if you allow the sense of ache and cold to penetrate your body as you listen. As *Cypress Grove Blues* unfolds it is revealed that the singer is living in New York but wants to leave because he is *"treated like a dog."* However, he is afraid to go back South because *"them people goin' kill me sure."* You may identify a similar time in your own life when none of the available choices seemed desirable and may remember a feeling of paralysis that can frequently accompany such awareness. The song closes with the line, *"I'm gonna sing this song and I ain't goin' sing no more. Because my time done got precious, Lord, I've gotta go."* We are left wondering whether the singer came to a new awareness, with an associated movement into action, or whether the song signals a giving in to the seductive call of death as a resolution to the emotional dilemma. The images provided in the song remain ambivalent and mysterious. Often songs, like dreams, don't reveal all during the first listening. It can sometimes be beneficial to replay a song numerous times – allowing you to sink more deeply into the atmospheric space created by the song and your own response to the song.

Obviously, *Cypress Grove Blues* places the listener in communion with darker emotional themes. However, the emotional textures of the blues cover the spectrum of human experience, e.g., lust, impotence, love, joy, dissolution, despair, arrogance, frivolity, resignation, acceptance, rumination, birth, death, loss, and awe. In active imagination, or in an imaginal encounter with the blues, there is no right or wrong response. The attitude to hold is simply one of maintaining a stance of openness and curiosity. Allow the images that float up in response to the song to have their own life and direction. Remember that imagining the blues also involves interacting with the blues. Imagining the blues is about cultivating a relationship to the emotional *prima materia* in your own life that is also reflected in the lyrics, rhythms, dynamics, and tones of the blues.

At the end of this book there is a list of blues recordings which can serve as a starting point for imagining the blues. Many of these songs are also available for listening through internet websites such as you-tube.com. The blues song selected becomes the acoustic stimulus and container for the imaginal experience, as well as becoming a window into the blue soul.

8

Conclusion

"The man that hath no music in himself,
Nor is not moved with concord of sweet sounds,
Is fit for treasons, stratagems and spoils;
The motions of his spirit are dull as night
And his affections dark as Erebus:
Let no such man be trusted. Mark the music."
—Shakespeare

Many aspects of the blues that are worthy of psychological exploration have been left unexamined in this book. For example, the themes of magic, the supernatural, and religion, which are important to the examination of unitary reality, are strongly represented in the blues. Also worthy of examination is the relationship between the sexes, including a discussion of *anima* and *animus* representations in the blues. Similarly, travel and geographical themes are prominent in the blues. Therefore, an examination of travel as a metaphor for shifts in psychological states and geographical references as an analogy of the inner world would be another interesting exploration. Finally, the prominent role of the erotic and the issue of race, deserve additional attention.

It is somewhat sad that many African-Americans no longer find solace in the blues. It seems that rap and hip-hop have now become the voice of much of the African-American community, although it also seems clear that these musical forms originated from the blues just as jazz and rock-and-roll did at an earlier time. These changes in the status of the blues have not occurred overnight and we can only speculate that this shift represents a change which is occurring on the level of the collective psyche. Big Bill Broonzy, commenting in 1953, said: "Young people have forgotten how to cry to the blues . . . Back in my day, the people didn't know nothing else to do but cry. They couldn't say about things that hurt 'em. But now they talks and gets lawyers and things. They don't cry no more."[279]

---

279 Quoted in Spencer, *Blues and Evil*, p. 123.

There are some who say that the blues is dying as this shift occurs. However, there is consolation in the words of Charles Keil who says: "Whatever the future holds, I suspect that men and women will have little trouble in finding excuses to fuss and fight. These basic conditions of friction are enough to ensure the continued existence of the blues for many generations to come, if only because no form of music yet evolved has been able to express so simply and directly the frustrations, satisfactions, and reversals of the mating game."[280]

The blues is a movement away from abstraction that helps us stay in sentient relationship with ourselves and others as well as in relationship to the events and experiences of our lives. The blues is about maintaining a close relationship to one's emotional life; becoming intimately acquainted with one's emotions and embracing what is painful, but also embracing what is ultimately enriching and meaningful. Blues music helps make life more bearable, often under unbearable circumstances. It creates and tells stories, builds community, and functionally provides a bridge between the poles of relatedness and alienation.

For me, the blues serves as a compensation for the more dominant aspects of my personality. As a person with a strong tendency to engage with life as an introverted thinker, I find balance in the associative, extraverted feeling of the blues. My natural inclination is toward the Apollonian rather than the Dionysian of the blues. It is the mutual interaction of emotional material in the blues which has made the blues so transformative for me. The blues has become a part of my personal mythology, a sense of connection to the emotion expressed by these men and women who create the blues. This music has allowed me to discover a wider range of emotional self experience. Incorporating the blues has enabled me to connect in a richer way to the archetypal elements of my own emotional experience, a means of glimpsing unitary reality. Perhaps Purvis Spann, Chicago blues disc jockey, says it most simply: "If you don't like blues, you've got a hole in your soul."

280　Quoted in O'Neal, *I Once Was Lost But Now I'm Found*, p. 387.

Postlude

The Premature Autopsy of the Blues
—Sermon by Stanley Crouch[281]

Though we are told to mourn it, we must know that it was a noble sound. It had majesty. Yes, it was majestic. Deep down in the soul of it all, where the notes themselves provide the levels of revelation we can only expect of great art, it formed a bridge. That's right, a bridge. A bridge that stretched from the realm of dreams to the highways and byways and thoroughfares and back roads of action. To be even more precise, let me say that this sound was itself an action. Like a knight wrapped in the glistening armor of invention, of creativity, of integrity, of grace, of sophistication, of soul, this sound took the field. It arrived when the heart was like a percussively throbbing community suffering the despair imposed by dragons . . . But when a majestic sound takes the field, when it parts the waters of silence and noise with the power of song, when this majestic concatenation of rhythm, harmony, and melody assembles itself in the invisible world of music, ears begin to change and lives begin to change and those who were musically lame begin to walk with a charismatic sophistication to their steps. You see, when something is pure, when it has the noblest reasons as its fundamental purpose, then it will become a candle of sound in the dark cave of silence. Yes, it was a noble sound. I say that it was noble because we are told today that this great sound is dead.

It is possible that those who listened heard something timeless from those who are descendants of the many who were literally up of sale, those whose presence on the auction blocks and in the slave quarters formed the cross upon which the Constitution of this nation was crucified. Yet, even after that crucifixion, there were those who rose in the third century of American slavery with a vision of freedom; there were those who lit the mighty wick that extended from the candle and carried it; there were those who spoke through music of the meaning of light; those who were not content to accept the darkness in the heart that comes of surrender to dragons who think themselves grand: those who said – listen closely now.

---

281 © Stanley Crouch, 1989.

I am here to tell you that there are some who do not accept the premature autopsy of a noble art form . . . You have to beware of premature autopsies. A noble sound might not lie still in the dark cave where the dragons have taken it. A noble sound might just rise up and push away the stones that were placed in its path. A noble sound might just rise up on the high side of the sky, it might just ring the silver bells of musical light that tear through the cloak of the dragon's shadow that blocks the sun. You got to watch those early autopsies. A noble sound is a mighty thing. It can mess around and end up swinging low and swinging high and flapping its wings in a rhythm that might swoop over the limitations imposed by the dreams of dragons.

Appendix: Recommended Listening

The blues has its origins in rural settings but evolved as bluesmen migrated to the cities and their instruments became electrified. The blues has become more diverse: country blues, Piedmont blues, jump blues, soul blues, Chicago blues, jazz blues, West Coast blues, North Mississippi Hill Country blues, and Delta blues – each possessing its unique characteristics – but still grounded in the same *prima materia* of everyday emotional life that forms the foundation of the blues.

In my opinion, there is no substitute for listening to live music of any genre. Only by being in the room can we pick up on nuances of the singer's voice, feel the movement of the sound waves through our bodies, sense the impact of the music on the other audience members, and fully participate in the ritual of the performance. However, when opportunities to listen to live blues are limited, listening to the recordings from this list will enhance and deepen the experience of the book and hopefully encourage you to begin your own blues journey.

R.L. Burnside – *Too Bad Jim*, Fat Possum

Rev. Gary Davis – *Harlem Street Singer*, Prestige/Bluesville

Buddy Guy – *Damn Right I've Got the Blues*, Silvertone

Son House – *The Original Delta Blues*, Columbia Legacy

Skip James – *Complete Recorded Works: 1931*, Document

Robert Johnson – *The Complete Recordings*, Sony

Blind Willie Johnson – *The Complete Blind Willie Johnson*, Sony

Junior Kimbrough – *You Better Run: The Essential Junior Kimbrough*, Fat Possum

B.B. King – *Greatest Hits*, MCA

Prison Songs: Historical Recordings from Parchman Farm 1947-,48, Vol 1 & 2, Rounder

Johnny Shines - *Johnny Shines with Big Walter Horton*, Testament

Koko Taylor – *Deluxe Edition*, Alligator

Sonny Terry – *Whoopin' the Blues: The Capitol Recordings, 1947-1950*, Capitol

Big Mama Thornton – *Ball N' Chain*, Arhoolie

Stevie Ray Vaughan – *The Essential Stevie Ray Vaughan and Double Trouble*, Sony

T-Bone Walker – *Stormy Monday Blues: The Essential Collection*, Half Moon UK

Little Walter – *His Best: The Chess 50th Anniversary Collection*, Chess

Muddy Waters - *The Definitive Collection*, Geffen

Junior Wells – *Hoodoo Man Blues*, Delmark

Big Joe Williams – *Shake Your Boogie*, Arhoolie

John Lee "Sonny Boy" Williamson – *The Original Sonny Boy Williamson: Vol 1*, JSP

Sonny Boy Williamson II – *His Best*, Chess

Smokey Wilson – *88th Street Blues*, Blind Pig

Howlin' Wolf – *His Best: The Chess 50th Anniversary Collection*, Chess

References

Ashton, P. & Bloch, S. *Music and Psyche: Contemporary Psychoanalytic Explorations*. New Orleans: Spring Books, *2010*.

Atwood, G. & Stolorow, R. *Faces in a Cloud*. Northvale, NJ: Aronson, 1993.

Balint, M. *The Basic Fault: Therapeutic Aspects of Regression*. New York: Brunner/Mazel,1968.

Bodkin, M. *Archetypal Patterns in Poetry*. London: Oxford University Press, 1934.

Bollas, C. *The Shadow of the Object*. New York: Columbia, 1987.

Bowlby, J. *A Secure Base*. New York: Basic Books, 1988.

Cammerloher, M. "The Position of Art in the Psychology of Our Time." In J. Campbell (Ed.) *Spiritual Disciplines: Papers from the Eranos Yearbooks*. Princeton, NJ: Princeton University Press, 1960.

Campbell, J. *The Inner Reaches of Outer Space*. New York: Perennial Library, 1986.

Charters, S. "Workin' on the Building: Roots and Influences." In L. Cohn (Ed.). *Nothing but the Blues*. New York: Abbeville Press, 1993.

Cohn, L. *Nothing but the Blues*. New York: Abbeville Press, 1993.

Cooper, M. "Luther 'Guitar Junior' Johnson: You Got to Have a Feeling for People." *Living Blues*, Issue 142, pp. 42-49, 1998.

Covington, C. "No Story, No Analysis?: The Role of Narrative in Interpretation." *Journal of Analytical Psychology*, vol. 40, no. 3, pp. 405-417, 1995.

Diggs, S. "Alchemy of the Blues." *Spring*, vol. 61, pp. 16-50, 1997.

Eliade, M. *The Sacred and the Profane*. New York: Harvest, 1957.

Eliade, M. *Shamanism: Archaic Techniques of Ecstasy*. Princeton, NJ: Princeton University Press, 1965.

Evans, D. *Big Road Blues: Tradition and Creativity in the Folk Blues*, New York: Da Capo, 1982.

Evans, D. "Robert Johnson: Pact with the Devil." *Blues Revue*, Issue 21, pp. 12-13, 1996a.

Evans, D. "Robert Johnson: Pact with the Devil, Part 2." *Blues Revue*, Issue 22, pp. 12-13, 1996b.

Finn, J. *The Bluesman: The Musical Heritage of Black Men and Women in the Americas*. London: Quartet Books, 1986.

Forman, R. "A Psychological Account of Meister Eckhart's Mystical Transformation." *Journal of Psychology and Christianity*, vol. 6, pp. 21-32, 1987.

Frede, A. "Words, Sound, Power: The Blues Vision of Corey Harris." *Living Blues*, Issue 126, pp. 22 -33, 1996.

Garon, P. *Blues and the Poetic Spirit*. San Francisco: City Lights Books, 1996.

Gentry, J. "The Subway Lounge: The Heart of the Blues in Jackson." *Living Blues*, Issue 132, p. 55, 1997.

Guralnick, P. *Searching for Robert Johnson*. New York: Dutton, 1989.

Gussow, A. *Mister Satan's Apprentice: A Blues Memoir*. New York: Pantheon, 1998.

Hamilton, E. *Mythology*. New York: Mentor Books, 1969.

Herman, P. "Big Mo and Little Whitt Sing the Moody Swamp Blues." *Blues Revue*, Issue 32, p. 32, 1997.

Hillman, J. "Alchemical Blue and the Unio Mentalis." *Spring*, vol. 57, pp. 132-148, 1993.

Humphrey, M. "Bright Lights, Big City: Urban Blues." In L. Cohn (Ed.). *Nothing but the Blues*. New York: Abbeville Press, 1993a.

Humphrey, M. "Holy blues: The Gospel Tradition." In L. Cohn (Ed.). *Nothing but the Blues*. New York: Abbeville Press, 1993b.

Johnson, R. *Inner Work: Using Dream and Active Imagination for Personal Growth*. San Francisco: Harper & Row, 1986.

Jones, L. *Blues People*. New York: Morrow Quill Books, 1963.

Jung, C.G. "The Psychology of the Transference." In *The Practice of Psychotherapy*, CW16. Princeton, NJ: Princeton University Press, 1946.

Jung, C.G. *Psychology and Alchemy*, CW12. Princeton, NJ: Princeton University Press, 1953.

Jung, C.G. "Problems of Modern Psychotherapy." In *The Practice of Psychotherapy*, CW16. Princeton, NJ: Princeton University Press, 1954.

Jung, C.G. *Symbols of Transformation*, CW5. Princeton, NJ: Princeton University Press, 1956.

Jung, C.G. *The Archetypes and the Collective Unconscious*, CW9i, Princeton, NJ: Princeton University Press, 1959.

Jung, C.G. *Alchemical Studies*, CW13. Princeton, NJ: Princeton University Press, 1967.

Jung, C.G. *The Structure and Dynamics of the Psyche*, CW8. Princeton, NJ: Princeton University Press,1969.

Jung, C.G. *The Red Book: Liber Novus*. New York: Norton, 2009.

Jung, C.G. *Psychology and Religion*, CW11. Princeton, NJ: Princeton University Press. 1969.

Jung, C.G. *Psychological Types*, CW6. Princeton, NJ: Princeton University Press, 1971.

Jung, M. "Acoustic Blues in Oakland." *Living Blues*, Issue 126, pp. 34-39, 1996.

Kawai, H. *The Japanese Psyche*. Dallas: Spring, 1988.

Keil, C. *Urban Blues*. Chicago: University of Chicago Press, 1991.

Kittelson, M. *Sounding the Soul: The Art of Listening*. Einsiedeln, Switzerland: Daimon Verlag, 1996.

Klein, M. "Notes on Some Schizoid Mechanisms." In J. Mitchell (Ed.) *The Selected Melanie Klein*. New York: Free Press, 1986.

Kohut, H. "Observations on the Psychological Functions of Music." *J. of the American Psychoanalytic Association*, vol. 5, pp. 389-407, 1957.

Kugler, P. *The Alchemy of Discourse*. Lewisberg, DE: Bucknell Univ. Press, 1982.

Laplanche, J. & Pontalis, J.B. *The Language of Psycho-Analysis*, New York: W.W. Norton,1973.

Levi-Strauss, C. *Structural Anthropology*. New York: Basic Books, 1963.

Levi-Strauss, C. *Myth and Meaning*. New York: Schocken Books, 1978.

Mitchell, S. *Hope and Dread in Psychoanalysis*. New York: Basic Books, 1993.

Moore, R. "Ritual, Sacred Space, and Healing." In N. Schwartz-Salant and M. Stein (Eds.), *Chiron: Liminality and Transitional Phenomena*. Wilmette, IL: Chiron, 1991.

Moore, T. "Musical Therapy." *Spring*, vol. 42, pp. 128-135, 1978.

Neumann, E. "Narcissism, Normal Self-Formation, and the Primary Relationship to the Mother." *Spring*, vol. 30, p. 81, 1966.

Neumann, E. *Depth Psychology and a New Ethic*. Boston: Shambhala, 1969.

Neumann, E. *The Place of Creation*. Princeton, NJ: Princeton Universit-Press, 1989.

Oliver, P. *Blues Fell This Morning: Meaning in the Blues*. Cambridge: Cambridge University Press, 1990.

O'Neal, J. "I Once was Lost but Now I'm Found: The Blues Revival of the 1960's." In L. Cohn (Ed.), *Nothing but the Blues*. New York: Abbeville Press, 1993.

Robertson, B. *Little Blues Book*. Chapel Hill, NC: Algonquin Books, 1996.

Rolla, G. *Your Inner Music: Creative Analysis and Music Memory*. Wilmette, IL: Chiron, 1993.

Rothenberg, D. "The Necessary Note." *Parabola*, vol. XXIII, p. 4, 1998.

Skar, P. "Music and Analysis." In M. Mattoon (Ed.). *Zurich 95: Open Questions in Analytical Psychology*. Einsiedeln, Switzerland: Daimon Verlag, 1997.

Schafer, R. *Retelling a Life*. New York: Basic Books, 1992.

Sharp, D. *C.G. Jung Lexicon: A Primer of Terms and Concepts*. Inner-City Books: Toronto, 1991.

Spencer, J. *Blues and Evil*. Knoxville, TN: University of Tennessee Press, 1993.

Stern, D. *The Interpersonal World of the Infant*. New York: Basic Books, 1985.

Storr, A. *Music and the Mind*. New York: Ballantine Books, 1992.

Streich, H. "Music, Alchemy and Psychology in Atlanta Fugiens of Michael Maier." In M. Maier *Atlanta Fugiens*. Grand Rapids, MI: Phanes Press, 1989.

Titon, J. *Early Downhome Blues: A Musical and Cultural Analysis*. Chapel Hill, NC: University of North Carolina Press, 1994.

Townsley, T. "Paul Geremia: Looking for the Sound." *Blues Revue*, vol. 42, pp. 8-13, 1998.

van Loben Sels, R. *Shaman: A Differentiation of Image from Instinct*, Unpublished diploma dissertation, New York Jung Institute, 1980.

von Franz, M. *Interpretation of Fairytales*. Dallas: Spring, 1970.

Whiteis, D. "The History of the Blues." *Living Blues*, Issue 121, p. 111, 1995.

Willeford, W. "Abandonment, Wish, and Hope in the Blues." In N. Schwartz-Salant and M. Stein *Chiron: Abandonment*,1985.

Winnicott, D. "Transitional Objects and Transitional Phenomena." International Journal of Psycho-Analysis, vol. 34, pp. 89-97, 1953.

Wolf, E. *Treating the Self*. New York: Guilford, 1988.

Wright, K. *Vision and Separation*. Northvale, NJ: Aronson, 1991.

INDEX

Navajo 64
Neal, Larry 63
Neumann, Erich 6, 25, 26, 27, 30,
    33, 36, 38, 39, 44, 45, 48,
    50, 51, 63, 70, 71, 75, 90,
    116
Newbern, Hambone Willie 45
Nietzsche, Friedrich 31
Nighthawk, Robert 16
nigredo 52, 80
numinous 35, 42, 57, 70

O

Odin 64
Odysseus 9
Oedipus 57
Ogden, Thomas 26
Oliver, Paul 5, 17, 31, 50, 60, 64,
    100, 116
omnipotence 40
O'Neal, J. 22, 48, 100, 108, 117
ontological time 33
oppression 14, 15, 16, 52, 71, 76,
    99, 100
Orpheus 8, 9

P

Pan 9, 41, 70
parable 25
Paracelsus 67
paranoia 40
paranoid-schizoid position 40
Parker, Little Junior 22, 51, 74
participation mystique 26, 47
passion 3, 35
pentatonic scale 13
performer-listener dyad 48
Persephone 8, 9
personification 7, 81, 82, 86, 87,
    88
Phillips, Washington 76
plantation 11, 16
Plato 8, 67
play 44

Pleasant Joe 41
Pontalis, J.B. 60, 116
possession 47, 50, 61, 62, 63, 65,
    66, 82
prima materia 10, 66, 112
prisoners 13, 99
profane 31, 44, 57, 85
psychic energy 71
psychoid realm 26

R

racism 14, 15, 76
Rainey, Ma 20, 82, 95
Rapunzel 73
reality field 26
Red Book 103
redemption 20, 75
Reed, Jimmy 43, 55, 100
reels 13
Reese, John 10
repression 15, 53, 76, 100
resurrection 20
rhythm 1, 11, 49, 65, 110, 111
Richardson, Mabel 19
ritual 44, 58, 59, 64, 71, 72, 92
Robertson, Brian 10, 13, 22, 54,
    59, 117
Rothenberg, David 58, 117
Rumpelstiltskin 73

S

sacred 3, 11, 31, 44, 57, 64, 71,
    76, 85
sadness 1, 10, 17, 22, 72, 75, 79
Santaria 86
Satan and Adam 33
Schafer, Roy 68, 91
Schopenhauer, Arthur 70
selfobject relationship 60
Sels, Robin van Loben 65
sensuality 21
shadow 11, 15, 70, 75, 76, 111
sharecroppers 13
Sharp, Daryl 3, 26, 117

You might also enjoy reading these Jungian publications:

The Creative Soul by Lawrence Staples
ISBN 978-0-9810344-4-7

Guilt with a Twist by Lawrence Staples
ISBN 978-0-9776076-4-8

Enemy, Cripple, Beggar by Erel Shalit
ISBN 978-0-9776076-7-9

Divine Madness by John R. Haule
ISBN 978-1-926715-04-9

Farming Soul by Patricia Damery
ISBN 978-1-926715-01-8

The Motherline by Naomi Ruth Lowinsky
ISBN 978-0-9810344-6-1

The Sister From Below by Naomi Ruth Lowinsky
ISBN 978-0-9810344-2-3

Like Gold Through Fire by Bud & Massimilla Harris
ISBN 978-0-9810344-5-4

The Art of Love: The Craft of Relationship
by Bud & Massimilla Harris
ISBN 978-1-926715-02-5

Resurrecting the Unicorn by Bud Harris
ISBN 978-0-9810344-0-9

The Father Quest by Bud Harris
ISBN 978-0-9810344-9-2

Phone Orders Welcomed
Credit Cards Accepted
In Canada & the U.S. call 1-800-228-9316
International call +1-831-238-7799
www.fisherkingpress.com